International Praise for *Tongues of Fire*

'The best sociological study of Latin American Protestantism to date.'
Theology Today

'Astonishingly rich . . . This is an important book that makes a new and significant contribution to a crucial debate. Very highly recommended.' *Choice*

'An excellent scholarly analysis that is accessible to the average reader and provides a good bibliography as well. Highly recommended.'
Library Journal

'Compelling in its reasoning . . . it is a worthy addition to anyone's library.' *Evangelical Missions Quarterly*

'A brilliant, richly suggestive book, accessible to any interested reader.'
Dow Jones

'Extraordinarily interesting.' *Church Times*

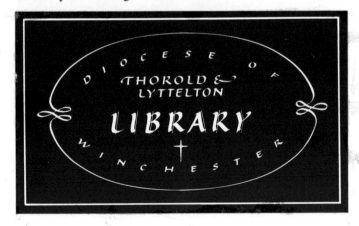

For Bernice

Tongues of Fire

The Explosion of
Protestantism in
Latin America

David Martin

with a Foreword by Peter Berger

BLACKWELL

Oxford UK & Cambridge MA

Copyright © David Martin 1990
The extracts from *Workers in the Cane* by Sidney Mintz are
reproduced by kind permission of Yale University Press, © 1974.

First published 1990
Reprinted 1991
First published in paperback 1993

Blackwell Publishers
108 Cowley Road, Oxford, OX4 1JF, UK

238 Main Street,
Cambridge, Massachusetts 02142, USA

British Library Cataloguing in Publication Data

A CIP catalogue record for this book is available from the British Library.

Library of Congress Cataloging in Publication Data

Martin, David, 1929—
Tongues of fire: the explosion of Protestantism in Latin America/David Martin; with a foreword by
Peter Berger.
p.   cm.
Originally published in 1990.
Includes bibliographical references and indexes.
ISBNs 0–631–17186–X (hbk.); 0–631–18914–9 (pbk.)
1. Protestant churches — Latin America.   2. Evangelicalism—Latin America.   3. Pentecostal churches—
Latin America.   4. Latin America—Church history.   I. Title.
[BX4832.5.M37 1993]
306.6'804'098 - dc20   93–15412
                                                                                          CIP

Typeset in 11 on 12pt Ehrhardt by
Hope Services (Abingdon) Ltd
Printed in Great Britain by
T.J. Press Ltd., Padstow, Cornwall

Contents

Foreword

This book deals with one of the most extraordinary developments in the world today – the rapid spread of Evangelical Protestantism in vast areas of the underdeveloped societies, notably in Latin America. What is also extraordinary is that very few people in Europe and in North America are even aware of it. Yet, if one looks at today's religious scene in an international perspective, there are two truly global movements of enormous vitality. One is conservative Islam, the other conservative Protestantism. Since the Iranian revolution at least a good deal of attention has been paid to the former in the West. Conservative Protestantism in its world-wide explosion remains, by and large, *terra incognita* even to otherwise well-informed people in the West. It is high time that this changed, for the potential impact of this religious phenomenon is likely to be very powerful indeed.

The growth of Evangelical Protestantism in Latin America, a continent still widely regarded as solidly Roman Catholic, is the most dramatic case. It is important, though, to see this too in a global context. The same type of Protestantism is also sweeping across large areas of East and Southeast Asia – most strongly in South Korea, but also in all the Chinese societies and communities outside the People's Republic as well as in the Philippines (Japan is the exception in the region). The South Pacific is another area of rapid expansion. And the same Protestantism, though here often in bizarre combinations with indigenous religious traditions, is growing throughout sub-Saharan Africa; it is there that it directly competes with militant Islam. Last but not least, the Evangelical community has been growing both in numbers and in social prominence in the United States, and its members are well aware of their important place within a world-wide movement. Needless to say, the phenomenon varies from country to country both in its religious characteristics and its social consequences. At the same time there are striking similarities everywhere: This is, truly, a global movement.

It is difficult to think of a better qualified scholar than David Martin to attempt an overview of the phenomenon. One of the most distinguished contemporary sociologists of religion, Martin has studied Protestantism in detail in its British and North American 'home territory,' and he has progressively widened his attention to other parts of the world. His earlier book *A General Theory of Secularization* has become an important point of reference in the sociology of religion. Here now he develops various ideas adumbrated in previous works of his with originality, verve and an astounding ability to weave numerous details into a fascinating portrait of dramatic dimensions.

It began in England, this great drama of world-transforming Protestantism. This locale is far from accidental. Martin cites Claudio Véliz's proposition that we all live in 'a world made in England' – from parliamentary democracy to soccer, from mass production to the clothes worn by sailors, and above all in the unchallengeable dominance of the English language. This should not really surprise: England, after all, is where the great institutions of modernity began with the Industrial Revolution. The origins of the phenomenon at issue here are in England as well, in all the little Nonconformist chapels and conventicles that grew around the margins of the Anglican Establishment. And, of course, the peculiar religion and morals formed in this milieu were successfully exported wherever British settlers moved, most grandiosely in the colonies of North America. The first internationale of world-transforming Protestantism, if that term be allowed, was predominantly Anglo-Saxon in provenance; we are now in the midst of a second Protestant internationale, which is moving freely across all language boundaries. Thus the new Protestants of Guatemala and southern Mexico are singing the old revival hymns – translated into Mayan. Max Weber and Elie Halévy have analyzed the manner in which the previous Protestant explosion transformed the world; Martin's book gives us a pretty good idea what this second wave is accomplishing.

Actually, Martin makes a distinction between three, not two, waves of Protestant cultural revolution – the Puritan, the Methodist and the Pentecostal. The second did not fully replace the first, and the third continues to co-exist with its two predecessors. All the same, the great wave of Protestantism sweeping across the Third World today is primarily Pentecostal – hence the 'tongues of fire' in Martin's title. The distinctive religious and social features of Pentecostalism – a white heat of emotional fervor – are important to understand, and Martin gives us vivid illustrations of what this *gestalt* of religious experience means in the lives of ordinary believers. It is different from the Methodist experience and very different indeed from the Puritan one. Nevertheless, the social and moral consequences of conversion to Protestantism continue to be remarkably similar to the consequences of the Puritan and Methodist revolutions: They are, when all is said and done, the components of what Weber called the 'Protestant ethic'; what is more, now as then, the ethos of Protestantism shows itself to be remarkably helpful to people in the throes of rapid modernization and of the 'take-off' stage of modern economic growth. The same ethos also continues to evince its time-honoured affinities with the 'spirit of capitalism,' with individualism, with a hunger for education and (last but not least) with a favorable disposition toward democratic politics. Now as then, these affinities are, in the main, unintended; they are the result not of explicated doctrine, but of the unanticipated behavioral consequences of both doctrine and religious experience.

Following the insights of Weber and Halévy, what one may expect is that the new Protestant internationale will produce results similar to those of the preceding one – to wit, the emergence of a solid bourgeoisie, with virtues conducive to the development of a democratic capitalism. It hardly needs emphasizing that this would be an immense event in Latin America as well as elsewhere in the Third World. Martin emphasizes that what is taking place now does not as yet constitute this event in its full force. The revolution-in-the-making is still very much *in statu nascendi*. It is occurring among very poor people, in the main, and their attention is still focused on the problem of survival. To steal from Marxist terminology, Latin American Protestantism is still in a 'pre-revolutionary' phase (Martin uses the term 'latency'). But the contours of the revolution that is to come can already be perceived in that 'free social space' (another phrase of Martin's) which the Protestant communities are carving out for themselves. Martin is a cautious analyst; he refrains from making too many predictions. His book is a severe temptation for this reader, at any rate, to be less cautious. Be this as it may, this is a book of very great importance. It should be read by anyone interested in the condition and the future of the Americas, but also by anyone concerned with the relation of religion and social change throughout the contemporary world.

David Martin's research which led to this book was one of the projects with which the Institute for the Study of Economic Culture at Boston University began its work some four years ago. The Institute, which it has been my privilege to direct, conducts research in several countries on the interaction between culture (including religion) and socio-economic processes. We are very gratified to have been in a position to help in bringing Martin's study to this happy conclusion.

Peter L. Berger
Boston 1990

Acknowledgements

This book has been about three years in the making and I am indebted to various people for helping me to make it.

First, and above all, I am indebted to Peter Berger and the Institute for the Study of Economic Culture (ISEC) for providing time and money to make it possible. Peter Berger originally suggested that I take up this topic when we met within a stone's throw of Aldersgate St, London. Arguably it was there that this story took off about a quarter of a millennium ago. Since that meeting he has constantly encouraged me and put the resources of ISEC at my disposal. Up to that point I had always written betweenwhiles and this was a rare opportunity to deploy the resources which are really needed for this kind of research. I am extremely grateful for the psychic support, for the free term provided and for the material resources.

Peter Berger and the staff at ISEC were so kind as to arrange a conference at Boston University of interested scholars with ideas which might bear on the progress of the book. The people who came to Boston were Dr David Docherty, Dr Steve Bruce, Dr Andrew Walker and Dr James Davison Hunter. I very much appreciate their coming to that conference and the excellent commentary they provided. Peter Berger was our intellectual host and Craig Gay our recorder. This was a pleasant and very fruitful occasion.

I also owe a very considerable debt of gratitude to Southern Methodist University, Dallas, Texas and to the donor of the Elizabeth Scurlock Chair, Mrs Laura Lee Blanton of Houston, Texas. It has been a great honour to be the first incumbent of that chair and to enjoy the friendship of Mr and Mrs Blanton. I hope they feel this book worthy of their intentions. My time at Southern Methodist University has been extremely pleasant. I have had every facility made available to me and enjoyed all the courtesies of a first-rate American institution. Conspicuous among the facilities have been the Fondren and Bridwell libraries. The people staffing these libraries have made my needs their pleasure. Southern Methodist University has turned out to be exile made easy and a place where good friendships could be had just for the asking.

My other debts are quite multifarious. Various people have helped in literature searches, including Chung Chin Hong and Hwan Kim, who sorted through materials on South Korea. Mrs Maire Howes provided me with a great deal of Latin American background and dug out fascinating Peruvian materials. I am only sorry that the economy of the book has not allowed me properly to incorporate much of what she uncovered. Cecilia Mariz carried out for me the first search of the Latin American literature, particularly that part of it written in Portuguese. She also helped me survive in Rio de Janeiro. I am most grateful to her for invaluable assistance.

Other debts were incurred on the research journeys made possible by ISEC and Southern Methodist University. They are, in the order in which they occurred, to Dr Rafael Cobos and his colleagues at the University of the Yucatan, Mexico; to the pastor of the Presbyterian Church, Merida; to the staff of ISER and Dr Rubem Fernandes in Rio de Janeiro; to Professor MacKenzie and Dr Barry Chevannes at the University of the West Indies, Mona, Jamaica; to Dr Philip Potter and Dr George Mulrain; to the curators of the research library in Antigua, Guatemala, and to Dr Virgilio Zapata Arceyuz, Rector of the Protestant University, Guatemala City; to Dr Jean-Pierre Bastian of the Institute of Advanced Studies (Mexico City) and the College of Mexico, and to Dr Carlos Garma Navarro. The work of Jean-Pierre Bastian has been of particular value to me; and his friendship more than encouraging.

I am very grateful to Judy Charvat at SMU for typing the fourth chapter (which was, as it happened, the first to be written), as well as for typing the first interim bibliography. Mrs Yvonne Brown at the London School of Economics typed the bulk of the manuscript with her usual faithfulness, kindness and efficiency. I am deeply in her debt over many years. Cheryl Badley saw through the last stages of the book, notably the endlessly revised and very long part II, and the final version of the bibliography. This was difficult work accomplished with tact, intelligence, kindness and forbearance.

Two final debts are of a rather different kind. One debt is to Dr William Abraham at Perkins School of Theology, whose interests overlapped mine very easily and who provided me with helpful criticism, suggestions, materials and ideas as to what further I should read. He was in effect a research associate with whom I could discuss my problems.

The other debt is to my wife, who read the manuscript at each stage, constantly encouraged me and accompanied me on all the research trips, except that to Rio. As ever, we discussed the whole content of the book. These were good and fruitful times and for these and all others my continual gratitude and the heartfelt dedication of this book.

David Martin
Southern Methodist University;
London School of Economics
Christmas, 1988

Introduction

In writing about a quite extraordinary and little-known development, I have adopted certain principles which I want to explain before I go on to indicate the problematic thrust of the argument, and the shape of the book.

First of all I have tried to be simple. There are few matters, if any, in sociology which cannot be made accessible to the ordinary reader. I have come to the conclusion that the technical language of sociology can be converted to ordinary speech almost without remainder. More than that I believe that a great deal of such language strains out the humanity of the actors in historical and social dramas, and too easily discounts their own understandings of what it is they are doing. They are reduced to sleep walkers driven by social forces and processes. So in what follows I want to present a world of actors, as well as of processes.

I would add that I also want to avoid 'framing' these worlds lived in by the Latin American poor in language of covert political hostility, or encasing them in grand notions of the right or main path of social evolution. It is a strange perversion of our intellectual culture that we so often want to have people and movements framed in this way in order to tell us if they are politically alright. We demand a secular version of the 'last judgement' here and now. That I will not and cannot give. Certain inhumane horrors apart I find the world in general ambiguous, and these particular worlds more potently ambiguous than usual. The language of sociology is not the language of political or cultural certification and docketing. It does, however, encompass humane sympathy and empathy. I write sympathetically, *not* to add to the repertory of approved attitudes.

Since I want to write simply and directly I have avoided certain kinds of discussion about sociological terms. 'Modernization', for example, is a much contested term and so too is 'development'. Hardly any word gets through the sieve of criticism, and yet we have to go on talking, trusting that readers will make their own intelligent reservations.

Parallel but different problems attend the use of religious and theological terms. To explain why I, from time to time, use 'Protestant' or 'evangelical' or 'Christian' or 'believer' is out of the question. So too is a minute analysis of all the varied theological differences lying inside and across these broad labels. Where my approach becomes problematic, as for example in the complexities of the Evangelical Revival and the genealogy that connects Methodism to Pentecostalism, I have indicated what has to be read.

One major problem about theological terms remains important for a sociological analysis, and that concerns the way we deploy the word 'charismatic'. I believe charismatic Catholicism to be something other than Pentecostalism and that is in part because it does take place within the Roman Catholic Church. Its aetiology and background I regard as largely distinct from the background of Protestant Pentecostalism. But I confess I do not sufficiently turn aside from the line of my argument fully to justify that position. Catholic Pentecostalism is, of course, a much less massive phenomenon.

A persistent technical problem concerns statistics. The major statistical source provided by David Barrett's monumental *World Christian Encyclopedia* is now almost a decade out of date, and the materials being collected by *Imdela/Procades* are not yet fully available. I have had to use varied sources and have only indicated very broad tendencies. A proper statistical survey together with all the appropriate caveats would take up another volume at least as long as the present one. The same applies to maps. Maps have been published from time to time covering Brazil, the Argentine, Chile, Mexico and Central America, but they are a decade, or even two decades, out of date. One has only to reflect on the vast labours associated with the cartographical work of John Gay in England, François Isambert in France and Aurelio Orensanz in Spain to gain some idea of what would be involved in producing anything of the right standard, which was contemporary and seriously informative.

At least two chapters, 11 and 12, have the character of reviews of the literature. Such reviews are not always easily assimilated and enjoyed in the way I would like. But insofar as I am building up a case it is important to do so by the citation of cumulative evidence. This kind of book depends on a multitude of small studies and it is only morally and intellectually proper to acknowledge them and expound them individually. Such a book also depends on certain earlier wide-ranging analyses which I want specifically to acknowledge, above all those by Walter Hollenweger, Emile Leonard, Christian Lalive D'Epinay, Emilio Willems and Bryan Wilson.

Aside from the attempt to communicate easily, there remain major theoretical concerns which I will set out. One is the clash of Hispanic and so-called 'Anglo' civilizations over the past four centuries. That provides the dramatic backdrop of the whole story. Another is the comparative study of why Protestantism makes an impact in (say) Brazil and Guatemala rather than in (say) Uruguay. To do that properly would require prolonged study of each separate country and culture, such as Jean-Pierre Bastian has undertaken in the case of Mexico. All I have been able to do is to indicate what I think are facilitating or inhibiting circumstances in this or that context.

The key problem areas from the theoretical viewpoint are the issues raised by Halévy about the advent and impact of Methodism, and the debate over secularization. So far as Methodism is concerned, my focus is on how the emergence of a voluntary form of faith in England (and Wales) and its full realization in the United States was part of the erosion of organic unities at the level of the locality and at the level of the state. What was the social role of Protestant networks for mutual support and the effect of new notions of self, of movement, mobility and individual initiative, once those unities broke up? These crucial questions are now transferred from the Humber to the other side of the Rio Grande.

The debate over secularization is relevant in two ways. First, it is relevant because up to 1960 Catholic societies and Protestant societies had entered upon 'modernity' by quite distinct paths, such as I tried to chart in my *General Theory of Secularization*.[1] Nobody expected the issues raised by Halévy to come alive again in Catholic Latin America. Yet they have. Not only has 'Anglo' civilization met the Hispanic world, but the characteristic Protestant pathway in its Anglo-American variant has been crossed with the Catholic one. The specific pattern of change persisting in Catholic societies from 1789 to 1950 has given way to a criss-cross, which is a genuine new moment in modern history. This moment cannot be dismissed simply as a transfer from North to South America brought about by cultural imperialism. What we have is an indigenous enthusiastic Protestantism rooted in the hopes of millions of Latin American poor.

The wider question is whether this new movement remains,

nevertheless, just part of transition within the larger and all-enveloping scope of secularization. Up to now the proponents of universal secularization have seen all Catholic societies as prefigured by France and all Protestant societies as prefigured by Sweden. But maybe Europe does not provide the universal model, and maybe Europe only illustrates what happens when social change occurs in states where religion has been tied to governments and to old elites. In the United States that tie was broken and religion floated free of the particular entanglements of status and power. Perhaps what is happening now in South America is a complicated dance in which both Catholicism and Protestantism are floating free and breaking out of the bounds set by the last two centuries. So not only is the great Anglo–Hispanic gulf symbolized by 1588 closing, but maybe the specific historical trajectory triggered by 1789 is finally petering out. As North American modes of socio-religious change combine with those of South America so the spirals of antagonism over religion which have dogged all Latin cultures are showing signs of terminal exhaustion.

How then have I organized my themes and planned my book? In the first place I have set out the dramatic confrontation over four centuries between the Hispanic and Anglo-American worlds. Back of that lie some remarkable assertions of Claudio Veliz. 'We were', he says, 'all born in a world made in England and the world in which our grandchildren will mellow into venerable old age will be as English as the Hellenistic world was Greek, or better, Athenian.'[2] To assert that is to distinguish sharply between the dismantling of an empire and its cultural reproduction throughout a large part of the world. Veliz goes on:

> In the last two generations or so, certainly since 1947, when Britain started dismantling her empire, the world crossed a barely perceptible but very real threshold into a quasi-Hellenistic period during which the cultural forms originated by the English-speaking peoples, especially at the time of their remarkably inventive Industrial Revolution and their brief imperial moment, have been consolidated effortlessly as principal strands in the common fabric of knowledge, habits, affectations and beliefs on which rest the quality and survival of civilization.[3]

The initial distribution of this culture lay, of course, in a series of cultural transplants from Britain, above all to the United States. Veliz adds, in a manner directly parallel to my own exposition, that the United States extended what was transplanted from Great Britain, though it is, of course, 'far more than an efficient distributor of English significances'.

Veliz then goes on to contrast this Anglo-Saxon cultural dynamic with the impact of the Spanish empire, which was arguably the most formidable since that of the Romans. In his view its cultural and vital significances did not prove transportable outside its own vast domain. Bull-fighting and Castilian remained bounded; football and English did not. The one was centralized and monopolistic and restricted to its own political imperium; the other was loose, plural, latitudinarian, and available for export.

The second chapter of this book is concerned with the religious aspect of this 'availability for export'. It examines the creation of a voluntary, fissile and participatory form of religion in Britain, its export to North America and its development as the core culture of the United States. There were three successive models of cultural reproduction: the mark 1, so to speak, which is Puritan, the mark 2, which is Methodist, and the mark 3, which is Pentecostal. (Behind mark 2 and 3 lies North European pietism, but that never took off because it was kept inside the monopolisitic confinement of the state-church system). Mark 1 and mark 2 proved difficult to transport from North to South America, except as minor reinforcements to anti-clericalism in the characteristically Latin struggle between Church militant and militant Enlightenment. Mark 1 and mark 2 acquired cultural influence but not numerical power.

Mark 3, however, succeeded in crossing the Rio Grande in force and proved reproducible on a mass scale. That was because it was equipped with local adaptors and easily became indigenous. Mark 3 passed with accelerating force through a whole series of conduits: to small people with some element of independence through a craft or through land or work as journeymen and watchmen; to those displaced by the advent of capitalist farming and anxious to defend or relocate themselves; to small disaffected tribes and to large subordinate ethnic groups on national peripheries, like the Maya and Quechua; and above all to those caught up and disoriented in the vast *movement* from hacienda to the environs of the mega-city. Part II describes the variable incidence of this religious inundation throughout the Hispanic world, evident above all in south-eastern Brazil, but almost equally evident in Chile and Guatemala.

However, the religious inundation represented by Pentecostalism and by other forms of conservative Protestantism was not confined to the world of Latin America. It spread in various contexts in the Caribbean which were of Anglo-American and Franco-American as well as Hispano-American provenance. So chapter 7 examines

Trinidad and Jamaica; Haiti; and Puerto Rico. Protestantism also spread in much more far-flung contexts, along the western Pacific rim: China, the Philippines, New Guinea, Indonesia and, above all, South Korea. Chapter 8 examines why South Korea should have proved so hospitable to conservative Protestantism, in the first place to Methodism and Presbyterianism, and now to Pentecostalism.

The advance of conservative Protestantism involves certain processes and transformations indicated by the key signatures of Pentecostalism: the discharge of guilt and of disease involved in *Sanidad Divina*, and the charge of power involved in 'betterment' of every kind. These charges and discharges are analysed in chapter 9, which shows how they have been propagated by songs and stories, and along chains of intimate personal and familial contact. They unite the tradition of black spirituality with the white tradition of religious enthusiasm, and combine the most ancient world of the pre-literate with the most recent world of post-literacy.

How the transformations are achieved at the level of microprocesses and in the texture of intimate personal biographies is analysed in chapter 10. The biographies are taken from Puerto Rican culture and located both in Puerto Rico and in the United States, in order to illustrate transitions and turning points in places that bridge and link the Anglo and Hispanic worlds, and also in order to show how they are linked to physical migrations back and forth.

The final transformations concern the economy and the polity. Here I aim to show how the cultural logic of participation, voluntarism, self-government and personal initiative lies latent. In the beginning the religious impulse assembles a network to which men and women lash themselves for safety. Initially most of their energy is expended on constructing the raft, devising fraternities and sororities of mutual aid, of communication, and useful connection. Those who guide the raft may well be politically very cautious and conservative, anxious to avoid the destructive turbulence of political contention and polarization. The question then becomes: what are the political and economic potentials lying latent in this conservative format? From that question follow others. How far will the oratorical skills and organizational capacities fostered in the 'free space' of the religious group be extended to a wider world? How far will the sense of individual humanity, generated and protected by the company of the faithful, be transmuted into economic initiative, into new priorities and aspirations? Chapters 11 and 12 try to answer just those questions.

PART I

Historical Genealogies and Theoretical Background

Chapter 1

Anglo and Latin: Rival Civilizations, Alternative Patterns

Some wars are of very long duration, with the actual fighting quite intermittent. The Hundred Years War between England and France helped create both countries and confer on them their national identities. The thirty years war from 1914 to 1945 between the Allies and the 'Central Powers' crucially weakened the initial participants and gave undisputed world-supremacy to Russia and America. One of the longest running of all wars is the four hundred year clash between the Hispanic imperium and the Anglo-Saxon imperium. On the one side are all the successor states of the Iberian Peninsula; on the other side are England and its mightiest successor state – the USA.

The moment at which this is written, in late July 1988, is currently being marked in England as the four hundredth anniversary of the defeat of the Spanish Armada. The school-book the author read over forty years ago was very clear about the world-historical issues at stake. In his *English Seamen in the Sixteenth Century*, J. A. Froude said: 'We shall miss the meaning of this high epic story if we do not realise that both sides had the most profound conviction that they were fighting the battle of the Almighty. Two principles, freedom and authority, were contending for the guidance of mankind.'[1] Froude, of course, exaggerated. Nevertheless, on the one side was the certainty of autocracy; on the other the potentiality for freedom. Had the Spanish Armada won there would have been no United States, not even Los Estados Unidos.

To find the right perspective on the current rapid explosion of evangelical Protestantism in Latin America, we have to place ourselves initially on some very high ground, rather as Thomas Hardy did in *The Dynasts* before his focus shifted from the macrocosmic to the detailed geography of events and even the interweaving of personal biographies. He said, quite correctly, that one had to 'close up Time' and 'traverse Space' in order to 'Link pulses severed by Leagues and years' and 'Bring cradles into touch with biers':

> So that the far-off Consequence appears,
> Prompt at the heel of foregone Cause . . . [2]

The high ground can be staked out quite briefly. What happens now in Puerto Rico or Brazil or the Philippines by way of mutations in culture, and especially in religious consciousness, takes place within frames established in the long clash of 'Anglo' culture with Hispanic (or Lusitanian) civilization. Both participants in this clash had been steeled for it through struggles for their own national and religious identity. The Spanish for their part had established a fanatical union of nationhood and religion in the course of an 800-year war with Islam. The English (along with the Germans and the Dutch) had for their part established a union of faith and people in the course of a revolt against Rome. Braudel has brilliantly characterized this revolt as a declaration of independence on the part of the northern European colonies against the Roman Catholic or southern Latin imperium.[3] That struggle was then renewed in the Americas between the heirs of the Reconquista and the heirs of the religious left wing of the English Reformation. The residual legatees of the Reconquista were to be, of course, the successor states to the Spanish and Portuguese empires. The residual legatees, or more properly, perhaps, the true heirs of the left wing of the English Reformation, were to be the founders of the United States.

To begin with the weight of power in the Americas remained with the Latins. Their claims, and heroic explorations, extended deep into North America and are today movingly marked out by the mission outposts in Texas, New Mexico and California. As for the British and the Dutch (and, of course, the French), their toeholds in north-east America were relatively recent and comparatively minor.

Yet gradually the balance tipped against the Latins. First the British eliminated their French rivals, who might well have strangled British North America in an encircling sweep from the Great Lakes to New Orleans. Then the French (and the Spanish and the Dutch) helped the American colonists gain their independence from Britain and thereby brought to birth the most potent challenger of Latin civilization. The defeated British for their part just held on to their key outposts in the Caribbean (which were at that time rather more important to them than the American colonies!) Later they proceeded to assist the South American colonists gain their independence in turn from Spain and Portugal. Interestingly enough, in South and North America alike a large proportion of the colonists did not so much achieve independence as have it thrust upon them.

The axis of this world-historical clash beween 'Anglo' culture and Hispanic civilization now turned more and more on the United States. The wars between the Americans and Mexicans resulted in the establishment of Texas and the annexation of at least one-third of Mexican territory. The military conclusion of the clash came with the Spanish–American war of 1898 when Spain lost Cuba, Puerto Rico and the Philippines. Thereafter the United States maintained unquestioned economic and geopolitical supremacy and backed this up with sorties and occupations in Central America as far south as Panama.[4]

Revolutions in Nicaragua and Cuba are as much nationalistic declarations of independence against the United States as they are also undoubtedly movements of the left. Independence movements in the Caribbean are likely to be left-wing if only as an expression of the principle of political contrariety. They fit into the long succession of such declarations: Northern Europe from Rome, North America from Northern Europe, Latin America from Southern Europe and – now – Latin America from North America. It is perhaps worth adding that the recent clashes between Britain and Guatemala, over what is now Belize, and between Britain and Argentina over the Falkland Islands, are quite minor though interesting footnotes to the wider clash in which the principal actor was unequivocally the United States.

The clash was also, of course, cultural and *ipso facto* religious. It occurred on the cultural plane and it was often perceived in religious terms. For some Latin Americans the culture of North America and the Protestant religion were alike intrusions of the barbarous alien, a view echoed by cultural nationalists to this day, with appropriate additions about economic imperialism and dependence. For other Latin Americans, more especially the liberal opponents of clericalism, American culture was to be emulated. It was empowered by certain progressive principles, among them being the principles of Protestantism. Some Latin American liberals and most liberal North Americans viewed the Anglo-Hispanic clash in terms parallel to those used by Froude about the Armada. The issues for them were, once again, those of freedom against authority, equality against hierarchy, individual conscience against organicism, progress against reaction, and peaceability and commerce against unproductive militarism. It was a case study framed, it would seem, to illustrate Herbert Spencer's famous contrast, put forward in his *Ecclesiastical Institutions*, between the peaceable and productive ministers and the unproductive and military priests. It might even be seen as a case study in the wider application of the Whig interpretation of history.

There is an irony written into this contrast between peaceable Protestant commerce and unproductive priestly militarism which is worth bringing out, since the creation of a peaceable culture and a pacific personality is indeed central to the liberal-cum-Protestant project. Informing the whole argument of this book will be a tension between the pacific ideals of personal and cultural development, promoted by certain varieties of Protestantism, and the ideals of the military and of male machismo. The cultural clash of 'Anglo' and Hispanic is in part fought out on this plane. However, the fact that it is 'fought out' indicates where lies the irony. To many Latin Americans the peaceable self-portrait painted by the imperial Protestant republic – *La République Impériale* – is an irony of a very simple kind. To them it is mere hypocrisy, looking the more odd in view of the crime rates of American cities. But the question is more complicated.

It is a matter of simple observation that pacifism as a doctrine and peaceability as an individual and personal ideal have been more widely disseminated in Britain and America than anywhere else. It has something to do with the relative safety conferred by the ocean, and a great deal more to do with the propagation of radical and Arminian Protestantism as a form of voluntary religion separate from the state, from the experience of power and the exigencies of *raison d'état*. Catholicism has been bound up organically in the nexus of those pressures; Arminian Protestantism has released itself from them.[5]

This is not to say that Anglo-Saxon Protestant cultures lack military traditions, or links between certain kinds of piety and military avocations. Indeed, in the British context there are notable traditions of evangelical military leadership, especially perhaps in Presbyterian Scotland and Ulster. It is to say that peace movements and objections to conscription have flourished in Anglo-Saxon cultures as almost nowhere else, and to emphasize the creation of a certain kind of pacific personality deeply averse to political or personal violence. The peace movements have varied roots, in semi-secularized versions of the left wing of the Reformation and Unitarianism and in the Sunday schools and social rescue movements of evangelicalism. Perhaps these pacific motifs are strongest where evangelicalism and the pacific ideologies of nineteenth-century liberal commerce overlap and reinforce each other. It might also be observed that no other cultures have nourished so much guilt about military and imperial expansion.

The irony arises from the manner in which the two peaceable and commercial nations of America and Britain have taken pleasure, profit and pride in military prowess, especially at the expense of Hispanic nations. In spite of the quite correct association of Protestantism with personal peaceability, there has also been a geopolitical and ideological association of Protestantism with preponderant power and worldly success. As a result, whenever peaceable liberals enter into warfare with 'backward' militaristic nations, they see themselves as crusaders for progress. The Americans are even better at this than the British, though the British are no laggards. Thus when President McKinley sought justification for the extension of United States sovereignty over the Philippines, he did so in terms of making straight the way of the Lord and allowing entry to the gospel. The spectacle of a United States President of Ulster Protestant lineage sanctifying the war in the Philippines in such lofty terms is to be savoured as an exemplary irony in the whole relationship between the Anglo and the Hispanic cultures.

The theme of peace and of the specific role of voluntaristic Arminian Protestantism in encouraging a pacific temper introduces the next large-scale process needed to frame the current diffusion of Protestantism in Latin America. That is the emergence of voluntarism itself and the breakup of the union of church and state, people and faith, local community and local church. The spread of evangelical Christianity in Latin America is contingent upon the breakdown of the organic unity of a given religion and national identity, and the general deregulation of religion. That breakdown has to be expounded in terms of the sociological differentiation of spheres of activity, whereby spheres such as medicine, education and social legitimation are successively secularized, and also in terms of dramatic contrasts between the way this differentiation has worked out in Protestant as compared with Catholic cultures. We look first at the Protestant pattern, which is itself divided into three variants: the North European, the British and the American. Each of these lies on a continuum from the union of church and state to the separation of church and state, and from the regulation of religion to the deregulation of religion. Each of them is also one of the successive declarations of independence just outlined. We begin with the particular variant of Protestant church–state relations dominant in the ex-colonies of continental Northern Europe.

Since the North European pattern is historically very complicated, the process has to be radically simplified and also concentrated for expository purposes in two instructive examples: Haugeanism in western Norway, and Pietism in Germany. What, then, is the North European pattern?[6]

Protestant Pattern A: Northern Europe

Broadly, in Northern Europe the unity of church and state, faith and people, was maintained, with a minimum of overt religious dissent or, at any rate, with few organizational breakaways. Crown and altar stayed in close proximity, with the altar generally subordinate to the crown except in matters of faith. Religious change occurred by way of alterations in devotional attitude or philosophical emphasis, or the emergence of cells and pressure groups. But not by way of mass movements of dissent and nonconformity. When such began to emerge, as in mid-nineteenth-century Sweden, they encountered counter-measures severe to the point of repression. Many Swedish Baptists, for example, preferred to emigrate. As a result, when Social Democracy gained power and influence among the people at large, it had few *major* traditions of religious dissent on which to draw, and often became anti-religious as well as anti-clerical. That remains true of every country in Protestant Northern Europe. There is, for example, plenty of evidence from mid- and late nineteenth-century Germany of the way radical politics look on an anti-religious polemic which, given the alliance of church and aristocracy, affected parts of the middle class as well as the working class.[7] The political division over religion was not so great as in most Catholic countries, but it was greater than in Britain and America. In the long run, this unity of faith and people tended to mutate into a degree of ideological homogeneity around a new Social Democratic consensus, at least in Scandinavia. The church, after a period of social exile on the right, gradually conformed to this consensus, and sometimes, as in Finland, did so quite enthusiastically. The Social Democrats, for their part, also mellowed, and might even, as in contemporary Finland, include 'Christianity' as part of their approved consensus.

This Northern European pattern may appear remote from issues relating to Latin America, but logically, sociologically and historically it is important and has to be included. Ultimately, of course, it is of prime importance because of the varied legacy of Luther and of Pietism, passed on alike to Methodist and Pentecostal nonconformity. Thus the Protestant University in Guatemala City immediately confronts you in the doorway with a genealogy going back to Luther and to Wittenberg. But more proximate reasons for including some reference to the North European pattern are that it represents the kind of union of church and state which successfully prevented the voluntaristic denominationalism from which Pentecostalism derives, *and* yet nourished the forms of piety on which Pentecostalism ultimately rests. The long-term progenitors of Pentecostalism are Spener and the German Collegia Pietatis. The exploration of a Christian 'affect' found in Pietism, and most familiar to us through the religious texts set by J. S. Bach, is part of the ancestry of Pentecostalism mediated to a large extent through Methodism. Not only is the 'affective' aspect of Pietism important, but so also are pietistic traditions of subordination to the powers that be and of withdrawal from politics. Contemporary critics of Pentecostalism continually fasten on what they call its apolitical 'pietism'. This is a broad and polemical use of 'pietism' but it correctly looks back to the traditions of Pietism proper in Northern Europe.

However, so round a characterization of pietism has to be qualified, since pietism is not necessarily apolitical. Throughout this book, it will be argued that this kind of pietistic faith passes through periods when it is politically latent and others when it is active. Furthermore, it will be argued that political activity when it does emerge will be quite varied, even though the cultural logic of Pietism itself points towards fraternal equality. The political expressions of Pietism depend on circumstances and I now offer my examples. They are Pietism in Germany and Haugean piety in western Norway. The first example bears most directly on the question of pietistic support for the status quo. The second example bears on the way Pietism may locate itself on a major regional and cultural periphery in confrontation with a secular centre: a theme to which the subsequent argument frequently returns. Haugeanism also illustrates the central theme of the relationship between styles of Protestant piety and the establishment of mutually supportive economic networks.

Thus in these two examples three elements in the thematic repertoire of this book can briefly be introduced: *the varied political attitudes attendant on fraternal kinds of religiosity; the relation of given forms of religion to the tension between centres and peripheries; and the contribution of religion to mutually supportive economic networks and to personal advancement.*

In order to discuss German Pietism, I draw on the work of Mary Fulbrook, which is concerned with the capacity of this kind of religion to achieve strikingly varied political expressions in different areas of seventeenth- and eighteenth-century Germany. Her analysis deals with two areas noted for the strength of their Pietist movements, Württemberg and Brandenberg-Prussia. In the one Pietism helped oppose attempts to set up an absolutist regime even though it was not aggressively political. In the other Pietism became in effect the state religion and a branch of the absolutist state.[8]

Pietism in Württemberg spread initially in the years from 1680 to 1720 as a response to the devastation of successive wars, compounded by natural disasters and the absolutist ambitions of Duke Eberhard Ludwig. The Pietists interpreted the various devastations as divine admonitions, as do Pentecostals today, and joined forces with those who inveighed against the iniquitous luxury of the court. However, with the advent of relative prosperity and peace the Pietists became rather passive politically, and (like John Wesley) showed considerable interest in the millennarian predictions of Johann Albrecht Bengel. As members of the bourgeoisie they tended to support the Estates' demands for the retention of ancient rights and privileges, but saw princely authority as of God and evil as part of the inevitable emergence of the Antichrist before the Millennium.

Pietism in Prussia owed a great deal to the influence of Francke, who initially conceived of the movement as combining strenuous charitable endeavours, reform, biblical translation and world-wide missionary, manufacturing and trading concerns. However, in spite of this activist thrust, it evolved into a branch of the absolutist state, partly because the Pietists were glad to exchange persecution elsewhere for state assistance in Prussia, and partly because state officials saw the usefulness of Pietism. Pietist organizations could be useful in ministering to the military (as are Pentecostal organizations today in parts of Latin America) and the Pietists themselves could help the state in its contest with the orthodox Lutheran hierarchy and its feudal patrons in the provinces. However, with the accession of Frederick the Great in 1740, the centralized state no longer needed Pietism to lubricate its bureaucracy and, for that matter, the inner intensity of Pietism itself ran dry and infertile.

Mary Fulbrook comments on the social location of the Pietists in Württemberg and Brandenburg-Prussia. In relation to the latter she quotes authorities who argue that Pietism could only have fought the alliance of the feudal aristocracy and Lutheran orthodoxy on its own and independent of the monarchy if it had possessed a base in a really self-confident and powerful bourgeoisie. Its genuine political thrust was, therefore, blunted by the need to compound with the centralizing monarchy. In Württemberg by contrast the state church and the bourgeoisie were closely related and Pietism was viewed by the authorities as a largely ministerial movement which offered little threat and could be tolerated. Württemberg had, in any case, a long democratic bourgeois tradition and the Pietists were themselves either independent bourgeois or small traders and artisans. In such a situation the Pietists might protest during the bad conditions of the early period, but once matters eased off they were mostly content to pray rather than to act.

Turning now to Haugeanism, we have a movement which was the core of several vital changes and initiatives. It infused the western periphery of Norway with piety and helped build up Norwegian nationalism and the local language against Swedish domination. It povided the social bases for the so-called 'old left' of Norwegian politics, which actually turned out later to be influential in holding the political centre just when Norway might have tipped in a communist direction in 1920. And it also created networks of people animated by a spirit of economic innovation.

The Haugean movement in Norway, like the Inner Mission later, stayed within the state church, in spite of the fact that Hauge received a more repressive response from the authorities in church and state than ever Wesley did in England. Haugeans, and Pietists more generally, regarded the orthodox church as the arm of an urbane and colonial elite, infiltrated by false 'Enlightenment'. The Haugean movement was to the Norwegian periphery what Methodism was to Wales and Cornwall. Like Methodism it created a network of communication. Its followers were active in economic ventures and provided mutual support. They mobilized local feeling and roused linguistic consciousness. Their movement was a primary intimation of voluntarism, of liberal rights and pluralism. Hauge and his followers and successors were harbingers of local democratic lay awareness and initiative. And this initiative showed itself in a willingness to migrate: a disproportionate number of those Norwegians going to the United States were Haugeans.

Moreover, the Haugeans were eventually successful. They were active in the mobilization of feeling in 1830–3 and in 1884, and they finally broke the power of the bureaucracy associated with the influence of the towns. Because of this role of the towns and also of the eastern part of the country, the rural counter-cultural struggle was largely separate from and cross-cut the cleavages eventually appearing in the east. The conservative party never gained rural religious support: it was associated with urbane, convivial drinking, as well as with the channels of foreign dominance. The religious revival tended to support the parties of the so-called 'old left' which now forms the centre. In the south and west where they were the core of a cultural defence system, they resisted the class polarization found in eastern and parts of northern Norway. They now provide a centre of support for the Christian Party. As in the cultural defence system of rural, small-town America, the issue of prohibition became an important rallying symbol for them; and as in contemporary Wales the issue of local language provided and still provides another focus of identity.

In the rest of the country, during the 1890s, radical polarization along class lines proceeded rapidly. Norway industrialized very crudely and very quickly and succumbed to considerable communist influence, particularly after the First World War when socialists joined the Second International for a short time. But the need to appeal to the electorate over a wide enough area and the existence of the relatively unpolarized south and west meant that eventually the Labour Party had to move closer to the centre. The superimposition of cultural cleavage and of class cleavage ameliorated the astringency of political combat. Nevertheless, the unitary element in Norwegian society reasserted itself in that Social Democratic dominance, once established in 1935, became permanent; the phrase 'from Danish bureaucracy to the one party state' indicates this continuity.[9]

By contrast with this major movement, combining as it did political and economic innovation with the upsurge of national consciousness on a geographical 'periphery', the other countries of Scandinavia remained relatively homogeneous. They experienced only small movements of free churches as in Västerbotten in Sweden, or North Jutland in Denmark, or else rural revivals as in the Finnish countryside. The film 'Babettes Feast' gives the flavour of this rural Scandinavian piety. Thus Haugeanism (with its derivatives) presents the nearest analogue to Methodism to appear within the North European pattern, but it was, nevertheless, much smaller and never fully broke out of the swaddling bands of establishment. For that breakout we will have to turn to the English pattern, and to its eventual realization in America. (Holland *might* have performed these world-historical tasks; it had the freedom of religion and a remarkable degree of decentralization but could not sustain its rivalry with England for a sufficiently long time.)

Before turning to Britain and to America, the point of adducing such examples is worth some further emphasis. They are offered, as suggested earlier, as cases of Pietism close to source and still bound into the organic frame of the unity of church and state, prior to the breakouts which occurred in Anglo-American culture. They illustrate how the political thrust of Pietism varies and how it may in one situation be blunted by adverse circumstances, or fade into apolitical withdrawal, or else emerge as the radical consciousness of a stratum or region. They therefore bear on the whole issue of the relation of Pietist religiosity to the politics of protest as well as the avoidance of violent revolution. The Haugean example in particular bears on the avoidance of violent revolution in Norway and also illustrates the way Pietism may be associated with a new economic ethos and the creation of networks of support. These cases are, therefore, introducing the economic and political problematic of the whole argument.

Protestant Patterns B1 and B2: Britain and America

The British and American patterns, so far as they exhibit respectively the partial and the complete collapse of the unity of faith and people, can be presented together. That is because America simply takes potentials partly realized in Britain and brings them to a logical conclusion. England itself retains some elements of aristocratic hierarchy, and of the relationship of church to state, while its Protestant peripheries in Wales, Scotland and Ulster, as well as its overseas extensions in Canada, Australia and New Zealand, variously evolved towards something closer to the American pattern. Just as there is a church–state continuum running from Scandinavia through England to America, so there is a sub-continuum running from England through Wales, Ulster and Scotland, and Canada, Australia and New Zealand, to the United States.

All the peripheries of Britain are more Protestant and egalitarian than England itself, and have contributed massively to the cultures of the 'white' Commonwealth and to the foundation of America, and – maybe – by extension to the overspill of American Protestantism into Latin Americas. One cannot help speculating on the high proportion of Scottish names among American missionaries to Latin America.

Indeed, it is worth underlining the long-term origins of the American awakenings in seventeenth-century revivals taking place in the nationally self-conscious 'peripheries' of the British Isles. The Great Awakening itself was a complex phenomenon with diverse social roots and varied locations in time and place, but it certainly found fertile ground among Scots and Scots-Irish migrants to British North America. Recent research by Marilyn Westerkamp traces a genealogy of large-scale and long-lasting emotional meetings back to Ulster and the Scottish lowlands in the 1630s.[10] This religious genealogy was not only emotional in tone but lay in character. In eighteenth-century America it might run in all kinds of ecclesiastical and ethnic channels, and traverse the whole gamut from modified

Calvinism to Arminianism, but it was everywhere recognizable for dealing in the heart and the affections, and in the vital activity of the Spirit, and for its emphasis on lay participation.

If we now consider just England and the United States rather than the intermediate instances, the centre of interest turns on three major waves of religious change, Puritanism, Methodism and Pentecostalism, and the different degrees to which they succeed in informing the two cultures. 'Methodism' in this context stands in for the Evangelical Revival in general. That the Revival had roots in modified Calvinism has already been indicated; and the way the Spirit of Revival eventually relocated itself in part in Baptist, conservative Presbyterian, Holiness, and Pentecostal traditions is part of the following argument.

In Britain, more particularly England, the unity of church and state became precarious quite soon after the Reformation.[11] The emergence of massive Puritan dissent created a major channel for combined religious and political change, and cleared the social space within which Methodism might develop. Initially Puritanism was not voluntaristic either in England or America; and it continued to fuse religion and politics in a manner that aimed at a godly theocracy, in old England and New England alike. But it also contained seeds of voluntarism and religious democracy, and gave rise to such a multitude of contenders that theocratic governance could not be maintained. In any case, in old England in 1660, the monarchy and state church were restored, and thereafter the voluntary sector constituted no more than a countercultural minority. It is reasonable to see the Glorious Revolution of 1688 as an extended realization of part of the Puritan programme in that monarchical absolutism and Catholicism were prevented from making a return, and Parliament successfully asserted its supremacy.

In America, however, the core cultures were more weighted towards dissent than in England, and the Church of England could only acquire a shadow of its English dominance even where it was strongest and most ambitious. Rhode Island, Pennsylvania, New Jersey, Delaware and (initially) Maryland all established religious tolerance and prepared the way for the final separation of the state from each and every church at the Revolution. After the Revolution, the Anglican church became no more than a culturally elite fragment. The American Revolution of 1776 was the final conclusion of the trajectory of the two English revolutions of 1642–9 and 1688, and the ripened fruit of John Milton and John Locke. Of course, it also owed much to the eighteenth-century Enlightenments in England and in Europe, and to the English 'country party', but the social base on which it rested was created by the forms, sentiments, implications and residues of Puritanism – and of enthusiastic religion.[12]

The Methodist and Pentecostal waves of voluntary religion also affected Britain and America differently. In Britain, Methodism and its various offshoots carried forward the religious counterculture of old Dissent and strengthened it to the point where, in the mid-nineteenth century, nonconformity and the establishment confronted one another almost on equal terms. Nevertheless, the established Church of England also revived and maintained an inclusive framework. It mostly held on to the high ground of culture and power. Things were quite otherwise in America, where – as the next chapter will indicate – the explosive power of Methodism and of Arminian evangelical Protestantism generally (for example the Baptists) undermined all establishments, including the old Puritan churches as well as the Anglican (Episcopal) Church. Arminian evangelical Protestantism provided the *differentia specifica* of the American religious and cultural ethos. Perhaps one marker of the way this fed into, created and expressed the difference between America and England is the American insistence on sincerity and openness rather than on form and privacy. The whole American style was, and is, 'Methodist' in its emphases, whereas in England the culturally prestigious style remained Anglican. 'Enthusiasm' of all kinds, religious, cultural and personal, became endemic in America; in England enthusiasm remained intermittent and the object of some mild curiosity. In this respect the two cultures took different paths.

Why evangelical religion maintained itself in the USA and not in Britain or Northern Europe is a question too large to be pursued properly here. It is important only to observe the fact. Nevertheless, one or two points can usefully be made. First, the maintenance of aristocratic hierarchies in England, and even in Northern Europe, created an association of religion with power and high culture which progressively alienated the majority from active observance, more particularly people in the working classes and the great cities. Faith became passive and non-observant. In the United States, however, where high culture was too weak to inhibit or restrict enthusiastic popular religiosity faith became active and observant; and the great cities did not sink into religious apathy.[13]

Second, the countries of Northern Europe, Britain included, were relatively small and mostly centralized; and their core institutions, including in recent times the media, bore down upon evangelical culture. In consequence, we see evangelical faith burgeoning only at the cultural and regional peripheries, in western Norway as opposed to Oslo, in Jutland as opposed to Copenhagen, in Wales, Ulster and the Scottish highlands and islands as opposed to London. In the USA, however, the spaces were so vast and the institutions so dencentralized that evangelical culture could remain self-sustaining, even if eroded at the margins in the way recently analysed by James D. Hunter and George Marsden.[14] It is true that evangelicalism had its strongest roots in a periphery of sorts, the American South (and parts of the South West), but that periphery is larger and more powerful than all but a very few nations. It is a world in and for itself, and can sustain independent generators of evangelical culture with enormous reproductive and missionary power.

What emerges from this in general is the importance of peripheries and regional redoubts, as will be illustrated later in my accounts of evangelical expansion in south-east Mexico. What emerges in particular in the context of a comparison between America and Britain is a point recently made with some force by Steve Bruce.[15] An evangelicalism established on the 'periphery' represented by Dallas, Texas has a future, whereas one established in the Western Isles of Scotland appears to have more of a past. Indeed, many of the most powerful impulses of American missionary zeal emanate from Dallas as well as from the 'old' South.

Apart, however, from such major differences between Britain and America, there are some common tendencies to be observed. One is for religion to shift away from the core structures of society, necessarily rooted in hierarchy, power and violence, towards the cultural realm. Methodism and Pentecostalism alike construct models of equality, fraternity and peaceability in the religious enclaves of *culture*, but do not generalize from these in terms of coherent political world-views. In others words, they set up communities, the political implications of which are fraternal, participatory and egalitarian, even though such communities can only survive if they also have vigorous structures of authority, Methodism and Pentecostalism are sociologically consonant with democratic polities and provide part of the popular cultural base on which such polities might rest. But they are not themselves basically political, even though a Wesley, for example, might well produce projects for communitarian reform.[16] Their mass momentum as manifest in vast open-air meetings is restricted to the politics and long-term dynamics of culture. Thus whether or not you take seriously their impact on a society as a whole depends on your estimate of the power of culture.

From this other things follow. A culture informed by Methodist or Pentecostalism does not generate a 'Christian' political party, except maybe at some insignificant margins. It may generate movements for moral regeneration which affect politics, but that is something much less than a fully fledged political party. America and Britain entirely lack 'Christian' parties.

Not only are there no Christian parties corresponding to the cultural mass movements of Methodism and Pentecostalism, but such movements are sufficiently distanced from power, violence and *raison d'état* to concentrate on the creation of a peaceable attitude. The issue of peace has already been touched upon and it arises again here in a slightly different context. To be cut off from the centres of raw power and the corruption of polities leads either to semi-pacifist understandings of the political realm, such as characterize modern Methodism, or else to an apolitical withdrawal and anti-political moralism and naivety such as characterizes modern Pentecostalism. Methodists and Pentecostals criticize each other over their different versions of social change, but both bifurcate from a shared reserve about power and its corruptions.

As will be seen later, this apolitical withdrawal by Pentecostals runs into problems once it moves out of a highly differentiated society like the United States into countries like those of Latin America, where politics, violence and religion remain closely intertwined. Thus Latin American societies remain relatively undifferentiated compared with societies in the North Atlantic world and do not permit any mass movement to work solely at the level of culture. To be peaceable and apolitical may not be problematic in the United States, but in Latin America it can easily mean that the effect of Pentecostalism is sometimes to shore up the powers that be.

However, the issue here is not only the relative lack of differentiation in Latin American societies but the dramatically different historic trajectory taken by Catholicism in its confrontation with modernity and change. In the most general terms, Catholicism maintained an organic and militant front against change and opposed the Enlightenment, whereas Protestant societies crumbled internally and devised enlightened versions of Christianity. It is to that radically different Catholic pattern that we have now to turn.

The Catholic/Southern Latin Pattern

The Catholic pattern of confrontation emerged in Europe after the French Revolution in 1789, and appears to be endemic in all societies where Catholicism is the faith of the majority *and* closely linked to the state. The only exceptions occur where a Catholic majority is ruled by a non-Catholic foreign state, as was the case in Ireland and Poland, or where matters have been complicated by an internal territorial and ethnic division, as between Flanders and Wallonia, and between Czech Lands/Moravia and Slovakia. In the two latter cases one ethnic group has been strongly Catholic and the other distinctly anti-clerical.

The Hispanic (and Lusitanian) world is one where societies have been polarized, and religion, or more specifically the church, has been a core constituent in the polarization. Societies have rocked backwards and forwards between revolution and counter-revolution and have been ruled alternatively by a conservative military or by militant radicals who are themselves often soldiers. The conflict manifests itself comprehensively in disputes over clericalism, over church property, especially land, over ecclesiastical education, and over the degree to which Catholic norms governing abortion or divorce are built into public law. Historically the proponents of militant change have identified the church as a massive rampart of superstition, social passivity and the structures of the *ancien régime*, and the Catholic Church has responded by anathemas, by a sweeping Syllabus of Errors, and where possible by organizing the faithful in a ghetto. The most frequent source of contention turns around Catholic control of education, particularly elite education, and that was a crucial source of friction in Chile between Allende and the church. It remains an issue in Europe even today, in Italy, Malta, Spain and France.

In Europe the confrontation reached its bloody climax in the Spanish Civil War, in which the issue of religion was irretrievably tangled with all kinds of other alignments.[17] In Latin America it reached an equally savage climax in the protracted Mexican and Colombian civil wars. Some of the confrontations have left the church very weakened, so that in Uruguay, Venezuela and Guatemala the range of its influence became quite minimal. Occasionally the impact of confrontation was particularly great in one area, for example, the state of Tabasco in Mexico. As will be emphasized later the incidence of conflict over the Catholic Church and of state-inspired secularization affects the degree to which Protestantism is able to expand. Protestantism has not, at any rate as yet, made much impact in the highly secular atmosphere of Venezuela and Uruguay.

Yet in Colombia, where *La Violencia* was particularly brutal and the issues and alignments remarkably confused, the church survived and somehow re-established itself. It wielded extensive power, even among the trade unions, and for long defined Colombian identity as coextensive with Catholicism.[18] That, too, plainly affects the pace and nature of Protestant expansion. Perhaps the optimum conditions for Protestant expansion exist where the church has been seriously weakened but the culture not secularized, as in Brazil, Guatemala and Chile. But to pursue that is to anticipate subsequent extensions of the current argument.

In general, the war between the church and militant secularism has resulted in a stand-off where both sides recognize the cost of confrontation and where the ecclesiastical elite has partially disengaged itself from its ties with the landed and military elites. The church has adopted several strategies deployed according to local circumstances and how these work out bears on the opportunities open to evangelical Protestants. The church may retain or renew its alignment with the old landowning classes and the military. However, this involves a degree of subordination to the state and of acquiescence in brutality which harms the church and arouses the opposition of many Catholics. In any case, the military associated with the national security state have evolved into a more efficient bureaucratic stratum and do not always regard the church as intrinsically bound up with their interests, partly because it is becoming increasingly unreliable, and partly because some sectors of Protestantism are willing to fill the vacant place.[19]

Another strategy open to the church is to refurbish the organizational supports of the ghetto, like Catholic Action and the Cursillos. However, Catholic Action has often developed a radical wing, particularly among its youth, student and worker organizations, which can lead to difficulties. Associated with this strategy there is often an implicit alliance with parties well-disposed to the church, which usually means the Christian Democrats, but has for certain periods also meant populist parties like the Peronistas. However, such parties may evolve in less friendly directions, as the Peronistas certainly did, or may execute policies which implicate the church in their unpopularity. The government of Frei in Chile was at times an embarrassing ally for the Church.[20]

A third strategy is provided by liberation theology and the base communities. The base communities are the main rivals to the Pentecostals, and fish in the same water. However, they are always in danger of cumulative politicization, and of becoming more Marxisant than Christian. They also threaten hierarchy and unity, and a divided church may lose some competitive edge faced with the evangelical Christians. The Catholic Church finds it not altogether easy to pursue equality in the wider world and retain hierarchy within its own ecclesiastical walls.

It may be that the church will adopt an intermediate option of pursuing a more 'laic' model shorn of the revolutionary implications of liberation theology. According to this model elements of participatory democracy will be gently encouraged within a hierarchical framework, and critical political comment continued with certain clear limits set to politicization, particularly among the clergy. This option often includes greater respect for Marian doctrines and the priestly role while, at the same time pre-empting elements of the appeal of Pentecostalism through growth strategies, modern mass communications, lay inter-action and Catholic charismata.

How these alternative options bear on the expansion of Pentecostalism and evangelical Protestantism generally will become clearer as the argument advances. Clearly they affect the form and speed of evangelical expansion. In some areas the social role, provenance, function and destiny of groups pursuing moderate reform within the church run parallel to the social role, provenance, function and destiny of Pentecostals, while in other areas the Catholic partisans of liberation both pursue some of the things also pursued by Pentecostals, but also present a militant political alternative. The old *integristas* and Pentecostals are rivals in a quite different sense. Like the Pentecostals the *integristas* define themselves as apolitical but their philosophy is aligned with a conception of the union of church and state for which Pentecostals are barbarous aliens.

The analysis up to this point has merely erected the broad frames within which the expansion of evangelical Protestantism, and of Pentecostalism in particular, needs to be placed. Those frames have been the clash of the Hispanic and Anglo worlds, and the dramatically different ways in which Catholic cultures and Protestant cultures have entered into what we call modernity. Pentecostalism has been identified as the third and latest wave in the successive socio-religious mobilizations which have affected the 'Anglo' world, especially America, but which have discernible roots in the Pietism of Northern Europe. Pentecostalism is also the first wave to cross the border from the Anglo to the Hispanic worlds on a large scale.

It is now possible to move from this high ground a little closer to the material and concentrate on the genetic relation between the Methodist second wave and the Pentecostalist third wave and on the way the third wave has overflowed into the Hispanic cultures. In what follows, Methodism will be examined to yield a model and a problematic which may be applied to its Pentecostal successor. Certain elements in that model and that problematic have already been foreshadowed. They are: the quite varied political roles of evangelical piety according to circumstance; its adoption of a fraternal and peaceable outlook for which all the structures of politics and power are highly problematic; its capacity to enter into the mobilization of particular strata with the provision of networks for mutual support and economic advancement; and its role in the cultural defence or even the cultural renaissance of regional or subordinate ethnic cultures.

The Methodist Model: Anglo-American Cultural Production Reproduced in Latin America

At this crucial juncture in the argument, I move to one central element in the Protestant pattern of social change as it has worked itself out in Anglo-Saxon cultures. That is Methodism. I have already pinpointed Methodism as the second of the three main waves of Anglo-Saxon Protestant religiosity and I now wish to show three things. First, I want to establish the close genetic connection between Methodism, as the second wave of Protestantism, and Pentecostalism as the third. That is a matter only of indicating a genealogy in the history of religious ideas. Second, I wish to establish that the structural relationship of Methodism to English society, and also to Welsh society, offers an instructive model for looking at the relationship of Pentecostalism to Latin America today. In that connection I shall emphasize how Methodism widened the rent in the 'sacred canopy' which the 'Anglican' Church tried to maintain over English society; how Methodism helped destroy what remnants of the sacred canopy remained in the United States; and how Pentecostalism now performs similar roles with respect to Catholicism in Latin America.[1] Third, I shall show how the problematic of Methodism, especially as established by Halévy, offers us a problematic with respect to Pentecostalism in Latin America.[2]

Protestant Waves Two and Three: The Methodist/ Pentecostal Connection

There is no great difficulty in establishing the genetic connection of Methodism and Pentecostalism. However embarrassing it may be to some Methodists, for whom the 'enthusiastic' past of Methodism is emotionally and historically remote, the early stages of Methodism in England and America closely resemble the present condition of Pentecostalism. There are hundreds of descriptions of Methodist meetings which sound like descriptions of Pentecostal services today. Joseph Barker, describing a revival in Sheffield round about 1835, referred to wild excitement, screams, 'jarring songs', and shouts of 'Glory', and also to people falling down on the floor or leaping over the forms. Such services went on for hours, as do their Pentecostal successors. And they generated similar reactions of hostility and occasional violence.[3]

What Methodism and Pentecostalism clearly share is an emphasis on the availability of grace to all, a millennial hope, and an intense search after 'scriptural holiness'.

Elements in Pentecostalism less evident in Methodism are exorcism, divine healing and speaking in tongues, though the early Methodists certainly rebuked the Devil and his minions, and also dispensed homely remedies to the sick.

The strongest of all the links between Pentecostalism and Methodism is the search after holiness. Vincent Synan in his *Holiness Pentecostal Movement in the United States* says unequivocally that 'the historical and doctrinal lineage of American Pentecostalism is to be found in the Wesleyan tradition, and the same argument is made out in Donald Dayton's *Theological Roots of Pentecostalism*.[4] The first Methodist sermon in America was preached in 1766 in New York City by Captain Thomas Webb and passed directly from justification by faith to receiving the Holy Ghost and to sanctification. A revival in Virginia in 1773–6 was 'the first instance of a pentecostal-like religious revival in the nation'.[5] From Virginia it spread to New England and to the frontier country of Kentucky. The camp meetings in Kentucky were full of godly hysteria, holy dancing and laughter. During a revival in the University of Georgia in 1800–10 the students even spoke in tongues.

Synan stresses the importance of Southern Pentecostal groups in developing the emphasis on holiness; and he also points out how Methodism was disturbed by the way a revival of holiness religion within the Methodist Church ignored denominational boundaries. By the beginning of the twentieth century most of the major holiness groups had been formed. In particular in the South there were the Church of God, the Church of God in Christ, the Fire-Baptized Holiness Church and the Pentecostal Holiness Church. These fed into the background of the famous Azusa St Revival of 1906, even though the single most important individual catalyst for the Revival was a black Baptist minister, W. J. Seymour. This Revival is usually accounted the commencement of modern Pentecostalism. As Aldersgate St, London was to Methodism, so Azusa St, Los Angeles was to Pentecostalism.

The interweaving of Methodism with Pentecostalism, even at the parting of the ways nearly a century ago, can be illustrated by the early histories of groups currently active in Latin America. The Church of the Nazarene, for example, traces its origin to the union of the Holiness Church of Christ and the Pentecostal Church of the Nazarene at Pilot Point, Texas, in 1908. All the various groups feeding into the combined church had been deeply influenced by the National Holiness Movement and *'had large contingents of former Methodists'*.[6] The Church of the Nazarene 'ardently defended entire sanctification as a second work of grace' but it denied any connection between speaking in tongues and the Baptism of the Holy Spirit.[7] This is why in 1919 it dropped the word Pentecostal from its name.

Most interesting and sociologically most significant is the story behind the emergence of the Methodist Pentecostal Church in Chile, which is briefly summarized by Walter Hollenweger in 'Methodism's Past in Pentecostalism's Present'[8] and is also covered in Kessler's standard history.[9] The genetic continuity, and the sociology of the discontinuity, more particularly in Latin America, is perfectly illustrated in Hollenweger's account. It shows how schism is endemic in the process of a church becoming truly indigenous and also how divisions turn around the 'coldness' of the educated and the warmth of the uneducated.

Hollenweger concentrates on 'the revival under Willis Hoover, the blending of Wesleyan and Chilean popular cultures, the clash which arose between the Chilean Protestants and the American missionaries, and the subsequent establishment of the first theologically and financially self-sufficient Protestant church in the Third World'.[10] It was in the closing years of the last century that an attempt was made to establish an indigenous and self-sufficient Methodist Church with official backing in Chile. Because this was not forthcoming, the missionaries who went to Chile tended to be drawn from the less cultured, revivalist fringe of American Methodism. Notable among them was Willis Hoover. So evident was the poor education of some of the Methodists that a Presbyterian lady was moved to comment both on their lack of worldly wisdom – and on their abundance of life and love. The Methodist work in Chile prospered. But then in the late 1900s better educated missionaries started to arrive who disapproved of Hoover's revivalism, of his friendship with the Chileans, and of his protests against financial dealings behind the nationals' backs. Hoover himself began to look to new horizons, which included the Pentecostal revivals, and also the work of T. B. Barratt, a Methodist evangelist in Oslo who was later to become the 'Pentecostal apostle' to Europe.

At that point, the Chileans began to take over responsibility for worship as they had already taken over responsibility for their church buildings. This shift helped bring about revival but it also created difficulties with the American missionaries. An English girl, Nellie Laidlaw, became converted and began to intervene in church services following 'leadings in the spirit'. Eventually on 12 September 1909, she and her supporters were restrained by the police, and that date came to be remembered as the Reformation Day of Chilean Pentecostalism. Soon afterwards Hoover himself was charged with teaching false doctrines; and a church commission passed resolutions condemning miracles and healings, and tears and visions consequent on the baptisms of the Holy Spirit. The Chileans recognized in this an oblique trial of their own revival and saw that it meant a break with the missionaries. They declared their independence and were immediately penniless. But, in the event, official Methodist expansion slowed down so completely that it took seventy years to double the membership, whereas over the same period the new Iglesia Metodista Pentecostal reached a membership of nearly one million.

During this crisis even the Christian and Missionary Alliance had felt impelled to describe the revival as a species of fanaticism with 'gesticulaciones grotescas'. It seemed some converts crowed like cocks, and others thought they were playing a stringed instrument; yet others lost all feeling in their bodies. Yet the revivalists maintained all the elements of Methodist doctrine and even of discipline, adding only manifestations which renewed the early history of Methodism itself. The implications were clear. Methodism could only recover its early enthusiasm through independent channels, and it could only expand in Latin cultures by breaking out into new organizations under Chilean control. In short, the power of Methodism could only be recovered by setting up another circuit: indigenous Pentecostalism.

Structural Analogies: Anglo-American Methodism, Latin American Pentecostalism

With the Methodist contribution to the genealogy of Pentecostalism established, we have next to outline the structural analogies between Methodism in England and in the United States, and Pentecostalism in Latin America. Those analogies need to be set out in skeletal form before being fleshed out, even at the price of repeating arguments made in the previous chapter. The backcloth to the whole drama is the unity of people and faith, church and state, local community and local church which the Church of England tried to maintain after the Reformation and which was partially re-established in 1660 after a brief period of republican rule and religious voluntarism. That establishment and that re-establishment provides a fundamental historical marker for this argument and happens to be crucial for any understanding of the subsequent social and religious development of England. In short, the sector of voluntary religiosity in England was kept in check after 1660 to a degree which was impossible in colonial North America.

Nevertheless, the voluntary sector was dramatically widened even in England by the rise of Methodism and, in time, grew to become a powerful counterculture, especially among the upper lower classes of England's industrial north.[11] In Wales it actually became the core element in a revived national culture, though, of course, not an established church on the old model. In North America, however, the countercultures of England became the defining core cultures of a new national society and provided the social and religious matrices out of which the United States emerged, aided, of course, by philosophical enlightenments more or less shared by England, France and North America. Methodism, and Arminian Protestantism generally, then went on to complete the corrosion of the old union of church and state which had originally proceeded *pari passu* with the historic evolution of the colonies under Puritan aegis. *What had been implicit and countercultural in England became explicit and definitive in the United States*, and a key element in a world-historical transition. In that transition the United States declared its independence in 1776; and the American Methodist Church declared its independence in 1784.

Over a century and a half later the same kind of process was repeated, as between North and South America, though with significant differences. This time the receiving culture in Latin America retained vigorous elements of the union of church and state, local church and local community. This time the sending culture was one in which religion and society, church and state, were officially, and even practically, highly differentiated. The First Amendment ruled.[12] What the 'advanced' culture of the United States offered to Latin America was, first of all, its own religious development in amalgamated form: Arminian evangelical Protestantism (Methodist and Baptist) in what were often conservative variants, and Calvinistic Protestantism (Presbyterian), again in rather conservative variants. That initiated a *minor* break in the principle of religious uniformity in Latin America conjoined to the political assault on the Catholic Church by militant liberals. Two or three generations subsequent to that Pentecostalism became the explosive agent of a *major* break in the principle of religious uniformity, acting as Methodism (and Arminian Protestantism generally) had acted previously in England and in the United States. And it, too, declared its independence, initially in 1909 but also in a whole series of subsequent declarations which established the self-government of the indigenous churches. More slowly and sometimes less explicitly the older Protestant churches also declared their autonomy.

This skeletal frame now needs fleshing out at one or two key points, not in order to provide yet another history, but in order to bring out the sociological fundamentals which inhere in the model. First, we consider significant elements in the success of Methodism as a counterculture in England and then elements in its success as a coreculture in the United States.

Methodism owed part of its success in England to a combination of the archaic with the modern, and also to potent ambiguity. Wesley himself, as John Walsh has shown, came close to desiring 'all things in common' and placed a sacred aureole around the head of the poor.[13] They had special spiritual gifts and deserved Christian charity. Wesley even started the first people's dispensary. Yet Methodism itself nourished individualists for whom the poor were simply idle and undeserving. Methodism utilized different elements in its wide and ambiguous heritage according to circumstance. It carried forward elements of high culture and could also pick up elements of popular culture. The most potent ambiguity of Methodism lay in its organization, which was authoritarian in mode and participatory in its intimate style. It thus had sufficient backbone to survive and yet could express all the resonances of equality before God and before man.

Methodism in England after 1738 was a *movement* and arguably one of the first mobilizations in the modern sense of that word. It developed an itinerant system because the population itself was becoming itinerant. It thus became a manifestation of increased physical communication between one area and another as well as an intensification of spiritual communication. Methodism directly addressed multitudes through its circuit riders and lay preachers.

It also broke up the unity of the local nuclei of habitation. Some of them remained too tightly integrated to be broken up but many more were ready for the Methodist fission. Many people at the margins of the social hierarchy found the pride of rank too neatly and offensively replicated in the parish church. By joining the Methodists they were able to make their autonomy visible without directly challenging the whole political order. To have challenged the bastions of local and state power directly, especially in the years of nervous repression following the French Revolution, would have brought about serious persecution and perhaps even the kind of legal control which smothered dissent in Sweden. People were also able to make their inner autonomy visible by the free expression of their feelings, anxieties and hopes in chapel worship and in large-scale open-air meetings. There, perhaps, protest stopped, at least for a while, but within the free space afforded by faith new and more egalitarian relationships could be explored and new positions of initiative and authority exploited. People not only expressed their nascent autonomy but learnt the skills of oganization, responsibility and public speaking. They became 'speaking men', and even, to some extent, speaking women, and they knew themselves as individuals possessed of a conscience. This personal sense of conscience and the allied capacity for conscientiousness had effects far beyond the formal frontiers of Methodism.

At the same time, they were bound together and assisted one another. The Methodist chapels, along with the chapels of other denominations affected by revival, harboured networks of people who might create libraries, or offer each other economic assistance, or unite in the defence of farm labourers or practitioners of a trade. The same networks might be the basis for singing together or attending an adult school. Sometimes such activities might expand to create very large organizations: the Sacred Harmonic Society of London or the Stockport Sunday School.[14] Even though these networks and their activities were not in themselves political, they were recognizable as the specific expression of a new social interest. Eventually that interest acquired its political correlative in the organization of provincial liberalism. And so it came about that political allegiance to the conservatives or liberals between 1870 and 1920 could be predicted from attendance respectively at Anglican or Nonconformist Sunday schools.[15]

Methodists clustered in particular places. You might find them in an industrial village like New Mills, or in the wool and cotton towns of east Lancashire and Yorkshire, or in the fishing and mining communities of Durham and Cornwall or South Wales, or in the Potteries. They also clustered in particular occupations where they might have some independence. They were artisans, or foremen, or small shopkeepers. Later they might become social workers and teachers. Since their resources were very limited and the educational ladder not yet in place, their social mobility was restricted. The ministry offerred them their best channel of advance. Mobility was a kind of offshoot of cleanliness and carefulness. A minority were successful on a more dramatic scale and became entrepreneurs in industries like flour-milling and jam-making, and even in mining. Even if they did not rise very far in the social scale, they ate well and were pioneers of good nourishment.[16]

This brief pen-portrait is offered as a template to be remembered as the characteristics of contemporary Pentecostalism in the developing Third World come into view. Above all, those who were caught up in this evangelical movement exhibited two novel kinds of rhythm which are highly relevant to Pentecostalism. One was the rhythm of work in the factory for which Methodists were well prepared by their emphasis on 'method'. The other was the rhythm of 'spiritual songs' culled from any source that would appeal, and the new metres of the hymns of the revival. The first rhythm was orderly, and the second was riotous; and they were complementary.[17] This orderliness in the sphere of work and effervescence in the sphere of grace links together the Methodist and Pentecostal movements.

The new social and religious rhythm was particularly powerful in the peripheries of England, above all the Celtic societies of Cornwall and South Wales.[18] At these edges and margins the new culture of relatively autonomous and/or marginal people became the core culture of the whole society. But it had to do that through distinctive, and sometimes separate, branches of the revival which could express the character of the country and speak its language. Thus the Welsh revival fed off its own Calvinistic resources, whereas Methodism on the English model affected only a smallish minority.

In Wales evangelical religion expanded in a whole variety of forms – Baptist, Congregational, Wesleyan Methodist and Calvinistic Methodist – and became the established dissidence.[19] Whereas in England it worked within a framework still Anglican and hierarchical, in Wales the erosion of the sharper edges of class distinction went much further, and the key difference came to be more between the respectable chapel-goers and the disreputable drinkers. These socio-religious changes fed into and expressed the way in which all the 'peripheral' cultures of Britain – in Wales and Scotland – were more egalitarian in tone than in England, and more tilted towards radical politics. Even if many of the Welsh chapels remained embedded in a modest liberalism, they provided the cultural background out of which emerged cadres of Labour leaders as well as Liberal leaders, and later some of the leaders of Welsh nationalism.[20] The clearest external sign of that is the way evangelical style of oratory has informed the speech of Welsh politicians, like the Liberal Prime Minister, Lloyd George, or the present Labour leader, Neil Kinnock, or George Thomas, for long speaker of the House.

Of course, it is a matter of controversy how far the revivals, which continued from the 1730s to the conflagration of 1904, helped revivify the traditions and autonomous culture of Wales. Some commentators have seen the various evangelical movements as Puritanical repression of the mores and sports of the people. Others have seen them as enveloping the people of Wales in a distinctive style of communal music-making and poetry which runs parallel to movements aimed at recapturing the ancient bardic tradition of the country, as well as restoring the language and Welsh political dignity. Certainly the classic translation of the Bible into Welsh was a major influence on Welsh culture. Neil Sandberg comments on how religion contributed to the survival of the language as people were taught to read the Welsh Bible. He adds that 'it was not unusual for 90 per cent of households in Welsh-speaking areas to be associated with a Sunday school . . . and the use of Welsh was seen as particularly appropriate for theological discourse and argument.'[21] The controversy about the relation of evangelical religion to language as well as to mores and nascent nationalism will reappear in the context of Jamaica and the Maya of the Yucatan and Guatemala.

The discussion now shifts to the relationship between the evangelical counterculture(s) of Britain and the much more central evangelical culture of the United States. The peripheral cultures and the dissenting faiths of Britain, and the mixing of those egalitarian faiths and egalitarian cultures, contributed powerfully to the evolution of the United States. Wales, Ulster and Scotland are culturally closer to America than is England. It was immigrants from Ulster and Scotland who constituted one-sixth of the American population at the time of independence and many of them contributed vigorously to the American revolution.[22]

They also made large contributions to Canada, Australia and New Zealand, which helped place those societies midway between England and the United States. Calgary, Ballarat and Dunedin are place-names which give some indication of that immense diaspora of Protestants from the British peripheries. Anglican dominance decreased along a crucial continuum from England, through Wales and Ulster, to Australia, Canada and New Zealand, until it is only a shadowy elite fragment in the United States. Each point along that continuum defines a set of cultural correlatives which go with a diminishing organic hierarchy and an encroaching voluntarism.

This is not the place to work back over the contribution of classical English Puritan dissent to the making of America, except to say that the leaders of 1776 were heirs to the English republican revolution of 1642–9, and that a line runs from that upheaval to the Glorious Revolution of 1688–9 and the American Revolution of 1776. If one wants recent expositions of the contributions of religious enthusiasm to American independence and of the way the Great Awakening of the 1740s prepared the slipways of cultural and political change in America, then such are available in David Lovejoy's *Religious Enthusiasm in the New World: Heresy to Revolution*, and (at a more local level) in Richard Pointer's *Protestant Pluralism and the New York Experience*.[23] Pointer shows how religious diversity and evangelicalism together undermined the shadowy canopy that Anglicanism had still maintained in parts of the colonies and had even hoped to reinforce. Some recent historical writing has stressed the power of the religious undertow of the revolution rather than the philosophical overlay which was subsequently able to present itself as the ideological key to the emergence of America.

The object here is to show how Methodism swept away many of the remaining supports of Anglican power and status, and how it came to constitute a core element in the social and religious constitution of the early United States, along with Arminian Protestantism generally. For that purpose I am deploying three sources. One source is Seymour Martin Lipset, one of the most distinguished of American political scientists. He maintains that American exceptionalism, meaning by that the existence of America as perhaps the *only* culture born in, and crucially informed by, Protestantism, is related to the emphases of Arminian evangelical faith. Another source is a study by William Williams of the local impact of Methodism on the Delmarva Peninsula from 1769 to 1802; and a third source is the study by Rodney Stark and Roger Finke of 'How the Upstart Sects won America: 1776–1850'. These are enough to outline the way the dissidence of Britain helped establish the core culture of early America.[24]

Lipset has put forward his argument in his *Revolution and Counterrevolution* and in numerous articles, as for example, in contributions to *Capitalism and Socialism* edited by Michael Novak.[25]

Lipset maintains that the Arminian emphasis on free universal grace as preached by Methodists, Baptists, and even some moderate Calvinists, paralleled the offer of free, universal participation in the rights of American citizenship. Moreover, voluntary religious groups like the Methodists and Baptists are under constant pressure to mobilize the support of their members. 'They are', says Lipset, 'the most truly Protestant of all denominations in the sense that the relationships between the individual and God, and between the individual and Society, emphasize the conscience of the individual'.[26] However corporate and close-knit the religious community may be, there is a personal conscience nourished at the centre, and this shows itself particularly in works of mercy, charitable organizations, movements of social purity, alterations in the treatment of women and family responsibilities, and in criticism of personal violence and war. Lipset adds that this Protestant matrix creates conditions which inform the attitudes of American Catholics and Jews almost as much as the attitudes of Methodists and Baptists. The Methodists and Baptists do not have to be the majority: they do, however, provide the differentia specifica.

Williams describes how the Methodists undermined the Episcopalians in the Delmarva Peninsula by providing them with a second 'English' church. The Methodists fitted in with what many inhabitants of the peninsula were seeking, because the Methodists had secured their own independence in 1784 and were in tune with the American ethos. Methodism on the peninsula, as often elsewhere, 'had its greatest successes in areas previously dominated by the Church of England and the descendants of Englishmen'.[27] This is why opponents of Methodism tried to discredit the English character of Methodism by referring to some Methodist preachers as 'nothing but a parcel of Irishmen who ran away from their country to keep from being hanged'.[28] The truth behind this is that American Methodism was fertilized in particular by Irish Methodism; and the broader sociological truth behind it is that religious dissidents are more inclined to migrate than the 'conformists'. They respond more to the pull and suffer more from the push.

The spread of Methodism exhibits an ecology similar to the later spread of Pentecostalism in Jamaica. The Methodists were successful in the country, among people suspicious of town life, and their itinerant system seemed ideally suited to reaching the isolated farmers and watermen who worked the flat land of the Chesapeake and Delaware bays. In the towns their places of worship were often on the outskirts. Another feature which is nowadays echoed in the spread of Pentecostalism was the disparity in manpower between a dozen or so Episcopalian clergy and the 'great company' of Methodist preachers, two hundred of them lay.

Williams adds that lassitude and a weakness for alcohol hindered the performance of the Episcopalian clergy, so that by the early 1800s one in five of the whole population was Methodist. He summarizes the reasons for this in a few sentences entirely applicable to Pentecostalism today. They underline both the supportive nature of the community and the change in the male personality.

> The Methodist prescription called for a revolution in values. In order to move from the ways of men to the ways of God, the Methodist message demanded the substitution of seriousness for frivolity, cooperation for competition, compassion for brutality, and egalitarianism for deference.
>
> To those seeking deeper human relationships than found in the surface camaraderie and the boozy haze surrounding the card game, horse race, or gala party, Methodist societies offered a supportive community. To a people facing a life-time of long, harsh days that drained youth and high spirits from its young and prematurely aged its adults, Wesleyan societies offered far more than just a way to fight the boredom and loneliness of farm life. They provided a real sense of psychological security as Methodist brothers and sisters offered physical and financial help, or lent a sympathetic ear in time of tribulation. Moreover, while the Methodist class meeting kept its members on the road to perfection, it also encouraged each member to bare the innermost depths of his or her soul. What a wonderful catharsis! This type of activity could not go on in the outside world, dominated as it was by the competitive, self-assertive values of the gentry, which regarded self-revelation, particularly among males, as a sign of weakness.[29]

Another tendency, familiar from later evangelical successes in Latin America, is the way some groups will only shift their allegiances when those above them set the example. For reasons of local history, some of the gentry found in Methodism the residual legatee of the Church of England, and thus encouraged many of the middling sort to follow suit. The professionals and the business people found Methodism quite congenial because it 'reinforced the very assumption that ambitious young men recognized as crucial to improving their own socio-economic status'.[30] Methodism gave them an ethic of work, a temperate manner of life, pacific temper, and an assurance of God's favour.

Furthermore, the Methodist 'Discipline' actually admonished Methodists to buy from each other and to employ Methodist craftsmen and attorneys: admirable incentives to conversion entirely in line with Weber's analysis of the way credit-worthiness operated among the American Protestant faithful.[31] At the same time, to be a poor tenant farmer made one particularly receptive to true religion, whereas success, as Wesley himself dolefully predicted, led some to forget that they were Methodists. For the poor white belonging to a Methodist class meeting could be a crucial economic insurance as well as a forum within which his frustrations, hopes and deeper feelings could find expression. There he could hear himself called brother by people of every kind, even if the better sort tended to take the positions of leadership. No doubt it was tensions over leadership which all over America helped incite schisms and breakaways.

Of first-rate importance is the well-documented appeal of Methodism to women, which provides a potent anticipation of a similar attraction exercised by Pentecostalism. Various explanations are offered. Methodism provided ways for women to come together, it assisted them spiritually in their training as wives and mothers and, above all, it offered the *only* place where they could experience independence, self-esteem and power. Women often joined the Methodist societies independently of their husbands, and encountered some resistance for doing so from men who suspected the kind of female solidarity engendered by an all-female class meeting. Moreover, Methodist sermons 'idealised such feminine traits as patience, love, gentleness, sensitivity, humility and submissiveness, and rejected the competitive values of the male-dominated spheres of commerce, politics, and sport'.[32] Here we have comments echoed exactly by Elizabeth Brusco's comments on the kind of personality bred by evangelicals in contemporary Colombia, as well as a hint that Methodist mobility quite often flowed through the service professions. The parallel between the Delmarva Peninsula in 1800 and Colombia in 1980 is quite striking.[33]

Blacks, too, were attracted to Methodism, since no other religious body, apart from the Quakers, treated them better. They appreciated the emotional appeal of a full-blooded Methodism, and it was often a black outburst from the galleries or the back of the meeting that proved a godsend to preachers unable to stir lethargic whites. Methodists preaching awoke echoes of an African past and also spoke against slavery, though this commitment was to weaken after 1810 and Methodism was, in the event, split over the issue of emancipation.[34]

The story of the split takes us beyond our legitimate concerns here, but it involved a shift to congregational autonomy and to independent black churches emerging nationwide in almost every denomination. Blacks, like women, lacked full access to power and only acquired their own free space through successful separations. Will B. Graveley, summarizing these developments, argues that 'black religious independence arose from communal initiative and corporate ethnic consciousness that expressed 'nationalist aspirations' at a pre-theoretical but practical, institutional level'.[35] Evangelical experience, whether among early Methodists or among contemporary South African charismatics, frequently breaks down ethnic barriers, but these tend to emerge again later in all kinds of religious separatism.

An incident which nicely sums up the relationship of Methodism to the tattered remnants of the 'sacred canopy' of Anglicanism is provided by the 'Great Pig Issue'. In 1791 Georgetown became the county seat of Sussex county, and Episcopalians, drawn in part from judges, lawyers and county officials, wanted the new community to become aesthetically attractive and properly sophisticated. Georgetown's Methodists, however, were either drawn from people lately in from the country or farmers on the edge of town. Their main concern was with the right to turn their livestock loose in the streets, and soon Methodist pigs were rooting up Episcopalian flower gardens: which thing is a parable.

The wider dissolutions of any suggestion of religious establishments continuing to form any kind of sacred canopy, even for specific ethnic groups, are dramatically conveyed by Stark and Finke in 'How the Upstart Sects Won America: 1776–1850'.[36] Their thesis is succinctly summarized by themselves:

> We shall argue that the fortunes of the so-called 'mainline' Protestant bodies began to decline rapidly in the late 18th and early 19th centuries, not in the 1950s and 1960s . . . we shall show that the Congregationalists, Episcopalians and Presbyterians truly dominated the religious scene at the start of the American Revolution. In less that eight decades, by 1850, they had slumped into numerical insignificance while the Methodists and Baptists swept over the land.[37]

What Arminian Protestants could not achieve in England they had ample opportunity to achieve in the United States, changing and expressing the emergent ethos of a changing society. That we do not notice this, Stark and Finke attribute to the fact that liberal Protestants are overrepresented in the seats of power, including the university chairs where the histories are written.

America after the Revolution moved from the toleration of variety to an unregulated market economy in religion. That ensured the more aggressive firms would survive. Unfortunately the highly educated and dignified clergy of the old semi-established faiths did not care to compete on the kind of vulgar terms necessary. Thus the evangelical upstarts increased their share of the market and the older denominations declined to the extent that they relaxed their moral prescriptions, embraced the world, accepted relativism, and ceased to care about missions. In 1776 only 17 per cent of the colonial population was in membership with a church, but once the evangelicals entered the market it doubled by 1850. Even in New England the Baptists and Methodists were ousting the Congregationalists. As for the Episcopalians, in the South Atlantic region, where they were strongest, their share of the market in souls dropped from 27 per cent of all adherents to just 4 per cent. The faith which experienced a truly meteoric rise was Methodism. (The question of the specifically ethnic churches is, of course, quite separate, though the denominational principle was to eat even into them.)

The newly successful bodies were democratic, participatory in style, and lay in their ethos. 'Unlike the Congregational, Presbyterian and Episcopalian ministers, who typically were of genteel origins and who were highly trained and well-educated, the Baptist and Methodist clergy were of the people' – and reflected their prejudices. That is the price of religious democracy. 'They had little education, received little if any pay, spoke in the vernacular, and preached from the heart.'[38] Exactly this is true of Pentecostalism today. The emergence of a trained ministry meant that social distance increased between pulpit and pew, especially in areas like the frontier and the South where people retained bitter memories of clerical superiority. Also the Methodist circuit rider could move with the people wherever they went. Methodism, as suggested earlier, was a *movement*.

Yet the meteoric rise of Methodism was short-lived. By the turn of the century Methodists were being passed by the more conservative and evangelical Baptists. Though they had caught up with Congregationalists in learning they were being passed by Baptists in soul-winning. On the contemporary scene, it is the Baptists and denominations like the Pentecostal Assemblies of God who retain or expand their holdings among the faithful.

And that pattern is now world-wide. In spite of the fact that it is the conservative and evangelical (and Southern?) among the historic denominations who have been more anxious to win souls in Latin America, the share of Pentecostals has risen to at least two Protestants there out of every three. The Methodists have been one of the least successful missionary groups, apart, that is, from the

Methodist Pentecostal Church in Chile. The Evangelical religion now spilling over from North to South America is primarily Pentecostal.

The same ripples run back to the original source of the evangelical message: today's secular England. Within the Church of England evangelicals are the most successful party and outside it the most dynamic churches are found among the Pentecostals and the freeranging evangelicals. The same is also true in the countries poised between America and England: Canada, Australia and – even – New Zealand. These have registered overall declines in participation, and increases in the proportions of evangelicals and Pentecostals.[39]

As Wade Clark Roof has amply demonstrated, the relative weight and power of conservative evangelical and liberal is being redistributed.[40] As it is in the United States, so it is also in England, the countries of the British Commonwealth and even in Europe. Moreover the flow chart of religious influences imitates the flow chart of overall cultural power. What passed from England 'to the American strand' in the second quarter of the eighteenth century is passed back to England in the last quarter of the twentieth. Methodism is almost everywhere in difficulties, at least in the developed world and in Latin America; Pentecostalism is almost everywhere expanding.

The Shared Problematic of Methodism and Pentecostalism

Clearly what has just been briefly delineated generates a problematic, and one which has already been widely discussed. This is the problematic set out by Halévy in relation to Methodism in England, discussed variously by such scholars as John Kent, Bernard Semmel, David Hempton, E. P. Thompson and Eric Hobsbawm. A parallel problematic has been set out by Christian Lalive D'Epinay, Emilio Willems and Jean-Pierre Bastian, in relation to Pentecostalism, though the continuity of the two sets of problems has not been adequately recognized. It is not at all necessary to summarize here the positions taken up by various authors. There are lots of brief accounts of the debate available, together with bibliographies, one being by Michael Hill in the ninth chapter of his *Sociology of Religion* and another being by Kenneth Thompson in *Religion and Ideology*, co-edited with Robert Bocock.[41] The one thing required is a statement of the issues raised in such a way that we are equipped with a questionnaire in our mind to place against the evidence cited later concerning contemporary Pentecostalism, more especially in Latin America and in South Korea.

The problematic engendered by Methodism is, in the broadest perspective, part of the collapse of the monopolistic relationship between a given religion and the state, and between that religion and the local community. It is also part of a process of differentiation which hives off religious mobilizations from political mobilizations. In Catholic societies the relationship between the political realm and the religious realm stays closer because religion is encapsulated in a politically conservative format in dramatic opposition to irreligion encapsulated in a liberal or socialist format. But, as already argued, in Anglo-Saxon cultures the political and religious components separate out, leaving only a symbolic resonance between religious movements and their political analogues and a partial overlap of personnel. In any case, the religious movements may even move in contrary motion to their political analogues if the interests of their adherents so dictate.

This needs explaining with examples. The last union of religion and politics in Anglo-Saxon culture was Puritanism. Thereafter, with the emergence of Methodism, religion ceased to be tied in with an all-inclusive political viewpoint. Some Methodists might be conservative at one time and place, liberal at another time and place, depending on their social location. The political component of Methodism is reduced to the level of cultural politics, so that it becomes a civil rights movement to remove the religious disadvantages encountered by its adherents, and it is pulled along in the wake of such political parties as suit or take up the social and moral aspirations of those adherents. Methodism becomes a movement which entertains and promotes forms of interaction resonating positively with certain political philosophies and parties, such as egalitarianism and participation. However, only some of its adherents may actually support those parties. The social location of Methodism could theoretically conflict with the natural resonance of its mode of interaction, just as the social location of Catholics in Anglo-Saxon cultures had led many Catholics to support non-hierarchical political philosophies and parties.[42] Thus the most that can be said about Methodism is that its preferred forms of interaction, and the cultural slipways it constructs, resonate with the logic of the liberal project. This focuses the problematic of Methodism on the resonances and consequences of its cultural politics.

Pentecostalism represents an even more advanced differentiation of the religious and political spheres. Pentecostal mobilization has not overlapped strongly with a particular political mobilization, though there have been observable relationships with the Moral Majority of recent years. Pentecostalism has radical symbolic *resonances* but takes an apolitical conservative *form*. Indeed, it operates in a sufficiently differentiated social sphere to revive Christian suspicions about power *as such* and, therefore, tends to discourage its adherents from overt political activity. At the same time, in developing societies where the political and the religious are still intertwined, Pentecostalism is forced into political positions foreign to its genesis in Anglo-Saxon culture. This allows its suspicion of politics and of corruption to be viewed as a conservative withdrawal from commitment to 'liberation'.

Thus both Methodism and Pentecostalism give rise to a fundamental question which concerns the extent to which their non-violent and apolitical quietism feeds the status quo, and how far the energies they evoke are drained away from the revolutionary or progressive political task. This is essentially the problematic argued by Halevy and answered in somewhat different ways by Marxist historians like E. P. Thompson and Eric Hobsbawm or Methodist historians like John Walsh and John Kent. When one refers to diverted energies, these include the catharsis of violence and power achieved in worship and the achievement of harmony through singing. There is, therefore, an extension of Halévy's problematic about the avoidance of revolution which includes music as well as the directly religious. A rich commentary on the musical aspect of religious change and social harmony is provided by Roger Elbourne in *Music and Tradition in Early Industrial Lancashire 1750–1840.*[43]

The problematic not only focuses on the incidence of religious enthusiasm as it either reinforces political enthusiasm or diverts it into 'safe' channels, but on the latent capacity of cultural changes held in religious storage to emerge over time when circumstances are propitious to activate them, or when things are safe enough for people to make open political claims. It is perfectly possible to see the American Revolution as moving along cultural conduits laid down by the Great Awakening, and to view the movement for black civil rights in the mid-twentieth century as an extrapolation from what had already been achieved symbolically in the 'free space' created by the black churches.[44] Thus Methodism and Pentecostalism can both be analysed as anticipations of liberty, initially realized in the religious sphere and stored there until either a shift in cultural underpinnings actually undermined the structural barriers, or protest moved from a cultural to a structural expression.

These cultural shifts are not only concerned with the symbolic affirmation and realization of liberty and equality in the religious sphere. They are concerned with the way particular strata so mobilize themselves and reorganize the psyche that they alter their social position. They may do this by establishing networks for mutual support, and even by creating a framework of therapeutic, leisure and educational institutions. Adventist hospitals and schools are precisely part of such a framework; so for that matter is Oral Roberts University and Hospital.[45] It is, in effect the autonomous creation, *ex nihilo*, of a system for welfare and for educational advance. These networks were seen by Max Weber as part of the problematic of evangelical religion in his essay on 'The Protestant Sects and the Spirit of Capitalism'.[46] The networks are paralleled in the psyche by the provision of opportunities for release in worship and opportunities for discipline and 'method' in work. Methodism dealt in grace on Sundays and works on Mondays. E. P. Thompson in particular has stressed the Methodist capacity to create a sector of the work-force which was disciplined from within.[47] Not only that but the inner discipline of the godly was matched by their outer cleanliness. Those who were washed in the blood of the Lamb also insisted on washing behind their ears. Those who sought holiness also developed tastes for wholesome food and priorities in their habits of consumption which stood them in good stead for the future.

The problematic of Methodism is thus one concerned with social and economic mobility, and that becomes automatically the problematic of Pentecostalism. The question is how far a religious frame of meaning also encapsulates a programme of social and economic self-help realized in everything from mutual economic assistance to community therapy, from leisure facilities to schemes for insurance. One also asks how far the skills of public speaking, exposition and organization devised and exercised in the community of faith are transferred to secular aspirations, to business administration and to political movements.

A further element concerns the attempt to curb violence in the self and avoid violence in the political realm. This is in turn linked to a feminization of the male psyche and a stance which abjures violence whether in domestic politics or between nations. Methodism rejects the culture of honour and shame and establishes a problematic about the cultural impact of peaceability. Pacifist movements and non-violent forms of moral protest have fed on evangelical roots as well as on the Quaker and Unitarian residual deposits of Puritanism.[48]

A final element concerns the impact of this peaceable culture on blacks and women. There is no doubt about the appeal of Methodism to women and the opportunities offered them in the early stages of religious effervescence and enthusiasm. There is also little doubt that religion can overrun the barriers of colour for a period, but the evidence so far as Methodism is concerned is that these gains become eroded over time by the cake of custom and inbuilt distinctions. Given the black origins of Pentecostalism and the fact that most

Pentecostals are women, this problematic obviously extends beyond Methodism to its Pentecostal successor.

To all of the above must be added a qualification. The problematic of Methodism has been presented as an integral part of the fragmentation of socio-religious wholes at the level of the state and the local community, and as a part of a social differentiation which separates off the religious realm from the political. However, there are situations when it – or evangelical religion generally – can inform a national or sub-national culture which is at the geographical periphery or in some way cut off or defeated. Methodism does not, of course, create a new national church but it does provide a distinctive ethos and potent markers of difference. And just as it animates a whole sub-national culture, so it imparts those special characteristics, such as egalitarianism, self-discipline and spontaneity, which otherwise are restricted to groups within a particular strata. This animation of a subordinate culture was carried out by evangelical Haugeanism in western Norway, by Arminian Protestantism generally in the American South, and by Methodism in Wales – and Fiji. Pentecostalism may to *some* extent play similar roles among the Maya, the Jamaicans and the South Koreans.

If this problematic were reduced to a questionnaire drawn from Methodism and asked of Pentecostalism, it would run as follows. Is the rise of Pentecostalism in this or that context related to the collapse of a comprehensive system of religious coverage? Can Pentecostalism provide the distinctive markers for a subordinate or peripheral national culture? How far does Pentecostalism express the radical social differentiation of religion from politics? To what extent does Pentecostalism draw off energies from the political realm? Does Pentecostalism help create networks of mutual assistance which build up the resources of groups hitherto denied them, for example through medical and educational facilities? Does it inculcate disciplines which assist personal advance, economically and socially? Does it provide an arena for the exercise of skills in speaking and organization later available for personal use, for economic propulsion and for political deployment? Does it make for peace in the psyche, in relationships at work and international relations? And, what does it do for blacks and women?

PART II

Latin America: History and Contemporary Situation

Chapter 3

Profiles of Evangelical Advance in Latin America

The advance of evangelical Protestantism over the whole of Latin America from Mexico to the Argentine began in small stirrings in the mid-nineteenth century, which sharply accelerated in the 1930s and reached hurricane force in the 1960s. It is part of a world-wide phenomenon affecting parts of the rim of the western Pacific, especially South Korea, and several countries in Africa, including Nigeria and South Africa.[1] Even in countries where Christianity is otherwise declining or static like Australia and New Zealand, the dynamic sector is evangelical, and in particular Pentecostal. In the United States, the epicentre of Protestant power and expansion, the conservative evangelical and Pentecostal churches are growing relative to the liberal denominations.[2] Arguably this extraordinary growth world-wide challenges comparison with the explosion of fundamentalist Islam, though Islam is usually intertwined with nationalist fervour and Pentecostalism usually is not.

The object of this chapter is first to give an account of contemporary changes, in particular the rapid expansion of Pentecostalism, and then to indicate the breaks in Catholic dominance, both as they have occurred historically since the mid-nineteenth century, and as they have widened dramatically over the past thirty years.

The Contemporary Scene

The broad dimensions and character of this explosion are easily indicated. In 1916 in the whole of Latin America Protestants were a tiny minority, and many of them were British, German or North American.[3] Missionary work was largely directed from North America, in particular by the Baptists and the Presbyterians. But in the next two decades things started to change. The membership of Protestant churches grew to 2.5 million and the Protestants were now mostly Latins. At the same time their buildings remained small and at least in some countries the believers came for the most part from the marginal and the poor.[4] Brazil was something of an exception in having a staid Protestant middle class; and in countries like Argentina and Chile the effects of social mobility, particularly among pastors, had taken Protestants into the lower middle class.

During roughly their first century in Latin America Protestants were regarded as alien invaders by conservatives and were targets of their hostility. From time to time local hostility and state restrictions made their life difficult. They were natural opponents of the alliance of church and state, and opponents of the teaching of the Catholic religion in state schools. Liberal governments and anti-clericals regarded them as allies of progress and friends of welfare. If they were not valued specifically for their faith they were at least valued for their schools and hospitals. Structurally they were part of the current of change in Latin America and had to count in the liberal column. Indeed in the Mexican Revolution many Mexican Protestants were identified as part of the vanguard.[5]

The take-off came in the late sixties. At the beginning of this period evangelical Protestants counted some 5 million members, excluding children, and their wider constituency extended to some 15 million. Two decades later that constituency extended to at least 40 million, which is remarkable even allowing for rapid growth in total population. It may even be the case that in parts of Latin America the number of Protestants regularly involved in worship and fellowship exceeds the number of Catholics.

The Pattern of Protestant Penetration

The depth of Protestant penetration and its variable incidence can be roundly demonstrated. The deepest penetrations have occurred in Brazil and Chile, in Nicaragua and Guatemala, and (outside strictly Latin America) Haiti, Jamaica and Puerto Rico. In Brazil up to 20 per cent of the population of 150 million is Protestant. According to the *New York Times* for 25 October, 1987, evangelicals in Brazil have doubled in numbers since 1980, to about 12 million, while another 12 million regularly attend services. In 1985 there were 15,000 full-time

Protestant pastors in Brazil compared to 13,176 priests. In Chile, much of the growth has been associated with a Pentecostal breakaway early this century from the Methodist Church. From 1930 to 1960 this church alone grew from 54,000 to 425,000. From 1930 onwards Chilean Protestantism rapidly expanded as a whole, though the rate of growth dropped during the decade of radical political change from 1960 to 1970. The current Protestant population of Chile is certainly well over a million and variously estimated at between 15 and 20 per cent of the total.[6]

The most dramatic changes in Central America are those in Guatemala. Guatemala is now over 30 per cent Protestant, and could in the view of some (perhaps) alarmist commentators find itself embroiled in a hot as well as a cold religious war. Nicaragua is now about 20 per cent Protestant and Costa Rica not far behind with 16 per cent.[7] In Puerto Rico the rhythm of Pentecostal and other Protestant expansion takes place against the long-term background of a Protestant incursion associated with Americanization following American victory in the Spanish–American War. In Jamaica Pentecostalism may now have a constituency of up to 30 per cent and clearly challenges all the older-established churches. Pentecostalism and a variety of evangelical missions have had parallel successes in Haiti.

Much less dramatic penetrations have occurred at the two extremes of the Hispanic world in the Argentine and Mexico. Protestantism advanced sluggishly in the Argentine until very recently, and in 1980 accounted for only about 3 per cent of the population, and much of that was found in ethnic enclaves. Recently, however, the statistics published by the Assemblies of God give prior warning of what may be a late visitation of Pentecostalism to the Argentine.[8] Something similar may be true of Mexico. Until recently the growth of Protestantism in Mexico was modest by Brazilian standards, not exceeding 4 per cent, but the most recent researcher, Kurt Bowen, suspects that the figure is now nearer 6 or 7 per cent, which suggests a constituency of some 4 or 5 million.[9]

In countries of very traditional Catholic loyalty like Colombia, Protestant expansion was initially slow, but it accelerated somewhat between 1930 and 1946 and even managed to maintain some momentum in the difficult and dangerous years of *La Violencia*. In the 1960s Protestantism surged forward and now includes about a million persons or 4 per cent of the population.[10] In the other Andean republics, Protestantism has been at least sufficiently successful to arouse Catholic concern. In Bolivia the number of groups actively proselytising goes into hundreds. In Peru itself perhaps 2–3 per cent of the population is Protestant. Where Protestantism has been least successful is in the highly secular and urbanized environments of Venezuela and Uruguay.[11]

The Shift to Pentecostalism

There have been certain fundamental shifts in the character of Latin American Protestantism over these decades of rapid expansion. The balance of numerical power has now passed unequivocally from the older denominations to the conservative evangelicals and, above all, to the Pentecostals. The older denominations were themselves quite conservative theologically, but they were fairly staid in style. The newer denominations are, if anything, more conservative and for the most part they are charismatic, rather after the manner of John Wimber's 'Vineyard Christian Fellowship'. Indeed, independent Christian fellowships are growing rapidly on the contemporary scene, for example in Argentina.

There are in fact two distinct genealogies of Christian faith and experience at work: the one conservative evangelical, which concentrates on the correct grammar of belief, and the Pentecostal, which stresses the gifts of the Spirit. In what follows, there is no attempt to distinguish all the varieties of either conservative evangelicalism or Pentecostalism, but it is at least important to keep the two genealogies separate. It is also important to keep in mind that there are two other genealogies propagating rapidly in Latin America: the Adventists, who are closely related to the evangelical family, and the Mormons and Witnesses who belong to quite different genealogical trees.

Just how great the swing to Pentecostalism has been is illustrated by the fact that in Central America in 1936 Pentecostals accounted for only 2.3 per cent of all Protestants, whereas in the sixties they accounted for over a third and in the eighties well over half.[12] In some countries, for example Chile, they account for over 80 per cent, though in Chile this predominance happens to be more long-standing than elsewhere.

Other shifts are towards autonomy and fragmentation. So far as autonomy is concerned the important point is the indigenous and self-governing character of the evangelicals and Pentecostals. North American personnel may be present but they are for the most part not in control. So far as fragmentation is concerned there has been a completely free market in competing versions of evangelical Christianity. Of course, most of the 'market' is served by about a dozen major organizations, in particular the Assemblies of God, but the number of alternatives on offer goes into hundreds.

There are other important changes. The older denominations had reaped some of the advantages of the Protestant Ethic and had made their way into the lower middle and professional classes. This was particularly true of the children of pastors. As Pablo Deiros put it in his study of Baptists in the Argentine, the Protestant religion 'generated an ethic conducive to a disciplined hard-working life so that by the second or third generation they were mostly integrated in the middle or lower middle classes'.[13] Pentecostals, however, constitute a much more extensive engagement with the poor and are the first popular manifestation of Protestantism. What is interesting is the way the flexibility and variety brought about by fragmentation both enables them to stay popular (in the sense of reaching the mass of the people) and to create offshoots which can be offered either to those who are ready for mobility or to those already in the middle class.

The mass appeal of Pentecostalism and the emergence of groups with a middle-class character is illustrated in the kinds of building now being erected. One kind is extremely large and includes some of the largest auditoriums in the world. The Jotabeche Cathedral in Santiago can hold some 18,000 people and the Temple of Brasil para Cristo even more.[14] Another kind is the multi-purpose community church, with amenities, air-conditioning and handsome appointments, such as may be found in any North American city. These can now be found all the way from Mexico City to Lima and to Rio.

The last shift is towards modern means of communication, notably television, radio, cassette and film. It is perhaps in this sphere that North American control is still evident. Television in particular requires vast resources and so too does large-scale evangelism carried on in vast public arenas holding 100,000 people or more. As a result much of the televisual material is part of the general output of the Electronic Church, and a great deal of the large-scale evangelism is carried out by North American evangelists.[15] But on a smaller scale indigenous Protestants also utilize modern technology, especially local radio. In that respect at least they are among the harbingers of modernity.

The Pentecostals, along with the recent wave of conservative evangelicals, have been for the most part opposed to communism, especially after the experience of Cuba. They frequently picked up and transmitted tensions from the Cold War and were often inclined to take a favourable view of the United States. This meant that the older conservative and *integrista* (organicist) hostility towards Protestants was now supplemented by a radical and nationalist hostility. Protestants were 'everywhere spoken against', by radical intellectuals, secular and Catholic alike, and by journalists of most political persuasions. They were seen as the insidious privy paw of American culture, or even as a 'low-intensity' operation sponsored by the CIA.[16] So far as liberal theologians and liberation theologians were concerned, this latter-day evangelicalism was a powerful current of regression, back on the one hand to a sectarian dualism and millennialism, and on the other hand to an almost classical Lutheran passivity before the dynamics of power and the state.[17]

Certainly the new evangelicals were for the most part strangers to the structural analysis of political change, and if they had any expectations at all of secular improvement they were based on the personal impact of virtuous people. Mostly, however, they were pessimistic with regard to the political realm.[18]

Thus while the ancient feuds between Catholics as such and Protestants as such faded away, a new bitterness emerged between right-wing Catholics and left-wing Catholics, between liberal Protestants and conservative Protestants. Only the liberal Protestants and left-wing Catholics had much time for each other, and made up the core of the ecumenical movement. The rest remained resolutely anti-ecumenical, and especially the new evangelicals and Pentecostals.

Not all elements in the new Pentecostal and conservative evangelical wave have been politically conservative. There are groups in most countries whose political approach runs parallel to that of the 'Sojourners' in the United States. The discussion of political stances in chapter 12 will document how people with this kind of commitment view their world, and the possibilities of political action may be gathered from the recent volume edited by Pablo Deiros entitled *Los Évangelicos y el poder politico en América Latina*.[19] At the grass roots, in rural Mexico, in Nicaragua, in the movement called Brasil para Cristo, and among some Pentecostals in Chile during the Allende years, there has been sympathy and support for radical change, though rarely for violence.

These, then, in broad strokes, are the main developments: an explosion of conservative evangelical religion, a shift towards Pentecostalism, a rejection of ecumenism, and the manifestation among many of those involved of the evangelical capacity to unite modern technology with political conservatism.

Such massive changes need to be set against certain important historical changes in Latin America over the past century and a half. Some of these changes, with respect to the oscillation of parliamentary and military regimes, the lopsided development of commerce and industry, the impact of inflation and indebtedness, the growth of population and of the mega-cities, will be part of the analyses undertaken country by country.[20] But there are other historic changes and background conditions which have special relevance to the growth and distribution of Protestantism. They are, taken in turn: the religious deposits left by non-Hispanic colonization; the indigenous peoples surviving under Spanish rule; the migrations of peoples within Latin America or from Asia and, above all, from Europe; and finally the condition of the Roman Catholic Church, in particular as concerns its relationship with the state and with the rival elites of Latin America today.

First Breaks in Hispanic Dominance

Taking first the breaks in Hispanic dominance these have been mainly at the hands of the Americans and the British, and are therefore part of the long-term clash of civilizations. There are a number of countries or areas where British colonization has created Anglican/Protestant enclaves, some major, some minor. For example, Barbados and Jamaica, and to a lesser degree Trinidad, reflect the long-term influence of the religious traditions of Britain. Again, the northern parts of Honduras, Belize, the Atlantic coast of Nicaragua, and Guiana, all show evidence of those same traditions. These then are long-term deposits of Protestant faith. A parallel United States influence, which grew stronger with the increasing power of the 'imperial republic', as well as the dispersal of US citizens, is to be found in Panama, Haiti, Costa Rica and Puerto Rico. This US impact is variable, depending on whether the incursions are economic, military or political, and on how long they persist. After the US victory in the American–Spanish War, Cuba and Puerto Rico both came directly within the US sphere of influence. In the case of Puerto Rico this led to virtual absorption in the United States and quite extensive deposits of Protestantism; in the case of Cuba it led to a successful defiance and thus to the evacuation of most of the fruits of several decades of US Protestant work.

Another break in Hispanic dominance comes as the result of migrations. These are of several different kinds. There are the migrations of Asians, Africans, and Afro-Caribbeans in search of work, often as indentured labour. One result of this is the presence of Muslims and Hindus in Guiana, Trinidad and Surinam. So far as Protestantism is concerned this may mean, for example, that black migrants carry their Protestantism to Panama. Another kind of migration occurs for specifically religious reasons and represents a South American variant of the original migrations to North America.

These are sometimes Protestant and may be motivated by persecution in their countries of origin or by utopian hopes centred on the New World or simply by a feeling that Europe is too set in its pattern of established churches really to offer religious dissidents full opportunities. At any rate, Lithuanian Baptists made their way to Brazil, Russian Mennonites to Paraguay, Italian Protestant Waldensians to the Argentine, and German Catholic Apostolics to Uruguay.[21]

Yet another kind of migration is the sort which occurred from Europe (and the Middle East) to South America, based on the search for new opportunities. These migrations involved the transfer of ethnic churches, some of which were Protestant. Thus there are large German churches in Brazil, in Chile, the Argentine, and elsewhere, as well as much smaller Scandinavian, Anglican, Scots-Presbyterian, and French Reformed churches. One may find a Scots-Presbyterian community in southern Chile or a Welsh Methodist/Presbyterian community in Mexico or Patagonia. As for the Catholic migrations, these also are relevant since in certain circumstances Catholics may find themselves ecclesiastically not at home in the receiving country. Thus the Italian community in Brazil provided a fertile seedbed for the origins of a Pentecostal denomination, Brasil para Cristo. (Conversely, the non-Catholic migrants from Japan to Brazil are now mostly Catholic!)[22]

A further religiously significant migration, if migration is the right word, is the forced movement of slaves from Africa to the New World, especially to the Caribbean, the Southern states of the USA, and Brazil. It is significant for two reasons. One is that the Africans maintained a partial continuity with the religions of Africa and these have now surfaced in myriad forms in Jamaica, Haiti, Brazil and elsewhere. In Brazil, Umbanda is the main rival to Pentecostalism. The other reason why the African presence is significant is that Pentecostalism in part originated in black culture – by John Wesley out of Africa – and Pentecostalism today catches fire among the brushwood of spiritist cults with African roots.

A final break in Hispanic (and Creole) dominance is located in the re-emergence of the aboriginal peoples of Latin America. The largest of these are the Quechua and Maya peoples, and these have sometimes been open to Protestant penetration. Indeed, the Maya people of south-east Mexico and Guatemala have a history of revolt against their conquerors, and their final revolt appears to be cultural and religious. Of course, there are also many smaller groups, some of whom have never been Christianized at all. There is a long history of Protestant missions to 'Indian' tribes, beginning under the aegis of British power with the Moravian mission to the Miskito Indians of the

Nicaraguan Atlantic coast. At any rate today one may find small Indian groups all over Latin America who have been missionized by this or that missionary society or denomination. Particularly active are the Wycliffe Bible Translators, whose work has been a source of recent controversy among anthropologists.[23] To take examples at random, there are many Adventists among the Aymara of the Andes, Pentecostals and Mennonites among the Toba of the Argentine, converts of the New Tribes Mission in Bolivia and converts of the Gospel Missionary Union in Ecuador. Whatever the critical estimates of this activity may be in terms of external and internal colonialism, it represents a heroic enterprise in continuity with those Jesuit enterprises among the Guarani which were finally closed down in the mid-eighteenth century.

The State of Catholicism, Past and Present

The final element in the background is inevitably the history and contemporary condition of the Roman Catholic Church. As for the history, the single most important fact is the *patronato*, offered by the Pope to the rulers of Latin America and claimed by the successor states after independence. The *patronato* subjected the church to the secular state as effectively as did the Scandinavian, German and English Reformations. In some countries during the Enlightenment, notably Brazil, the church was neutered and barely recovered. It is true that the Brazilian church was eventually Romanized again in the twentieth century, but the years of attrition left it perilously weak. In other countries the association of the church with the state and state patronage, as well as the landed wealth of the regular clergy, meant that when revolution came the revolutionaries mercilessly savaged the church. The Guatemalan Revolution of 1871 was particularly destructive.[24] Thus the Roman Catholic Church has suffered both from the way it was established and the manner in which it was disestablished.

Curiously, in view of the stereotypical view of Latin America as securely and devoutly Catholic, the culture of the people has been quite resistant to Catholic teaching. This is very understandable in those areas where subject peoples have maintained an underground resistance to the religion of their masters. But it is also evident among the Hispanic and Creole populations, for whom such practices as priestly celibacy are unintelligible and who regard actual attendance at church as suitable only for the very young, the old and the women. Quite apart from this resistance there have been far more dissident and sectarian movements than is usually realized, especially in Brazil.[25] Those regions where the stereotype of devotion holds are in a minority, and are often to be found in quite remote areas like Catamarca in the Argentine and the Antioquia in Colombia. South-western Mexico is another area which conforms to the model of universal Catholicism.

Thus the coverage provided by Catholicism is very varied. Perhaps less than 20 per cent of Latin Americans are regularly involved in the church, and that global figure will include rural areas where the vast majority practise, and, at the other end, *bidonvilles* (shanty-towns), where regular practice is as low as 2 or 3 per cent. The strength of Catholicism historically has not lain in attachment to its central doctrines but rather in cultural and national identifications. Catholic leaders themselves refer to this when they attribute the success of Protestantism to the inertness of conventional Catholicism.

A further relevant fact about contemporary Catholicism is the degree to which the priesthood is thinly spread and composed of foreigners. In the period before independence the 'foreigners' were *peninsulares*, with Spanish roots and loyal to Spain; in the twentieth century the foreigners may be Dutch or American. One cannot say that either a low ratio of priests to people or the alienation produced by a priesthood drafted in from elsewhere weakens the Catholic Church crucially. It all depends on the configuration of circumstances. But it is at any rate evident that when other negative factors are operative, shortages of personnel and the fact that they are foreign can make things worse.

Similar considerations apply to the adoption of liberation theology or alternatively to the maintenance of conservative alliances. It cannot be said in general that the adoption of a radical or a conservative stance assists the growth of Protestantism or of other signs of alienation from Catholicism. It depends on the circumstances. It is true, for example, that both liberation theology and Protestantism are powerful in Chile and Brazil, but then both of them are responses to the specific circumstances of those countries.

What does seem plausible is that divisions in the church over political issues universally assist the growth of Protestantism. It is also plausible that when the church proves unreliable as a pillar of society, or rather of government, then right-wing rulers and the military may welcome the growth of Protestantism as an alternative source of support. Pentecostal pastors have frequently responded to this offer of a place in the sun, seeing in it a form of acceptance by the authorities hitherto resolutely denied.

In general, with regard to the relationship of the Catholic Church with society and with government, the optimum chances for Protestantism exist where the church has been drastically weakened and yet the culture has remained pervasively religious, as in Brazil, Chile and Guatemala. If, however, there has been a comprehensive secularization of culture then Protestantism makes little headway. For example, in contemporary Uruguay and Venezuela there exists a general scepticism about religion *as such* which militates against any form of conversion.

Such general considerations offer an initial perspective within which to place the contemporary explosion of Protestantism, and they lead naturally into more specific considerations focused on particular nations. These illustrate in varying ways the great political and economic changes currently occurring in Latin America. Of course it is not possible to cover all the countries involved. This is in part because information for some countries is fragmentary. It is also in part because the trajectories in Guatemala and Nicaragua are dealt with in chapter 12 under the head of Protestantism and politics, while the Caribbean is covered quite separately in chapter 7.

The strategy is to deal first with Brazil as the most important and complex case (chapter 4). After that follows an analysis of the 'southern cone', in chapter 5, turning on a comparison between the Argentine and Chile; Colombia and Peru are also discussed, as being the two major Andean republics. Then come three contrasted smaller societies, Ecuador, El Salvador and Guatemala; the last country discussed in chapter 6 is Mexico which, like Brazil, is important and complex. Apart from Brazil and Mexico, each case is dealt with in relation to some salient feature, since dealing with the complete situation every time is plainly impossible. Mexico is used to provide an interim summary by noting how certain features which it exhibits are to be found in this or that country already discussed. Before the final and general summary there is a brief digression on the tribes.

Chapter 4

Brazil: Largest Society and Most Dramatic Instance

Brazil is, of course, half a continent and regionally very varied. About half the Protestants of Latin America live in Brazil, and Brazil was the one country in which Protestantism was moderately successful in the earlier periods. Nowadays it also contains two massive movements which are rivals to Pentecostalism, the base community movement and Umbanda. Indeed one might say that Pentecostalism itself is a form of base community plus the therapeutic recourse to the Spirit found in Umbanda.

Modern Brazilian history is often divided up into the century prior to 1930 and the period from 1930 to the present day, and the latter period is then subdivided by the crisis year of 1964 which saw the advent of the military dictatorship. In the time roughly from the mid-nineteenth century to 1930 the structure of preponderant power remained in place, and yet there were important shifts toward modernity. The structure of power stayed oligarchical; and the economy remained dominated by agricultural exports which proved highly vulnerable to outside movements.

Several middle classes emerged, notably a modest bourgeoisie engaged in commerce, handcrafts and small manufacture, but also an officialdom employed by government and large-scale industries, some liberal professionals, and there were also some small independent landowners. Basically social stagnation was avoided through the existence of the entrepreneurial class and through the arrival of millions of immigrants, in particular Germans but also many Italians. The primary economic focus shifted from north-east to south-east, and from sugar to coffee. And modern urban centres grew rapidly in response to industrialization and migration, as well as in response to the arrival of ex-slaves from the countryside. Perhaps it should be emphasized that the cities grew to some extent whether or not industrialization occurred, and that they were often not 'cities' on the European model. The important point here is that they were open to change and to ideological novelties, which included republicanism, Positivism, freemasonry – and Protestantism.

These ideological novelties overlapped each other in a common culture of dissidence similar to that which developed in Mexico in the later repressive stages of the *porfiriato* at the turn of the century. They reflected French, British and American influence roughly in successive phases. Parenthetically, if French influence is scanted in what follows that is because it does not bear directly on the issue of Protestantism. According to David Gueiros Vieira, liberalism, republicanism, freemasonry and Protestantism together stood for progress. He refers to the eleven years between the Liberal Cabinet of 1878 and the end of the monarchy as characterized by a programme of liberal reforms, such as civil registration of marriages and complete religious liberty, the separation of church and state, as well as the abolition of slavery.[1] This programme was the substance of discussion in the progressive clubs of the time – as in Mexico – and was expanded to include scientific and economic progress and a policy of immigration favourable to Germans and Anglo-Saxons, and therefore to Protestantism.

It was in the new cities that the republican elites combined with an army swollen by the Paraguayan war to overturn the monarchy. The Catholic Church had no special reason to side with a monarchy which had offered it civil toleration rather than positive support. Yet the church remained caught in a social trap, on the one hand exposed to the civil power and the contemporary version of the *patronato*, and on the other tied in to the plantation system. It was also, in common with the church in most of Latin America, hamstrung by poor coordination and poor communications. Catholicism on the ground had degenerated into an agglomeration of folk practices and pilgrimages.[2] This tally of weaknesses pushed the church toward cooperating with whatever political forces might protect its interests, which in turn meant entanglement in political partisanship and the interests of its backers.

The separation of church and state came about in 1891 in the early years of the Republic. It at last offered scope for change after humiliations which had continued for over a century from the time of Pombal. Reorganization was taken in hand, new dioceses created, and an attempt made to recover Roman norms, in particular some serious revival of the monastic vocation. These changes are often referred to as 'Re-Romanization'.

Unfortunately, recovery was not altogether easy. Brazilians, in common with many other Latin Americans, were not well disposed towards priesthood and celibacy, and rarely sought ordination. This meant that priests had to be brought in from abroad. The stereotype of a priest in Brazil even to this day is of somebody who has a foreign accent and fails – in every sense – to communicate. Nationalists were irritated by these foreigners and some Catholic apologists found themselves hampered in their efforts to link national identity with Catholic faith. What this means is that the equation between Catholic faith and being a patriotic citizen has had less force and less success in Brazil than in many other parts of Latin America. Proposals to adopt some other ideology such as were put forward for Positivism in the nineteenth century or for Afro-Brazilian religion today are not inherently implausible.

In what ways then did Protestantism enter the competition to provide a viable faith? Along what social slipways might it hope to make headway? In the early stages when educated Brazilians first looked longingly at the advantages of modernity, Protestantism was assisted by its Anglo-American associations. Later, as admiration mingled with resentment, some Protestants tried to reverse this association by claiming to be more nationalist than the Catholics. Such a seemingly implausible strategy was made plausible by the initial attitude of conservative Catholics to the advent of the Republic. Since Protestants were forward-looking people they were allies of the republicans and *ergo* fervent patriots. Their biggest problem, in Brazil as in all other Latin American countries, was that their Republican allies merely regarded them as the least offensive version of the backward superstition known as Christianity. The polarization of opinion in Latin society over the church had resulted in so vehement a rejection of all religion as a bastion of irrationality that Protestantism could not cross the divide.

Insofar as Protestantism did trickle across this divide it had to do so in a schizophrenic manner, not only as both foreign *and* patriotic, but as modern *and* conformable to Brazilian values and culture. Thus the Protestant emphasis on universal criteria had to give way to nepotism, and its emphasis on individuality had to acknowledge the supremacy of the family over the individual.[3]

Initially it was the Presbyterians who made most impact, as the upright and rigorous representatives of classical Reform. Theologically they tended to be from the conservative wing of Presbyterians, partly because theological conservatives see more reason to evangelize, and partly because there was an influx of conservative-minded Southerners after the American Civil War. Brazilian Presbyterians gained their organizational independence from the United States in 1888, responding to and expressing the rising current of nationalism, but like the Brazilian nation at large they found economic independence less easy to achieve. The question of nationalism was not one they found it easy to be agreed upon, and they were equally divided about the proper balance between education and evangelism, about the training of pastors, and the appropriate attitude to freemasonry. Insofar as Presbyterians were successful, they were so among the more middling, independent sort, though a few individuals were converted among the upper reaches of Brazilian society. Presbyterians made some converts in the rural areas of eastern Minas Gerais and Espirito Santo and also gathered a tiny minority of followers in the urban middle class.

The main rivals to the Presbyterians were the Baptists, who like them were theologically conservative and came disproportionately from the American South. Baptists found themselves as divided over issues like the balance of education and evangelism etc. as were the Presbyterians, but in the upshot they tipped the balance more in favour of evangelism. As in the United States, so in Brazil, the tilt proved to be popular in every sense of the word. Baptists had a more demotic and participatory style and they were ready and/or able to reach some of the poor and the coloured. Moreover, schism seemed to cause less disruption among the Baptists than among the Presbyterians. They were already decentralized and a schism was little more than an overt manifestation of decentralization.

The growing success of Baptists relative to Presbyterians presaged the future success of the Pentecostals. The Pentecostals were in most respects like the Baptists, only more so. As the Baptists overtook the Presbyterians in numbers so the Pentecostals were to overtake those evangelicals, whose primary concern was with the grammar of doctrine. The relative failure of the Methodists was, and for that matter still is, minatory. They should by the nature of their tradition have been the ones who gathered in the harvest. But they were overcentralized, they resisted local independence, and they tilted the balance towards education rather than evangelism. The possibilities for Methodism are indicated by the expansion of the Methodist Pentecostals in Chile, which was originally an enthusiastic movement within Methodism forced out by rigidities of organization and adamant liberal distaste. Methodists made a signal contribution to the education and welfare of Latin Americans without adding to the church.

Ronald Frase in his magisterial dissertation on Protestantism in Brazil, gratefully used by this author, sets out the several paths along which Protestantism could move.[4] They are surprisingly numerous. For example, the messianic movements of the interior had at least established a tradition of dissidence. The brotherhoods had introduced the idea of lay initiative, and the kind of extraordinary regional cult which grew around Padre Cicero had demanded ascetic standards of behaviour. So the right elements were present for the success of enthusiastic Protestantism. Other paths were laid down by the openness of mind found among some of the many foreign immigrants and the questing spirit of people living on the frontier or caught up in the dynamic expansion of the coffee industry in the province of São Paulo.

A more localized pathway for Protestantism was provided by the situation of the rural middle class, referred to earlier with regard to the penetration achieved by the Presbyterians. Such people were not so beholden to the large landowners as those below them and could exploit their margin of economic independence. In his study of Minas Gerais, Emilio Willems found Protestants most frequent in *municípios* where landownings were of medium size. Thus we see that Protestantism could find an opening either where there was movement, as on the frontier, or where there was modest independence.[5]

Wherever they were in this early period of penetration, Protestants remained a peculiar people marked out by their dislike of alcohol, promiscuity and dancing, and by their attachment to work and social mobility. Their pastors, who came for the most part from the rural middle class, were specially notable for their spirit of emulation, and their progeny often moved up and away into the professional world. As elsewhere, the pastorate provides an escalator to be walked on to and in a later generation stepped off. Within the small and dynamic subculture of Protestantism the pastors were power-brokers and patrons in proper Brazilian style. Protestantism certainly nourished individuality, but the assumptions retained from Brazilian life at large ensured that the pastors in their churches and in their own families retained an authoritarian spirit. Protestantism was therefore ripe for the factional divisions, the generational rivalries, and the political differences which tore it apart in the twentieth century.

The year 1930 marks the end of an era for Brazil – and for Protestantism. Vargas came to power in a coup and the interests of agricultural exporters no longer dominated Brazilian policy. The country began to industrialize and by the 1950s the process was very rapid, especially in the south-east. Population soared and vast urban areas appeared which were not so much cities as loosely connected agglomerations of neighbourhoods, slums and encampments.

The great fact of Brazilian politics after 1945 was the emergence of ordinary people in these vast agglomerations as political actors, able to provide a base for Vargas and the Brazilian Labour Party. This is not to say that patronage disappeared. Rather it extended downwards from the middle classes who had deployed it since the 1930s, to include much of the working classes. Naturally this extension generated considerable anxiety in the middle class and it was the accentuation of this anxiety by inflation which helped bring about the military take-over of 1964.

It was during this period of population growth, of movement and of intermittent populism that Pentecostalism expanded most rapidly. Pentecostalism was fully indigenous and able to provide an all-encompassing world-view for marginalized people, especially in the vast urban agglomerations in the south-east and São Paulo. Pentecostalism was the religious form of a raised consciousness and quite literally of a raised voice. It cut people off from the wider society in order to raise them within a new religious framework. They were 'peculiar' in order to be something different.

And the difference was on the one hand the acceptance of a discipline and on the other the offer of participation to all. Participation was not only offered but required. All who desired to be reborn and who exhibited the spiritual gifts attendant on rebirth could and must sing, play an instrument, organize, share, assist each other, praise – and spread the word. Anyone could rise to the top if equipped with spiritual gifts, and if those gifts did not find room in one Pentecostal church another church rapidly appeared where room could be found.

Frase sums this up by saying that Pentecostalism offers the fruits of honesty and thrift and a surrogate family, as well as the chance of participation, and a sense of worth, meaning and empowerment.[6]

So it came about that a group which, in 1930, accounted for only one in ten of Protestants accounted in 1964 for between seven and eight, excluding the ethnic church of the German Lutherans. The Assemblies of God alone numbered over a million, while Brasil para Cristo and the Christian Congregation each numbered some 300,000. And the spread of rival charismata ensured that there were dozens of other churches, all insisting on local autonomy and total participation.

As the movement grew certain changes occurred. Brasil para Cristo became noted for its use of modern communications, for participation in secular politics and for its amazing headquarters temple. To have a temple of this size and to engage in vast rallies increased the sense of power and of (literally) *counting* for something in society. Those behind were coming up front, at least in their own independently created sphere. Brasil para Cristo also began to provide services of worship and other services specifically designed to attract the middle class. For that matter the constituency of Pentecostalism at large began to widen without any loss of roots or of power among the poor. Certain groups simply extended the range of their offerings or emerged specifically to speak to the middle class. For example, the Church of the New Life, founded in 1960 by Robert McAlister, and centred in Rio, speaks to people in the Brazilian middle class. It puts out regular broadcasts, and its building in Botafogo is a handsome edifice, with gallery and with air-conditioning.[7]

One of the potential changes attendant on those just outlined is a move towards theological education. This has indeed occurred but with caution and on a small scale. Pentecostals are a people obsessed with the one thing necessary, and that one thing is not a knowledge of Gadamer and the hermeneutic problem. They also sense that theological education by its nature separates off even those whose original roots are among ordinary people from the language and experience of ordinary people. It simultaneously inhibits the preacher and draws a cordon around a clerical caste. Pentecostals recognize that their life-blood depends on breaking the cordons of clerical caste, Protestant or Catholic. Religiously that is their *raison d'être* and in the symbolic realm it dramatizes their emigration from the class barriers of Brazilian society. They are, if you like, establishing their own special realm in the world of Brazil, and its name and title for them is the Kingdom of God.

So large a movement, now including about one in six of all Brazilians, has clear political potential. Yet Pentecostal success and the possibility of adherents creating their own free space is predicated on the avoidance of secular entanglements, among which politics are included. Pentecostals are people imbued with hope and with what they discern as 'power', but they have little hope of power through politics. The best that political experience has hitherto offered them has been as clients in the patronage networks of the populist era. For the most part they are pessimists about the efficacy of political action and have written off the public forum as an avenue to personal dignity and civic participation. They do, after all, come from among those who have been dumb or whose voice has been strangled for centuries. They also know political action is dangerous and prefer to survive.

It is probably the case that most Pentecostals, or at any rate most of their leaders, gave tacit support to the military take-over in 1964. Since the *abertura* (or opening to democracy) and the later more extensive instalments of democratization their votes show a cautious support for the right and the centre. Of the thirty-three Protestants among Federal Deputies, most belong to the Liberal PFL, or the Brazilian Democratic Movement (the PMDB) or the Social Democratic Party (PDS). But Protestants are also to be found in the opposition parties, especially so among the new Deputies. Amongst these is a black woman who belongs to the Assemblies of God and represents the Workers' Party. Rolim comments that in the past some Pentecostals were active in the Peasant Leagues, where they redeployed their ability to create cohesive cells, and showed themselves capable of fraternal solidarity with others in facing up to concrete problems.[8] However, their relation to such Leagues has at times turned sour. In general, it can be said that such interest as Pentecostals show in politics is of a piece with Brazilian political life as a whole: votes given by clients to patrons for services rendered.

Since Pentecostals are withdrawing from society and thereby creating a space outside the injuries of class and preponderant power, their contact with blacks is important. Brazil is far from the colour-blind society sometimes depicted, and any breaks in the lines of colour in the religious sphere are highly significant. It seems that Pentecostals have to some extent succeeded in making these breaks. At any rate Villeroy noted more black people among the Pentecostals than were to be found in the other denominations: 70 per cent in Bahia, 45 per cent in Pernambuco.[9]

The data on Pentecostal religion and race are not really available, but an interesting difference emerges between the way Pentecostalism affects black people and the way the older denominations have affected them. The modest appeal of the older Protestantism was to mulatto and black elites. It came about in part because Protestantism was opposed to slavery and permitted no discrimination on grounds of colour in its schools. Nowadays those blacks who belong to the historic denominations are identical in their attitudes to their white co-religionists. They are, and always have been, puritanical, thrifty and literate, interested in mutual support and social advancement, and deeply averse to superstition.

Things are somewhat different among the Pentecostals. According to Bastide, control has given way to ecstasy, and faith-healing plays a major role. This is as you would expect. Yet Bastide still discerns the motifs of personal advancement and of the assimilation to 'Western' norms among the black Pentecostals. He argues that at the very moment when the black 'seems closest to Africa – shaking and trembling, speaking in tongues, possessed by the Holy Ghost – he is actually farthest from it, more Westernized than ever before'.[10] It is difficult to assess this kind of argument, though it plainly belongs with those arguments which see Pentecostalism as introducing modernity and perhaps American culture by a concealed conduit.

However, what Bastide goes on to say is also highly pertinent to the concerns of the present argument.

> To the black joining any Protestant denomination is in itself an advance. A cultural advance because Protestantism is the religion of the book and therefore of literate people; it is the religion of the United States, of a world power. A social advance because on every level the Protestant tends to rise and enter the middle class. And lastly a religious advance.[11]

As will be indicated elsewhere, the conclusion about social advance is disputed so far as concerns Pentecostalism, but Bastide's view does in fact sum up much contemporary research.

Two other aspects of religion in Brazil need briefly to be touched upon because they complement or rival Pentecostalism: Umbanda and the base communities. Umbanda is a faith offering therapy, catharsis and healing by access to the spirits, and it has expanded alongside Pentecostalism over roughly the same time-span. The base communities have emerged within Catholicism since the sixties under the stimulus of liberation theology, though they have some continuity with the radical wings of Catholic Action and the Cursillos de Christianidad.

Umbanda and cultic movements of similar provenance offer the greatest single challenge to Pentecostalism. Indeed Gary Howe, writing as recently as the late seventies, saw the growth of Pentecostalism as unremarkable by comparison.[12] Obviously, a proper treatment of Umbanda would require a historical retrospect. It would also require an analysis of its complicated relation to Spiritualism and Afro-Brazilian religion, as well as an account of regional variations and processes of 'whitening' and Africanization. Anyone wishing to pursue such matters cannot do better than consult the work of Peter Fry, Gary Howe, and Diana de G. Brown.[13]

The first Afro-Brazilian churches emerged in the nineteenth century in the wake of the decline of the *irmandades* or brotherhoods. As elsewhere these brotherhoods preserved African elements alongside and inside Catholic forms, and their decline released an ancient underground stream of religiosity into Brazilian society. The specific origins of Umbanda were in the practices of collective spirit possession in Afro-Brazilian religion and also in Kardecist spiritism, a version of spiritual evolution imported from France and for a while popular among the more affluent and educated Brazilians. However, Umbanda is more than mere eclecticism. Diana de G. Brown comments that 'what was new in this religion was that its early leaders organized the Afro-Brazilian churches of Rio and other southern cities in a relationship of classes, through religion, and brought new values, ideology and organizational forms to it.'[14] Diana de G. Brown goes on to characterize the members of this new faith in terms strikingly similar to the earlier recruits to historic Protestantism. They were small business men, bureaucrats, military officers, journalists, teachers, lawyers and some immigrants. Interestingly, these people were concerned to 'whiten' and to purify Umbanda. This 'whitening' was later reversed as 'negritude' came to be evaluated more positively. The ambivalence of Umbanda towards blackness both masks and perpetuates racial prejudice.

From 1930 to 1945 Umbanda was subject to repression but after 1945 it gained increasing acceptability and visibility, and acquired political representation, mainly for the sake of self-defence. It expanded down the class spectrum and built up a patronage system perfectly adapted to the populist politics of the later Vargas era. Indeed, its whole cosmology was a reflection of patronage, mediation and decentralization. In the view of Gary Howe it represents the obverse of Pentecostalism, with its vehement denial of mediation and its 'centralized' monotheism. Howe sees Umbanda and Pentecostalism as rival but accurate reflections of the double nature or duality of Brazil: one decentralized, the other centralized. Umbanda actually provided one of the main means whereby politicians could extend the tentacles of patronage to the urban poor.[15]

When dictatorship supervened in 1964 the change made as little difference for Umbanda as for Pentecostalism. Umbanda was seen as a conservative influence. Its cosmological articulation of Brazil's supposed racial democracy and its cross-class appeal complemented the nationalism of the government. Again, by a striking parallel with Pentecostalism, Umbanda probably gained from the worsening relationship between the Catholic Church and the state, and received some tentative state support. Since the *abertura* (or time of political opening) and the slow return to democracy nothing much has changed for Umbanda, apart from the revival of Umbanda's role in organizing clienteles for politicians.

There are two other elements worth emphasizing when drawing parallels between Umbanda and Pentecostalism. Firstly, 'Western' medicine in Brazil was never so completely established as to drive out alternative forms. Both Pentecostalism and Umbanda offer alternative sources of health, one through the Holy Spirit, the other through the spirits. Secondly, as indicated earlier, Brazilian Catholicism has not been able to impose any kind of hegemony for a very long time. Brazil has in the past been rife with serious dissent and is now rife with serious contenders for the key position of the Catholic Church and for a major role in expressing the core values of the society.

Of course, the other rival to Pentecostalism is the Catholic Church's own response to the various challenges to its hegemony and to the course of state policy since 1964: the base communities. These represent the emergence of a form of voluntaristic, participatory and lay organization within the Catholic Church itself. They are incipiently Protestant in those respects, and are therefore dangerous to the hierarchy as well as instruments of it. They simultaneously express a residual hegemonic purpose on the part of the church *and* threaten its structure.

To analyse the base communities in detail would be to stray too far from the main focus of this analysis. All that can be done is to underline certain similarities and differences with respect to Pentecostalism. The main difference is that base communities are concerned to raise the political and social consciousness of the whole community. They are not turned inward and they have a structural view of the nature of social problems. Another difference is that they recruit more from the direct producers. This, at any rate, is the view of Rolim, though other observers believe that base communities draw on a social constituency almost identical with that drawn upon by Pentecostals.[16]

In two respects Pentecostals and members of base communities are similar. One is that they both apparently vote in roughly the same way. This is surprising and intriguing if true, since the political leadership of base communities is certainly to the left of the Pentecostal pastorate.[17] One might almost surmise that among Pentecostals and base communities the leaders lean respectively to the right and left while their followers stay in roughly the same place. The other similarity is to be found in an increasing appeal to the middle class. W. E. Hewitt in his study of base communities in the archdiocese of São Paulo shows the extent to which this recruitment among the middle class is going forward and comments further that this involves 'the politically influential middle classes directly in the social reform movement in Brazil'.[18]

Up to this point concern has focused on the great mega-cities, but change is also occurring in the inland regions. Useful research has been done in the Sertão by Scott William Hoefle and it provides a brief overview of one of the interior zones of Brazil.[19] The Sertão is an arid region, thinly populated, and still characterized by very sharp class differences. At the same time changes are occurring there quite rapidly. There has been an economic penetration from the more developed centres of Brazil. And the older forms of religious dissidence, in particular the millennarian movements, are giving way to Afro-Brazilian spiritism and evangelical Protestantism.

Of course, Catholicism remains the dominant religion, tied in to the life-cycle of the individual and of the community. Yet regularly practising Catholics are 60–85 per cent female, and are found most frequently among the widowed and the elderly. Men often regard concern with the church as unmanly and the priestly vocation as incomprehensible. For some of them whoring and gambling are the natural attributes of the proper male.

Thus the Catholic Church is both strong and weak: strong with respect to traditional and organic continuities, weak with regard to respect for the institutional church and an understanding of Catholic teaching. Protestants resolutely define themselves over against Catholic beliefs and Catholic behaviour. They emphasize spontaneous participation in worship, personal interpretation of the Bible, and personal financial and practical involvement in maintaining their church. They reject *compadres* (god parents) as unscriptural and thereby cut themselves from a major institution for maintaining communal links. They also cut themselves off by rejecting drink and promiscuity, and by avoiding the people who drink or are promiscuous. Hoefle comments that this temperate approach to life helps them in establishing a responsible work ethic, but since they are poor it does not give them much of a chance to become entrepreneurs. Individual eonomic success is less important for them than brotherly aid and mutual support. In stressing abstinence and mutual support Hoefle reinforces findings by Novaes in rural Pernambuco, though Novaes, as it happens, does not see much evidence of a changed attitude to work.[20]

Protestant adherence in the Sertão increases with the size of community. Thus Protestants number 0.2 per cent in the smallest communities, 4.6 per cent in a coastal city of modest size and 8.6 per cent in Greater Recife with a population of over 2 million. However, this clear relationship is to some extent confused by other evidence cited by Brandão, who finds instances where Catholicism is weak in very undeveloped areas, and strong in urban areas.[21] Such variations exist in the Mexican data and point to the need for more localized explanations to complement the general trend. Of course, if Protestants are relatively more likely to migrate from the country to the towns than Catholics, this further complicates the picture. Some commentators attribute some of the difficulty of maintaining successful Protestant churches in the countryside to the way Protestants are more ready to leave for the towns.

Hoefle also discusses the Afro-Brazilian and Spiritualist cults which have been active in the Sertão since the 1930s. He comments that the leader of the *xangô* sects does not regard himself or herself as being an intermediary between humans and the spirit world in the sense of being set apart. The leaders and their followers still see themselves as good Catholics and for the most part they attend mass. Only Protestants see their faith as excluding them from participation in these Afro-Brazilian rites. From the figures cited by Hoefle it would seem that the followers of Afro-Brazilian religions are relatively few in the countryside, though these figures may well be an underestimate given the fluidity of membership.

This discussion of the situation in the Sertão concludes the survey of Brazil, which is simultaneously the world's largest Catholic country, the scene of the largest spiritist movements – and the home of maybe half the evangelical believers in Latin America.

Chapter 5

The Southern Cone:
Chile and the Argentine Contrasted

Turning to the 'southern cone' of South America, to Chile and the Argentine, the object is not to give extended accounts of the growth of Pentecostalism but to address the remarkable difference between the eastern and western sides of the Andes. Pascal's remark about all jurisprudence altering with 1° of latitude could not be more apposite. Pentecostalism has long flourished on one side of the mountains and languished on the other, at least until very recently.

The coming of independence to Chile and to the Argentine in the early nineteenth century presaged a general opening up of the continent, in particular to commerce, and to Anglo-American and German penetration. The elites of Chile and the Argentine wanted to share in the manifest destinies and the progress of countries in the North Atlantic tier and this meant liberalism and a modicum of religious tolerance. The Catholic Church had in any case lost prestige through the Spanish sympathies of the upper clergy and the political haverings of the Pope.

However, the elites of the newly independent countries initially wanted no more than a Catholic Church under their own control, less rigid and less inquisitorial. They did not want to jettison the church as a valuable pillar of national unity nor did they contemplate conversion to Protestantism. As elsewhere Protestantism came in the baggage of liberalism and included certain benefits like schools and modern views of education. Protestants might be modest allies in the liberal attempt to rein in the political power of the church. For the most part Protestantism existed as a faith of foreigners, to begin with British business people and British engineers of Anglican background, followed by members of other historic denominations from North America, Germany or Scotland.

Christian Lalive D'Epinay shows how the greater part of the missionary work in both countries between 1880 and 1920 was linked to immigration, leaving aside some missions to the Indians.[1] He adds that the cultural influences at this time were more European, less North American, than was the case further north. The change from European to North American tutelage was not completed until the First World War.

It was round about the turn of the century that the histories of Protestantism in Chile and the Argentine began to diverge. The peopling of the Argentine up to 1930 came about by the arrival of millions of migrants, some of them Protestants. The Protestantism of the Argentine was, therefore, mostly a matter of ethnic churches, and (what is just as important) *defined* as such. Chile, on the other hand, received many fewer migrants, which meant fewer ethnic Protestants. Chilean Protestantism would have to expand through conversion, and this came about in the main after the onset of economic revolution in 1930. Conversion accompanied the rural exodus, partial industrialization and import substitution. Thus, the main increase in Argentinian Protestantism was by migration prior to 1930, and the main increase in Chilean Protestantism was by conversion after 1930.

This basic difference in turn affected the territorial distribution of Protestants in the two countries. In the Argentine the great migration ensured that the weight of population tilted very strongly and rapidly to the coastal regions and urban areas. The location of Protestants reflected that tilt, and the density of the various denominations naturally depended on which nationalities went where. The highest relative density of Protestants was in Missiones and Entre Ríos.

Even the migrants who intended originally to go to the country were inclined to turn in their tracks and swell the proletariat in the cities. Those who did settle in the rural areas often went to reservations set aside for them, for example in Patagonia. As for the long-standing populations of the interior, they tended to stay where they were, territorially – and religiously. For example, not much Protestantism was to be found in the remote and Hispanic province of Catamarca.

The crucial fact about Argentinian migration is that it drew mainly on Italians and Spaniards. They were, of course, mainly Catholic, even though the Italians included a number of Protestant Waldensians. These migrants inevitably included many anti-clericals opposed to all religion. The migrants who later followed them were often people for whom religiosity and identity were bound together, and who might be immigrating in order to find political safety, such as Jews, Russians, Poles and Ukrainians. Such groups would not lightly give up a union of peoplehood and faith forged under political threat to convert to Protestantism, especially when that was primarily associated with the ethnic identity of Scots, Welsh, English, Scandinavians and Germans.

Another relevant consideration is that once migration from (say) Italy reached a critical mass, it was not necessary to view the Catholicism of long-standing Argentinians as strange or unwelcoming. The cultural distance between the Italians and Argentinians no longer mattered since the migrants were numerous enough to stay within their own familiar Catholic environment. This was in contrast to the Italians in Brazil. There the Catholicism they encountered was not only weak but experienced as foreign. So many Brazilian Italians felt sufficiently alien to 'reform' themselves both socially and religiously, and convert to Protestantism. The impact of religious or anti-clerical traditions in different regions of Italy cannot be ruled out.

Thus religion in the Argentine was an ethnic trait: of Catholic Argentinians, of Catholic migrants or of Protestant migrants – or of Jewish and Orthodox migrants. It would require a longish period of shaking down before conversions were likely, and that period has lasted until the early 1980s.

Such conversions as did occur in the Argentine are nevertheless interesting. One form of evangelization is to be found in the provinces of Neuquén and Rio Negro. In these provinces about one person in ten is of Chilean origin, and the Chileans have brought with them their lively evangelical religion. It is, however, largely restricted to Chileans. Another form of evangelization is to be found among Indian tribes in the subtropical north of the country, for example the work of the Mennonites and the Pentecostals among the Toba.

What then of conversions of people in the mainstream of Argentinian society? Most of the increase in the Protestant population from 2.0 to 2.6 per cent between 1947 and 1960 has to be attributed to evangelization, much of it running parallel to the kind of evangelization found elsewhere in Latin America – that is, among the working classes who have moved from country into town, especially into Greater Buenos Aires. The most successful efforts have been those of the Plymouth Brethren, the Baptists and the Adventists. The Adventists in particular are well organized. They tithe, they build schools for their converts, they make use of radio – and they campaign against smoking as part of a broader emphasis on health and a sensible diet.[2]

Some comments on the relative successes of the various Protestant groups in the Argentine may be useful. Elsewhere in this study not much is said about the varied appeal of different Protestant churches. As just indicated, the most successful groups in the Argentine in the past have been the Brethren, the Baptists and the Adventists. Arno W. Enns remarks on the 'astonishing surge' of the Pentecostal churches, even though that is much less astonishing than in other Latin American countries.[3] There is also a discernible impact of the new wave of independent charismatic churches, in particular the Vision of the Future movement, with over 150,000 members. The main thrust of Enns's argument is the role of fervour in sustaining dynamism as compared either with a focus on correct credal grammar or on social involvement. Those churches who foster a dry concern with dogma at the expense of spiritual dynamic and freedom remain relatively ineffective. The same is true of those churches which stress liberal theology, tolerance, ecumenism and social engineering.

Enns singles out the Methodists as an example of a static body suffering from diluted conviction, theological liberalism and over-weighty organization.[4] The Methodists arrived early in Argentina and held fast to the status of 'elder brother', in that respect coming once more to resemble their Anglican origins. They have many kinds of ministry, and show a genuine social concern, which is especially evident among the substantial middle-class membership. The Methodists have distinguished theologians among them, as for example José Míguez Bonino, and are open to European theological trends. They also retain their early emphasis on secular education, much of it directed to influential middle-class families. The Pentecostals have none of these things: and it is they who grow.

In turning to Chile the object is solely to emphasize the contrast with the Argentine. Whereas Protestantism in the Argentine is largely a cultural trait imported by migrants from Protestant countries, in Chile Protestantism is a result of evangelization carried on by Chilean working people among those of their own class as they gathered in the environs of the great cities. It took off from an electric spark struck locally by W. C. Hoover, but parallel with a whole series of sparks struck at roughly the same time in Los Angeles, Armenia, Wales, Korea and South Africa. In Chile, as Lalive D'Epinay puts it 'les critiques assaillent les inspirés, singulièrement semblables à celles dont, cent soixante-dix ans plus tôt, la hiérarchie anglicane accablait les frères Wesley.'[5] The spark was struck within Methodism but the explosion took place through Pentecostalism.

The earliest missions to penetrate Chile were, as Lalive D'Epinay puts it, merely 'vegetative'. The Anglicans restricted themselves to

Anglo-Saxons or the Araucan Indians. The Lutherans were active only among the German migrants. However, the Baptists made modest progress rather like their co-religionists in the Argentine. The Methodists, having given painful birth to the Pentecostals, had to watch their errant children expand until, in 1960, they were four out of every five Chilean evangelicals. From 1940 to 1952 Protestantism expanded in the provinces of Concepción and Arauco and above all in the Central Valley, where land tenure was dominated by great estates. The expansion ran *pari passu* with a rupture in Chilean society signalled in a great rural migration. This was motivated less by the attractions and opportunities of the cities than by crisis in the countryside, notably rigidity in agriculture and in extractive industry. By contrast with northern Europe such movements of population were not primarily provoked by industrial development. They were provoked rather by opportunities in the tertiary sector related to the rapid development of bureaucracy, to the commercial export of 'monoproduction' and to the import of consumer goods and equipment. Between 1940 and 1960 personnel working in the service sector tripled, but those working in manufacture increased only by half. Many who sought employment failed and had to subsist uncertainly as small artisans or travelling salespeople. It was among these that Protestantism was most successful.

Christian Lalive D'Epinay comments that the great estates from which the migrants came at least offered the security of authority. The estates were in fact an ensemble of families under the protection of the *patrón*. In his view Pentecostalism reconstituted the social unity, security and authority of the hacienda, as well as offering a certain human dignity within the supportive community of the faithful.[6] Each member could participate and felt animated by the common task of evangelization. Pentecostals preached in the language of the people and provided a channel for symbolic protest.

They also shared in a broad national sensibility still impregnated by faith, even to some degree by magical thinking. Chile, like Brazil, was and is a society pervaded by religiosity, if not by institutional practice. On the one hand the church is weak, on the other the culture has remained religious. In such a situation Lalive D'Epinay sees nothing astonishing in the emergence of two basic responses, both of them Latin America mutations of foreign ideas: a religious creed which is apolitical and a political creed which is atheistic.[7]

Lalive D'Epinay in his study of Pentecostalism in Chile provides the most detailed account of the social geography of Pentecostal expansion currently available and it is therefore important to summarize his argument. He restates the co-incidence of the economic crisis in a dependent economy and the growth of Pentecostalism, and taking off from that premise he aims to show how far the regions and groups most affected by 'destructuration' are also those where Pentecostalism had most impact.[8]

Taking first the northern and southern extremities of Chile, these are areas where Pentecostalism has not taken off. They are distinguished not so much by *type* of production but by a *mode* of production, which is oriented to the world market and controlled from abroad. They are peripheral enclaves, far from the centre, and contain relatively large foreign minorities.

The north in particular is scarred by the closure of its mines, and many places are as sadly deserted as some of the valleys of Wales. So many people left the area that the Methodist Church, for example, had to close many of its chapels. As for Punta Arenas, the Panama Canal ensured it a fate comparable to that of Liverpool. And as in Wales and Liverpool, the people became highly politicized and combative. In short, a combination of depression, the departure of the people and politicization has meant that Pentecostalism has made little progress. In any case in an elongated country like Chile these extremities are both remote and shut off.

The second region examined by Lalive D'Epinay extends from Ñumble to Llanquihue and comprises nine provinces where Pentecostalism has spread most. The area includes 'the Frontier', which was a place of pioneers where the great estates did not exist and small farms were prevalent. It also includes some Indian reservations which have been resistant to any form of Christianity, and mark the area out as the heartland of earlier pre-colonial peoples. Taken as a whole, the region has no consistent pattern of tenure or of social organization, and it was, in fact, only integrated into Chilean society about a century ago. In some of its provinces the coverage provided by the Catholic Church is quite fragmentary.

It may seem difficult to discern why Pentecostalism should take off in a region with such varied characteristics. Unlike Willems, Lalive D'Epinay does not look for the relevant opening where the farming is small-scale and precarious, as, for example, in Cautín. The existence of such farms may play a role, as it did earlier in Brazil, but Lalive D'Epinay stresses rather the general fragility of social order in the whole region. The pioneering character of the region and its relatively recent integration into Chilean society both give rise to this fragility. By significant contrast those provinces integrated into Chile at the time of the original colonization have been much less responsive to Pentecostalism.

The third area is the Central Valley. This is distinguished by large and small estates. Pentecostalism arrived late and up to 1940 moved slowly. But then it expanded very quickly, establishing itself in the countryside and even penetrating the closed social structures of the hacienda. Pentecostalism entered where Marxism and syndicalism had been vigorously rejected, providing the one form of organization which belonged entirely to the exploited. It was their free space just as was the black church for the slaves of the US South. At times it seemed that the Catholic priest was chaplain to the great house and the Pentecostal preacher chaplain to the workers. In that role he was almost tolerated, maybe because the element of symbolic protest and cultural revolution did not immediately threaten the structures of the established order.

As for the '*provinces-villes*', the people there have also responded to Pentecostalism. However, in Valparaiso and Santiago where Pentecostalism was born, the proportion of Protestants has not increased. Instead Pentecostalism radiates out in parts of the countryside and among those on the move from country to city. Pentecostals become a case of *rus in urbe*. Lalive D'Epinay here turns to studies carried out in the sixties of two areas in Santiago. These studies showed that four out of five Pentecostals did not own the small parcels of ground on which they lived. Nor did they include many individuals from the stable working class, but rather journeymen and peripatetic salespeople, watchmen and porters, as well as some people in the lower middle class.

Interestingly enough Pentecostals were those who had some individual niche in the interstices of society, however precarious that niche might be and however subject to chronic under-employment. It is precisely such people who disproportionately make up the Christian congregations in the Soviet Union – that is to say, people partly outside the downward thrust of power from above and in part released from constraining lateral solidarities. Lalive D'Epinay's broad conclusion about the social location of Pentecostals jibes nicely with Rolim's in Brazil: 'the under-proletariat from the country'. His broadest characterization is that Pentecostalism in Chile represents the cultural aspect of economic and political dependence.

The Andean Republics: Colombia and Peru

Colombia is important because it is the most traditionally Catholic of all the major countries of Latin America. It stands at the opposite end of the continuum from Uruguay and Venezuela. Whereas they inhibited Protestant expansion because they were comprehensively secularized, Colombia inhibited Protestant expansion because it was comprehensively Catholicized. In Colombia there has been up to very recently a church on the Spanish model, vigorous and adamant, dogmatic and triumphalist, ready to identify the church with the nation. Whether in the older conservative framework or in the radically critical framework of today, the Colombian church seeks and assumes hegemony. Even after the withdrawal from political partisanship that began in the bloody shambles of *La Violencia*, the Catholic Church offers herself as the moral guide and mentor of her Colombian children. She tolerates Protestantism, but guardedly.[9]

It was perhaps because of these claims and assumptions that anti-clericalism was more fervent in Colombia than anywhere else, apart from Mexico. However, that anti-clericalism is now mainly a thing of the past. It reached two high points, one in the 1850s, during a period when the Liberals were in power, and again in the time of upheaval from 1930 on, which concluded in *La Violencia*, or more accurately in the Civil War.

The important point is that in the mid-nineteenth century the Catholic Church eventually won, and in the mid-twentieth century fought its opponents to a draw in which most of its powers and influence remained intact. Thus, according to the Concordat of 1887, the church gained control over education. Equally today it retains massive influence through its schools. Two-thirds of all secondary schools are Catholic and they are educationally superior to their state rivals. Indeed in the 1940s the church, through Catholic Action, actually developed successful trade unions, as well as adult education programmes and community projects.

The clergy of the Colombian church have not only promoted *Hispanidad* in the past, but they have been mostly natives of Colombia. They have the advantage of being both numerous and native. Another advantage is that they have to some extent offered avenues of social mobility to the poor and, in a rather ambiguous manner, have stood between the poor and the exploitative zeal of the upper classes. Though they have generally supported the centralizing ideology of the right, they have at the same time sometimes tactically retired to a federalist viewpoint when wanting to defend their provincial strongholds.

This means that certain areas of the country, like the Antioquia, are resolutely and fervently Catholic, and resistant to all alternatives. As José Sanchez puts it, 'In the 1960s the Colombian clergy remained a powerful group. The primitive social and educational levels in rural areas provided them with a continuing dogmatic hold.'[10] Not surprisingly, the entrance of Protestantism was late and at first only effected seriously in those areas under Liberal control. One of the first serious missions to arrive was the Christian and Missionary Alliance, which came in from Ecuador in 1923.

There was one other consequence of the overarching claims of Catholicism and its emphasis on *Hispanidad*, and that was the lumping together of Protestants, liberals and communists, under a single head. Something similar occurred in Guatemala during the counter-revolution of 1954, and the same identification sometimes occurs in Peru today, though for somewhat different reasons. At any rate those clerics who were most tempted in the thirties and forties by the lure of the Colombian versions of Francoism were inclined to lump Protestants along with communists. Again later, in the confused turmoil of the early stage of *La Violencia*, the same identification was made. Many Protestants were among the hundreds of thousands murdered at that time, and Protestants were effectively forced underground into house churches. Of their schools 270 were closed and of their churches 60 were destroyed. The result was a peculiar pride in being the people who held their Bible in their own hands. The Bible became a sign of the independent person deciding his faith for himself, and a talisman of endurance. At least from the Protestant viewpoint, the claims of the church were such that their movement was automatically a demand for civil rights irrespective of creed. This was particularly the case with regard to the laws of marriage and divorce.

Since the 1960s the church has withdrawn from political partisanship and followed in the path of a minority of clerics who had for some time advocated disentanglement and/or social criticism. The new neutrality is now combined with a radical social critique though this critique resolutely rejects liberation theology. Both disentanglement and critique rest on the foundation of a Catholic presidency over the unity of the nation. As Daniel Levine comments, 'it is easy to imagine the Colombian Church favouring more equal income distribution, agrarian reform and the like; but it is considerably harder to envision its leaders willingly turning over to others . . . the moral authority to develop norms in these areas without reference to the Church.'[11] As I have suggested elsewhere, even liberation theology itself remains part of such a hegemonic project, at least in the field of norms if not in the field of substantial political power.

One very interesting feature of Catholic moral theology as developed in Colombia is its approximation to what is usually called the Protestant Ethic. What the church actually teaches, as distinct from what its more Laodicean members practise, closely resembles the teaching of those Protestants most vehemently opposed to it. It recommends hard work, regular savings, a personal discipline, and sets forth the social ideal of the small independent owner. It is as if Protestants were demanding an adherence to this moral teaching. Of course, the other side of their protest is the rejection of all mediation and all elements of clerical caste, along with their withdrawal from the church as anciently aligned with an oppressive and all-encompassing social environment. Nevertheless the close correspondence of Catholic and Protestant in the matter of moral and social aspirations remains interesting, and acts as a reminder of all those movements of ascetic activism which have remained within the church. Catholics *can* be *morally* very 'Protestant', and especially so in the most Catholic of countries: the Republic of Ireland, Spain – and Colombia.

The foregoing has, of course, simply recapitulated the ecclesiastical side of the development of Colombia and it is necessary now to trace the general social and economic developments and the opportunities they have offered to Protestantism. One of the main sources for doing this is Cornelia Butler Flora's book published in 1976 under the title *Pentecostalism in Colombia: Baptism by Fire and Spirit*.[12] Interestingly, Flora's arguments about the parallelism of economic and cultural penetration as well as about the mobility of Pentecostals follow similar lines to those of Lalive D'Epinay. Basically she treats Pentecostalism as the religious aspect of economic dependency, and runs her economic account closely alongside her religious account. Put less baldly, she is saying that foreign capital brings about a commercialization of land and proletarianization of labour and that the consequent dislocations and movements offer entry to Pentecostalism.

Initially Colombia attempted to develop in isolation. The rural landowners transformed themselves into urban capitalists and continued an unimpeded oligarchical rotation of the great and the 'pure'. To that extent Colombia remained economically and religiously inviolate. Thereafter foreign capital effected an entry at the margin in the primary sector, and American missionaries also appeared at the margin, notably a few Presbyterians who set up some prestigious schools. Then, finally, in the fifties and sixties foreign capital entered Colombia on a broad front and with it came the rapid commercialization of land, the proletarianization of labour and indigenous Pentecostalism. At the same time vast urban agglomerations grew up, above all the mega-city of Bogota. The migration to Bogota was only in part a result of industrialization. Like other great Latin American agglomerations it offered precarious employment about half of which was in the domestic and service sectors. The migration was as much a flight from violence and murderous squads of guerrillas as it was a realistic search for industrial employment.

The difficulties of the present time of transition are so dramatically illustrated in Bogota (as in São Paulo, Rio, Lima, Guatemala City, Mexico City) that they need brief enumeration. People in the *barrios* of Bogota live in conditions of total frustration bordered by unattainable hope. In the near distance are vast insurance blocks; in the immediate vicinity there are women leading donkeys carrying firewood and homeless urchins importuning passers-by or squabbling in murderous gangs. Unemployment is chronic, and over-employment in terms of hours worked for money received severe. If you want a job, competence is only half the relevant qualification: the rest depends on your network and family connections. The Colombian city-dweller is familiar with the desertion of wives by husbands, and the short duration of a fractured childhood. Desperate women have recourse to prostitution. The city-dweller suffers from sleeplessness and irritability and even from poor hearing, all brought on by noise and confusion and the tremors of continuous uncertainty. The nightmare breeds a mal-aise, dis-ease, and dis-tress, in which the physical and the psychical are intermingled.[13]

Into this transitional zone of pullulating city life, emerging within the context of rapid and warped economic development, comes the new message proferred by the Pentecostals. The Pentecostals speak the language of the people, either through vast campaigns or through the intimate invitations of relatives, friends and evangelists. They propose a restoration of scarred and fractured relationships, a repudiation of corruption, a discipline of life, an affirmation of personal worth, a cancellation of guilt, a chance to speak and to participate, sisterhoods and brotherhoods of mutual support in sickness and in health, and a way to attain *Sanidad Divina*. The *Sanidad Divina* deals precisely in the psychical and the physical viewed as intimately bound up together. Pentecostalism offers the old fiesta in the form of lively worship, the old trances in the form of spiritual ecstasy, and the old networks in the form of the brotherhood. Perhaps, as Donald Palmer has suggested in his Colombian study *Explosion of People Evangelism*, it is the autonomy, the self-support, the liveliness, and the chance of release and participation which count for most in the Pentecostal appeal, plus a sense of having something which nobody else has.[14] So far as the Pentecostals themselves are concerned their conversion is a matter of being literally 'shaken' by a total reorientation of the heart and the will in order to join the ultimate fiesta: 'Estamos de fiesta con Jesus; al cielo yo quiero ir . . .'

This contrast between the confused city of man and the ordered city of God has to be drawn in dramatic and empathic language even to hint at how it is that people can pass from an all-encompassing world of their past to undertake this combined social and religious transition. But (reverting to the proper sobrieties of sociology), Cornelia Butler Flora points out just how down-to-earth the concerns of Pentecostals actually are.[15] They want the removal of those things which (literally) bedevil them and a salve for their sorrows and diseases. They put boundaries between themselves and the outside world precisely to protect the space within which they can make gestures of equality and proclaim that 'the first shall be last'. The boundaries put up do not, in her view, prevent them seeing the upper class as corrupt, unworthy and antagonistic to their achievement of a better life. Nor does their apolitical stance prevent them from voting for the populist candidates rather than for the old rotations of liberals and conservatives. They take part in water-strikes just as much as others in the same social situation. What she does regard as doubtful, however, is the efficacy of their aspiration to be in business for themselves. That may have been realistic for Methodists in the early stages of English industrialization, but in her view it is anachronistic in the conditions of Colombian capitalism today.

While tracing the general trajectory of Protestantism in Colombia, it is worth referring in the briefest aside to Venezuela, which was earlier characterized as highly secular. The important point here is that in Venezuela it was the liberals who eventually won the battles, not the conservatives, and that the church was totally reduced with respect to its property and its social functions. (Indeed, it has been questioned whether Venezuela was ever successfully converted to Catholicism.)

The other crucial point is that Venezuela was totally altered by the impact of oil, together with the activities of a strong state and the emergence of mass-based political parties. The complicated nexus between these cannot be pursued here. The upshot is that while Colombia has been dominated by preservation, Venezuela has been concerned with novel creation. In those conditions the church in Venezuela shifted out of its early right-wing identification, embraced the return to democracy in 1958, and accepted the presence of the Democratic Action Party. From that point on the Catholic Church sought to maintain a stance of critical neutrality.[16]

The modern, urbanized Venezuela is the most secular country in Latin America after Uruguay. The predominant pattern of education on offer inculcates secular perspectives in the world. Its Protestant membership as recorded by David Barrett in *The World Christian Encyclopedia* (1982) amounts only to 0.5 per cent of the population.[17]

Peru, like neighbouring Bolivia, has a population which is half Indian, and the Spanish suppression of Indian identity is only the last of a series of conquests and suppressions. Today the country has been semi-industrialized and some two-thirds of the people live in urban areas. Related social changes were clearly on the way by the 1950s as political clientage developed towards populism, as grass roots movements appeared, and a group of reformers emerged in the Church. As an institution the Church was not well placed for a major role in social change, given that rates of active participation were low and the clergy short handed. Very few priests were recruited from the indigenous population, and illiteracy was general.

The coup of October 1968 brought a reforming military government to power. By this time many Catholics, especially bishops and female religious were ready to support such a government. Indeed many radicals such as the distinguished liberation theologian Gustavo Guttierez and the young urban priests associated with the National Office for Social Information, offered critical support from the left. Catholic organizations now acted alongside popular organizations, and the Church provided trained personnel to help in the task of social reconstruction. Yet in the late seventies further shifts occurred in the military, this time mainly to the right and after some protest the Church itself seemed to fragment into various positions – liberation theology, the charismatic movement, as well as a neo-conservative thrust such as is associated with Opus Dei. In any case, the hierarchy had always been conscious of the minatory example of Cuba. As change and disorder accelerated, the Church also became aware that Protestantism was making headway even in Peru, and in 1986 sponsored a report tracing the type and extent of Protestant expansion.

Following the general strategy of this survey what follows concentrates on two salient aspects of Protestantism in Peru: the role of Protestant education and the work of evangelical missions among the indigenous population.

With regard to education the most notable impact on Peruvian society was achieved by the American Methodist Episcopal Church. The Methodists, like the Presbyterians in many other parts of Latin America, played a surprisingly significant role in offering new perspectives, new areas of competence, new conceptions of self and of personal discipline, through their schools. What they lacked in numbers they made up for in influence and in contributions to social change.

When the Methodists first began to work in Peru in 1889 the country was still engaged in reconstruction following the disastrous war with Chile. The Catholic Church for its part was still allied with feudal elements and held tenaciously to a religious monopoly which was to last in practice until 1915 and constitutionally until 1979. At the same time the balance of foreign economic power affecting Peru was tilting away from Britain to North America. The arrival of American Methodism was therefore parallel to the arrival of American capital, and both encountered an alternation between acceptance and hostility.

Methodist work in Peru over the following two generations focused on social transformation. Just as in Mexico, Methodist schools offerred a social alternative and embraced quite ambitious ideas of moral and intellectual renovation. The journal *La Nueva Democracia* provided a forum for liberal and radical leaders, including the legendary Haya de la Torre and other politicians of the Alianza Popular Revolucionaria (APRA). The Methodist schools aimed at the newly influential middle classes, but also provided education for workers. What they offered was a business and commercial competence allied to a strong emphasis on punctuality, discipline and truthfulness, as well as access to English. They also offered an advanced pedagogy and a progressive curriculum for women. After 1930 the Methodist schools ran into problems with anti-imperial sentiment and found their moderate radicalism overtaken by the more extreme polarities of Latin America political culture. But the way they helped forward the modernization and liberalization of Peru at a crucial juncture in national development is clear and is fully documented for example in the work of Rosa del Carmen Bruno-Jofre.[18]

The Adventist schools were rather different but also influential. They were established originally as the forward posts of Adventist work among the Quechua and Aymara. Conversion among these tribal groups was not so much through individual choice as through processes of collective decision-making. What the Adventists provided was a new collective faith and the basic infrastructure of health and education. In such a situation education and evangelization were inevitably bound together. In time Adventists became the largest Protestant church in Peru, and for that matter also in Bolivia.

The most recent advance of Protestantism came with the great migration to the cities, and it involved a massive relative growth of Pentecostalism, as well as the expansion of several other groups, such as Mormons and Witnesses. In the earlier years the most conspicuous Protestant presence in Gran Lima was the Christian and Missionary Alliance. Nowadays it is the Assemblies of God. In 1940 Protestants in Gran Lima numbered under 1 per cent, but in 1961 they were 1.44 per cent and in 1987 3.54 per cent. In a study recently carried out by Manuel Marzal in the Agustino district of Lima 12 per cent of heads of families declared themselves to be Protestant. As usual the vitality of Pentecostalism provides an indication of the vitality of Protestantism as a whole.[19]

There are, however, some slightly unusual aspects of Protestant expansion in Peru. One is that Protestants are still sometimes identified as political subversives and are shot impartially by guerrillas and the army. Perhaps this is just part of the growing anarchy of contemporary Peru. Another is the extent of non-evangelical conversion, especially to Mormonism or to the Jehovah's Witnesses. Missionaries of the Bahai faith have been active, and indeed in neighbouring Bolivia some 160,000 Indians have become Bahais. The Society of Friends also has areas of influence. And, most curious of all, two groups of 'Israelites' have broken out of the fold of Adventism. Maybe this relative success of non-evangelical faiths has something to do with the way schisms have come about in Peru from the earliest years until now. Whereas elsewhere schism has usually been a sign of vitality, in Peru it has actually drained the contending bodies of energy and credibility.[20]

Chapter 6

Smaller Contrasting Societies – Ecuador, El Salvador, Guatemala – and Mexico

There follows now a brief account of the trajectory and contemporary condition of Protestantism in three very much smaller societies, Ecuador, El Salvador and Guatemala. The evidence for Ecuador records a modest expansion, but one reflecting the general profile of Protestant history for most of Latin America.[1]

If we leave aside intermittent activity on the part of individual members of British and American Bible Societies, organized Protestant work in Ecuador really became possible only after the liberal revolution of 1895. Prior to that the Catholic Church was tied in with the landowning elite, and it controlled education and the organs of censorship. When Protestantism was eventually established on a serious footing, the comity agreements of 1916 helped ensure that it was mainly evangelical and fundamentalist and promoted moreover by lay mission boards. The historic churches did not have a serious impact until the 1930s. Yet despite the emphasis of conservative Protestants on evangelization, the Protestant membership, between 1909 and 1949, only increased from 10 to 1,030 which constituted 0.03 per cent of the total population. In 1973 Protestants were only one in two hundred and today perhaps one in fifty.

The initial impact of Protestantism was on the coast rather than in the sierra. Even so recently as 1973 one in three of Protestants lived in the sierra, whereas one in two of the total population did so. This has much to do with ethnic, political and economic influences. The coast contained the main liberal bases, it was Creole rather than Hispanic, it supported plantations rather than haciendas, and its patterns of land tenure were less extreme. Greater access to land and more rapid industrialization on the coast allowed for greater mobility among the rural people. Moreover, the power of the Catholic Church in this area had been broken since 1895.

At the same time there has been a major evangelical movement among the Quechua-speaking peoples, and churches have grown up among the Hispanic population in the highlands. The mid-sixties saw the arrival of several Pentecostal groups, followed by Southern Baptists and the Church of Christ in 1970. About half of the Protestant community is now Pentecostal, while the other half is conservative evangelical. It is interesting that David Preston, commenting on the impact of missions to the Chimborazo, notes that those converted have improved their living standards and are more likely to migrate.[2]

Most Protestants today belong to the lower middle or upper lower classes. Characteristically they are skilled artisans, small shopkeepers and white-collar employees, though there are a few manual workers and some professional people, especially teachers. The existence of professional people is connected with the Protestant emphasis on education, including the provision of evening courses.[3]

A more lively picture emerges in El Salvador. The material available for El Salvador concentrates more on the Pentecostals. Beginning in the 1880s, successive regimes abolished communally owned Indian lands and forced subsistence farmers to plant coffee trees. Land gradually fell into a very few hands and the country people were cut off from the advantages available in the towns. The vast majority were subject to illness and they were illiterate. Next to nothing has improved since, and the military coup of 1979 in the end did little but add more blood to the tally of misery. Today many Salvadoreans have joined the guerrillas or have emigrated.

Over this past sombre century sectarian Protestantism did not initially offer the kind of option it offered in other Central American republics. Even as late as 1940 Protestants accounted for only 0.17 per cent of the population. This failure was perhaps the more marked given the traditional anti-clericalism of the upper classes. E. Everett Wilson comments that although the evangelical churches created a favourable climate by their educational efforts, they tended to become narrowly constituted urban churches that even as early as 1940 reached an institutional plateau.[4]

Pentecostalism arrived in 1915 by way of an offshoot of the Central American Mission. Most groups met on the land of a member or sympathizer and conducted noisy ecstatic scenes into the early hours. Occasionally all came together in a Pentecostal counterpart of the country fiesta. Their emergence paralleled a general increase in associational activity among Salvadoreans, as for example, self-help and savings groups, burial clubs and trades unions.

However, this early manifestation of the Pentecostal spirit was undisciplined and lack of discipline proved dangerous in a society where cohabitation was the norm. The arrival in 1929 of a Welsh migrant, Ralph Williams, led to a reorganization, out of which two principal Pentecostal churches eventually came to pre-eminence: the Assemblies of God and the Church of God (Cleveland). Another signal result of this reorganization was the *Reglamento*, which provided a constitution widely adopted in Latin America, and includes a provision whereby every initiate pledges himself to respect civil authority and to refrain from political involvement. It allows for congregations to elect their pastors, and sets up a governing board consisting of both men and women.[5] The *Reglamento* proved a powerful instrument for integration. Members had to regularize their marriages, straighten out their affairs and pay a tithe on their income. Here we see how a restriction in political activity arises directly out of a specific historical crisis threatening the very existence of the church.

In spite of being suspected of involvement in the peasant insurgency of 1932, and having several members executed in the appalling aftermath, the little Pentecostal churches prospered. They had little outside contact and became models of indigenous evangelism. The Assemblies of God had a membership of 2,000 in 1935 which rose to 75,000 in 1981. Several smaller groups also engaged in evangelism, for example the Guatemalan church called Prince of Peace. Its principal leader was a woman, Carmen Mena Fuentes, and after her death the movement attracted many country people who were disappointed by the worldliness of some of the upwardly mobile urban Pentecostals. Clearly John Wesley's warnings about the relationship between success and flagging devotion applied in mid-twentieth-century El Salvador as much as in eighteenth-century England.

In the mid-1950s, El Salvador, in common with several other countries, experienced a period of revivalist campaigning. Many changes came about through the initiative of North American missionaries. Pentecostals not only attracted the marginalized urban population but began to penetrate the middle class by organizing the kind of activities which might appeal to professionals. They made use of modern technology and even organized a comprehensive school system. An estimated two-thirds of the Pentecostal congregation now owned real property and Pentecostals received recognition for their efforts in education and social service. Everett A. Wilson comments that the strength of Pentecostalism, which makes up 90 per cent of the Protestant total, lives in 'popular, diffused institutional authority', which at the same accommodates social change.[6]

Guatemala has to be included here in spite of being dealt with extensively elsewhere, especially in chapter 12, because it exhibits the highest proportion of Protestants in all of Latin America. In what follows, the focus is on the complicated way Protestants fitted into the internecine oppositions of Guatemalan politics.

In 1871 the triumphant liberal revolutionaries in Guatemala treated the church with great severity, depriving it even of legal personality.[7] But as was the case with so many other societies, the culture itself was not secularized. The Maya, who are in the majority, devised a kind of syncretic religious practice and used the *cofradias* (fraternities) as vehicles for conserving some of their pre-Columbian traditions. Though the liberals invited Protestants in as agents of progress and providers of services, they had little success. They were regarded as alien, and in any case the plantation-owners (like those in Jamaica at an earlier period) did not want the convenient fatalism of their labour force disturbed.

For a while in the 1920s it looked as if Protestants might be under pressure from nationalistic governments as agents of foreign culture, but the atmosphere eased under the influence of Roosevelt's 'Good Neighbour' policy. With the advent of a government under Arbenz interested in land reform the Protestants were divided in their response. Some US missionaries reflected the intensely anti-communist stance engendered in the Cold War; on the other hand many native Protestants became involved in land reform and in peasant organizations.

Then in 1954 there was a military coup, backed by the CIA, which inaugurated intermittent reigns of terror. It also partially restored the position of the Catholic Church, helped by US government which saw Catholicism as a barrier to communism. The Protestants found themselves under suspicion and were occasionally punished.

At this point more US missionaries arrived, many of them from the Latin American Mission (LAM) in Costa Rica. They were of a strongly conservative cast of mind and certainly helped Protestants lose the dangerous stigma of communism. The LAM missionaries stressed shared religious feeling rather than divisive dogma, and proceeded to modernize the local religious style, with novel techniques of planning, marketing and communication. This was quite successful, and provided persuasive American role models, but it was also resented as a foreign importation. An independent Presbyterian Church emerged in the Mayan highlands and also an independent

Nazarene Church. Fragments broke off from the Assemblies of God, for example the Prince of Peace group. This splitting preceded a rapid indigenous expansion, as it did in Brazil and also in Chile. Rapid growth was helped forward very much by translations of the Bible into the very numerous dialects of the Mayan language, in particular by members of the Central American Mission (CAM). It is insufficiently realized just how much threatened cultures have been revitalized in Latin America, as also in Africa, by translations of the Bible.

At the same time very rapid urbanization was proceeding in Guatemala. Nearly one-third of the total population was now living in Guatemala City. Yet there was only one priest there for every 30,000 persons. Then in 1976 there occurred the great earthquake. Aid and personnel poured in from North America and a major shift of the social landscape began to come about. The spread of Protestant groups, above all of Pentecostals, pulled people away from alcoholism, petty crime and corruption. Conversion was also a protest against violence and the disintegration of the family brought about by the male macho personality. The new faith encouraged savings and discouraged smoking and generally inculcated habits which might make for some modest economic advancement following the slogan 'From the dirt to the sky'. Part of the welfare infrastructure was by now associated with the Protestant churches, above all clinics. For the Maya the clinics dispensed magical power and so too did the Pentecostal healers. Even some of the middle class were converted to evangelical religion, for example the church known as Verbo, to which General Rios Montt belonged. Montt's brief and controversial time as President combined a drive against violence and corruption with a ferocious and effective attack on the guerrillas offering beans – or death. However, this temporary association with power did not appear to harm evangelicals very much. Some of them, of course, sided with the opposition, and mostly escaped the country in company with members of the Catholic left. Probably most Protestants supported the regime of Montt.

The very rapid expansion of Pentecostalism and conservative evangelicalism may mean that Maya culture is being re-formed in Protestant terms and that the communal organizations of the Maya are being renewed in the thousands of chapels to be observed everywhere in Guatemala from the *barrios* of Guatemala City to the jungles of El Petén. What is particularly notable about the Guatemalan case is the way the apolitical character of Pentecostalism is pulled into the polarized identifications of a Latin American society.

Mexico: The Case Exemplifying All the Tendencies

Turning finally to Mexico, we are dealing, of course, with a country populated by some 80 million people, making it the second most populous in Latin America. The remarkable variety of Mexican culture allows it to be used to bring together the limited aspects selected for attention in the countries surveyed earlier. It exhibits the same parallelism between Protestantism and freemasonry found in Brazil, and also the kind of influence of Protestant education found in Peru. It offers a dramatic case of conflict between church and state such as also racked Colombia, Venezuela and Guatemala – and indeed most other Catholic countries in some form or another. It has a large Indian population, in some areas unusually open to evangelical penetration. And it is also experiencing the great migration to the mega-cities, so that Mexico City is now the largest urban area in the world.

Let us take these parallels in turn. A new era opened with the granting of religious freedom in the constitution of 1857 and the disestablishment of the Roman Catholic Church two years later. However, as the corporatist state of Porfirio Diaz developed it became a massively conservative force increasingly in tune with the Catholic Church. At that point opposition emerged from three overlapping heterodoxies: spiritualism, freemasonry and Protestantism. In a manner reminiscent of the years of intellectual and social gestation before the French Revolution of 1789, there was a rapid expansion of lodges, mutual aid societies, spiritualist circles, liberal and patriotic clubs, and associations of free-thinkers. In a major work of historical documentation Jean-Pierre Bastian has described how Protestantism found its niche in this revolutionary milieu.[8]

Such a combination of freemasonry and Protestantism also recalls the way in which Protestants and freemasons were on the same political side during the Third Republic. Those in particular attracted to the Protestant societies included ex-soldiers of Benito Juarez and some ex-priests, as well as miners, textile workers and schoolmasters. Such people sought after some kind of 'civil religion' to replace what was for them an all-encompassing corporate system, political on the one side, ecclesiastical on the other. Thus the 'societies of ideas' and the Protestant schools came to celebrate a civic calendar based on 5 February (the Constitution), 18 July (the death of Juarez), 5 May (the defeat of the French at Puebla) and 16 September (Independence). They also created a democratic language and devised models of administration based on direct democracy. Jean-Pierre Bastian characterizes the Protestant churches of this period as 'pre-political groups' ranged against corporatism of every kind.

In the course of another recent book, *Protestantismo y Sociedad en México*, Bastian points in particular to Methodism and Methodist schools as an example of the consonance between religious dissidence and radical liberalism at this period.[9] He gives an account of the remarkable variety of Methodist initiatives designed to reach the workers of Mexico. Much of this Methodist work accompanied the operations of British engineering, mining and railway companies. Indeed, the Methodist circuits around Oaxaca run parallel to the railway lines. The Methodist congregation in Mexico City was the centre of a whole educational complex. Apart from the fifty-three 'temples' with 6,283 members, fifty schools were built at primary and at secondary level.

Indeed, for the Methodists, this work was their 'new frontier' beyond the Rio Grande, and one where the violence and opposition came from the entrenched powers of 'Christo-paganism'. They saw their mission as a war simultaneously against evil and ignorance, and as an exercise in civility, to be carried out with trenchant optimism and a touch of triumphalism. Their weapons were temperance and education, journals, libraries, Sunday rest, love for the brethren and reform of character.

Bastian sees the Methodism of that time as exhibiting diverse aspects. It was an expression of Anglo-American idealism in its pursuit of education and also in its attempts to rein in threats of American military invervention. It was a democratic religion which demystified the world and abolished mediation, and which diffused a lay morality and a personal conviction adamantly opposed to corrupt practices. Instead of the fiesta and its wasteful 'potlatch' it founded the library and the school. Methodism existed as a kind of mutual aid society chiming in with and overlapping other popular organizations for mutual assistance. As such, it helped along groups of workers in their passage from the country to the factory or the mill. The Methodists were the religious face of progressive liberalism and potent sources of anti-oligarchical sentiment, a point of critical reference against the repressive and hierarchical social order of the *porfiriato*. Clearly the Methodists in Mexico played a role parallel to their role in Peru.

In spite of their position in the revolutionary vanguard, the course of revolution proved difficult for Mexican Protestants. As the war grew increasingly violent and bloody the Protestant churches found themselves pulled into the spirals of religion versus militant secularism. The new constitution of 1917 curtailed the freedom of all religious groups. In 1926 it was decreed that all foreign clergy should leave the country, though in the event Protestant clery were less harshly treated than were Catholic. When the Cristero rebellion followed, Protestants once again found themselves in trouble, this time from the other (anti-government) side in the Catholic areas of central and southern Mexico. They were between the hard place of anti-clericalism and the hard rock of Peter. In 1934, when all education was declared 'socialist', Protestants found even their schools under pressure.

Fortunately, in the late 1930s the ferocious attack on all religion eased off and Protestantism began rapidly to expand. Whereas total population grew by 31 per cent between 1940 and 1950, Protestantism grew by 86 per cent. Even though growth slowed in the decade from 1960 to 1970, by 1970 Protestants were nearly a million in number, making up about 2 per cent of the Mexican population. They had acquired hostels and bookstores, and they operated sophisticated radio ministries. And they had also begun to set up large churches with a wider social appeal, offering musical ministries and even instruction in such subjects as business administration.

The period of the mid-century was one in which the historic churches did reasonably well. The Methodists and the Southern Baptists, as well as the Adventists, made rapid progress. Between 1935 and 1960 the National Presbyterian Church increased eightfold, and was particularly successful in the provinces of Chiapas and Tabasco.

However, in the sixties there began what Bastian regards as the 'rupture' in the history of Mexican Protestantism. Up to that point Protestants had been in the main mestizos, and had included modest intellectuals, many of whom were also uncertified doctors. They had valued their schools, and sought advancement through education as well as through hard work and self-discipline. But the movements which expanded in the sixties lacked this verbal culture, and drew increasingly on the semi-literate and on the Indians. The national distribution of Protestantism also altered. Whereas initially they had been concentrated in the northern provinces close to the USA, they were now concentrated in the south-east.

Bastian distinguishes between the kind of national Protestantism developing in the great cities and the kind of local Protestantism which has emerged in the countryside. The former he regards as bureaucratic, technologically sophisticated, often conservative, theologically as well as politically, and disposed to transmit US cultural influences. The latter he sees as a radical withdrawal from the structures of local power, particularly on the part of those marginalized by the advance of capitalist agriculture. However, these distinctions appear quite opaque to what has now become a vehement opposition. Catholic writers and journalists alike have taken up the critique of Protestantism developed by anthropologists and dismiss it *tout court* as a divisive and joyless intrusion of mercenary Americanism.

Both the urban and the rural forms of contemporary Protestantism have been investigated by Carlos Garma Navarro.[10] He describes how in Mexico City the Protestants gather in the marginal districts, many of them migrants from the countryside. There, they form an increasingly visible minority, concentrated in particular among those who have some small measure of independence or of private space in their sphere of work. By their discipline and sobriety, they often achieve some minor social advancement.

To a greater extent than in the countryside the urban evangelicals are rivalled by other active dissident groups, in particular Witnesses and Mormons, though the latter at least have had notable successes in some rural areas. Evangelicals in the cities are also faced by a more aggressive Catholic counter-reformation, occasionally in the form of base communities, but more frequently in the form of charismatic Catholicism, modelled along Pentecostal lines.

So far as the rural areas are concerned it is often Pentecostalism which provides the core of a resistance against the combined power of mestizo *caciques* (local power-holders) and mestizo clergy. As almost everywhere in Latin America the symbolic core of the old order is represented by the fiesta, and the withdrawal of Pentecostals constitutes a break in the social machinery of control, not to say a diminution in the profits from alcohol.

Just one example out of many of this resistance is provided by Carlos Garma Navarro. He describes a group of Totonac Indians in the state of Puebla. They had made their livelihood mainly by subsistence farming until commercial cultivation was undertaken in the 1950s by the Mexican Institute of Coffee. At that juncture the mestizo minority took on the role of middle-men, firstly between the Indians and the market, and secondly between the Indians and the dominant political party. At the same time a member of the Summer Institute of Linguistics came to work in the area, and various churches emerged including a Methodist 'temple'. After local opposition and various splits the church which emerged as the most vigorous and expansive was the Pentecostal Church of the Living Water.

With the help of Catholic coffee growers and led by their pastor, the Pentecostals first formed a coffee growers' union and a cooperative store. They then tried to assert themselves against the mestizos in the official party, and when that failed they occupied the municipal building – and joined the Partido Socialista Unificado de México. This instance of local political leadership provided by the pastor is only one of many which can be cited. Quite how this episode ended is uncertain since the area has now been taken over by the army.

One of the areas most affected by dissidence is in the mountains of Chiapas. Local Indians, Protestants and some progressive Catholics tried to establish their own channels for communication between the state and the indigenous population. According to the findings of Gabriela Patricia Robledo Hernandez the response to this initiative was violent.[11] Indeed in the elections of 1974 the candidate representing the *caciques* (or power holders) declared that all evangelical believers should be expelled from the *municipio*. The believers were accordingly forced to migrate as enemies of 'tradition' and 'custom' and had to set up new communities in San Cristobal de las Casas.

The varied evidence for this resistance is nicely summarized by Bastian. He describes how villages divide into rival territories and how whole groups of Protestant *campesinos* (agricultural workers) set up villages of their own. Bastian firmly rejects the notion that such symbolic and physical withdrawals from the structure of overarching power are simply manifestations of North American influence and penetration. Rather, 'El súrgimiento de las sectas protestantes y, en particular del pentecostalismo, parece sér el medio privilegiado para que ámplios sectores rurales subalternos expresen su protesta social y políticá.'[12] Contrariwise, the *caciques* responded by deploying their control of the symbolic apparatus of Catholicism.

A major problem of evangelical penetration among Indians has been the very large number of Indian languages. In this area considerable progress was made by the Wycliffe Bible Translators. One of the most interesting developments from the viewpoint of this book occurred among the Otomi. The Otomi have been mostly converted to an indigenous form of Pentecostalism. This was introduced by a miner in Pachuca in 1923, and is nowadays organized in the Union of Evangelical Churches. About half of the Otomi do not speak Spanish and about a third are illiterate. In the early period of evangelization the Pentecostals experienced considerable Catholic hostility. However, that hostility, as elsewhere in Mexico, is mostly a thing of the past. In the *Encyclopedia of World Christianity* edited by David Barrett it is claimed that 'All [the churches] are self-supporting, and there are Pentecostal cooperatives, large collective farms, and textile factories, and in consequence, members experience phenomenal social mobility.'[13] This provides a round assertion entirely appropriate to the conclusion of a historical and contemporary survey of Protestantism in Latin America.

A Digression: The Smaller Tribes

One aspect of the spread of evangelical Protestantism cannot be properly covered in the course of the kind of argument pursued in this book, and that is the missionary work undertaken among the tribes. The situations vary too much from tribe to tribe and from country to country; and the outcomes of missionary work are equally varied. All that can be attempted is a brief overview of the characteristic problems, supplemented by comments derived from a few ethnographic accounts. However, a great deal of other material on the tribes is utilized in different parts of this book, in particular in those chapters dealing with economic and political issues. Since the Maya of Guatemala and Mexico are discussed in some detail elsewhere, the analysis here is largely restricted to the smaller tribal groups.

An overview of the issues is most easily achieved by examining the controversy over a major evangelical Protestant organization, the Wycliffe Bible Translators or Summer Institute of Linguistics (WBT/SIL). For that purpose David Stoll's *Fishers of Men or Builders of Empire?* is important as well as a special issue of *América Indígena* devoted to the controversy.[14] The use of these sources is not entirely unproblematic since some of the material, especially that by Stoll, is polemical in tone. A great deal of interesting analysis is embedded in strongly coloured rhetoric which seems to invite adverse moral judgements, in particular on the founder of WBT/SIL, Cameron Townsend. In order to obtain a different view, the points in contention were discussed with missionary anthropologists at the WBT/SIL Centre in Dallas, Texas. Some missionary narratives also proved helpful, such as *Uncle Cam* by James Hefley and Marti Hefley, and *Maya Mission* by Lawrence Dame. A short defence of WBT/SIL is to be found in *The Other Side*, and further discussion in Karl Franklin (ed.), *Current Concerns of Anthropologists and Missionaries*.[15] So far as this book is concerned, the issues have to do with Americanization, with 'modernization', and with the relationship between evangelical Christianity and cultural and political self-defence.

The WBT/SIL organization was formed at a time when it was difficult for Protestant missions to enter some parts of Latin America. WBT/SIL found a more acceptable way to effect entry by making contracts with governments to engage in linguistic work with the native languages, including in that work the translation of the Bible. The seed thereby dropped did not come from any denominational packet and was not to be accompanied by over-active watering. It might, however, be accompanied by the offer of medical supplies, education, technical assistance, and in particular by WBT/SIL's own system of air and radio communications. On occasion it implied considerable changes in tribal organization, since fluid and dispersed groups might be encouraged to concentrate and become sedentary. It was worth noting that such concentration was not only something which might follow from missionary activity but was almost a *sine qua non* of effective political and cultural self-defence. For such tribes, cultural defence itself implied massive cultural change. In other words, pristine isolation from religious or cultural change was not really an option.

For some while governments looked with favour on contracts with WBT/SIL in spite of pressure from the Catholic hierarchy, from cultural nationalists and some anthropologists. The missionary linguists were, by inclination, apolitical and even if minded to be otherwise, were conscious of their precarious contracts and their vulnerable position as long-term visitors. Governments were tolerably happy to have what could be classified as development work carried out by Americans at their own expense, particularly since not much else of a humane character was going forward in that area. Moreover, the Americans might also be viewed, or used, as the privy paw of internal colonialism. Whatever their personal intentions might be, the bilingual approach of the missionaries meant not only saving the native language but introducing natives to the wider national culture.

Eventually opposition to the missionaries/linguists of WBT/SIL became quite clamorous. They were suspected of being CIA agents and accused of being evangelists for alien ways of life and North American culture. In spite of claims by WBT/SIL representatives to pay special attention to the corrosive effects of modern technological culture, they were seen as insensitive in such matters. Opponents argued that they were damaging the ecology of native life and introducing divisions. Furthermore, the WBT/SIL organization was attacked for being a two-headed monster. In Stoll's view it was the WBT in the United States in order to obscure its scientific purposes and the SIL in Latin America in order to obscure its evangelical purposes.

It is true, of course, that the moment any tribespeople encounter a major world religion they are divided into those who accept the new faith and those who do not. Such divisions are exacerbated when there are several missions at work ranging from Roman Catholics to Jehovah's Witnesses. Groups may emerge who are sceptical of all faiths. At the same time, a missionary faith may sometimes reintegrate a society which is under severe stress from other agencies of the wider world, some political and others economic and commercial. Elmer Miller's well known study of Pentecostalism among the Toba of the Argentine suggests that for a time at least Protestantism brought about revitalization as well as disintegration.[16] Fundamentalist missions may even adapt more easily to local cultures, given that they often share the local belief in the spirit world. Ted Lewellen, in his study of Adventism among the Aymara of Peru, rebuts the notion that Protestants are 'anomic marginals joylessly repudiating their heritage while lusting shamefully after Western goods'.[17]

The political issue is equally complicated. Members of the WBT/SIL deny that they are in thrall to central governments or agents of Americanization and capitalism. They claim rather to seek justice and tribal rights and integrity through existing channels and by peaceful means. In their view critical rhetoric may let off moral steam but does little good to the local people. They also argue that spiritual transformations at the level of culture are an essential and ultimately efficacious form of social change. Anthropologists are more inclined to argue that many missionaries actually try to clamp down indigenous resistance, but that local Protestants take from the message just those elements which make for their own survival. There are plenty of examples which bear out the argument that local Protestants *can* become enthusiastically involved in indigenous resistance, and some of these are discussed in chapter 12. One of the studies cited below shows how that may come about. I do not intend entering into the prolonged debate about how far Christian millennarian expectation fuses with myths of returning culture heroes and about the Marxist categorization of religious rebellion as 'pre-political'. This is a vast field and those interested in a scholarly overview could not do better than consult Bryan Wilson's *Magic and the Millennium*.[18]

I now utilize three localized studies: first David Stoll's comments on WBT/SIL among tribes in Peru, second Joanne Rappaport's study undertaken in the southern highlands of Colombia, and third Blanca Muratorio's analysis of evangelization in rural highland Ecuador.[19]

Stoll begins his two long chapters concerned with SIL's work among Peruvian tribes with a succinct summary. He points out that no other Christian mission in the Amazon matches SIL's network. 'Here the base–airplane–bilingual school evangelizing machine became a model for other branches as far away as the

Philippines. . . .'[20] SIL has operated for a long period, with government backing, and has acquired considerable authority and power of patronage in native communities. Stoll maintains that SIL bridged the gap between dozens of tribes living beyond the subjugated Quechua peasantry and the wave of national expansion financed by the United States.

WBT/SIL was confronted by a system of exploitation dating from the rubber boom round the turn of the century. The Indians ended up in debt to the mestizo *patrones* who were in turn in debt to usurers in the towns. Either they fought the intruders off or else they fled to inaccessible regions under missionary patronage. Thereafter the building of roads, and the expansion of state bureaucracy and corporate investment, brought most Indians into contact with modern culture. They came to live in fixed villages by the larger rivers, often run by missions, and they depended on all kinds of brokers – traders, foremen, bureaucrats and missionaries. It was an era of civil rights movements, patronage battles, and fights to retain Indian refuges.

The missionaries operated both ahead and behind their commercial rivals. They brought the small semi-nomadic bands into a fixed area and provided them with sanctuary. In Stoll's view the effects of missionary work were simply ameliorative. True, they reduced oppression, and brought medicine and schools. But they also reduced resistance to colonization teaching native peoples that they now belonged to Peru or Ecuador and inculcating new kinds of leadership and economy. In short, the missions were the most humane versions of a new kind of political and economic socialization.

That context provides a background for Joanne Rappaport's detailed study of evangelical missions in highland Colombia. Nowadays entire villages among the Paez and Guambiano are composed of evangelical and Pentecostal Protestants, and they have in her view integrated their new beliefs with traditional thinking so as to legitimize political action aimed at self-determination.

The Paez and Guambiano number respectively some 80,000 and 18,000 people. They occupy the eastern portion of the department of Cauca and enjoy modest autonomy on their *resguardos* (reservations). Protestantism first came in 1929 with the Christian and Missionary Alliance, but the really sizeable evangelical populations emerged in the 1960s with the entry of the WBT/SIL. Since then, however, conflicts over land have led to the departure of the missionaries and the work has been carried on by local native pastors. Among the Paez in particular Protestant visionaries have emerged travelling from community to community with drawings which the faithful regard as significant for their moral welfare. New Protestant villages have also been founded by Pentecostals from a neighbouring department, and by Alpha and Omega, a dependency of Campus Crusade for Christ.

Joanne Rappaport describes the Paez and Guambiano as highly politicized.[21] Earlier this century they provided a base for *indigenista* (or pro-native) agitation and a headquarters for peasant leagues affiliated to the Communist Party. During the civil war in the years following 1948, the area was devastated. The local social and political organization was in ruins and many Paez thought it best to migrate to the western slopes of the Cordillera or to the Cauca Valley. The Paez still recollect the support given to the conservatives by Catholic priests and the murderous depredations of the military police.

Apart from these misfortunes, the Paez had to cope with the inroads of agro-industry and the effects of being linked to local market towns by new roads. Between 1945 and 1970 five Paez *resguardos* were extinguished, producing communal lands for the free market and leaving some communities without a territorial base from which to defend their rights. Meanwhile, the Guambiano were growing so much in numbers that many preferred to leave their home territory. The rest were deeply divided among themselves over development projects and over local governance.

In these circumstances indigenous resistance began to revive again in the 1960s and 1970s by establishing a cooperative and founding a regional organization, the CRIC, to reclaim stolen lands. Some people, however, were dissatisfied with this organization and founded another, also called the CRIC, based on the traditional structure of the *resguardo*. It seems that, at this juncture, Protestantism looked increasingly attractive as a faith which spoke to crisis and was uncontaminated by the reputation of Catholicism. In any case, some of the guerrillas from the time of the Civil War had been Protestants and had kept up good relations with tribespeople. Protestantism encouraged worship without non-Indian intermediaries and this meant that native visionaries could speak directly to the people, drawing on their own ancient messianic traditions. Once the missionaries had reduced the language to written form, Paez believers delighted in their ability to read the Bible and other books. They were also very pleased to have schools and medical facilities and to receive agricultural counselling.

What is interesting here is that Paez evangelicals and Pentecostals allied themselves with the Indian movement, more especially when the SIL missionaries were absent. Indian pastors and the evangelical faithful incorporated their new faith into the ancient myths which had helped motivate their struggle for land. The Christ who will one day return is also the mythic hero who once defended the Paez against European invaders. And the fiesta which once served to mark out territory has been revived in Protestant form, so that exchanges of hymns now replace exchanges of alcohol. The further details of the syncretism do not matter. The central point lies in Rappaport's conclusion, which is that the highland peoples have made Protestantism a part of their struggle, jettisoning only the 'foreign' elements of submission to the powers that be. The conclusion fits very well with arguments put forward by Jean-Pierre Bastian with regard to Protestantism in rural Mexico.[22]

The third study is another detailed analysis carried out by Blanca Muratorio in rural highland Ecuador and published in the *Journal for Peasant Studies*.[23] This is a Marxist analysis of a group of Quichua- (or Quechua-) speaking Indians living in Colta in the province of Chimborazo. Muratorio's interest is in the way capitalistic forms relate to pre-capitalistic forms and how the latter may even expand as capitalism advances. He is concerned with how the complicated layers reaching back into the remote past persist into the present and with how changes in the most recent generation have opened the way for the exercise of new religious options.

When Muratorio worked among the Indians of Colta in the late 1970s, they had gained somewhat from agrarian reform and now owned their own land. This provided them with a private space in which to exercise options. No longer were they under forms of personal control and patronage exercised on the hacienda, nor were they in need of priestly mediation. The contemporary mediators were the lawyers and the bureaucrats not the priests, and the Indians were having to acquire the skills of self-assertion needed to deal with these new functionaries. So, to the acquisition of private space was added the necessity of acquiring new selves for the public presentation of personal and collective requests or demands. One corollary of this was withdrawal from the ceremonial enactment of the older roles which was embodied in the fiesta. The fiesta itself was a form of mediation whereby representatives of the whole social system as anciently articulated sought the aid of the saints and the regional Virgin. It involved costs and alcohol. Protestantism constituted a comprehensive withdrawal from its pressures, its costs, its 'waste' and its sacred legitimation of the social hierarchy.

The minute differences between plots of land did not encourage a developed class consciousness among the Indian peasants. Yet they were acutely conscious of the strains and difficulties of their position. In the background there were the social definitions which held them in place as inherently inferior. And there were the current effects of increasing population on people whose portions of land were already quite small. One of these effects was indebtedness to merchants or money-lenders. Indians had, therefore, to invent new forms of solidarity for themselves, even if this was not class consciousness in the Marxist sense. Some members of households had to find different means of making a living, becoming petty traders, going to the coastal plantations, or working in the city, part-time or full-time. Somehow this newly invented solidarity would have to link those who left with those who remained behind. It would need to provide a *network* of contacts and of people who trusted and supported each other. The solidarity and the network were provided by Protestantism, a faith which offered a definition of 'self' which contained the idea of choosing in a private space, and which was symbolically and actually opposed to all the ancient definitions and circumscriptions embedded in folk Catholicism. Protestantism offered the *hermanos* and the *hermanas* a unity 'in Christ' as a substitute for the old solidarities of the *compadres* and it offered a new sense of the person. It dramatized the collapse of the old definitions and the desire to withdraw from the immemorial attachments and the mediations that they required.

It also offered a deity who spoke directly in the Quechua language and the ability to read for oneself what that deity had to say. A mestizo expressed her horror at what this implied by complaining that 'savages' were now presuming to talk to God in *that* vulgar tongue. As often elsewhere this new power of language helped forward a new sense of ethnic dignity. Indians started to speak proper Quechua, without so many Hispanic elements. But they also were better placed to learn Spanish, and that could easily mean assimilation. Here we recognize the same elements as were found in the polemic over WBT/SIL.

Armed with a new ethnic sense and self-assertiveness, the Quechua Protestants were well to the fore in demands for better roads, for more medicine, for more sewage and electricity. Through their local Association of Evangelical Peasants they could cooperate to deal with the state and other agencies. The state, for its part, was willing to work with peasants so patently interested in modernization, and especially so since they respected the powers that be and censured those of their members who took landlords to court for back wages or land disputes. St Paul, after all, forbade legal disputes among the brethren. However, Muratorio comments that these censures were not all that successful. Moreover, when strikes occurred evangelical Indians were also involved in them.

However, their 'respectful attitude', in combination with the new sense of ethnic and linguistic dignity and with the newly acquired corporate initiative, did seem to work with the state authorities. The Protestant Indians also exhibited a 'folkloric' attitude of which the state approved and which increased the income from tourism. All this did not mean that evangelical Indians were better off than their Catholic neighbours. In any case, the incursion of Protestantism is rather recent for such differences to be expected. What Muratorio stresses is a new pattern of consumption and new priorities: not alcohol, tobacco or wasteful ceremonial obligations, but tape recorders, medicine, bicycles and education. This brings Protestants more into touch with the modern market. The Protestants' sense of selfhood is expressed through making their bodies fit temples for God's mercy and indwelling. Muratorio's basic point relates to the advantages and mutuality conferred by a network of brothers and sisters: free (or cheaper) room and board when you go to the city, somebody to replace you on the plot while you are there, friends whom you consider more honest and hardworking, lodging provided for those children able to attend secondary school.

This Marxist analysis is interesting in that its empirical observations closely coincide with those of non-Marxist anthropologists. Its focus is, of course, on the way in which an oppositional consciousness may be formed which is not, however, a class consciousness equipped with a sophisticated theory of change. The analysis lacks any anthropological lament for the fabric of older relationships, even 'idyllic' paternalism, since it assumes a process of development. What all the studies indicate is the self-creation of new identities and the invention or adaptation of new forms of mutual exchange and solidarity. That this devides the community may be viewed as a tragic breakup of ancient ties or part of what is involved in social differentiation, in change, and in the opening up of private space.

Summary

What then, in summary – and leaving aside the local variation surveyed in Part II above – are the key features of this momentous encounter between 'Anglo-American' and Hispanic civilizations? Clearly over the past centuries since Spain ruled the old world and the new, the 'Anglo' culture has gained in preponderant power, first in its British form and then in its American. That preponderant power has been expressed in the realms of politics and the economy, as well as in culture and religion. Sometimes political conquest paved the way for religious expansion, as happened in British colonies like Jamaica or British Honduras (Belize), or as happened in places under

US political control, like Puerto Rico. This is not to say that the Protestant religion always acted as an arm of Protestant colonial power. It did not, but it did find openings where political control eased entry.

The major channel of Protestant religion was created by economic and cultural change rather than by direct political control. The states of South and Central America opened themselves up to the economic power and some of the cultural forms of Britain, the United States and Germany, hoping to share in what appeared to be the movement of progress. The radical elites of these countries wanted the same advantages for the southern tier of Latin countries as were now evidently enjoyed by the northern tier of Anglo-Saxon countries. Protestantism was a minor motif in this emulation of the advanced societies of the North Atlantic, valuable less on its own account than for its associations, and for its provision of welfare and its emphasis on the separation of Christianity from the state. What happened in this early phase is nicely indicated by the way in which the formation of groups of Brethren in the Argentine followed the railways built by the British.[24]

But this religious penetration, much of it linked to cultural emulation, was minor. It was often held in check by law, sometimes rebuffed by nationalism, and always neutralized by the mere fact of being foreign. Protestantism was written off by most Latin Americans as the peculiar property of ethnic wedges like the Germans of Brazil and the Argentine, or as a curious and almost unsellable import brought by zealous American missionaries. Only in Brazil was there any discernible take-up of the new faith.

In the 1930s, however, a much vaster economic revolution began to overtake Latin America, pulling it into the wake of a world-wide industrialization and urbanization. Politically this meant the onset of mass participation, mainly through the patronage networks of populism, and this in turn triggered counter-revolutions managed by the new military controlling the national security state. Religiously it meant the onset of mass participation, in evangelical and above all in Pentecostal form. As people moved from the countryside and the world of the patron to the pullulating and anomic world of the *favela* they were given new orientations, new meanings, new individual dignity, new supporting networks, new chances of leadership, by evangelical Protestantism. As the changes and disorientations around them increased, in particular from the sixties onwards, so the reorientation offered by evangelical Protestantism grew in power and appeal, especially in Chile and Brazil, but also in places like Guatemala and Jamaica. As was shown in the analyses country by country, the expansion occurred most dramatically where the Catholic Church had been attacked or undermined but the culture itself had retained a diffuse sense of the world of 'the spirit'. Where culture itself had been secularized, as in Uruguay and Venezuela, expansion was slow. Ethnicity also played a role, mostly holding back expansion where there were large migrations from Europe, helping it forward where extensive native populations had historically been resistant to Catholicism.

On the surface the new faith might not appear the most promising candidate for the empowerment of a major mass movement in Latin America – of all places. But it had certain advantages, notably on account of being sociologically advanced and theologically 'backward'. It was sociologically advanced in tracing a genealogy back through America to England – a genealogy which was rooted in the separation of the power of faith from the power of the state. It was, in other words, the harbinger of a breakup of the organic unity of faith and community, both at the national and at the local (or tribal) level. It therefore corresponded to what was currently going forward at hectic pace in Latin America.

Evangelicalism was religiously 'backward' in that it set up a protective screen around the enclave of the faithful and insisted on carrying out a series of social experiments almost entirely within that enclosed space. This 'backwardness' can be labelled dualism, or even simply a reversion to primitive Christianity, but it was and is socially realistic. New cultural practices had to be initiated in a free space which was circumscribed against the intrusive and hostile 'world'. Outside was bedevilment and corruption, machismo and violence, as well as personal and familial disintegration. Inside, however, there began a new order of the world, full of *Sanidad Divina*: soulful release and physical healing. For those people gathered in the free space a signal break had been made with the old ways. All the mediations between them and God were abolished. They were now a redeemed community with direct access in and through the Spirit, and by implication they were also above or beyond all the mediations of society as a whole, not merely the mediations of the priestly caste. All the criteria of power and worth which oppressed them in daily life were removed or reversed, and replaced by one criterion alone: God's sovereign favour, freely available to all. Once that criterion was fulfilled all the 'gifts' were theirs.

These changes, occurring within the constantly expanding free space of the brothers and sisters, were initiated by a faith forged in a fusion of white enthusiasm with ancient black power. Through the long trail of potent mutations it had passed from the margins of industrializing England to the American frontier, then to the impoverished whites and blacks of the American South, and then finally across the last frontier of the Rio Grande del Norte to the industrializing societies of Latin America.

This genealogy has been equally of the poor and of the socially mobile. It has been politically passive at some periods and active and reformist at others. But so far as concerns the burgeoning Pentecostal strain now active in Latin America it is mostly poor and mostly passive. Being a religion of the poor (rather than a religion *for* the poor) it lacks sophisticated structural views of society and of political change. That is what you would expect from a movement which picks up the mute and strangled voices of those unheard throughout Latin American history. At least in the sphere of faith they are a now giving 'tongue'. They are making their voices heard in vast assemblages where they finally *count* for something.

Naturally those who 'make the break' bring with them a past: the respect for authority and a responsiveness to leadership. Their pastors are unequivocally leaders not 'enablers', and they would be ineffective even as 'enablers' were they frightened of leadership and authority. Authority grants definition and direction, and both are desperately needed. Yet leadership is open, and when temporarily closed in one group is opened again by the emergence of other groups. Opportunity is ensured by fragmentation just as equality of access is ensured by the rejection of criteria based on theological training or general education.

Those who have found themselves in this new enclave experience both discipline and release. They embrace new controls and discover new sources for unburdening themselves. They enter a community of mutual support and solace. And beyond that they acquire skills of organization, of self-help, of self-expression which make them articulate and self-reliant. They understand what it is to create a new social cell, to exhibit a '*Nova Vida*', and to propagate a new view. And with all that they come to have command of the new technology of conversion. So, if to the social and psychological changes just outlined is added an entry into the world of technology, then it is reasonable to view evangelicalism as offering an induction into modernity.

The Pentecostal movement (and evangelicalism generally) is a symbolic and literal emigration, appealing in particular to those freed from constraining vertical and horizontal ties, by individualized and personal employments. It is the re-formation of those ties, the re-creation of those bonds. The *compadres* become the *hermanos* and the *hermanas* as well. Of course, that logically also implies division: the fracture of ancient tribal unities and, in the wider megalopolitan world, a break between those who embrace the new orientation and those who do not. All that is inevitable and it is part of the rapid expansion of the range of cultural communication and the differentiation of society. The old patriarchal harmonies of the hacienda and the unities of the tribes are equally lost, and it is a measure of the power of Pentecostalism and evangelical religion that it is able to create voluntary and chosen networks of mutual support where once there were the inevitabilities of tribal unity and rural hierarchy.[25]

PART III

Comparisons and Parallels

Chapter 7

Caribbean Comparisons: Jamaica and Trinidad; Puerto Rico and Haiti

At this point it is useful to extend the cultural range of this discussion and look at selected countries in the Caribbean, more especially Jamaica. The religious changes in Jamaica are at least as dramatic as those in Guatemala and are in many ways similar. Conservative evangelical religion, and in particular Pentecostalism, is expanding to the point where it may soon command the allegiance of the majority.

The rationale behind the comparisons attempted in this chapter is based on a contrast between the expansion of Pentecostalism in the vast Hispanic world and an expansion in the small insular worlds of what some Americans have viewed as an American lake. Thus all the countries in the Caribbean have been exposed to intense cultural radiation from North America (including Canada) and have at the same time been historically subject to a whole variety of European influences, British, French, Spanish and Dutch. The countries selected have therefore combined a proximity to America with another major cultural influence, British in the case of Jamaica and Trinidad, Spanish in the case of Puerto Rico, French in the case of Haiti. The interesting point is that the established religions of these societies, whether Protestant/Anglican or Catholic, are proving as vulnerable to Pentecostal penetration as societies in Latin America.

Jamaica: Pentecostalism in an Area of British and United States Influence

In size Jamaica is comparable with many of the Central American states. Its population numbers 2.5 million (1987), which is roughly the same as those of Nicaragua and Costa Rica. Kingston is a capital which has grown very rapidly in the same style as Guatemala City and Mexico City, and now contains over three-quarters of a million people. Inevitably Jamaica lies within the gravitational pull of the United States, economically, culturally and politically. More than three centuries of British rule have meant that Anglo-Saxon culture encounters few major barriers, certainly not the kind of barriers erected by Hispanic history and the Spanish language. At the same time Jamaicans have created a highly distinctive and creative culture; and though they easily understand British English and American English, their own variant of English successfully keeps at least the casual visitor at bay.

From time to time Jamaica swings right or left, which has in the past meant towards the United States when the Jamaica Labor Party (JLP) is in power and away from the United States when the People's National Party (PNP) is in power. These swings occur within democratic limits, and though a degree of political violence and intimidation broke out in the seventies there was nothing to rival the institutionalized warfare found in many Central American states.

This democratic stability has at least something to do with the Anglo-Saxon Protestant pattern of social change, and may even exhibit the virtues of cricket into which a great deal of Jamaican passion has been poured. The matrix out of which Jamaica has emerged began in a relatively open relationship of the Anglican Church to the state, which disintegrated in the late eighteenth and early nineteenth centuries without fundamental social revolution. Thereafter religion followed the voluntary and pluralistic mode originating in Britain and developed to its fullest extent in the USA. The Anglican Church retained its power only in the shadowy form of a large constituency among the more powerful social strata, such as it also retained in Canada, Australia, New Zealand – and for that matter in the USA itself.

What is almost unique about Jamaica in the Western hemisphere is the extent to which it is a country of the African diaspora. There has been some racial mixing and there has been some migration from Asia. And there is a relationship between class and colour which means, for example, that paler skins are more frequently to be seen among the elite. But overwhelmingly the ancestors of today's Jamaica were brought to Jamaica as slaves or immigrated to Jamaica in the nineteenth century. The result is that both of the indigenous and long-term religious traditions of Jamaica are rooted in an African consciousness. Rastafarianism and what is known as Revivalism are the religions of blacks and in different ways of black protest. Rastafarianism is, as everyone knows, the most dynamic and sohisticated expression of a specifically black African consciousness in the Americas.[1]

This has implications for the way we analyse the openings for Pentecostalism in Jamaica as compared with openings in other countries. Almost everywhere in the Americas Pentecostalism can take fire among the tangled brushwood of spirit cults, and Jamaican 'Revivalism' is just one branch of that near-universal spiritism. But only in one or two countries does Pentecostalism (and conservative Protestantism generally) run into serious rivals rooted in indigenous practices. The most obvious instance is provided by Umbanda in Brazil, which in some of its forms has predominantly African roots and often appeals to a mainly black constituency. But Rastafarianism has a higher profile, nationally and internationally, than any other African faith of the diaspora, and its appeal is perhaps comparable only to that of Ratana among the Maoris of New Zealand.

As always it is only possible to understand the disposition and distribution of contemporary religion by returning to the historical relations of religious life and political life. Of the original Arawak inhabitants of Jamaica nothing remains culturally, and very little physically. The same is true of the Spaniards. They ruled the island till 1655 when it was taken by the British as part of Oliver Cromwell's 'western design'. The Church of England, re-established in England itself in 1660, after the Commonwealth, instituted a territorial division of parishes still operative today. The old framework also remains visible in the way many Anglican churches lie at the centres of towns, sometimes in symbolic proximity to the police station. However, the early planters were irreligiously inclined and barely more addicted to piety than the pirates who infested Port Royal. They disliked missions and from the arrival of the Moravian missionaries in 1754 onward suspected that religion encouraged rebellion. Not until the early nineteenth century were Christian clergy present in Jamaica in considerable numbers.

Meanwhile African religion survived underground, though without opportunity for open ritual expression. All Africans recognized the often menacing power of Obi and of Obeahmen.[2] The tradition of African religion was reinforced by successive arrivals from Africa.

According to Mervyn Alleyne it was the Africans of Akan descent who formed the most powerful group, and it was their gods which tended to prevail, without however obliterating traces of Bantu and Yoruba religion. Akan religion took two paths. One conserved the old traditions as far as possible and was particularly active amongst the groups of escaped slaves known as Maroons who for a long while maintained successful rebellion. The other path emerged into the open under protective guise provided by Christianity, and it too soon acquired a rebellious aspect. Alleyne remarks: 'From the very inception of slave society, therefore, religion and rebellion became associated in a symbiotic relationship.'[3]

What is interesting here and of particular importance for the argument of this book, is that evangelical religion, especially in its Baptist form, became a channel of protest, rebellion and reform.[4] Clearly evangelical religion is capable of sustaining and inspiring protest in certain circumstances, just as in other circumstances it may inculcate passivity toward the ruling powers 'ordained by God' and recommend political withdrawal. At the minimum it creates a space within which a repressed group may express itself and organize itself religiously. In Jamaica it created much more than a space. The period of Baptist resistance, which took active as well as passive forms, ran from the 1780s to the 1860s. It included two wars, the first in 1831 led by a Baptist deacon Sam Sharpe, and the second in 1865 centred around a native Baptist leader named Bogle.

The early period of nonconformist incursion from Britain and America, and of incipient rebellion, can be seen as a first watershed in the making of modern Jamaica. The missionaries were mostly opposed to slavery and often persecuted for their opposition. Under evangelical and Quaker pressure, and also for economic reasons, Britain abolished slavery in the 1830s. But the missionaries recognized with some unease that the long-term results of their preaching could run in channels outside their control. Indeed there emerged both African variants of Christianity and features reminiscent of the radical Anabaptist Reformation.

Among the white families and slaves who arrived from the USA in 1783 were two former slaves, George Lisle and Moses Baker, who took up preaching. Lisle himself remained orthodox. Baker for his part took a strict line on such issues as concubinage, polygamy and idolatry, but revived a radical Anabaptist strain by introducing the washing of feet, abstention from recourse to law, and anointing of the sick. When a representative of the British Baptists named Burchell arrived in 1824 some of the local converts adhered to orthodox Christianity but others did not. The heterodox engaged in controversy over the relative powers and roles of Jesus and John the Baptist and above all tended to stress the supremacy of the Spirit. An Afro-American preacher by the name of Gibb encouraged candidates for baptism to seek spirit visions and dreams in the wilderness, rather like initiates to West African secret societies. Some converts even slipped towards the antinomian heresy, sinning the more that grace might abound the more. What is important about all this for the Jamaican future is the permeability of religious boundaries and the supremacy and universal availability of the Spirit.

A major opening for organization among the oppressed was the religious 'class' system, which gathered people together into cells under the tutelage of class leaders. In the case of the Methodists, says Alleyne, the leaders were selected from freedmen or whites, but in the case of the Baptists they were generally slaves and therefore illiterate. This is how native religious leaders saw a chance to make their subterranean religious practices legitimate. The local ruling class made attempts to prohibit these practices and to prevent all unlicensed noncomformist activity but prevailing liberal opinion in Britain ensured that these attempts were unsuccessful.

As just indicated, the Spirit (in good and in evil manifestations) provided the emerging framework of Jamaican religion. Alleyne emphasizes the permeability of boundaries, arguing that where power was being sought from rival spirits and deities we have a continuum of more – or less – orthodox religion. 'Religions identified by names such as Revival Zion, Pocomania (called here Pukumina), Convince, Kumina, are merely zones abstracted from this continuum. . . .'[5] Alleyne goes on to argue that in a parallel manner several varieties of language operated then and today still operate in the same way. A speaker may locate himself vaguely within a zone along a continuum from standard English to a Creole. He may switch zones and appear to be operating two different systems according to his needs in different contexts.

Syncretistic religion and degrees of Creole both emerge so that people may achieve some modicum of communication with the ruling class and also retain an instrument of cultural defence or actual revolt. In this way the invocation of the Spirit and the development of semi-secret languages come to play a major role, to be fully exemplified later in Rastafarianism and in Pentecostalism. Alleyne adds that what distinguished Methodists and Presbyterians from other groups was their resistance to spirit possession, though individual Methodists and Presbyterians might well become quietly possessed by the Spirit. Those Christian groups which today encourage possession, like the Pentecostal Holiness and Shiloh

Apostolic Faith, are demarcated from groups like Pukumina and Revival (Zion) only by allowing entry solely to Christian powers rather than to the ancestral spirits.

The oscillations set up in the early period were equally to be observed in the two major events of the mid-century, which were the settlement of freed slaves in central Jamaica under the aegis of the churches, including the Anglican Church, and the Great Revival of 1860–1. Actually the abolitionists in Britain were divided between those who proposed land reform and those who were against it. In Jamaica at any rate the new settlements were set up on land bought by the churches, an arrangement which actually enabled the ancestor cults to continue. The creation of settlements was an ambitious attempt to create communities with autonomous interlocking systems of social control, recreation and communication, and open to the adoption of new crops and agricultural methods. It was even proposed to introduce education on the model of London's new university. But there was vicious local opposition to any schemes which might make blacks eligible for the vote. In any case the state of the economy worsened after 1840 and with it the viability of the settlements and the popularity of orthodox Christianity. The spirit cults revived, and also the Native Baptists led by black class leaders.

The Great Revival of 1860 was intended to reverse this disintegration and at first seemed to do so. Many of those 'living in sin' got married and many also forsook rum. But then the pace and tone of the Revival shifted towards dancing, flagellation, possession – and speaking in tongues. Peter Wedenoja, in a study made in the late seventies, argues that at this particular watershed we can see two Jamaicas emerging, one of the folk religions, the other of the metropolis. The popularity of the missionaries slumped once more and many of them abandoned the peasants to identify with the colonial establishment and emerging middle class. The Anglican Church, for example, offered education to blacks within church schools, and saw religious belief as a civilizing influence, but the blacks recognized that the education provided was not that offered to the whites.

Within the folk religion of revivalism Barry Chevannes discerns a continuous 'expression of struggle against the white man's political and social control'.[6] As underlined already, this tradition slips in and out of Orthodox Baptist and Native Baptist forms, and combines with African forms of possession and initiation. By way of a contemporary aside (1971) Chevannes goes on to add that 'none understand this tradition of resistance better than the politicians who at the same time as they are courting "Africa" do not hesitate to class Rastafarians as criminals. . . .'[7]

In the 1880s there emerged the messianic figure of Alexander Bedward. He drew on precisely this revivalist tradition and proclaimed a healing mission at Mona by the waters of the Hope River. In 1920 he failed to achieve a promised ascent to heaven and went instead to a mental hospital, but he none the less provided a link both to Marcus Garvey and to Rastafarianism.

Garvey is, of course, a major figure. He was created a National Hero by independent Jamaica and his centenary was officially celebrated in 1987 at ceremonies attended by Mrs Coretta Scott King. Garvey's vision had an international scope and he combined appeals for international black separatism with appeals for repatriation. His Black Star Line was just one part of his plan to repatriate blacks to Africa.

Rastafarianism combined elements taken from Bedward and Garvey with elements of Revivalism. However it seems that Garvey himself did not approve of the millennial and 'Ethiopian' stress in Rastafarianism. According to Robert Hill the Ethiopian stress and the divine honour accorded the Emperor Haile Selassie owed a great deal to Leonard Howell, a seaman who returned to Jamaica from the USA in 1932, and was himself influenced by a sect called the 'Israelites'.

It is not necessary here to follow these tangled spiritual genealogies. The 1930s bring us up to the modern period in which the trade unions became powerful, notably under Bustamente, and in which party politics took the centre of the stage, with the Jamaica Labour Party and People's National Party in acute rivalry. The Second World War also vastly widened the perspective of many Jamaicans. The island began to prosper in 1950, until the bauxite market declined twenty years later; and in 1962 the country became independent, though still within the British Commonwealth. It might be expected that such an expansion of secular approaches and opportunities might draw away religious energies or convert them to politics. Maybe that did happen for a while so far as the Revival cults were concerned. But this same period also included the rise of Rastafarianism, which once more mixed rebellion and religion.

Rastafarianism is the main rival to Pentecostalism and to conservative evangelical religion. It resembles many radical groups on the margin of Christianity in its adoption of a true Zion elsewhere, in this case in Ethiopia. It also exemplifies a tendency among millenarian faiths to oscillate between withdrawal and physical militancy. Rastas physically controlled West Kingston by 1958. They adopted the 'Rude Boy' attitude as part of a new personal and collective model, and frightened many people with the nihilistic 'Natty Dreads'.

Rastafarianism passed through phases in which it was ignored –

and derided – and then feared, until in the late sixties it achieved a kind of vanguard role. From being stigmatized as near-criminal the Rastas found their symbols widely adopted by politicians. In 1972 the leader of the PNP, Manley, threatened the 'corrupt rich' with 'the rod of correction'. In the 1976 election both parties used reggae. Rastafarianism was now regarded as 'progressive' and it began to appeal to one or two members of the middle class, such as the occasional lawyer and university teacher. It is unlikely, however, that this represents a social mobility stimulated by the Rasta faith itself, though Rastas generally have no objection to a bit of individual entrepreneurship.

Yet by 1980 the Rastas had lost some of their influence on political symbols. Their dream of real power had died with the death of Haile Selassie, even though his departure could be accommodated theologically. The death of the reggae star Bob Marley in 1983 was also a blow. The bulk of the upper class still disliked Rastafarianism, and Edward Seaga as leader of the (right-wing) Jamaica Labour Party and as Prime Minister began to shift towards Revivalism, in its old form and in the new Pentecostal version. Indeed Seaga approached the co-option of symbols from the viewpoint of a sociologist specifically interested in religious traditions. Although himself from a Catholic Maronite (or 'Syrian') background, he had in earlier years sympathetically analysed Revivalist beliefs and practices, especially the Pukumina cult.

This shift on the part of Seaga perhaps reflects a shift in the weight of religious power in Jamaica towards Pentecostalism. Pentecostalism had arrived in Jamaica in 1907 through American missionaries sent by the Church of God. By 1943 some 4 per cent of Jamaicans were Pentecostal, in 1960 13 per cent and in 1970 20 per cent. They currently bid fair to rival the established churches in numbers. In the parishes of northern Clarendon and northern Manchester studied by William Wedenoja they are already on equal terms.[8]

Pentecostalism bears some relation to the older Revival cults, except that it has to a large extent brought the old oscillation between African and other identities to an end. Wedenoja comments that some revival cults have only been able to compete by themselves becoming Baptist or Pentecostal. In Wedenoja's view the Pentecostal churches have a 'far greater affiliation than Rastafarianism'.[9]

This growing influence is somewhat reluctantly acknowledged by the Jamaica Council of Churches, and various different denominations are imitating Pentecostal practices. Many Anglican churches have introduced altar calls and the laying on of hands, as well as baptism by immersion. Even some Presbyterians have begun to speak as the Spirit gives them utterance. Charismatics are in regular evidence in the Roman Catholic cathedral in Kingston. Of course it may well be that Jamaicans, at least for a time, keep a foot in the older denominations. In any case they refer to a division of labour based on the New Testament injunction to worship God 'in spirit and in truth'. The old denominations worship Him in truth and the Pentecostals worship Him in spirit.

At the same time there is bound to be some discomfort felt in the older denominations, since they have also taken part in Jamaican and Caribbean Councils of Churches which share the political outlook of the World Council of Churches (WCC). This outlook stresses the need to find a Christian identity which is authentically Jamaican rather than superimposed. Jamaica has to be decolonized spiritually and its indigenous and African contributions taken seriously. The trouble is that in actual practice this decolonization runs alongside the decline of the more liberal denominations and the growth of Pentecostalism. It is disconcerting to well-meaning Christians and liberal Anglicans or Methodists when the faith which in practice picks up the traditions of Jamaica is a conservative faith originating in the USA.

Pentecostalism is in part of United States provenance, but in part independent. The extent of US religious influence and the degree of US control and support vary in different parts of the Caribbean. In Wedenoja's view 'Pentecostalism reached Jamaica by means of returning migrants rather than by foreign missionization.'[10] There was not so much a direct implantation of US culture as an adoption of US style and a deployment of US skills in leadership. The US aura carried a message of modernity and of a power to be shared more widely. Only secondarily did it signify colonization.

United States influence and money is most visible in the major crusades and in television slots bought by evangelists like Oral Roberts and Jimmy Swaggart. But probably it is the local evangelicals who will be the main beneficiaries when the new second channel is opened up on Jamaica television. For every major crusade there are many minor crusades run locally in small towns and villages; and there is a level of fissiparous expansion well away from any direct US influence.

Those most alert to US cultural colonization tend to be members of the Jamaican intelligentsia, and such people are anxious to probe other sources for the definition of Jamaican identity. For them the most dramatic instance of the relationship between religious and cultural invasion was provided by the proposed visit of an evangelist to Jamaica in 1987. It seems his campaign was actually to be called 'Invasion Crusade'. Letters from the evangelist came into the hands of the People's National Party, as well as tapes of television broadcasts. In the letters and tapes he earnestly solicited funds, in particular to help save Jamaica from communism.

The basic reason for the expansion of Pentecostalism, quite apart from any aura of modernity or any external financial help, is its capacity to combine a 'New Man' with an ancient strain of spirit possession and healing. It is at once the most recent expression of Christianity, and in touch with the therapeutic cults embedded in a world-wide 'archaic' religiosity. Furthermore it is colour-blind and encourages local leadership and participation. The 'higher' churches are more white or at any rate more brown. Pentecostalism takes up a deeply ingrained Jamaican faith in the ability of the Spirit to seize each and every one.

Pentecostal churches are usually led by males of fairly low status, though perhaps not of the lowest, who can speak for their people in the accents of their people. It is widely suggested that the Pentecostal pastorate provides men with some social mobility, offering them authority and modest economic improvement. Whatever may be the case with the average Pentecostal it seems very likely that taking up the pastorate brings some prosperity and can lead to further mobility in the next generation. A few of the pastors have now gained diplomas or wear clerical garb.

How far Pentecostals taken as a whole advance themselves is difficult to document precisely. The search for respectability engaged in by those below the middle class involves at the minimum habits likely to promote some advancement. Jamaican society has for a long time been divided into 'sinners' and 'Christians'. The latter seek meekness, joy and temperance; the former, at least by repute, like to cheat, drink, curse and boast. The New Testament promises that he who seeks shall find, and Pentecostals seek both health and wealth. They quite frequently believe that being a Christian brings rewards in this life as well as hereafter. Pastor (or Bishop) Blair has declared his liking for pie now as well as pie in the sky, and it is said he has not been disappointed. From time to time successful people attribute their good fortune to their good faith. But of hard evidence there is none.

In trying to assess where Pentecostals end up socially one needs to know where they come from, and the evidence here is sketchy and disputed. Ashley Smith writes of chapels located in areas of seasonal labour and geographical mobility which lie close to the sugar estates or bauxite mines or are tucked in the urban fringes.[11] Chapels are also to be found in clusters of slum dwellings just on the margin of higher-income housing. Smith suggests that Pentecostals are numerous among people like yardmen and household helps, and that suggestion would fit with the evidence provided by Rolim in Brazil which characterized them as in the personal service and minor white-collar jobs.[12] Clive Stilson Cato sees Pentecostals as among the better off of the poor.[13]

Whatever is true about the social location of Pentecostals Wedenoja unequivocally sees Pentecostalism as conferring a new individual identity. It gives people a personal voice which is dramatized in possession by a new and powerful spirit. Wedenoja goes further and makes similar claims for Pentecostalism in Jamaica as Burnett made for it in Guatemala. In his view it is 'facilitating the creation of a unified national culture'.[14] It does not do this by political revolution but by psychic mutation. Many would dispute Wedenoja's claim, particularly those who see change as arising from the kind of political mobilization which alters structures. The silent changes of the soul and identity do not in their view constitute 'real' politics.

Jamaican intellectuals would probably question whether Pentecostalism can provide a viable public symbolism, such as Rastafarianism offered. A glance round the remarkable Jamaican National Gallery in Kingston gives no clear answer to this. Most of the paintings and sculptures have religious themes, giving evidence of a society in which religion provides the modalities of expression (and where churches are more numerous per person than anywhere else in the world). There is a lot of Rasta influence on the gallery as well as some Jamaican religious primitivism. But undoubtedly the most impressive works are by Kapo, a sculptor and a painter who is also a Revivalist preacher.

A key point made by Ashley Smith relates to female identity and the approach made by at least some Pentecostal churches to the situation in which young unmarried mothers find themselves.[15] The older churches in the past often did not get beyond condemning concubinage and child-bearing outside marriage. In Jamaica the onus of moral behaviour rests on the women. They find themselves pressured by men for favours and yet they are often disinclined to use contraceptives. In any case they may well see childlessness as a curse. For them Pentecostalism offers a new beginning and quite often a chance to contract a marriage in a 'respectable' atmosphere where mutual trustworthiness may be assumed. Outside in the 'sinful' world the Jamaican male tends to set religion apart in a compartment and to dally as fancy takes him with several women. He may also suspect the authority exercised by the preacher and the heavy atmosphere of sublimated sexuality exuded in the chapel. That the chapels act as a refuge for women and for the family, and that most members are women is undisputed.

How far this readiness to include the unmarried mother is really peculiar to the Pentecostals at the present time is disputable. Dr Caroline Sargent, an anthropologist working in Jamaica, is of the opinion that with so many young mothers unmarried and the majority of members in all the churches being women it is unlikely that any church took a harsh view. Indeed she mentioned an occasion in her experience when the preacher at a well-known Baptist church omitted 'fornication' from a Pauline list of sins in Holy Scripture, showing (she presumed) a proper sensitivity to the condition of a fair proportion of his congregation.[16] It seems agreed that a great many young Jamaican women get into difficulties and also that women bear the onus of family integrity, as they do throughout much of the Caribbean. They also stand aside from the widespread violence in the male community. Dr Sargent quoted an informant who suggested that having your husband 'born again' would decrease the likelihood of regular beatings.

Both Wedenoja and Smith stress the heavy load of guilt carried in the Jamaican psyche.[17] Jamaican upbringing apparently involves quite severe punishment and – in their view – concomitant guilt. A highly emotional faith is able to deal with this guilt. Perhaps the roots of the widespread desire for adult baptism by total immersion are nourished here. Jesus Himself is seen as a figure of unqualified mercy: at once gracious mother and faithful husband.

Of course Jamaica provides only one instance of the way Pentecostalism has taken off in the Caribbean. In almost all the islands spirit possession is a central experience, and the various cults are almost merged with or alternatively at some distance from orthodox Catholic or Baptist or Methodist or Anglican Christianity. It is impossible to survey the situation island by island. The background provided by British or French or Spanish or Dutch colonial rule is too varied, and the mix of migrants and religions is too complex. All that can be done is to utilize various studies of Pentecostalism which happen to have been carried out in Haiti, in Puerto Rico and in Trinidad, and indicate any distinctive insights they may offer. For this purpose I lean on a volume edited by Stephen Glazier.[18]

Trinidad: Pentecostalism in Another Area of British and United States Influence

In Stephen Glazier's study of Pentecostalism in Trinidad the focus is on the way Pentecostalism handles beliefs concerning Obeah and demon possession. He begins by saying that a church may play a modernizing role without growing very much, *and vice versa.* In Trinidad Pentecostalism has 'developed a very modern way of dealing with [Obeah] beliefs which may, in turn, have an unexpected modernizing influence on the life of the individual'.[19] It has also grown spectacularly, increasing from some 4,000 in 1960 to over 20,000 in 1970. Churches grew rapidly larger, so that one building in 1978 could accommodate 2,000 people and there were plans to build another able to accommodate 7,000. Pentecostalism may influence more people than are actually in membership, since many Trinidadians are in the habit of sampling several churches a week, among which Pentecostal churches will be included.

In Trinidad Obeah beliefs are very widespread. They serve to explain bad luck and good luck and provide a channel through which to express malice and aggression. In particular economic success is explained by magic, since so rare a phenomenon must have a supernatural explanation. Success is suspected as due to magical malfeasance, and this suspicion may well be a drag on general economic development. To counteract such malfeasance is very expensive, at least if pursued through traditional channels.

All churches have in different ways come to terms with these beliefs, and exorcism is widely available, from ministers or from priests – or for that matter from practitioners in the syncretistic cults. But Pentecostal rites are by far the most popular. They are relatively anonymous and they are free. They are also, Glazier maintains, the first step towards a naturalistic understanding of disease.[19] Pastors encourage all who seek relief and pass by the altar to seek medical attention, and they may also make direct referrals. The exchanges between pastor and demon (or demons) are humorous, and Glazier sees this as arising in part from a tension perceived between modern and traditional beliefs.

This is a complex matter. The situation in Trinidad would need to be compared with those situations in Guatemala for example where both exorcism and medical treatment were viewed as 'miraculous'. The category of 'miraculous' is always difficult to handle, and you can even hear sophisticated commentators on public television in the United States referring to new drugs as 'semi-miraculous', meaning – perhaps – that they are unbelievably powerful.

Glazier contrasts the conditions of Pentecostal exorcism with those of Obeahmen and cult healers. The Obeahman may try to run the life of the supplicant, telling the client what he may eat and when he may have sex. He may also make more and more exorbitant demands, buttressed by threats of further illness. By contrast the good offices of a Pentecostal pastor are standardized, public and predictable. Clearly

Glazier is here emphasizing how Pentecostal practices can be seen as part-way along the road towards Weberian rationalization.

Glazier also describes another version of the relationship to the USA (and to Canada). At the point where other local churches have sought financial independence Pentecostal churches seek ties with North American sister churches. The pastor visits the United States; US churches help with contributions. An informal employment agency develops which helps a limited number of converts to find jobs in the USA. However, Glazier does not agree with those who see this as a mode of adjustment to modernity. Domestic service, for example, does not in his view provide much by way of an adaptation to industrial life.

Glazier is also uncertain about the relationship of Pentecostalism to personal economic advancement. He quotes Angelina Pollak-Eltz in her study of Pentecostalism in Venezuela where she suggests that pressure to legalize marital unions and to maintain them leads to more money spent on home improvement and education, and thence to upward mobility. In Glazier's view sermons advocating either church marriages or abstinence and sobriety run too much counter to Trinidadian culture. Moreover it may be that the churches in Trinidad are much larger than those in Venezuela, so that their influence is more superficial and diffuse. All the same it seems that some of those who seek improvement will at least find themselves commended and confirmed in their ambitions from the pulpit. They are assured that when Solomon found favour with the Lord he also grew rich, and that there is nothing holy about being poor! Liberation theology may seek 'an option for the poor' but it seems many of the poor have their own options in mind.

How these options work out is illustrated in a study by Eila Helander. Helander provides information specifically about evangelicalism among socially mobile university students in Trinidad,[20] and shows how it has survived both the experience of university and the challenge of Black Power. Of course, evangelical students, most of them in the Baptist and Holiness–Pentecostal traditions, found they had to respond to Black Power criticism of the American origins of their faith, especially in the seventies. Nevertheless, they managed to achieve a more distinctively Trinidadian form of devotion, for example, the use of steel bands, without being prised out of their basic commitments. Indeed, evangelicalism actually expanded among university students as well as among most of the different ethnic and status groups in the society at large. As in Jamaica, much of this expansion took place at the expense of the mainline Protestant churches.

Many of the student evangelicals saw academic success and prosperity in general as a testimony to the power of faith, although some believed they were called to a simpler life style alongside the vast masses of the impoverished. According to Helander, evangelicals mostly came from the lower or maybe lower middle groups and were seeking betterment of every kind. That search for betterment is in part realized by a rejection of the cinema, Carnival, jewellery, alcohol and tobacco. As for political vocations they are perceived as tainted and pessimistically dismissed as bound up in a tissue of corruption.

Puerto Rico: Pentecostalism in an Area of Hispanic and United States Influence

In Puerto Rico Pentecostalism has burgeoned both in the independent churches and in traditional bodies such as the Episcopalians, Presbyterians and Roman Catholics. As in Jamaica Pentecostalism has been present for three-quarters of century, and it expanded to some extent during the depression years of the 1930s. In 1942 Pentecostals constitued 8.5 per cent of Protestants and in 1962 about 25 per cent.

In the fifties and sixties Puerto Rico experienced a rapid economic growth like that in Jamaica: industrial plants appeared, an American-style middle class expanded, and city and suburban networks grew into sprawling conurbations. It was in this period that Pentecostalism burgeoned until now it comprises about one-third of the Protestant population, which in turn is one-sixth of the total population. Most Puerto Ricans remained poor, however, often hopelessly so.

Anthony L. LaRuffa studied Puerto Rican Pentecostals in the late sixties, so his work is now about two decades old.[21] He argues that the growing visibility of economic disparities and of consumer society in Puerto Rico accelerated the growth of Pentecostalism. The warm community of faith offered hope and emotional release. He makes three points about the relationship of Pentecostalism to personal economic advancement.

First he emphasizes the way the pastorate offers new opportunities, in particular because it provides a network of contacts. He describes one pastor whose position as district pastor enabled him to find customers for his appliance business. There are also, as apparently in Jamaica, 'evangelists who bask in the limelight of fame and comfort'.[22] Second he mentions the way Pentecostalism can adjust itself to increasing affluence. Some churches have grown more staid and include a professional constituency. Third, he sees Pentecostalism as reinforcing the process of Americanization, and in Puerto Rico that has a particular meaning. Pentecostals supported the American 'commonwealth' status of Puerto Rico. They were deeply alarmed by any prospect of a communist take-over such as might occur after independence, and preferred Puerto Rico to remain a satellite of the United States.

Perhaps it is also worth adding that in the case of the particular group which LaRuffa studied the 'missionary' was a native-born Puerto Rican woman, who became converted in New York, and then returned in the thirties to found a church at home. This does seem to be a very frequent pattern.

Haiti: Pentecostalism in an Area of French and United States Influence

In turning to Haiti something at least must be said about the political background. Politics in Haiti whirl in a vicious dance around issues of colour, class and language, as well as town and country – and religion. What follows relies for the most part on David Nicholl's book *Haiti in Caribbean Context*.[23]

There are several similarities between the French-speaking and English-speaking Caribbean. There is the same dualism in religion and language deriving from colonialism and from slavery. Though a considerable part of the society has for a long time consciously rejected those impositions, they have recognized how survival, preferment and all kinds of access involve the adoption of French and of Catholicism.

Again, in Haiti as in Jamaica, the African religious inheritance has played a role in resistance. It is possible that Voodoo was one of the symbols of resistance in the successful revolution of 1804. Certainly the leaders of the rural *cacos* revolt in 1918–19 against the American occupation drew inspiration from their African religion. Another intriguing parallel is that François Duvalier, like Edward Seaga in Jamaica, had extensive interests in ethnology.

A further similarity worth noticing here, because it extends to the whole Caribbean and also because it bears on economic advancement, is the role and political stance of ethnic minorities. In Haiti, as in Jamaica, Trinidad and the Dominican Republic, there is a substantial Middle Eastern minority. It is often 'Syrian' in origin, which usually means Christian Lebanese. Such groups have become entrepreneurial in their attitudes and illustrate Simmel's view of the stranger as the potential trader. This form of economic advancement is decidedly not rooted in the 'Protestant Ethic'. Since the politics of Haiti are more determined by ethnicity than is the case in the Dominican Republic, the favourable effect of their economic initiative has been more noticeable in the latter country. On the whole migrant groups prefer strong government, even dictatorship; and they sometimes have reason to fear black power movements. The Chinese and the Jews tended to leave Jamaica in the seventies. East Indians in Trinidad are also entrepreneurical in their approach, and have preferred stability, in spite of including many very impoverished people. Certainly middle-class East Indians in Trinidad have been totally opposed to black power.

These similarities apart, Haiti has its own specific characteristics. It is 180 years since political independence was first achieved, not just twenty-five as in Jamaica. Independence was gained by force exercised against a system that was dominated by the military as well as centralized. So the army has become a preponderant force in Haiti and it has offered the main channel by which poor blacks might rise to power. The rulers of Haiti for a century were soldiers.

Inevitably the colonial impact was less direct than elsewhere and the educational penetration was also quite limited: 85 per cent of Haitians are illiterate. Moreover the distinctive attitude of the Catholic Church towards Voodoo, condemning and accommodating it, has implications for even the religion of the elite. Though members of the elite are 'Catholic' (and speak French) they know about Voodoo (and understand Kreyol). In particular they learned about Voodoo and Kreyol as children through their black servants and nursemaids.

Protestantism has played an interesting role in relation to Kreyol which is linked to a complicated cultural symbolism and to the polities of culture as practised by François Duvalier. Duvalier was anti-elitist and populist, and many of his followers in the early years of his movement took an ethnological approach to Kreyol, emphasizing its importance. Kreyol also became a medium of criticism in the late 1970s. At the same time Protestantism was a powerful influence for Kreyol, using it as the main medium of communication in the countryside. If we add to this the access offered by Protestantism to English we can see that the cultural stance of Protestantism acquires some definition as *not* aligned with French. The orthography of Kreyol was devised by a Methodist minister, and it is, of course, frequently the case throughout the Americas that an orthography for an oral tradition is constructed by missionaries.

Up to the time of the Duvaliers the Roman Catholic Church was identified with the old Francophone elite. François Duvalier's rise to power was based on the black middle classes, rural as well as urban, and these exercised control over the ferocious Tontons Macouttes. Duvalier first of all systematically reduced elite power in the unions, in business, in the intelligentsia, in the army and in the church. Gordon K. Lewis has suggested that the regime of his family can plausibly be seen as a kind of Creole fascism.[24] It was violently anti-communist. It promoted a state ideology of *noirisme* and *négritude* based on systematic violence and terror. And it attributed a variety of secular sainthood to the leader.

By the mid-sixties Duvalier had decided to stabilize his regime by negotiating with the power bases of the old elite, and in the case of the army and the church this was achieved by changes of leadership. However, the ecclesiastical changes had unanticipated long-term consequences. The French clergy, mainly Breton, were repatriated, and replaced by native leaders. Many of the younger Haitian priests eventually became radicalized by liberation theology.

On its own, however, the church could not have toppled the system, though in the later years of the Duvalier period it became more and more a defender of human rights – much as it did in the later years of the Trujillo dictatorship in the neighbouring Dominican Republic. But the advent of Jean-Claude Duvalier ('Baby Doc') had brought about new shifts in the power base of the regime which led to instability. The new dictator moved further towards the mulatto elite, and towards technocrats and business men who might assist with international connections. This worried the black middle classes who had controlled the countryside and it also confused sections of the Tontons Macouttes. The regime then tried to make populist appeals direct to the masses, which further eroded its power base. Thus in early 1986 the high school student body aided by the church was able to initiate the overthrow of 'Baby Doc'.

Quite what the role of Protestants and of Pentecostal has been in this is unclear. Clearly the connections with the United States are unusually close; and the United States has veered between periods when it has pressed for more liberal measures and periods when it has supported the Duvalier regime as anti-communist. It also appears that Protestantism was encouraged and expanded considerably during the period of François Duvalier's struggle with the Roman Catholic Church.

Certainly Protestantism gains from current disputes between liberation theologians like Father Aristide and the Catholic hierarchy. A correspondent in the *Manchester Guardian Weekly* (13 September 1987) speaks of the Catholic left and the Protestants competing over the same corners of the field. He also speaks of some 500 Protestant 'sects' currently 'influencing' about a third of the population.

At the minimum Protestantism is involved in quite characteristic mutations at the level of culture. Just how consistent the effects of Protestantism are from one generation to another can be gauged by a quotation from Louis Joseph Janvier. Janvier was one of the most vigorous Haitian writers on national independence, and argued that economic development required an appropriate ideology. Catholicism he viewed as encouraging external loyalties and a carefree, irresponsible life-style. In the late nineteenth century he wrote: 'The protestant is thrifty, a respecter of the law, a lover of books, a friend of peace, rich in courageous hope and perseverance. He is self-reliant, knows how to turn immaterial forces into material capital. He suppresses carnival and the festivals. . . . Everything which trades, cultivates, manufactures, earns, gets rich, prospers, is protestant.'[25] The point about 'carnival' is particularly interesting. It was precisely the tendency to eliminate 'carnival' and the old rural pastimes that E. P. Thompson lamented in his critique of the impact of Methodism on rural England.[26]

With that general Haitian background sketched in, we can turn to a local study undertaken by Frederick Conway.[27] Conway points out that Haitian Protestantism is supposd to exclude both Catholicism and Voodoo. In fact Protestants call upon the army of the Great Spirit to defeat the legions of the evil one. Pentecostals in particular summon up the Holy Spirit and are possessed by Him. These 'manifestations' are easily understood in Haitian culture but in Conway's view their efficacy as a sign of spiritual power can only be understood in relation to the healing functions of the Pentecostal congregation. For conversion to Pentecostalism to be an effective form of divine healing it must involve a new relationship to *Bon-Dieu* coming through the spiritual power of the whole congregation. This involves prayer for and over those who are ill both during services and by groups in peoples' homes. Pentecostalism offers comprehensive and divinely guaranteed insurance against all evil – free.

Conway discusses the organization of Pentecostalism and links it more explicitly to the United States than do authors writing about other societies. For many Haitians Protestantism is part and parcel of American enlightenment and social development and brings with it American prosperity as well as American handouts.

This can mean that the local Pentecostal chapel is the most imposing building in the village. It also means the availability of patronage, at least for those who are part of the administrative hierarchy of the church. Some Pentecostals spoke more truly than they knew when they mixed French with Haitian Creole to produce

'Celui qui chef trouvera': he who is the boss shall find. Certainly the pastors acquire social skills, and English, and an opportunity to go to the United States.

Americans are widely perceived as open-handed missionaries, in spite of the fact that the missionary is a rather remote figure at the head of a hierarchy. The United States itself often is seen as the source of all good and all goods: it nourishes a chosen people. Pentecostalism inducts people out of African origins and out of practices which are held to mire them in poverty, and leads them towards the happiness of the American Zion.

As is usual in these studies Conway has comments to make about the place of women and, again as usual, there is a distinctive twist to be noticed in the Haitian situation. Conway focuses this in relation to a tension between the concern with health and the organizational side of Pentecostalism.

Most converts are women and this is because the women are primarily responsible not only for morality but for physical well-being. Women receive the benefits of healing and are themselves healers. Men often encourage women to convert and spread the benefits of health, but avoid converting themselves and dodge the disbenefits of being castigated for their male behaviour. However, the pastorate and the key administrative jobs are mostly reserved for males. Women are therefore shut out from the role of broker in relationships with the American missionary. The charismata fall on whom they will, male and female, but the line of organization is reserved to the male.

Conway comments that the Pentecostal network and hierarchy may become a means of integration at local, regional and national levels. At the village level it seems that Pentecostals have to retain relations outside the congregation. But in the towns their networks are more self-contained. The brothers and sisters interact between themselves and assist each other in the job market, somewhat to the chagrin of those outside the faith. However, the chances of real economic advancement will only be realized over time, when the economic opportunities are there and the small industrial sector expands. God helps those who are least are supplied with *some* means to help themselves. As in the parable you need at least one penny to be getting along with.

As regards the situation in Haiti's sister state of the Dominican Republic information is sparse. The Roman Catholic Church suffered expropriation in the mid-nineteenth century and has been damaged by close association with Trujillo dictatorship in the mid-twentieth century. Priests have been few and practice has been minimal. However from the end of fifties on the church edged away from the government and began to defend human rights. Protestantism has made much less impact than in other Caribbean countries and accounts for less than 2 per cent of the total population. In a way, however, the usual pattern has been repeated on a smaller scale. Many fundamentalist missions arrived after the Second World War; and the Pentecostals by now comprise a third of the Protestant population. According to Wipfler, writing in the sixties, they have been the fastest-growing element, and are led almost entirely by native Dominicans.[28]

General Comments

This is a useful point in the argument to make more general comments about the evidence presented from different parts of the Caribbean. I begin with one or two points made by the theologian George Mulrain.[29] He stresses how Caribbean culture is one which is spoken and sung rather than written down. It is also informal, spontaneous, flexible and infinitely varied. Clearly such characteristics offer a potential harvest to a religion which is oral, informal and constantly splitting in order to adapt. Mulrain points out that it is the communication of the whole self in gesture, in expression and in the modulation of the face which counts. Here, he says, it is the Pentecostals who are the professionals. They are also professionals at sermons which tell stories rather than expound arguments.

What is above all most evident is the capacity of Pentecostalism simultaneously to conform and to transform. It finds out the morphology and shape of the local society and participates in the life of people. At the same time it provides new networks of participation and offers lines of organization and communciation along which signals of modernity and symbols of equality may travel. In one area it edges towards modernity in some particular respect, as for example in providing medical help or making medical referrals. In another area it may subtly alter the position of women and attack the traditional psychology and behaviour of the men. Sometimes, as in Jamaica, Pentecostalism is fiercely independent, at least at the local level. At other times, as in Haiti, it seems quite closely bound into US organizations.

Of course, the criticism is inevitably that Pentecostalism reflects the paternalistic relations of the plantation, that the equality it proclaims is merely realized in the group, and that the attitude it produces is recognizably akin to the Protestant Ethic. Certainly the economic advancement desired by many Pentecostals depends on the existence of facilitating economic conditions and may take a generation or two to achieve. People advance by the margins which are available to them, pressing on their constraints rather than breaking out of them. To achieve individuality and to break down barriers of class and colour even in a limited social space is a signal advance, and one from which new advances to broader equalities may be achieved – in time.[30]

Chapter 8

Instructive Parallels: South Korea and South Africa

This chapter is concerned with some other societies where developments are to be observed similar to those in Latin America. The main society under scrutiny is South Korea, partly because the growth of evangelical and especially Pentecostal religion there is so dramatic, and partly because first-class material is easily available. South Korea is also worth scrutiny because it exhibits a somewhat different relationship between religion and economic ethos from that obtaining in Latin America. An examination of South Korea helps underline the way the nexus of Protestant religion and economic ethos – and political involvement – varies according to context. The same inference is to be drawn from some concluding remarks on South Africa, another country where 'conservative' and/or charismatic religion is making rapid progress.

Broader Parallels?

Ideally a study of South Korea would be set in a context of comparisons between all the countries of East Asia exposed to religious and cultural radiation from the USA. It does not detract at all from what I argue about the successful indigenization of Pentecostal and evangelical religion to see countries in East Asia and in Latin America as affected by Anglo-American culture, sometimes initially in its British form, but latterly in its American form. It would have been particularly interesting to compare the degrees of evangelical penetration in Japan and in the 'four little capitalist dragons' of Hong Kong, Singapore, Taiwan and South Korea. As it is, comment has largely to be restricted to South Korea and Japan, two societies which can at least be said to exhibit striking and significant contrasts.

Of course, the proper universe of comparison would be the complete rim of countries subject to US influence, from Indonesia to China. Within the religious sphere that would have concentrated attention on the difference between those societies where there was still a strong relationship between ethnic solidarity and a given religion, or a given religious pattern, and those where that relationship was absent. Clearly a strong relationship exists between Buddhism and Laos and Thailand, and between Islam and Peninsular Malaya. The nexus of religion and people also exists in a different mode as between the Buddhist–Shinto complex and Japan. It barely exists at all in South Korea, nor is it really present in the Philippines and Indonesia, in spite of the strong entrenchment of Catholicism in the Philippines and of Islam in Indonesia. Equally, a unitary religious institution is absent among the Chinese peoples present throughout most of East Asia. To draw attention to this difference is to emphasize yet again that the theoretical backdrop of this study is the breakup of the union between religious adherence and communal belonging. Incipient pluralism is the necessary, though not sufficient, condition for penetration, indeed almost tautologically so.

That is what makes it so significant that only one country has really experienced a transition to large-scale pluralism – South Korea. In some other countries one has elements of a plurality of organic cultures in the sense originally discussed by J. S. Furnivall, but not pluralism.[1] (Singapore is 'plural' in that more limited sense, though it is now affected by a more modern and wider pluralism. Those interested in its religious condition can consult an excellent recent monograph *Religious Switching in Singapore: A Study in Religious Mobility* by Joseph Tamney and Riaz Hassan.)[2]

The Chinese, it must be admitted, are an odd case. So far as they are concerned, one has almost universal cultural forms and structures which, however, admit of different religious colourings: 'folk Chinese', Buddhist, Taoist, Islamic and Christian. The last two become problematic in Chinese contexts by reason of their own structural specificity and their distinctive and monotheistic claims. They are the two religions which have cut salients in Chinese culture. Part of the interest of a wider comparative study would have been the penetration of Christianity, especially evangelical Christianity in small cell-like forms, into eastern China and into most of the communities of the

Chinese diaspora. Enthusiasts claim that the penetration of these small (and virtually invisible) cells has spread deep in mainland China and may even involve some 50 million persons. Even unenthusiastic people believe the numbers to be considerable. To be apolitical may properly be regarded as an evasion in South Korea, but it is highly advantageous in China, and may even be an essential condition of survival, let alone expansion.

Apart from China and the Chinese communities, the only candidates for a comparative scrutiny of countries touched by the appropriate pluralism would have been the Philippines, Indonesia and – perhaps – New Guinea. The last is a very fragmented society and would have to be discussed in a way similar to the discussion of tribal groups in Latin America. It is certainly experiencing very active evangelization. As to Indonesia, it is a country so multi-centred, and populated by so many peoples, that it is difficult to discuss as a unit. It has a broadly sub-Islamic colouring, with substantial Christian and other minorities present in this or that ethnic, tribal or ecological sector. The evangelical presence is distinctly visible and evangelicals are very active. But such a mosaic of rival faiths operating among some 160 million people is simply beyond the scope of the present study.

The Philippines is the society which would have provided the most significant case study next to South Korea. It is a Catholic society (with a Muslim minority on Mindanao) which is, on the one hand, affiliated to the Hispanic world and to Latin America, and on the other hand, has been brought forcibly within the American sphere since the Spanish–American war. So it is a mixture which exhibits within a single state precisely the interaction of Hispanic with 'Anglo' cultures. It also contains many tribal and lingusitic subgroups in a way which parallels Latin America, and these are currently subject to eager evangelization.

Moreover, the penetration of the whole culture by conservative Protestantism is well advanced. Massive evangelical and Pentecostal rallies are held in the Philippines, and the Catholic Church is very conscious of 'the problem of the sects', as are the historic Protestant, separatist and Anglican churches. 'The problem of the sects' is held by some to be exacerbated by the activities of political infiltrators from the USA. The Philippines would, therefore, have provided a prime candidate for discussion as a kind of fascinating hybrid existing between the Hispanic, Anglo-American and Asian worlds. Only space and some difficulty in obtaining materials at a distance require it reluctantly to be excluded.

That brings us back from our detour to the specific and dramatic case of South Korea. South Korea *is* a plural society. The key fact about South Korea is that it has been broken down, broken up – and opened up. It is a society hammered to pieces by Japanese overlordship, by political division, and by US cultural power, and it is trying to find some manner whereby a viable self-consciousness and *modus vivendi* may be achieved. The old traditional Korean framework failed, the cultural alternative offered by the imperial Japanese was repugnant, and so alternatives with an American provenance were relatively attractive. They were the gateway to modernity and success. Those alternatives included Christianity. Like the Philippines, South Korea is a kind of meeting point between North America and Asia.

Korea: History and Political Geography

It may be useful to set out schematically the background to the rapid expansion of Protestant Christianity in Korea, before touching on the specific trajectory of Pentecostalism. Korea is placed, like Judaea, at a crossroad of peoples, and has been subject to many invasions and interventions. Above all two invasions provided the psychic impetus to seek a new and messianic deliverance. One was the Japanese annexation in 1910, and the other was the invasion from the north after the Second World War which cut the country in two. The deliverance came from an American Protestantism which in its first Korean incarnation was apolitical and pietistic, and reflected American ideas. The atonement and eschatology were central to its theological understanding. It was, in fact, identical with the Protestantism which arrived in Latin America and had the same large component of theologically conservative Presbyterianism.

The consequences of this apolitical tradition turned out to be paradoxical. In one way it assisted survival since the Americans tried to steer the churches away from sharp and damaging clashes with the Japanese overlords. In another way it allowed the Americans to be seen as devoid of serious colonial ambitions. They were the friends of the Koreans, especially given that the Japanese were the enemies. What followed from this was the adoption of Christianity by many Korean intellectuals as a political vehicle of nascent Korean nationalism. Almost everywhere else in Asia Christianity had some association with what was alien. But in Korea, given that Koreans were doubly alienated, from their ancient background and from the Japanese, Christianity went native and became genuinely popular.

There were, however, other elements in the rapid expansion during the early years. Protestant Christianity first arrived in 1884 and came to be regarded as an attractive alternative to the corrupt bureaucracy of the Yi dynasty and the Confucian ideology with which it was bound up. In particular, North Koreans found themselves discriminated against and it was they who most enthusiastically turned to Christianity. There is here a faint echo of the way that many of the Samurai in Japan, ejected from power at the Meiji restoration, embraced Christianity. This indicates how a new faith can be picked up by frustrated or ejected counter-elites and fits very well with E. Everett Hagen's analysis a generation ago of 'achievement motivation' among such people, whether 'dissenters' in Japan or literal dissenters in early industrial England.[3]

It seems that, through this amalgam of predisposing circumstances, Christianity came to be associated with Western learning (*soehag*) and with scientific knowledge. The parallel with the situation in late nineteenth-century Latin America is clear. Kim Ilsoo points out that 'A number of Korean literati turned to Protestantism in order to learn Western knowledge and English at the modern schools founded and administered by American, especially Methodist, missionaries.'[4] (This process is comparable to what is currently occurring in Singapore, where there is some modest association between acquiring English in university and adherence to Christianity.) Data of this kind suggest just how important it is to distinguish two different social locations open to penetration by a new faith: the upper lower class and the lower upper class. The latter, whether in nineteenth-century Brazil or in twentieth-century Singapore, may embrace a combination of Christianity, modernity, the England language and even 'Anglo' culture as part of a package offering further mobility.

However, Christianity would hardly have combined modernity with nationalism had it been rooted solely in the English language. US missionaries made a remarkable contribution to Korean culture by using the despised Korean tongue, teaching the Korean alphabet (Hangul) and publishing in Hangul. As Song Kon-Ho comments: 'In those initial years, being a follower of Christianity meant enlightenment. Followers mastered Hangul and were able to read the Bible; and, in the process of having access to a new western culture, science, and world news, developed a sense of nationalism.'[5]

Suh David Kwang-Sun has described something of the extraordinary educational and medical enterprises that led simultaneously to modernization and to nationalism.[6] In 1885 Dr Horace Allen opened the first missionary hospital, known as the Widespread Relief House, and now part of Yonsei University, indicating that Christian medical facilities were to be open to all. So, too, were the educational facilities. In 1887 the Rev. Henry G. Appenzeller opened the first school providing modern education for boys, known as the 'Hall for Rearing Useful Men'. Learning in the new American school came to mean skills as well as letters, science as well as the New Testament, Korean studies as well as English. Indeed, in the two decades from 1900 on, US missionaries established a Western system of public education from primary school to college. It was in these schools that the students' patriotism came to be expressed in physical education classes and through training in debating teams, as well as through political ceremonies. All this runs remarkably parallel to the way American Protestant schools in Brazil, for example, introduced science and physical labour, provided channels of social mobility and (after the fall of the empire) moved into the current of Brazilian nationalism.

At this point explanations have to run along two separate tracks. One track has already led to the combination of the aura of modernity with Christianity, especially Protestant Christianity. One may incautiously speculate that this appealed more to the 'lower upper' groups. The other track leads to the combination of Christianity with the aura of the most archaic layer of Korean religiosity: shamanism. One may again speculate with equal lack of caution that this appeals more to the upper lower groups. (In default of data hypotheses are free, though it may be as well to recollect that spiritism in Brazil has an appeal to the middle classes almost equal to its appeal to the less sophisticated groups.)

This relationship between conservative Protestantism (Presbyterian or Pentecostal) and shamanism is perfectly natural, even though it perhaps comes as a surprise. The world of New Testament Christianity contains 'demons' and it announces victory over 'the powers'. That world is, in fact, a common substrate all over the five continents. Even in Northern Europe and North America we dimly apprehend potent fragments of it in childhood. Shamanism and spiritism are nearly everywhere, just below the surface or actually on the surface of contemporary life. Certainly it is on the surface in the Yucatan, in the Sertão and in Seoul. Hexham has shown that even Afrikaaner Calvinism, to be discussed later, harbours an undergrowth of vibrant spiritism passed on by black African servants to their Afrikaaner child charges.[7]

Kim Illsoo quotes from an American missionary report published in 1907 which makes the point very well. 'Many of the religious characteristics of the Korean people mark them for discipleship in the Christian faith. Believing as they do in the universal presence of spirits, it is not difficult for them to accept the doctrines of the spiritual nature of God.'[8] The report adds, picking up the relationship of Christianity to a kind of natural moral law, that 'Confucianism, with its age-long insistence on the fact that man is a moral being and must obey moral law, prepares them sincerely to exemplify Christian ethics in their life'.[9] You can have utilitarian techniques to expel the daemonic and a Kantian respect for the majesty and universality of the moral law: *and* you can be saved. So Pentecostalism picks up the ancient Korean in the forms of shamanism and of Confucianism, as well as introducing the modern American.

Today's Efflorescence

A further double track may be followed with respect to the background of today's efflorescence of Christianity. There is, first of all, the mass migration of rural workers to the mega-cities, there to be received by the mega-churches, which in Korea happen to be the largest in the world.[10] This is a transmigration of souls as well as a migration of bodies since it is a search for spiritual security in a world changing with astonishing rapidity. The Korean churches, especially those in the Pentecostal tradition, are once again 'havens for the masses'. On the whole they abjure active political involvement. This occurs against a background of communist threat from the North, real enough even though exaggerated, and political turbulence at home. It is as well to remember that many hundreds of thousands of North Korean Christians fled from the North to what is now South Korea with the advent of communism, and that they know North Korea to be a totalitarian state of Albanian implacability and brutality. Some of those that fled were Catholics and the conservative attitude found among a minority of Catholics even today derives, in part, from that experience. This was the period and this was the experience that generated other messianic responses apart from orthodox Christianity, such as the 'Unification Church'.

There is in the second place, another track leading to an identification of Christianity with opposition to the fascistic and corrupt elements in South Korean society. Given that Korean Christians have a tradition of opposition to corrupt Confucian bureaucracy and to Japanese overlordship, this is now revived in an opposition to autocratic government. Political opposition is associated with students, intellectuals and some industrial workers, and it tends to come from the historic Protestant churches and from the Roman Catholic Church. Its distinctive ideological vehicle is 'Minjung theology' which is a variant of the Latin American 'option for the poor', but drawing on Korean resources.[11]

Kim Illsoo, in what is a very insightful analysis, pushes behind these familiar circumstantial bases for Christian expansion and lays his finger on the traditional propensity of Koreans to seek 'personal community'. This term refers to 'personal networks through which persons or members exchange help, affection, loyalty, status symbols, material resources and flattery'.[12] Here we have a clear parallel to the role of networks discussed in chapter 11 of this present work in relation to economic self-help and mutual insurance. Kim Illsoo argues that this propensity to seek 'personal community' explains the fact that Presbyterians in South Korea outnumber Methodists by 5 to 1 whereas in the US Methodists outnumber Presbyterians by 3 to 1. The Presbyterians came from the US, Canada and Australia, and they adopted the 'Nevius Plan' based on self-propagation, self-government and self-support. The idea was to toughen up converts by removing the cushion of foreign funds.

Kim Illsoo then indicates how the Protestant Ethic thus released was able to coalesce with cultural traits already oriented towards achievement. Indeed, this may be the most crucial observation in all the varied materials on Korean Christianity. He writes: 'In view of the achievement oriented, individualist character of Koreans [the Nevius Plan] opened a Pauline opportunity for a true believer to set up a "frontier" church upon which he depended for livelihood.'[13] Had Presbyterians in Brazil done the same then Pentecostalism might have been otiose.

There was another element in the Nevius Plan which allowed Christian organizations to coalesce with the unit of local democracy known as the Kye. The Kye was a traditional cooperative embodying friendship, mutual assistance and common beliefs, and it was used by the peasants to defend themselves against exploitation from the central government. This meant, firstly, that when an important member of the Kye became a Christian the whole group would often go with him, and, secondly, that small-scale Christian organizations and the Kye might well become coextensive.

The further indigenization of Presbyterianism was pushed forward, perhaps all too easily, by allowing the church to approximate to the Confucian ideal of the five cardinal relations beteen ruler and subject, father and son, husband and wife, and so on. The result is startlingly similar to the patronal relationships reproduced inside Brazilian Presbyterianism out of the patterns which obtained in the hacienda. Pastors and elders try to stay above the laity and insist on enjoying superior privileges. Thus the universal brotherhood of Christianity is rather too successfully toned down to limited and particular relationships. A further point of Kim Illsoo's analysis is to indicate that Presbyterianism made these transitions where Methodism did not. The sociological conclusion is (almost) tautologically obvious. Those who wish to become indigenous and popular must pay the full costs in losing much of their original character. (By the same token, in Japan a radical and critical theologian seeking to make his faith indigenous finds that this involves the principle of harmony rather than the duty of criticism.)

When these personal communities are unloosed from their rural moorings and begin to float in the open seas of urban anomie and competition, they prove very efficient means of retaining personal relationships and staving off impersonal bureaucracy. The wider results are astonishing. They breed enormously and they subdivide very fast. There emerge vast organizations which are really floating towns lashed together out of thousands of small units. Thus one Pentecostal church alone, the Full Gospel Central Church in Seoul, comprises 500,000 members, making it the largest church in the world, followed by the Jotabeche Methodist Pentecostal cathedral in Santiago, Chile, with 80,000 members. At this point 'scientific church-growth' principles have combined with the practical inventions of Korean society. Kwang Lim Methodist Church has grown to over 12,000 members from 82 in 1950 and 680 in 1970. Young Nak Presbyterian Church, which began as a tent church ministering to refugees from the communist North, had 60,000 members in 1984. These comprised some 10,000 households and were served by twenty pastoral staff members, fourteen pastoral assistants, and four thousand deacons (mostly women). There were in all 1,562 cell groups. All this reflects rates of growth in the wider society whereby Korean Protestantism tripled between 1940 and 1961, doubled between 1961 and 1971 and tripled again in the following decade, until in the early 1980s Protestants alone accounted for 20 per cent of the population.[14]

This explosive growth was matched by subdivision, and most commentators argue that schism assists growth rather than hampering it. As in Brazil fission is nuclear and it unlocks power. Almost everything in Korea splits and grows. By 1981 Korean Presbyterians had broken into forty-five separate pieces, a phenomenon known to Korean journalists as 'individual churchism'. The Methodist Church has lacked the benefit of these schisms and shows correspondingly low rates of growth. It seems that the ancient practice known as 'sheep stealing' keeps the Christian pastors keen, lean – and efficient. Theirs is literally a spiritual enterprise culture. The chief pastor/ executive combines many secular roles, as, indeed, he does in Brazil. He is a social worker and employment exchange official, a kind of store manager and a broker, an educator and a fixer. He is also, if in the top echelon, a kind of international manager 'in the spirit', who knows the labourer is worthy of his hire, and whose worthiness may well extend to staying at the Hilton rather than at the YMCA. Do not even the Americans so? Moreover, these pastors and their many assistants 'honour' each other in typical US style. It is worth adding that these characteristics are to be found in the churches which serve a Christian majority among the three-quarters of a million Korean migrants in the USA, keeping them in a continuous state of pullulating activity.[15]

What is interesting in all this is the seeming paradox of piety and technological pragmatism, scientific administration and Christian shamanism, which is actually no paradox at all. Dr Cho Yonggi, who is chief executive-cum-Pastor Pastorum of the Full Gospel Central Church, has degrees in law and technology. These subjects need have only a marginal overlap with what is understood by 'liberal' or 'humane' education, or with the enlightened views that often go with it. A technically sophisticated society, such as exists today in South Korea, does not require as by some inner necessity a humanist intellectual sphere equipped with appropriate moral, political and epistemological perspectives. It may advance, and advance spectacularly, by combining instrumental technical skills with conspicuous instrumentality in the sphere of religion. Dr Cho offers prosperity and healing on the wings of personal salvation, and does so by the most ancient means of prayer and the healing touch. The genealogy of his approach combines the Mechanics Institute of early industrial Britain with the expectation of personal miracle. Many thousands of pilgrims ascend his prayer mountain every year seeking relief and restoration, and some medicine of the soul which will redress the strain and stress of their everyday existence.

According to Yoo Boo Woong in an article on 'Response to Korean Shamanism by the Pentecostal Church', Dr Cho's philosophy is to "Find need, and meet need". Yoo Boo Woong goes on: 'Why do the Korean working class, and particularly women, go to the shaman? Because they need health, wealth, fertility and success in their life ventures. Dr Cho's preaching meets those needs exactly.'[16] Cho's favourite text is that 'All things are possible'. Like Oral Roberts he lays great stress on the third epistle of John 1: 2, where the writer links faith and health with things 'going well' for the believer. Cho is a 'positive thinker' in the mould of Vincent Peale and Schuller. He is also an exorcist and charismatic who heals the sick and drives away demons in the holy name. His approach heals enough of the people some of the time to be said to 'work'. He offers himself as evidence that healing and redemption work. Indeed, not only do they work: they help you *to* work.

The Pentecostal Upsurge

At this point it is worth turning to look at Pentecostal growth in particular before dealing with three specific topics: the role and place of women, economic ethos and political involvement. With regard to Latin America, these three are dealt with in separate chapters, but so far as South Korea is concerned they are best dealt with as integral parts of the discussion. It is interesting that part of the material I now use is based on a doctoral dissertation by Lee Jae Bum undertaken at the Fuller Theological Seminary School of World Mission, and therefore coming out of the 'scientific church-growth' perspective.

Lee Jae Bum sets his own question paper: 'Why is the rate of growth of the Protestant churches five times greater than the growth of the Korean population? Why are churches with Pentecostal distinctives becoming increasingly more effective in drawing Koreans into the churches?'[17] He mentions the various circumstances already referred to, including the importance of evangelization of the family and carried out through the family web, and he goes on to stress the relationship of rapid church–growth to the extraordinary economic expansion, the urbanization – and the dislocation, of the 1960s and 1970s. Christian expansion and economic expansion went hand in hand (though the nature of the connection is mediated rather than direct). He then states his main objective, which is to show that the strength of the surge in Christianity, its extra thrust, can be attributed to distinctive characteristics of Pentecostalism which also happen to be incorporated in the super-churches. Five of these churches provide the core of his analysis, one Pentecostal, one Presbyterian, one Methodist, one Baptist and one Holiness. Each church it the largest in its denomination. (He mentions on p. 9 his own experience of healing and subsequent ministry at the Antioch Church founded originally by his wife.)

Dr Lee then traces a historical genealogy of Pentecostalism concluding with John Wesley and Edward Irving (of the Catholic Apostolic Church), and proceeding from there to three events: the Topeka, Kansas, revival of 1901 (which led to the Azusa St, Los Angeles Revival), the Wonsan, Korea, revival of 1903 and the Welsh Revival of 1904. The key to further Pentecostal outpourings in Korea was apparently found at a meeting of Methodist and Presbyterian missionaries at Pyongyang in 1907. In five years from 1906 to 1910 the net gain to the churches was nearly 80,000 persons, more than the total number of Christians in Japan after fifty years of Protestant work. It seems the influential figure at this time was Pastor Sun Joo Kil, who represented the Princeton rationalistic fundamentalism then dominant in conservative Presbyterianism.

During the period of Japanese occupation 1910–1945 Lee Jae Bum mentions the concurrence of the independence movement and Christianity and suggests that many Koreans expressed their hostility to the Japanese by becoming Christians. The political complexities of this period are dealt with below in relation to politics, but a major issue in the 1930s was Japanese insistence on worship at Shinto shrines. (It may be recollected that several Pentecostal pastors in Japan lost their lives following refusal to comply with this demand.)

Pentecostalism proper came to Korea in 1928 with the arrival of Miss Mary C. Rumsey, who had taken part in the Los Angeles Revival. She and a Salvation Army secretary, Hong Hur, established the first Pentecostal Church in 1933. However, expansion was slow all through this difficult period of the World War and the Korean War. By 1953 some eight churches with 500 members in all came to constitute the Assemblies of God in Korea; and in 1961 revival rallies were held. It seems that the turning point for Pentecostalism did not arrive till 1973, and that around about this time the Full Gospel Church became a focus of growing Pentecostal dynamism.

By 1982 Pentecostal churches made up the third largest Protestant body in Korea with nearly half a million members, compared to 885,650 Methodists and 4,302,950 Presbyterians. They had experienced a decadal growth rate of 742 per cent compared to a Presbyterian growth rate of 135 per cent and a Methodist growth rate of 130 per cent. They were in seven different groups, though over half belonged to the Assemblies of God. Several mammoth non-Pentecostal evangelistic rallies, including a vast rally with Billy Graham, were held over this period, and at these Pentecostals came into contagious contact with other evangelical Christians. Lee Jae Bum concludes that the Pentecostal emphasis now affects most Protestant Christians in Korea.

Lee Jae Bum offers a familiar comparison between the kind of concern for the poor found in Pentecostalism and the 'option for the poor' exercised in Minjung theology. The one locates evil in the spiritual world, the other in structures. Pentecostals and exponents of Minjung theology mean rather different things by 'liberty to the captives' and 'jubilee'. The Pentecostal emphasis in Korea is really to see 'the Kingdom' both future *and* present in the signs of the Kingdom, especially healing and the 'baptism of the Spirit'. Unlike some of the older evangelicals they are not pessimistic, but want the kingdom *now*.

What then are the 'distinctives' (meaning by that the distinct characteristics) which Lee Jae Bum cites as helping on the special growth of Pentecostalism? He shows, first of all, the roots of all Protestants in preparation through the Sunday school, and indicates that the majority share a conservative Biblicism. He also describes their emphasis on prayer, including 'loud prayer' and prayer all night and in the early morning. 'Specifically exorcisms, healings, and miracles prominently occur in the growing churches of Korea.'[18] 'Furthermore, Korean pastors occupy positions of strong authority by means of their preaching and administration of their church.'[19] They do not act merely as 'enablers'. Also, many lay people are trained for their work and give a great deal in time and money. Every church has its own cell groups, which act as sources of mutual help in sickness or other adversity. The home cell is the centre of church activity. Social services are encouraged, such as collecting rice and clothing, and maintaining orphanages, kindergartens, widows' homes and homes for the elderly. Above all, church leaders establish *goals* as a strategy to encourage growth.

Lee Jae Bum cites some unusual statistics with regard to a minister well known for his emphasis on exorcism. It appears that since 1961 this minister has raised seven people from the dead, three of them before their funerals. This would certainly be a potent source of growth and popularity. Apart from that, he cast out demons from 400,000 people, fifty-nine of whom were crippled. Maybe Christianity itself began in a similar manner.

Lee Jae Bum concludes by making some useful points about the class background of those who belong to the five super-churches. They are, it seems, middle-class churches, with the exceptions of Sung Rak Baptist Church and Central Evangelical Church, which are lower middle-class. It appears that four out of the five pastors have experienced Pentecostal healing. It is also the case that the church with the fastest rate of growth, Sung Rak Baptist, lays stress on casting out demons. Lee Jae Bum relates this once again to the animistic tradition in Korea, and even cites one source as declaring that Christianity made the greatest impact 'out of the purely animistic area of Korea'. By contrast Pentecostal prophecy is less in evidence.

Specific Issues

Women

It is now appropriate to discuss the role and status of women. That is a major focus of this study and what appears here should be related to material in chapter 9 in particular to the work of Elizabeth Brusco. Here I rely on an article by Yi Hyo-Jae, Professor of Sociology at Ewha Women's University in Seoul, supplemented by comments supplied by Dr Chung.[20] Ewha Women's University is itself a piece of relevant evidence, since it was the first such university in Korea and grew out of a Christian girls' school.

Yi Hyo-Jae surveys a scene in which two things are clear. One is the role of Christianity in 'enlightening' Korean women; the other is the fact that Christian women, who constitute 70 per cent of the church, do not share proportionately in its operations and governance.

Before the modern period, women in Korea kept the family in being, biologically and as a day-to-day working unit. When Christianity arrived there was an enthusiastic response from women and they were catalysts in the revivals at the beginning of the century. The foreign missionaries tended to see the 'helplessness' of Korean women as deriving from their shamanistic practices, and their preaching offered women a salvation which would include the whole family. Once converted, Korean women came to play a prominent role in evangelization, working alongside women missionaries. The Women's Home Mission Society, founded as early as 1897, was in fact the first organized women's movement and Christian women were prominent among those who demonstrated against concubinage. Naturally the experience gained in these organizations and movements opened their eyes to new possibilities and to the different place of women in Western society. But they did not imbibe much by way of a platform of reform from their colleagues and mentors. The main effect derived from Christianity was due to the longer-term consequences of Christian schooling.

Women, nevertheless, did become self-conscious, and also conscious of the humiliation of their country. They took on more responsible roles in the church, much more so among the Methodists than the Presbyterians. So far as their hopes for Korea were concerned, the 1920s and 1930s were times when their union of faith with patriotic fervour had become very dangerous. Many restricted their activities to an apolitical Pietism and most felt obliged to conform to the Japanese demand that they offer worship at Shinto shrines. Even after the war and right up into the sixties, no substantial advance was discernible in the position of women. In this period Christian women's movements tended rather to defend the status quo. Then in the 1970s the wave of modernization in every sphere resulted in the diversification of evangelical activities, which involved women taking up posts in social work but not really acquiring novel capacities. Eventually, however, the increasing tempo of repression in Korean society during the 1960s and 1970s did involve women in 'various movements for democratization and humanization',[21] covering economic problems, women's issues, human rights and the nuclear question. In short, two things have happened: the creation of important roles for women, though these are ultimately subordinate to male roles, and the participation of women in the general current of rising social and political protest against a society devoted wholeheartedly to wealth creation. Perhaps this new consciousness may reflect a very general feature of Christian action in Korea, which is the transmission of whatever shifts are taking place in United States society.

Politics

Something further and more specific has to be said about the relationship of Christianity to political life in Korea, since it provides the essential background to Christian expansion and also offers clues for understanding the relationship of Christianity to Korean economic life.

As has been pointed out earlier, the initial expansion of Christianity stemmed from a collapse of Korean society, accelerated by the Japanese victory over the Russians (seen as a triumph of Western arms), and also by the Dong Hak peasant revolt. Christianity arrived with an aura of emancipation for commoners and for women, and it also came to be associated with Korean national aspirations. As a result a large number of Christians were to be found among those thirty-three nationalist leaders who signed the declaration of independence in 1919. The churches found themselves providing a network of communications for nationalist agitation, and the YMCA in particular served as a base for the independence movement.

However, many of the church leaders, and most of the US missionaries, were embarrassed by a youthful Korean militancy, which included violence as well as demonstrations. Some analysts have suggested that the concentration of the missionaries on revivals was in part undertaken as an alternative to political involvement. Certainly, the missionaries feared expulsion and an attempt by the Japanese physically to extirpate the church. They emphasized peace and reconciliation and also went so far in dissociating the church from political agitation that they were accused of adopting the role of quislings. In adopting this approach not only were they reflecting an apolitical and pietist tradition, but were influenced also by American geopolitical calculations which, at that time, favoured cooperation with Japan at the expense of the Korean nationalists. As in Latin America the Protestant emphasis on personal and political peaceability lost them considerable prestige with the male militants.

After Korea was liberated from the Japanese an abrasive struggle arose between the pro-Japanese pastors, who had been part of a church forcibly united by the Japanese, and other pastors who felt very strongly about the disgrace involved in consenting to Shinto worship and who wished to return to their denominational loyalties. (A parallel struggle occurred inside Japan itself.) Mostly the pro-Japanese stayed in control but at the expense of multiple schisms.

Meanwhile, two events had reinforced a turn to a purely inward piety strongly linked to anti-communism. One was the Korean War, as already indicated, and the arrival of Christians displaced from North Korea. The other was the arrival in power of many of the militant nationalists of the earlier period, including a Christian President, Syngman Rhee. To be in favour of Syngman Rhee was to favour the US liberators, including their economic system and their religion, and to be intensely anti-communist. As the Syngman Rhee policy was continued under the Park regime and, indeed, extended to encourage the participation of Japanese multinationals alongside US business, many students and intellectuals became increasingly alienated. Out of this political turmoil and the cultural chaos of Korea emerged yet further divisions. Many hundreds of thousands took refuge in sectarian groups, particularly the Pentecostals. There they sought a definition for the self and a network of communal support. These groups fitted well with the surrounding culture. They picked up the utilitarian tradition of Korean shamanism, and also expressed some of the age-old Korean respect for authority, especially bureaucratic authority. At the same time, they sought after prosperity and material blessings. Indeed, they mirrored the economic system in several ways, in their competitive spirit, in their quest for bigness and in the way they were stratified. A pastor at one end of the scale might earn $25,000 a year, another at the other end might earn less than $1,000.

A number of people in this sector of Korean Protestantism offered tacit or open support to the government. Park Chung-Hee himself sponsored the ecclesiastical career of Billy Kim, director of the Korean Campus Crusade for Christ, and this politico-religious partnership apparently sponsored evangelical crusades in the Korean army. Presidential prayer breakfasts were convened on the American model and two of the largest evangelical rallies ever were held in 1973 and in 1974.

On the other side were the advocates of 'Minjung theology' and an increasingly radicalized Catholic Church. These groups probably formed a minority among Christians and were allied with those, especially students and production workers, who felt most strongly their exclusion from the political process. This alliance emerged originally out of protests against the humiliating terms of the Korean–Japanese treaty and the inroads of Japanese business. The focus of dissent was located in the Korean National Council of Churches and in a human rights committee set up by the Council in 1974.

As to the Catholic Church, it was itself split. Some people belonged to an older Catholic political tradition and/or had been traumatized by the Korean War with its mass expulsions of Christians from the North. Others were members of the Korean CIA and/or had regional or family ties with the regime. The Catholic Church itself had changed from a small rural ghetto to a community with urban roots growing rapidly through the fifties and sixties. Its new membership, and especially its younger clergy, were no longer quiescent. As early as 1972 Cardinal Kim had issued a warning to President Park at the Midnight Mass of the Nativity in Myongdong Cathedral. Perhaps the real mobilization of the Catholic community came about with the arrest of Bishop Tji, and a major confrontation occurred in 1976 when the Catholic Church joined with the National Council of Churches in issuing a 'Declaration for Democratic National Salvation'. Soon after that, Kim Dae-jung, a Catholic and one of the two best-known leaders of the opposition, was arrested. Confrontation has continued intermittently ever since, with the church and the NCC (National Council of Churches) relying on international connections and American public opinion to protect them from the more severe forms of repression. In this context, the Catholic Church has revived a memory of martyrdom which stretches back some two centuries in Korea, and combined it with the methods of modern mass protest.[22]

One further element in the politico-religious mix remains to be identified and, as with all the othrs, it relates to Korean national aspirations and a deep and depressed sense of sad indignity (*han*) engendered by centuries of Chinese and latterly Japanese domination. Koreans have so often been losers and desire so much to be winners, as their performances at the Olympics indicated. The new religious movements grow in the context of folk beliefs which see Koreans as a chosen people and look for the coming of a True Man who shall establish a holy capital in a land of peace and safety. Plainly, the experience of Korea at a junction of stronger and more powerful civilizations has an overlap with that of Israel and has produced a similar response. Also, part of the continuing Korean religion is the 'Eastern Teaching', which is an immanental, this-worldly doctrine. Followers of the 'Eastern Teaching' were against the corruption of the old dynasty and also opposed to the Japanese.[23]

There are many syncretistic groups emerging from such traditions and they run parallel to the numerous splinter groups in South Africa as well as the Iglesia na Cristo in the Philippines. The Unification Church is just one such and combines elements from the Presbyterian background of its leader with spiritism and an eschatology in which Korea and a Korean Messiah figure prominently. The Unification Church also represents a strong orientation towards the USA and has been accused of fostering connections with the Korean CIA and right-wing groups in the USA.

Economic Life

In discussing now the relationship of religion, and of Christianity in particular, to economic development in Korea, some initial account must be taken of the broader question about the relationship between Confucianism and economic development all over East and South-East Asia. Whereas Weber regarded Confucianism as not conducive to economic dynamism and entrepreneurial initiative, some modern commentators have reversed his position and see in the Confucian ethic an East Asian 'functional equivalent' for ascetic Protestantism. In arguing this case they have necessarily emphasized the role of culture in creating a significant context for the rise of capitalism. Of course, they do not suppose that any culture, Confucian or otherwise, can of itself create a favourable context for economic development, only that it may be relatively receptive and help along the tide of change when the right set of conditions are present. Other commentators play down the role of culture altogether and do not think much is to be gained by contemplating the effect of so general and (in their view) so passive a variable. They lay stress rather on the right set of institutions and correct economic policies. They emphasize that these have the further advantage of being manipulable.

If you pay any attention at all to cultural factors, as the present author certainly does, two points need to be made with respect to the role of Confucianism and, more particularly, its role in Korea. Certain elements in the Confucian ethic do at least assist economic advance. These elements are to be found in an attitude which focuses on this world and in an emphasis on orderliness, discipline, respectfulness and group solidarity. At the same time, the mandarin mentality is concerned primarily with a scholarly and gentlemanly appreciation of the classics rather than practicality or commerce. That means that the most helpful kind of Confucianism has to be one which has undergone transmutation, so that, for example, the gentleman scholar or bureaucrat has been transformed into the knowledgeable and practical technocrat.

The second point applies more specifically to Korea, and it requires some recapitulation of points made earlier. Confucianism in Korea became associated with the corruptions of the Yi dynasty and with the overbearing influence of China. It belonged, as has been pointed out, to a decrepit system about to lose power and legitimacy before the impact of the Western technology. Paradoxically, this Western impact was channelled, in part, through Japan, and Japan was, after all, a country with an Eastern tradition. So one might think the example of Japan could have restored the prestige of Eastern traditions in general. However, Japan was the least Confucian of Eastern nations and, more importantly, was the current oppressor of Korea.

Korea, then, lay beteen two Eastern powers, each more – or less – Confucian, but both of them were regarded as inhibiting Korean national aspirations. In other words, as suggested already, this was a situation where the intrusive Western power, in this case the USA, was defined as much less intrusive than other Eastern powers. Indeed, the USA could be seen as relatively sympathetic to Korean aspirations, in spite of some intermittently hostile geopolitical gyrations, and the whole US package of economic dynamism, progress, egalitarianism – and the Protestant religion – could be welcomed by many forward-looking Koreans as good for them and good for Korea. This is pretty well the limit of the association of Protestantism with economic advance in Korea. It was the forward party of US influence in general, transmitted most effectively through missionaries and their educational institutions.

Hence, Kim Kyong-Dong in his discussion of this whole issue of religion and economic development in Korea,[24] locates the primary impact of Protestantism precisely at this early period. Insofar as other commentators, for example Gill Hyun Mo, attribute any weight to the religious aspect, they also refer to this early period. Gill Hyun Mo suggests (in a private interview with Kim Hwan) that when Christianity spread about a century ago, initially around Pyongyang, and the north-western provinces generally, its adherents were more industrious and better off. However, this was not a time of major industrialization, and the Japanese during their occupation were not interested in encouraging a Korean development to rival their own.[25] Presumably the main channels of mobility in the quasi-class system established by the Japanese were either the schools set up by them or else the schools set up by the Americans.

Kim Kyong-Dong sees no special connection between the expansion of Protestantism and the Korean economic take-off in the 1960s, even though both occurred with remarkable rapidity at the same time.[26] What one has to say is that this dual expansion of the 1960s was in itself also related to complex influences derived in important measure from America, whether or nor we are dealing with the cultural radiation which emanates in a general way from the powerful Protestant culture of the USA. That, of course, is a problem present in varying degrees throughout the whole discussion in Latin America as well as in Korea.

The expulsion of the Japanese opened up a new era of development for Korea and for Christianity. Here again some recapitulation is necessary to provide background for the economic issue. Two elements were crucial. One was the inward-looking revivalism which had been a concomitant of Japanese repression and the other was a legacy of militaristic thinking. The egalitarian and emancipatory motif in Protestantism had been severely attenuated during the Japanese period, and the mentality of many Koreans, including Christians, combined Confucian reverence for authority with the effects of Japanese education and training. During and after the war from 1948 to 1951, South Koreans had to rely on the military for survival and to serve in the army. They lived, and still live, with a siege mentality. During this formative period for the new Korea, ties with the USA were close, and Korea was dependent on US economic aid. Koreans gained experience of American culture from the US army and later many went to study in US universities. It is symptomatic of the nature of these ties with the USA that those Koreans who migrated there were and are disproportionately Christian.

After the Korean War, Protestantism was part of the link between the US government and the authoritarian regimes of Syngman Rhee and Park. That also bears on the question of economic development and Protestantism. These regimes placed economic advance before due democratic process, and for that purpose relied on a combination of Protestant quietism and those long-term elements in the Korean psyche which accepted authority provided it showed some (modest) paternalistic concern and, above all, gave evidence of success. Protestant fundamentalism helped prevent the political system from blowing up, thereby illustrating again one of the classic contentions of Halévy with regard to Methodism and revolution in England. It also joined forces with all those elements in Korea which sought mobility and rising material standards. If Protestants were not marked out as *more* successful than other people, they nevertheless enthusiastically joined in the frenetic search after prosperity. Most Koreans cared more for bread than for votes, and many of them found even a rising gap between rich and poor tolerable provided at least the poor were somewhat better off. The results of such single-mindedness were startling in terms of GNP, of changes in social structure, and of a vast migration to the cities. What the expanding fundamentalist churches offered was a hope, a therapy, a community – and a network. They fended off chaos and anomie. In the end some Christians also returned to the liberating and emancipatory theme, but that has already been discussed.

Some of the churches also partook of the utilitarian spirit of traditional shamanism, which again bears on the economic issue. Peter Berger has drawn attention to the utilitarian attitude towards the gods themselves in 'low' Confucianism.[27] If they do not deliver they are demoted. The Christian 'Spirit' in the eyes of devotees did deliver in terms of health and wealth, and He was therefore promoted. The Korean religious scene, Christian or otherwise, was one of rivalrous syncretism and pragmatic adaptability, thereby paralleling what was happening in the economic sphere. Given that religion did not *cause* the economic 'miracle', it certainly developed in parallel style and offered its own miracles. It may also be that the variety of religious firms on the market helped along a general climate of pragmatic adaptability. Kim Kyong-Dong has suggested that the underlying element in fostering Korean development is not Confucianism or Christianity, nor even Confucian/Christian shamanism, but the sheer syncretic adaptability found in the folk layer of religion.[28] In that respect Koreans like the Japanese, are absorbent; they encompass everything gainful as need arises.

In just one other respect Christianity offered an acceptable mode of stabilization and that is with respect to exorcizing the layer of the Korean psyche infected by *han* – rancorous grievance. As Koreans groped for personal and group self-definition, Christianity offered a means of self-expression and release, as well as an emphasis on peaceability rather than violence. After centuries of oppression and emotional and material impoverishment, some channels of peaceable effervescence were at last open, and Koreans could begin to redefine themselves as new men and even more as new women.

The Korean experience is, in certain respects, the obverse of the

Japanese; in other respects the two societies are very similar. Some brief comparison may be useful. The Japanese are the imperial nation for whom the Americans were rivals, and the Koreans are the colonized nation for whom the Americans were liberators. Japanese culture was protected by insularity; Korean culture was devastated by peninsularity. To be an island is much safer than to be a peninsula – or a bridge. What the Japanese were forced to accept from the Americans was a democratic polity; what the Koreans more or less took freely from the Americans were cultural elements which included Conservative Protestantism. Both cultures are very absorbent and blend whatever arrives from elsewhere with pre-existing elements, and that includes new religions. Christianity has been reshaped in the image of Korean shamanism, and it has also been incorporated in the Japanese '*wa*', the system of discreet 'harmonization'.[29]

Both cultures have salvaged their structures of local community and taken them into the industrial age. In the Japanese case the salvage operation has been undertaken both by the industrial corporate community and the neo-Buddhist groups. In the Korean case the salvage operation has been undertaken more by the Christian churches and not so much by the neo-Buddhist groups.

And here, of course, we arrive at the religious difference; and it becomes reasonable to suggest that the services undertaken by neo-Buddhist groups in Japanese culture are undertaken in Korea by the Christian churches. The defeated imperial culture of Japan gave birth to the new groupings that the new situation required out of its own Buddhist resources. Korea as an ex-colony whose resources were depleted or discredited on account of their alien character absorbed new resources from elsewhere. Of course, the Japanese 'rejection' of Christianity is not so straightforward a rejection as it might seem. Many motifs were borrowed from the Protestant Ethic in the early period of Japanese construction under the Meiji restoration, as Ronald Dore has indicated.[30] And as scholars like Jan Swyngedouw and David Reid have argued, Christianity is included for certain limited purposes within the overall Japanese *wa*.[31] It has also been absorbed through education and through the influence of the displaced samurai who were among the early converts. That influence extends to a sizeable segment of Japanese society, especially in the upper reaches of education. But the dramatic contrast remains between a Korean recovery, in which Christianity more and more largely figures, and a Japanese recovery, where it is kept more firmly at the margin than in almost any other East Asian society.

The Further Parallel: South Africa

It remains now to explore one further area of suggestive comparison. Clearly, Pentecostalism is making inroads in many parts of Africa, for example, Ghana and Nigeria, but current and usable information is available to the author only with respect to South Africa. South Africa attracts interest because it exhibits an Afrikaaner culture with a 'covenant' background and an American egalitarian potential which has gone tragically awry through adverse circumstances.

I repeat that South Africa, more specifically Afrikaanerdom, had the kind of religious resources which helped make the USA, and formed part of the original American 'charter'. In that respect it resembles Ulster, which not only had those resources but also contributed manpower to the American Revolution and still retains close cultural ties with parts of the United States. South Africa (again like Ulster) has lacked the vast 'open' space which America could utilize for the realization of its ideal. Given empty space, Afrikaanerdom might have created a variant of American society. It is, in fact, confronted with numerical majorities which ensure that it takes up an offensive–defensive posture to retain its racial privileges. South Africa is the more determined to retain these given that it has already experienced a trauma of dislodgement in the time of the Great Trek. Ulster, too, is still working through its trauma of dislodgement. So, in observing this American style of religion 'take off' in South Africa, one observes a fresh 'input' of American religious material, retaining important elements of egalitarianism, yet tuned to the apolitical preferences of a population feeling its moral and political isolation.[32]

In my comments I rely in particular on material assembled by Karla Poewe and, Irving Hexham, but I also use critical comment by Elda S. Morran and Lawrence Schlemmer. Karla Poewe draws attention both to the founding of huge black independent churches some decades ago and the contemporary emergence of white independent churches out of stirrings in the mid-sixties. In the heart of the city, or in the new, spacious and affluent dormitory townships surrounding them are emerging charismatic super-churches parallel to those in São Paulo and Seoul. 'Here', she says, 'the young and middle aged, from the middle and upper classes, go through the emotional turmoil of leaving the old and embracing the new. This drama is replete with prophecy and weeping, with repentance and hope, with victory and celebration'.[33] Not only does this involve greater sensitivity to one's environment and grasping new opportunities, whether for interaction or entrepreneurship, but also reaching out to non-whites in education or in multiracial pastoral teams or in crusades to Indian, coloured and black townships. In the view of Karla Poewe and Irving Hexham, this represents a beginning of detribalization for the Afrikaaner and a crossing of boundaries.

The main interest of Poewe and Hexham was in studying the ministers and ministries of these churches as they are currently found in Durban, Johannesburg and Pretoria (and in making some comparison with much smaller manifestations in Canada). The ministers were mainly people who had left successful secular careers and they were now redeploying their skills and personal assets in building up successful religious enterprises. The nine biggest churches studied each attracted between 1,000 and 5,000 persons to a Sunday service. Most of these churches use English, even though they include large numbers and sometimes a majority of Afrikaaners. They exist within a loose structure provided by three umbrella groups, the International Fellowship of Christian Churches, the Relating Churches, and the Christian Fellowship International.[34]

So far as politics are concerned, these churches mostly aim to work at the cultural level by showing rather than speaking. They create open and/or integrated congregations and multiracial leadership and the vast majority of their members are in favour of removing the groups areas. Each church tends to concentrate on a particular area, music or art or science or business. All the churches are superbly organized, one on the model of the Full Gospel Central Church in Seoul.

As in Korea there is emphasis on prolonged prayer and also on what is called 'travailling' and on weeping. This is seen as part of a dependence on the Spirit. There is also an emphasis on the coming of 'the Kingdom', a concern with coincidences in God's plan, offers and experiences of healing, and an element of the gospel of prosperity.

Karla Poewe suggests that such churches prosper where there are volatile economies or major social traumas, and where there are transient congregations of diverse denominational and socio-economic backgrounds. They are geared to handle depression, disillusion and anxiety. They derive from roots in a poor man's Pentecostalism which has been transmogrified to include a middle-class charismatic movement. They also offer a release which is associated with a shift to an oral culture and to stories which assist the rediscovery of immediacy and enable the individual to reconstruct his biography within an aura of hope. The atmosphere created by churches in this tradition is literally 'spirited' and tends to affirm love, life, health and abundance rather than to dwell on inadequacies. It also seems that this affirmative atmosphere is one that can assist women who are going through difficult experiences and/or are managing single-parent families. In that respect there are parallels with what was noticed in the Pentecostal (and other) churches of Jamaica.

What Karla Poewe and Irving Hexham offer is an enthusiastic account of movements which affect some 35 per cent of the total population and plainly represent an opening from the side of the white majority. They are genuinely integrated. However, there is another viewpoint, as always in this area, and one which criticizes the reliance of these churches on subjective rather than structural change and their belief in the efficacy of peaceful means. A critical account is to be found in *Faith for the Fearful? An Investigation into New Churches in the Greater Durban Area* by E. S. Morran and L. Schlemmer.[35]

This investigation suggests that members of the 'new churches' are in lucrative but relatively insecure occupations, and also without any clear political home. The members are inclined to submit to those in authority and are politically more conservative than people in the mainline churches. One sign of this conservatism is that they believe they are doing enough if their services are multiracial; perhaps another sign is that they accept the gospel of prosperity. 'New church' members clearly appreciate the services they attend and are attracted by the clear, unambiguous leads they are given. An intriguing finding is that not only members of the new churches but also people in the mainline churches believe there is too much political comment from the pulpit.

In their comments summarizing their overall impression, the authors suggest that the mainline churches can retain the commitment of their members only if they are given genuine fellowship, especially in informal groups based on the home. They should offer more and demand more, and seek out the anxieties brought about by the current situation. They also need to be less hesitant about criticizing the new churches.

At the same time, these new churches

> are not small eccentric sects getting on with their business in small derelict halls. They are attracting enormous numbers of converts ranging from film stars to politicians, sportspeople and ordinary people in all the major cities of South Africa. The popular media, although often critical of the new churches, has tended to concentrate on their more sensational aspects: healing, glossolalia, being slain in the spirit and cash flowing.[36]

The authors conclude that these churches 'are tailor-made to suit the needs of guilty consumers',[37] and offer instant consumer gratification.

They help lessen the traditional gap between Christianity and consumer capitalism.

Perhaps the conclusion which follows from the discussion of South Korea and South Africa has to pinpoint the common element of very rapid social change and considerable threat. So much is obvious, and does not offer anything new to our understanding. It is more important to observe the specificity of the conditions in each case: a rising group in an authoritarian society, and a group in an authoritarian society which has quite a lot to lose. In each society the new churches reflect the authoritarian structure around them. They also create structures which are in some ways parallel to what is found in the economic sphere. Whereas the Protestant Ethic was once supposed to assist business, in these cases the business ethos helps reconstruct the churches with efficient organization and undeniable consumer gratification. On the one hand they ameliorate some of the problems of their respective societies by breaking down barriers and providing secure orientations which assuage anomie. On the other hand they easily assimilate to the norms of consumer capitalism and defuse fundamental attacks on the social order. Of course, how you evaluate that depends on how you evaluate consumer capitalism.

PART IV

Re-formations

Chapter 9

New Spiritual Communications: Healings and Tongues; Songs and Stories

Evangelicalism, and more particularly its Pentecostal variant, is a system of communication. It has to do with 'signs' both in the sense utilized by the fashionable science of semiology and in the sense used by Pentecostals themselves i.e. 'signs – and wonders'. These signs form part of a complete 'field' which is integrated around the key notion of transformation. The distinctive signals of transformation for Pentecostals are speaking in tongues, and testimonies to 'blessings'. That is what happened at the first Pentecost as recounted in the second chapter of Acts and it is what has been recovered in the twentieth century after an intermittent and often underground history within Christianity.

This chapter is given over, therefore, to Pentecostal communication as it is manifested in the healing touch, in ecstatic speech, in stories and testimonies and in music, and also in an atmosphere of participation in which those hitherto voiceless, including women, make their voice heard. The chapter which then follows is concerned with the means and modes of transformation, and that involves some coverage of the outer pattern of conversion and of its inner trajectory as evident in individual biographies.

Multiple Sources: The Ancient and the Modern, the Black and the White

Walter Hollenweger, who is the distinguished doyen of Pentecostal studies, reminds us that this extraordinary, expansive, flexible and vibrant system of communication represents the encounter between a specifically Catholic spirituality mediated through John Wesley and the American holiness tradition, and 'the black spirituality of the former slaves of the United States'.[1] It is the same kind of potent amalgam we find in the union of hymns and spirituals and protest songs which gave rise to the blues and to jazz. It crosses the most ancient layers of 'the spirit' with the most modern manifestations of spirituality, and it amalgamates the traditions of white enthusiasm and mysticism with the traditions of black enthusiasm and mysticism. These potent combinations now express the pains and aspirations, material and spiritual, of hitherto tongue-tied populations in the developed, and above all in the developing, world. The tongue-tied become 'inspirited', which is part of what it means to have your consciousness raised. They speak and sing in what Charles Wesley called 'a thousand tongues'. This ecstatic speech, song and dance, is also related to the recovery of dignity for indigenous languages. Just as the translation of the Bible into English and German (or, for that matter, into Welsh and Finnish) confirmed the secure arrival of those languages, so the translation of the scriptures as well as of 'hymns and spiritual songs' into indigenous languages helps perserve cultures even at the very point when they are being opened up to an intrusive, and corrosive, wider world.

Part of the argument of this book has been concerned with the paradoxes of ancient and modern as they are found in the meeting of imperial Hispanic and 'Anglo' cultures with indigenous cultures and, therefore, with the substrate of an almost universal spiritism. In Africa, in the Americas, even in Europe, there is a shared substrate of the animated and the animistic, both of which are literally synonyms for 'the Spirit' in all its guises. Friedrich Heer, the Austrian historian of ideas, has written about this universal substrate which underlay (say) Catholicism in tenth-century Normandy as much as it still underlies Catholicism in Guatemala, or Calvinism in South Africa, or Protestantism in Korea, or Orthodoxy in Northern Greece, or Islam in the Sudan.[2] It is the kind of inspirited and entranced view of the world discussed by Ioan Lewis in East Africa and which we see within a hair's breadth of our own European consciousness in the work of Keith Thomas and James Obelkevich.[3] The oddity and the power of Pentecostalism resides in its capacity to unite such apparently 'modern' inventions as the encounter group and community-based medicine with ageless techniques of spiritual restoration.

Spiritual Healing: A Case Study in Mexico

The easiest way to gain some initial sense of how these ancient and modern elements combine and how the Pentecostal system of spiritual communication actually works on the ground is to pick on a particular study. For that purpose I am utilizing material collected by Murl Owen Dirksen and presented in 1984 as a Ph.D. dissertation at the University of Tennessee, Knoxville.[4] The dissertation is entitled 'Pentecostal Healing: a Facet of the Personalistic Health System in Pakal-Na, a Village in Southern Mexico'. In this study we see most of the elements which Walter Hollenweger identifies as characterizing Pentecostalism and (in his view) deriving from its original roots in black culture. These are an emphasis on the spoken as much as the written; the 'telling' of faith and giving of testimony through stories; the extension of participation to all, including women; the inclusion of dreams and visions in personal and public worship; and 'an understanding of the body–mind relationship that is informed by experiences of correspondence between body and mind',[5] most strikingly through healing in constant prayer. Having regard to this unity of body and mind, Pentecostalism also attempts to unify individual and community by affirming that healing is a public and communal activity. This is important. Given that Pentecostalism is widely criticized for a dualistic attitude to mind and body, it is interesting that in this context the 'holy ghost' well and truly animates the whole biological 'machine'.

Hollenweger summarizes very eloquently what the study by Dirksen illustrates. 'For them,' he says, 'the medium of communication is, just as in biblical times, not the definition but the description, not the statement but the story, not the doctrine but the testimony, not the book but the parable, not a systematic theology but a song, not the treatise but the television programme, not the articulation of concepts but the celebration of banquets.'[6] Pentecostals are, therefore, in his view, quintessentially a case of the union of ancient and modern, since they combine the pre-literate with the post-literate: Lévy-Bruhl, so to speak, and Marshall McLuhan.

The overall argument as presented by Dirksen is worth summarizing before elements are picked out for emphasis. Dirksen compared the degree of recourse to three different sources of healing – folk, religious and medical – among Pentecostals and non-Pentecostals. It emerged that the Pentecostals were more 'personalistic' than the non-Pentecostals in their search for healing, but 'both groups showed little involvement with traditional curers and both showed high confidence in religious elements including church, prayer, and Bible.[7] Uniquely Pentecostal sources of healing included a dedicated life-style, visions, possession by the Holy Spirit, and the use of sanctified oil. Though non-Pentecostals were better disposed towards modern medicine, the younger and more socially mobile Pentecostals were steadily integrating modern medicine into their personalistic framework. Most Pentecostals cited healing as a reason for joining the congregation, and for about a quarter of them it was the main initial draw. Often they were brought by some member of the family and then the whole family became involved in the church. To enter into church membership meant joining a quasi-familial network of brothers and sisters who would gather round and (literally) touch you in time of sickness or trouble. They would also preserve you from the fear and the isolation of the hospital. What the invocation of the saints is for Catholics, communal healing is for Pentecostals.

Most villagers, whether Pentecostal or not, recognize the evil eye and sorcery as responsible for illness or misfortune, but for Pentecostals the holy spirit, often working through the personal holiness of the pastor, expels or exorcizes the evil spirit. Each year a Pentecostal convention is held on the outskirts of Pakal-Na at which a major service is devoted to healing, which can be viewed as a kind of mass expulsion of evil and ill-health. Some 5,000 people gather at this convention, including many marginal believers and spectators. The press is so great that temporary restaurants are put up to meet their needs.

Dirksen characterizes Pakal-Na as a mestizo area of in-migration, of modernization, and of commercial or industrial growth, and argues that Pentecostalism helps forward adjustment to these changes, even though the rather strict and sectarian atmosphere retards assimilation to the mainstream of modern urban life. In Dirksen's analysis, two other general points emerge. One concerns women. Women have long been accepted in Pentecostal churches as evangelists. Pentecostalism was introduced into Mexico by a woman, who began dozens of churches in Sonora, and 'Pentecostals have offered women roles of unprecedented leadership'.[8] In Pakal-Na the only organizations controlled by women are the Pentecostal women's groups. Moreover, groups of Pentecostal women move freely about the community seeking health, or themselves becoming healers. As such they are crucial to understanding the search for health in Pentecostalism.

The other point bears on social mobility. In Dirksen's view Pentecostals are not the well-off or the poor but 'appear slightly more prosperous than the general population of their community'.[9] Almost twice as many among Pentecostals have relatively expensive concrete roofs as among the rest of the people in Pakal-Na. This 'aspiration' within the Pentecostal community is, in their view, literally impelled by the Spirit, but in two significantly different modes. 'Traditional Pentecostals consider God's spirit to be a functional power providing subsistence in a "daily bread" fashion, while more progressive Pentecostals view spirit possession as a means of achieving the good life so that "daily bread" prayers become unnecessary.'[10] What is promoted by their faith is an inclusive definition of 'the good life': betterment.

The elements of main interest in Dirksen's ethnography relate to healing and to worship: the tactile and the vocal aspects of Pentecostal communication. Pentecostal healers lay on hands and anoint with oil. They fast; and they engage in constant communal prayer around the sick, both in church and in the home. At the same time, they offer practical assistance. Pentecostals identify more than one source of sickness. 'They often recognize an immediate naturalistic cause, but they also believe that a spiritual cause ultimately lies behind the illness.'[11] This may lie in personal evil or demonic powers. Cures are never complete beyond relapse until open testimony is given to the efficacy of faith.

Sometimes the understanding of sickness includes a magical aspect. Thus the Bible can be used as a talisman of spiritual energy, particularly perhaps by those unable to read it. One Pentecostal described how 'I lay down on the cot, and I had my Bible with me. I began to read the Bible and I became sleepy, and I put the Bible on top of me. I went to sleep and the pain was gone when I woke up.' Another Pentecostal described listening to a religious radio programme from Guatemala. 'I put this small jar with oil in it on the radio, and I told [my friend] to put this oil on the sick parts of his body, and to do it every day.'[12] As several other commentators have noted, the Pentecostal methods of healing have one very clear advantage over sorcery and that is the fact that they are free and not calculated to threaten or to frighten.

If healing is participatory and tactile, so worship is participatory and vocal. Whereas the older Protestant denominations stressed literacy, which might turn out to involve a longish process of learning to read, Pentecostals work with the oral tradition, aided sometimes by the visual icons of religious television and the cinema. In Pakal-Na services run from 7 p.m. to 9 p.m., and are preceded by a half-hour or so of cleaning up the building and then of prayer. By the time the service is to begin, a large crowd has gathered and the murmur of passionate prayer resounds even outside the church. For an hour or so singing and prayer alternate.

The repertoire of songs is small because some of the church members are illiterate. The initial songs are simple choruses known by all participants and sung repeatedly while everyone claps to the strong beat emphasized by the guitar player. A single chorus may be sung for as long as ten minutes. The longer the song is sung, the more involved the congregation becomes; and when a particular emotional level is detected by the lay leader, he either enters spontaneously into verbal prayer or directs the congregation to pray with him.[13]

After that a pre-selected group is asked to sing a series of songs and recite scripture. The people are solemnly numbered and their activities during the week duly recorded. There follows the sermon, delivered with verve and authority and punctuated by praise, acclamations and shouts of approval. As the sermon ends the congregation breaks out into loud wailing and prayer, while the pastor moves among them, praying for or with them and laying his hands on them. At the conclusion members move around the church shaking hands and saying 'God bless you'.

Dirksen adds that the style of leadership is extremely authoritarian. This is a very widespread observation. It is similarly argued, for example, by Thornton with respect to situations in Colombia, that if the leadership is not firm and assured, participation falls off and membership becomes static.[14] Such intense participation *depends* on strong leadership. The 'leadership principle' seems fundamental in Latin America, as also in Korea, and to act only as 'enabler' is to ensure ill success. A Pentecostal preacher speaks 'as one having authority and not as one of the scribes'.

Various themes in this account must now be picked up individually, such as those relating to music, tongues, and female participation, but before doing so it is very useful, briefly, to compare the efficacy of Pentecostalism as a system of communication in a Mexican context with the efficacy of a rival movement of the spirit. This is Spiritualism. As has already been indicated, throughout Latin America, above all perhaps in Mexico, Haiti, and Brazil, the signs and wonders of the religion of the Holy Spirit are in competition with the signs and wonders of the world of the spirits. The pastors are rivalled by the mediums. To switch images, both the pastors and the mediums fish in the deep waters of the ageless spirit world and, at the same time, convey intimations of modernity.

Rivals in Spiritual Communication: A Second Case Study in Mexico

According to Kaja Finkler, Spiritualism in Mexico is an 'important health care delivery system',[15] which arose when the country was 'plagued by internal dissension, foreign invasion, and the early inroads of industrialization'.[16] Finkler follows Vivian Garrison's argument concerning Pentecostals to the effect that *within* a given social sector those who become involved are distinguished by their personal experiences, notably, of course, by illness. However, these experiences, of fear and stress, let us say, and/or of chaos, need to be woven into an overall sociological account. Thus the attraction of Spiritualism also springs from its ability to meet demands for social equality through its rituals, and in particular its ability to offer authoritative roles for women. Spiritualism, like Pentecostalism, both protests against the involvement of Catholicism in the social hierarchy *and* supports the status quo, especially the nationalism of established Mexican society. Spiritualism, like the early incursions of Protestantism, was a North American import active in the general atmosphere of liberal reform in the third quarter of the nineteenth century. At this time many liberals embraced Positivism and technology, and whereas Protestantism was associated in a more general way with progress, spiritualism was associated with currents of para-scientific thought which claimed there was positive evidence for communication with discarnate spirits. This current affected many parts of Latin America, above all Brazil. But in Mexico it became attached to a certain Father Elias of mixed Indian and Hispanic-Jewish descent, who proclaimed himself incarnate 'de Spiritu Sancto' and proceeded to inaugurate the Age of the Spirit in the manner set out in the millennial prophecies of the Abbot Joachim. In this last Age of the Spirit, God speaks directly to His people face to face, and it is the mediums who are the 'radio transmitters' of the message. That, in itself, is fascinating since it provides an analogy with the way the Protestant pastors mediate the abolition of mediation.

In the original direct transmissions from God twenty-two commandments were 'irradiated', including prohibitions against alcohol, abandoning one's children, and taking up arms against brother Mexicans. In time Mexico emerged as the New Jerusalem to which 'all nations should come'. The parallel with Protestant moral emphases is very clear: the central evils are drink, violence and family instability.

The rituals of Spiritualism are just as significant as the commandments and operate in a very ordered format. The more developed adepts sit closest to the podium and others are seated in turn as they arrive further and further away. Kaja Finkler adds that 'Spiritualists evince regularity and order not only in their irradiation ceremony but also during daily ritual activities.'[17] Tuesdays and Fridays are dedicated to healing the sick, and the sick are recommended to listen to the divine irradiations as part of the cure. Though Spiritualism originally attracted a rather loose band of dissidents, it now comprises an alternative hierarchy, with the mother temple (or 'womb') in Mexico City at the pinnacle. Each subordinate temple must have a head, who is frequently a woman.

Some further observations by Finkler bear closely on the comparison with Pentecostalism which is our chief concern. First, Spiritualists complained that services in the Catholic Church were 'disordered' and gossipy in such a way that they felt derided for their overall stance and their presentation of themselves. Thus the equality which the Pentecostals achieved by vigorously controlled but expressive participation was achieved among the Spiritualists by sheer steadiness, order and regularity. Second, males who become *adherents* are often seeking a way to side-step the obligatory machismo of Mexican society. They stop drinking, which is economically advantageous; and for their wives there is the distinct benefit of a husband who now treats them decently, has stopped wandering, and does not beat them up. Third, most adherents are recruited because of illness, and in the course of seeking a spiritual cure they bring their relatives along with them (or alternatively it is the relatives who bring them). Thus Spiritualists, like Pentecostals, are recruited in families and along networks of relatives.

The next point of significant comparison with Pentecostalism relates to the adamant anti-Catholicism of both groups, expressed in a negative attitude to almost all Catholic practices and feasts. Both movements are the reverse of Catholicism, formed by negation: in a word, Protest-ant. What Catholics make concrete Spiritualists make abstract, so that candles become irradiations. Mediators of all kinds, such as the saints and the Virgin, are repudiated as part and parcel of the social-cum-spiritual hierarchy. What has to be emphasized here is that spirit*ism* is integrated in folk-Catholicism or what some call 'Christo-paganism', whereas Spirit*ualism* is definitely outside the Catholic ambit. Spiritism retains the fear of evil spirits; Spiritualism overcomes it. This needs to be cross-referenced against the situation in Brazil where spiritism used to be more or less integrated into folk Catholicism, but is now increasingly attacked by reformist Catholics and, therefore, begins to emerge in massive non-Catholic cults.

However, although Spiritualism as a system of dissident communication is defined over against Catholicism and over against the general notions and realities of mediation and hierarchy, the countervailing power of the Spirit does not build up into cohesive political potency. Direct individual interaction with spiritual power fragments any cohesion that could arise, even more so than in Pentecostalism. God elects not to improve His people's lot, and their devotion of time and money to His service even detracts somewhat from their economic advancement. The one clear exception to this is the temple head. For her, and occasionally for him, the temple 'affords a modicum of social mobility'.[18] Here we have a very clear parallel with Pentecostalism in that the pastors provide the clearest evidence of social mobility. Both movements, then, are systems of signs for providing what counts as unmediated communication to the voiceless and by the voiceless. Speech, at least, is direct and equal and approximates to Habermas's notion of untrammelled 'communicative competence' within the limited enclave. This equality of communication is, as pointed out earlier, realized in the biological family as well as in the quasi-family of the faith. In that sense Finkler argues that Spiritualism is highly 'adaptive' with regard to the situation of the nuclear family in an industrializing society. The parallel with all the evidence on Pentecostalism is obvious. The general point about family cohesion and the status of women will be reinforced by further evidence about specifically Pentecostal practice given below.

It remains only to note that Spiritualists tend to be persons who have a lengthy experience of wage labour migration, enjoy limited interaction with immediate neighbours, and are probably not integrated into the national political structure through the programmes of land reform. Crucially, however, and perhaps to some extent consequent on their itinerant status, Spiritualists have been differentially exposed to major emotional and physical traumas. Thus we may say that in almost every respect Spiritualists run parallel with Pentecostalists, except that their provision for release and for expression of 'power' is in a less dramaturgical mode.

Communication in Tongues: A Third Case Study in Mexico

We turn now from significant comparisons of Pentecostalism with a potent rival 'in the spirit' to examine the unique distinguishing mark of Pentecostal communication, which is speaking in tongues. It will be recollected that this specific 'note' of Pentecost was in the Book of the

Acts a sign of universal communication reversing the misunderstandings of Babel. It was a recovery of spirit and a voice by those previously voiceless and dispirited. The technical question as to what kind of 'other' language it represents is thus quite secondary. Speaking positivistically one can reasonably say, with Hine, that to participate in glossolalia significantly changes personal attitudes and social behaviour, affects cognitive organization and emphasizes the break with the non-Pentecostal world. However, this is only a redescription in more clinical terms of what Pentecostals claim in their own theological terminology. It does give rise, of course, to an issue which cannot be discussed here, which is whether this 'ecstasy' is a breakthrough to a higher unitive life or a breakdown into baby talk. It will lead quite naturally to the role played by the extra-verbal stimulation of music.

To discuss speaking in 'tongues' I will utilize another Mexican study, that by Felicitas Goodman of Apostolics in the Yucatán.[19] This is particularly interesting in that the ecstasy of the holy spirit, aroused in anticipation of a Second Coming, turned into what came to be regarded as the subtle intervention of the Evil One and then mysteriously tailed away into silence. It thus parallels the famous instance known in the anthropological literature as Vailala Madness; and it also parallels my own recollection of the student movement, which one of my own students at the time enthusiastically characterized as a form of secular Pentecost. This unusual episode in the Yucatan offers some helpful insights into ecstatic speech.

As indicated elsewhere, the Yucatan is mostly Maya territory and it nourishes memories of the Caste War and of later struggles for land. Spanish is the prestigious tongue but Mayan remains the language of the villagers and their loyalty is less to Mexico than to the Yucatan. The Maya are peasants who are mostly undergoing an economic squeeze and suffering from the increasing scarcity of land. And they are becoming aware of a different way of life, especially through tourism, in which their work is divested of its sacred quality. The world of the Maya is conceptually hierarchical, like the steps of the ancient Maya monuments, yet the Mayan peasant is invited into an alien world where equality is proclaimed and nowhere in evidence. He finds that he most desires what he most hates. Thus his 'world' is on the point of imminent destruction – or a most wonderful renewal.

The upsurge of enthusiasm began in the early summer of 1970 when certain pieces of cargo were sent from the mysterious other country of the United States. They were a public address system, far too powerful for its purpose, and a record player. The deposit of these items among the Apostolics of Utzpak was, if the term may be misused, to stimulate 'deviance amplification'. The effects were not unlike those fictionally depicted in the film *The Gods Must be Crazy* where the occupants of an aeroplane casually tossed a Coke bottle into a tribe of hunter-gatherers in the Kalahari who had never before encountered a hand-manufactured object.

The Apostolic Church grew along a new highway from Merida that simultaneously offered hope and spread disorder. Initially, local villagers fended off the Apostolics by force, but eventually some accommodation was reached. As Felicitas Goodman says, 'The persons who make the first, more or less accidental contact with the evangelist are usually innovators, in the sense that they are searching for religious satisfaction outside the Catholic Church.'[20] They may have tried other Protestant groups, and characteristically once they are converted start bringing other members of their family. Thereafter propagation travels along a neighbourhood pattern or along clusters of kin. What was true of the local Apostolics was also true of the local Presbyterians. If the family is under strain the apostolics come to represent a new version of the 'great family' as it was found in the older social structure. In the new family *compadrazgo* (godparenthood) is eliminated because all are parents and brothers and sisters 'in God'. The Apostolic movement spreads mostly in the villages, as Jean-Pierre Bastian has argued, and barely infiltrates the cities, though the urban churches do provide friendly havens.[21]

At this point one comes to the system of communication established by the Apostolics and sees how flexibly it can enter into the crumbling world of the Maya. In this instance Pentecostalism restores a hierarchical ordering of reality and promises a new and purified world. Those parts of the Bible are selected for emphasis which deal with 'sin', though there happens to be no word for sin in the local Mayan language. The Apostolics convenant together to leave the sinful world, notably the seductions of the city, such as smoking, drinking, cosmetics, dancing, pictures, fighting and adultery. To avoid the City of Destruction and enter the Kingdom of Heaven they must have their sins washed away and give evidence of being for ever sealed by the Lord through speaking in the spirit. It was this experience of trance and speaking in tongues which most excited the believers and equally stirred up their opponents. They were eventually accused of witchcraft. Indeed, they became distinctly unpopular. They had, in fact, established a new form of exclusive communication, not only by speaking in tongues, but also by using their own everyday greeting: Paz de Cristo. As a result other villagers refused to reconize them. They, for their part, consigned the villagers to perdition. Interestingly enough this condemnation of the wider

Catholic world is a strong version of a very general disparagement of the church indulged in by most of the Maya. It is their traditional riposte to the Spanish conquerors.

Felicitas Goodman analyses the experience of trance, and the special crisis which subsequently emerged when 'prophecy failed' among the Apostolics of Utzpak. As people are entranced they become dissociated from their surroundings and oblivious to external stimuli. They may perspire a great deal or salivate. Once they begin to 'speak in tongues' they vocalize very rhythmically, alternating rapidly between accented and unaccented syllables. Vocalizing begins at a normal pitch and then may rise higher and proceed faster before dropping quite suddenly. During this time people experience joy, hope and relaxation; afterwards not much can be remembered apart from a general sense of euphoria. Often the capacity for entering into trance weakens over time and the believer then experiences anxiety, perhaps attributing his loss to moral failure.

Among the Apostolics of Utzpak the rhythm of ecstatic speech and the power of entrancement reached maximum intensity under the guidance of Brother Lorenzo. Lorenzo was a charismatic preacher with a rather patchy personal history who announced the coming dissolution and restoration of the world. It is worth mentioning this patchy history because there are a fair number of cases on record of the warmth of religious enthusiasm and the violence of congregational interaction tipping over into sexual indulgence. As the careers of Jimmy Swaggart, Paul Tillich and others illustrate, such episodes are not confined to the Yucatan.

The passionate preaching of Lorenzo drew increased membership; and the participation of women gained in importance. Indeed, some of the women had difficulty in responding to the bell which signalled returning to mundane reality after speaking in tongues. As for the men, certain of them clearly found tongues a relief from almost unbearable tension. With the tempo of enthusiasm quickening a bright light was seen in the sky and the Devil personally observed in the Utzpak jail. Other visions were received as excitement mounted in periods of intense prayer, some going on all night or, at least, occurring every evening. Relationships became disordered. Some of the young girls accused older members of lack of consecration, and then a demand grew for everything red to be thrown out. Fears grew that Satan was attempting to enter the church, and all doors and windows were locked. At this point arousal began to taper off and some members averred that Beelzebub had been at work and not the Holy Spirit. The tongues nearly ceased and the changes instituted in the whole upheaval all disappeared. Interestingly enough the congregation neither reverted to the Maya status quo nor remade themselves in the image of the city. Goodman drily reports that the Presbyterians said Satan never attacked them because their religion was better than that of the Apostolics. The Apostolics for their part replied that Satan had no need to attack the Presbyterians since he was sure of them already.

It may well be, of course, that in many parts of Latin America, perhaps even in the area of Mexico studied by Goodman, Pentecostalism feeds upon underground channels of traditional entrancement and even maybe visionary Catholic spirituality. Karl Westmeier suggests that in Colombia, for example, intoxication and the knowledge of God still remain intermingled. He argues that the enthusiastic Protestant cults as practised in today's Bogota provides a cathartic experience in the city-dweller's monotonous life such as was once provided by the cycle of rural fiestas.[22] In contexts all over the world occasions multiply of urban dancing in which all the differences of status and colour are, for the time being, dissolved. In South Africa, which presents the greatest resistance to the breakdown of categories of colour and class, there have been some of the most dramatic instances of communal dancing 'in the Spirit'.

Communication in Spiritual Songs and Musical Sounds

A parallel form of ecstasy is of course music, and there is a variant on the Halévy thesis, mentioned earlier, which claims that the power of music is also an influence toward social harmony. Music is anciently credited with charms 'to soothe a savage breast'.[23] A Woodstock is as much a harmless release as it is an incitement to change the world. Above all it unites across boundaries. Perhaps one should say that music initiates precisely that kind of potent cultural change initiated by religion, and in much the same way slowly corrodes the outer forms of social structure. At any rate, the power of Pentecostal harmony has been commented upon again and again, and the Roman Church has been stirred to emulation by the imperative need to enter the musical competition for souls. Pentecostals actually accuse Catholics of attending their services in order to steal their musical clothes.

In her account of the Apostolics, Felicitas Goodman mentions that the church possesses some rattles, a high-pitched little bell, an electric guitar and a marimbol, which is a native instrument with a wooden resonator and attached metal pipes. All singing is accompanied by guitar and marimbol. The hymns are lively and constantly repeated and their vigorous rhythms are accentuated by the rattle and hand-clapping. During the type of short hymn known as a *corito* the clapping becomes very intense. Dirksen and Aulie also refer to the use of the electric guitar and even of a 'mariachi' style in religious services. Aulie clearly believes that music is the most powerful of all agents for the propagation of 'the gospel', so much so that in the Chol country where he was a missionary believers were labelled 'singers' by their irritated neighbours. In his view Spanish popular music is more appealing than Anglo-Saxon hymns. The Chols like to play the guitar and 'follow the rhythms of the radio and mariachi groups'.[24] Next to the healings it is the rhythmic music and hand-clapping of the Pentecostals that provides their biggest attraction. When the Presbyterians cling to the older more hymnic styles and quieter kinds of service they lose ground to the Pentecostals. In this, as in almost all matters except morality, Pentecostals are ready to adjust to whatever the demand requires. In the Caribbean world they use percussion instruments, in Chile the guitar, in Brazil the string orchestra.

A good illustration of the power of Pentecostal music and its capacity to coalesce with indigenous spiritual practices is provided by Elmer Miller's well-known study *Harmony and Dissonance in Argentine Toba Society*.[25] Miller describes how Toba society went through a period of disintegration under outside pressure and was then renewed for a while by forms of Pentecostalism brought initially by the Church of God, Pentecostal of Cleveland, Tennessee.

After emphasizing the importance of direct individual communication with the divine, Miller describes how a Toba service comprises singing, praying, preaching, dancing and healing. Services last several hours and begin with the congregation singing along for anything up to an hour. There are about a dozen *cancionistas* (singers) who stand together on the platform, and there are usually four young men who enjoy travelling around and picking up new hymns and choruses, often from *criollo* services in neighbouring towns. Some of the *cancionistas* acquire additional prestige by composing their own songs. Congregations like to sing all the songs right through and generally have them off by memory, or else they join in without forming the words. A loud and joyful noise to the Lord is considered virtuous and, in addition, helps scare the Devil off the premises. After the warming-up period, songs punctuate and mark out the whole liturgical order.

For example, it is usually the period of most intense singing which leads up to an episode of dancing. That, too, is musical in that individuals join hands or arms and audibly and rhythmically breathe out and in, while stomping about and shouting in ecstasy. Eventually individuals fall down entranced and still, until consciousness returns and they tell of their trance experiences. The concluding parts of a service are likewise sealed off by singing. As the preaching ends, the worshippers sing 'The Great Physician' and the sick are brought forward to the *dirigentes* (leaders) who lay their hands on them and loudly call on the demons to come out of them. The healing is in turn brought to a close by a song of benediction.

Initially, the singing of the Toba was unaccompanied but eventually a small band was formed with tambourines, guitar and drums. The music was adapted to a five point pentatonic scale and the rhythm and timing manipulated to create close harmony. Prayer itself was practised as a kind of *Sprechgesang*, beginning with murmurous petitions in unison and rising to clamorous shouts and vocalizations which then abruptly tailed away.

This adaptation to the local music, and the invention of new music also occurs on a world-wide scale. To give an example far removed from the Indians of Mexico or the Toba of the Argentine there was a Father Devadas who, early in this century, founded the Bible Mission in South India. Devadas was brought up a Lutheran but was influenced by a Pentecostal minister known as the Apostle Samuel. According to P. Solomon Raj, Devadas practised 'waiting on the Holy Spirit', exorcism, and spiritual healing, as well as a cult of cleanliness. P. Solomon Raj goes on to describe how Devadas was a writer of songs and composed over fifty fervent devotional ('*bhakti*') hymns. 'Whereas the mainline churches for a long time used only translations of the western hymns, the folk churches of India used more bhajans, and namasankirthans (praises in the name of God).'[26]

Communication in Ordinary Speech: Oral Tradition, Narrative, the Vernacular

Naturally Pentecostals (and Neo-Pentecostals within the mainstream churches) do also employ ordinary language as a medium of communication. But as Walter Hollenweger has emphasized the communication is more oral than it is written, more extempore than bound by a text. This is what gives it spontaneity, power and immediacy. George Mulrain in his work on Haiti has argued that this preference for narrative and stories rather than arguments helps give Pentecostals the edge over the more literate denominations of historic Protestantism and anchors them more securely in black culture.[27] In a curious way this restoration of the oral mirrors the emphasis on

religion as a story found in some modern liberal theology. Once
again, Pentecostalism links the very ancient with the modern.

Karla Poewe quotes the South African Pentecostal, David du
Plessis, to bring out the oral character of Pentecostal communication.
Du Plessis vigorously denied the influence of literacy in the
transformations sought and wrought by Pentecostalism, and that is as
true of the middle-class charismatic tradition he propagated as of
poor man's Pentecostalism. Karla Poewe asks: 'But if literacy does
not drive this religious cultural phenomenon, what does? The answer
is, of course, oratory. What we see in the movement is a restored
emphasis on an oral tradition, spoken spiritual autobiographies.'[28] The
oral culture is fostered in Christian lay organization and it comes to
fruition in testimonies, miracle stories, tales of encounter, celebrations,
ejaculations and prophecies, all of which make up a unifying common
code. The means and modes are technically sophisticated, running
from tapes and videos and radio to films and television. In Karla
Poewe's view these code words and gestures create a complete all-
enveloping environment within which a person may live his or her
life, whether in a slum in Guatemala City or in a middle-class suburb
of Calgary or Johannesburg. She adds, what is patently true, that the
movement takes myriad forms. It comprises a series of overlapping
and competitive religious groups operating on an open and bullish
market in souls.

This oral culture also propagates itself on a very large scale and
with an international circuit of star performers. On the one hand are
the Pentecostal pastors of the Yucatan, many of them old magi writ
just a little larger, and on the other hand there is an international
circuit in which power is transmitted and made palpable by the sheer
vastness of buildings and open-air gatherings. In Asuncion, Paraguay,
the (lately defrocked) Jimmy Swaggart may speak to 100,000; in
Seoul, Korea, a Billy Graham may speak to a million; in Guatemala
City half a million may foregather to celebrate the centenary of
Protestant missions. Not all these vast assemblages are Pentecostal
but most of them involve large numbers of Pentecostals. Such open-
air services are the distant but discernible lineal descendants of the
meetings at the Foundry in London over two centuries ago addressed
by John Wesley, and of the famous meetings of miners at Kingswood,
Bristol which were addressed by Wesley and Cennick.

Of course, there is a margin of triumphalism here whereby the
communicators become drunk with their own oratorical power and by
the sight of a constantly shifting panorama of faces. At a much quieter
and more local level, however, there is a serious linguistic rescue
service operating under evangelical aegis. It is active in hundreds of

small cultures from Korea and the Philippines to West Africa and the Argentine. Away from the television shows and public address systems, the Bible is translated into dialects sometimes spoken by very small groups indeed.

Some anthropologists have severe reservations about this activity, or at least about the concomitant attempts to evangelize and alter tribal mores and ways of life, but it is certainly the case that languages can be provided with a systematic notation and revived through the efforts of evangelical translators. There are a lot of problems which follow from this activity since small societies are often being simultaneously opened up by all kinds of agencies to much wider, more powerful and corrosive national cultures. Evangelization may at one and the same time confirm the validity of a local language and turn its converts into potential mestizos, or rootless urbanites. The results of communication cannot be controlled, and they may be deadly as well as vitalizing.

Sometimes, however, the results appear almost wholly for the good. The author recollects very well being sung to by a group of adolescent girl evangelists in Mayan and in Spanish to the sound of a small guitar. This happened at the Presbyterian Bible School in Merida and it seemed to the author that the little band of girls were the Yucatecan equivalents of a miners' choir drawn from the chapels of South Wales. The music was borrowed, so the pastor freely admitted, from the Pentecostals, but the words were of proper Presbyterian provenance. Adjoined to the school was a small hospital entitled 'La Esperanza' and served by a woman doctor, to which came the poor, sick and aged of the surrounding ramshackle suburb. The pastor was clearly a person of theologically conservative views trained in a conservative seminary in the United States. At the conclusion of my time with him he handed me the fruit of a life's work which was his participation in the translation of the Bible into Mayan.

A highly favourable light has been thrown on this world-wide process by Lamin Sanneh, a Gambian and a convert from Islam who now teaches at Harvard. He begins by saying how frustrated and confused he was by the resistance of liberal and guilt-ridden Methodists to accepting him as a convert. (If this resistance is at all widespread it would certainly help explain why Methodism has so little impact in Latin America.) Sanneh goes on to argue that it is more worthwhile to observe the effects of missions in the field than to speculate on the ambiguous motives of missionaries who acted, sometimes critically, sometimes enthusiastically, in the ambience of Western imperialism. The claims he goes on to make for missions are very high ones, and also of considerable sociological interest.[29]

Sanneh points out that more than 1,800 languages have been involved in the world-wide translation movement, and that this extraordinary effort has brought missionaries close to the intricacies of culture, with consequences alike for them and for the native. Such an effort must involve the creation of a vernacular alphabet where one is lacking, and may also involve recasting an existing esoteric literary tradition in popular form. Precisely this happened in Korea, where Hankul was rescued by American missionaries. In this manner local believers acquired a new interest not only in the vernacular but also in recording their history and collecting accounts of 'indigenous wisdom'.[30] Sanneh goes on to say that converts armed with a written vernacular scripture called into question the legitimacy of all schemes of foreign domination – cultural, political and religious. Here lay the paradox, since the impulse to question colonialism came through an alien agency. More than that. In societies where religious languages had been bound up in secret societies and professional priestly castes, the impact of a faith in the vernacular propagated by Tom, Dick and Harriet introduced the first intimations of populism. 'Women in particular discovered an expanded role.'[31] And in many cases the missionaries were themselves converted in the sense that they became identified with their adopted culture and, like Frank Laubach in the Philippines, protested against the encroachments of imperial power. They even laid the foundations for new national historiographies. Sanneh goes on to put forward the interesting argument that Islamic gains are related to the existence of a lingua franca, and Christian gains to the existence of vernacular pluralism.

I have chosen this formulation of the argument because it presents a criticism of guilt-ridden liberalism from a source which guilt-ridden liberals may be disposed to hear. It also, in my view, happens to be true and is relevant to the controversy over the evangelization of the tribes which is discussed elsewhere. The important point here is that Pentecostalism and the various faith missions do succeed in becoming indigenous expressions of faith, couched in the vernacular and spread by ordinary men – and women. The Latin American situation is not the African situation, because of the legacy of Hispanic hegemony, but even in those instances most vehemently controverted one has this sense of an implantation of a major text, the Bible, in a vernacular, and with that the formal and substantial rescue of yet another human language. That comes across with remarkable clarity in the biographical accounts of such controversial figures as William Cameron Townsend and the Legters. As a Cakchiquel Indian is reported to have said 'This is wonderful! God speaks our language!'[32] It may be, as the earlier argument implies, that Pentecostals are less concerned than others with literacy in the mother tongue, though the evidence I have surveyed suggests that quite often this proceeds alongside an accent on the oral tradition.

Communication from Females; Feminized Communication

From everything that has been suggested so far, it is clear that women are among the 'voiceless' given a new tongue in the circle of Pentecostal communication. Since this is likely to cause surprise given the emphasis of some American conservative evangelicals on female subordination, it is worth recollecting that one source of female emancipation in the nineteenth century was the evangelical tradition (as well as the Unitarian and Quaker traditions). Olive Banks has given some account of how this was so.[33] In bringing out the impact of contemporary evangelical religion on the ability of women to speak and to consolidate their position, I lean initially on a particularly sensitive doctoral dissertation by Elizabeth Brusco. It will be obvious that a great deal of the groundwork for this book has derived from the investigative acumen of female anthropologists from the United States. They have, moreover, been open to the idea of massive cultural and even psychological change, whereas male social scientists have concentrated on the more macho notion that culture is primarily dependent on structure. Machismo is not something that only infects 'the natives'.

Brusco's thesis can be economically stated.[34] Evangelical religion as studied by her in Colombia preaches an ideology which can be used by women to domesticate men. It does this partly by promoting a form of personality inimical to the stereotype of the Colombian male and partly by a strategic alteration in the priorities of consumption. The family has been perforce the main location for evangelical impact, since Protestants were not allowed to emerge in the public forum. Separation and ostracism allowed the evolution of a new domestic ethos. Brusco noticed that when an evangelical male gave an address his speech was tuned to a female wavelength and had the undertones of nurture rather than of assertion.

This alteration in attitude is particularly important in contemporary circumstances where the old cooperative units of domestic production have mostly broken up. Men are frequently unemployed and frequently leave the woman husbandless. Evangelical religion literally restores the breadwinner *to* the home and restores the primacy of bread *in* the home. The woman finds her refuge in the church and tries to bring her husband along too, if he is still around, or else she finds a supportive husband from within the fellowship. Quite often the conversion of the man comes about through sickness. Once sick he is pushed back on the assistance of his wife and comes to see vice and illness as in some way connected. Conversion follows and the atmosphere of the home changes. Perhaps the man relapses because of the ostracism of his peers or ridicule directed at him from the bar, but quite often he attends often enough to be intregrated into the standards of the community. His wife, meanwhile, has joined a whole series of women's organizations, and attends women's services, where the dominant images are those of cleanliness and good food. Moreover, the person who usually presides at these meetings is the pastor's wife. Brusco says in an interesting aside that the females begin to be interested in educational activities, for themselves maybe but certainly for the next generation, and that evangelicals can much more easily make headway in medicine and agronomy than in the more 'alcoholic' professions of business and the law. This again draws attention to the atmospheres generated by evangelical religion: peaceability and nurture not violence, education not aggressive exploitation.

Of course, not all Protestant groups successfully afford shelter for women or make inroads on male machismo. In particular, some Protestant groups adopt legalistic moral standards of such severity that women in difficulty or distress are ostracized or made acutely aware of their problematic status. Dirksen describes how a pastor refused to marry an engaged couple seen holding hands. The search for respectability claims its victims and the literature offers many examples of such victimization. And, of course, the directing roles are mainly male. Given, however, that Protestant groups are in the main composed of females, it follows that those who exclude the 'lost' on grounds of respectability are not likely to expand as rapidly as those which are more open and accepting. In some societies, for example in the West Indies, the proportion of abandoned women, or of women in common-law relationships, is so high that severity means a pretty empty church. Even if a church is 'respectable' it can deploy that 'respect' to cover all those who come to it for assistance and restoration.

It is perfectly reasonable to see in the motivations which assist conversion a substantial move to recover the family. Observation of the literature on offer at evangelical bookstalls suggests that the stability of family life is a major concern. If we return for a moment to the 'transitional' community as described by Dirksen, something of the variety for which Pentecostalism caters becomes evident. The oldest families are in a traditional extended form.

One of Pakal-Na's original Pentecostal households was an extended family whose modest ranch was one of the first residences in the community. The rancher, aged 64, lives in a small rectangular dwelling to which rooms have been added for his daughter's family of seven. A second family structure in Pakal-Na is the modified extended family; i.e., nuclear families residing in individual dwellings as near to the parents' home as availability of land allows. For example, a 33-year-old married Pentecostal male lives with his brother and family in a cement block home adjacent to their parents' house. The independent nuclear family is also common, particularly among young married couples and recently arrived families. One example of an independent Pentecostal family is a young married couple with no children. The husband sells groceries and owns a restaurant. In their early twenties, they have a modern cement block home with contemporary furnishings and plan to have only two children because of the expense of raising a family.

Other deviations from traditional family forms arise from unusual life situations. One of the most luxurious homes in the community is owned by a female who has established a matrifocal family. A recent Pentecostal convert, she cannot become a church member because she has three children by a wealthy older man who has seven wives and families. Among the village Pentecostals one also finds a number of single women whose husbands have left them. This situation is exemplified by a middle-aged Pentecostal female living with her two daughters and a grandson in a sparsely furnished two-room apartment. Her husband beat her when he left her, she moved from their *rancho* to Pakal-Na and rented a room.[35]

Elizabeth Brusco provides many examples of a similar kind.[36]

Tracing these basic themes of Pentecostal communication through several variations brings out one or two features with dramatic clarity. One is the union of the ancient and the modern, above all the pre-literate and the post-literate. The power of the Holy Spirit as conceived by the believers also fuses the ancient world of the spirits, in Korea or South Africa or Brazil, with a spiritual emanation from the world's most advanced industrial nation. This brings together in a single, if fissile, communion those who are trying to edge out of total poverty in the Yucatan or the Sertão with poor whites in Oklahoma who are trying to invent own religious and social support systems. In short, it brings together a Brother Lorenzo and a Brother Oral Roberts. What is manifested as a small clinic in Guatemala City is manifested on a different scale in the hospital of Oral Roberts University. Equally in both contexts healing is conducted in the community, a technique bringing together tribal forms of healing and the most modern understanding of community care.

It is not clear the extent to which this union of ancient and modern can be placed on any clear evolutionary ladder. Such ladders are full of missing steps; and terms like 'transitional' are too fragile to take much theoretical weight. What is clear is that Pentecostalism can enter flexibly and easily into all kinds of milieu, mingling miracle with magic in Guatemala, or miracle with modern medicine in Johannesburg. In some contexts people are too immersed in pre-literate worlds to make judgements about medical efficacy and may deploy 'too much faith', as has often happened with tragic consequences. In other contexts, especially where trained personnel are involved, the psychic and spiritual element in cure may be integrated into a system of referrals by pastors to doctors, such as has been observed in Trinidad. It is, of course, possible to see that as a stage in rationalization, in which case there would be some case for using words like 'transitional'. But that raises the whole question as to whether or not such phenomena as we have just surveyed are a passing phase in a grand scheme of secularization, and a question of that magnitude will have of necessity to wait till the concluding chapter.

Chapter 10

Conversions: Transformations and Turning Points

The material which I now deploy follows quite directly on what was discussed in the previous chapter. There the focus was on Pentecostalism as a system of signs fostering spiritual communication; here the focus is on personal and familial transformation. That transformation is conventionally called 'conversion', which etymologically simply means 'turning' or 'turning around'. People are 'turned around'; and they arrive at turning points. There are crises which lead sometimes to a spiral of disintegration and at other times to revisions and reorientations. This chapter is about 'visions and revisions'.

Pentecostalism declares itself to be pre-eminently about 'life' and power. Other churches are not so much wrong, although they are usually that, as dead and powerless. In order to see how life is 'received anew' or brought to a new birth I have selected some Puerto Rican life histories. The advantage to be gained from these particular life histories is twofold. In the first place they exhibit personal visions or transformations to be studied at the crossing points of Hispanic and 'Anglo' culture. Puerto Rican life is unusually rich in that respect. In the second place they help us to follow the paths of social mobility, leadership and educational aspiration as they have worked out in the lives of Puerto Ricans who went to mainland USA. The source books for these personal transformations are Sidney Mintz, *Worker in the Cane: A Puerto Rican Life History*, dating from 1960, and Alex Huxley Westfried, *Ethnic Leadership in a New England Community: Three Puerto Rican Families*, published in 1981.[1]

However, before these transitions and transformations are followed through, an earlier stage needs to be canvassed which has to do with the way Pentecostals, or other evangelical sects, find favourable niches in different microclimates within the whole field of a given culture. It is important to know not only how converts are drawn by healing or by music or by opportunities to participate, but also by what *processes* people in this or that structural and cultural milieu become susceptible to conversion.

We know well enough that the social climate of the landed aristocrcy does not encourage dancing in the aisles. We also know that there are ways of life deep in the desperate underclass which are very resistant to any 'redemption' in the Pentecostal manner. But we still cannot quite envisage the local processes whereby certain people remain structurally and culturally enclosed while others are to this or that extent exposed to a novel religious solution. Almost the only study which outlines this enclosure and exposure is by Ruben Reina and Norman Schwartz, and it deals with the El Petén district of Guatemala. So, I begin by leaning on the genuinely insightful work of these two anthropologists.[2]

Microclimates for Transformations: A Guatemalan Case Study

An inclusive hypothesis which can be stated at the outset is that people do need to be relatively independent before the prospect of individual conversion can become part of their horizon of hope. This independence can take various forms. You can be engaged in work where you possess your own tools or your own little business or some modest piece of land (or right of usufruct), or where you offer some personal service which does not actually incorporate you 'body *and* soul' into a vertical hierarchy. Alternatively, your independence may be a more desperate matter since you have become bereft of those visible means of communal and familial support which might tie you in to the pre-existing system. Your ties have all been broken. You are, perhaps, on the move and see the dangers of falling into the bottomless pit of crime, incapacity and destitution. You are seeking relationships that will support you, connect you with others of like mind and authoritatively redefine your moral universe. This is where millions of abandoned or mistreated women find themselves and something of their life situation has already been touched upon. The concern of Reina and Schwartz, however, is mainly with situations where people have some solid independence.

El Petén is in that northern part of Guatemala adjoining the Yucatan, and we are dealing, therefore, with two peripheries within a broader Mexican and Guatemalan area much affected by Protestant missions. The Peteneros look back on a history in which the region was colonized long after most of the rest of Central America, and it is, therefore, a history without the traumatic shock of the first conquests. They have never experienced the hacienda system or pervasive relations of patron and client and view themselves as more egalitarian and independent than other Guatemalans. Their relative freedom is reinforced by a system of land tenure based on inherited usufruct, and the ratio of man to land is not such as to generate serious competition.

At the same time, economic exploitation and the emergence of powerful economic cliques in the nineteenth century have created a class system, especially in the one 'city' of Flores. The people of Flores are – at least in their own eyes – urban sophisticates. Flores and the other less developed communities of San Andrés and San José are locked into each other through different kinds of exchange, and each exhibits a different degree of socio-economic differentiation, of ethnic diversity and ratio of natives to migrants. To this broad characterization must be added the fact that the Catholic Church penetrated El Petén only lightly, as was also the case in the Yucatan. Churches have traditionally been run by lay committees, and a reformed, more activist Catholicism only made its appearance as recently as 1954. In any case adult men rarely participate in church services.

Turning now to the different communities, we begin with San José, which is the poorest and most homogeneous, ethnically and religiously. Most of the men cannot live by the *milpa* alone and are engaged working in the forest. Their work and the fact that they live in more than one place leaves them little time either for communal activity or for religious activity in the *cofradia*. At home they all speak Yucatecan Mayan. They are bounded in their community and also take seriously their mutual obligations one to another; in particular, the duties of co-parenthood contracted at baptism. They lack envy or deviance or mobility or, indeed, anything much by way of formal leadership. They deal with the outside and alien world of business men, officials and clergy either as individuals, or unitedly in defence of their forest patrimony. In this world of inward-looking community and of the forest, it is the beliefs and rituals of folk Catholicism and Maya tradition which go with them in hunting, which help them to avert all kinds of ill, and which enable them to communicate with each other and the world of spirits. Those who do not fit leave. Certainly no one gets converted.

San Andrés is more of a town, and the forest plays a much smaller role in work and in consciousness. There are even some relatively large-scale producers of single crops, and most people encourage their children to complete their time in primary school in order to find work in the town. Some are hired labourers on small sugar-cane *ranchos*. About one in five of the population is from elsewhere and the town is ethnically and linguistically heterogeneous.

People in San Andrés emulate those in Flores, and seek after the signs of modernity: more money, new hair styles, white bread. They are economic individualists, concerned to use the market, and they are somewhat more utilitarian than people in San José in their relationships and their attitude to the forest. They 'give place to envy'. There are factions in the town and powerful cliques of rival leaders. There are also Protestants, who make up about a quarter of the population and can be identified (as were republicans in France!) by the way they name their children – after nations, flowers and fairy-tale figures.

The Protestant section of the population grew because in the late 1930s and 1940s several Protestant converts, Mayero (Indian) as well as Ladino (Hispanic), received secondary education from the missionaries. This meant that there were now some Mayeros better educated than some leading Ladinos. Such people were able to take advantage of the effects of the 1944 revolution and of changes in the chicle industry to acquire wealth and influence. The pyramid of power with Ladinos exclusively at the top collapsed into rival elites. Moreover, the previously dominant clique could no longer organize the patronal festival. Thus the emergence of the new elites and of the new Protestant faith together signalled the end of such all-inclusive occasions.

In Flores, the capital of El Petén, everybody speaks Spanish and, moreover, Spanish in a superior style. Wealth, occupation, education and power all mutually collude and there is little social mobility. The six main families and the upper middle class of small merchants, officials and teachers, consort together to some extent, though not without tension. Likewise, lower-class people, the menials, *chicleros* and labourers, have little choice but to keep company with their fellows. The group which is most dissatisfied is found in a lower middle class of small shopkeepers, and of artisans, such as carpenters, barbers, shoemakers and masons. Florenses in general are inclined to be suspicious of each other, and the elite groups in particular affect an urbane distance from the surrounding peasant world, except when a touch of exemplary control seems necessary. Protestants are less successful in Flores than in San Andrés. They accounted in 1960 for only about 5 per cent and were naturally concentrated in the lower middle class.

With this scale of development and differentiation briefly delineated, it is now possible to see how both Protestant and Catholic missions have impinged upon it, and given vent to its different interests, factions and frustrations. As already pointed out, the 'forest' community of San José treats all religious personnel as extraneous and continues on its ancient course, which happens to centre, so far as ritual goes, on a curious cult of three skulls on the main altar in the Catholic Church.

San Andrés presents a much more complicated picture and one that is very instructive. First of all, a reform movement within Catholicism has itself included some 'Protestant' elements, notably the prohibition of dancing and drinking and spiritistic practices. This has irritated some Catholics who see it as clerical interference in their customary behaviour. Second, Protestantism has arrived in two waves, the Nazarenes in the 1930s, and the Pentecostals in the 1960s. The rivalry of the Protestants among themselves and with the old and new kinds of Catholics has resulted in the emergence of some who are indifferent or who believe but have no church connection.

What then is the resultant pattern of allegiance among the rival groups in San Andrés? Those who were part of the original pyramid of power saw that their interests and affections lay in continued alignment with Catholicism, including the current of catechetical reform. Several reasonably well off Ladinos followed suit. However, some other Ladinos who had earlier been dislodged from power and had then counter-attacked politically following the 1944 Revolution, became religiously labile, converting, reconverting or drifting into indifference. The poorer Mayeros also stayed Catholic, often showing intense hostility to Protestantism, or else if they became Protestant, they did so late and in the protective shadow of other more influential Mayeros. Quite a number eventually joined the Pentecostals and so, too, did a number of Kekchi Indian migrants. The better-off among the Mayeros early became Nazarenes, and sought chapel offices more actively than Ladinos. They thus achieved a fresh sphere of independent fulfilment *without* actually arousing the kind of tensions which might have followed on a direct challenge to the ethnic distribution of power. This is a paradigm of Protestant activity. 'Like the Protestant Ladinos,' say Reina and Schwartz, 'they were quicker than most Catholics to utilize the opportunities, particularly economic ones, generated by the Revolution of 1944 and *thus continued a pattern of upward mobility which had been initiated prior to their conversion to Protestantism*' (my italics).[3] They then brought poorer kinsmen and kinswomen and followers into the chapel and proceeded to lead it. This sequence fits precisely into the model of mobility – Protestantism – mobility proposed by Sexton in his study of the Guatemalan town of Panajachel.[4] People look about them, reach after certain 'goods', then embrace Protestantism and are equipped with an inclusive vision, the better to pursue those 'goods'. The process is cybernetic in its complex feedbacks.

The situation in Flores is also instructive. In Flores the upper classes consider that customary Catholicism grants leadership in religious matters to them and resent clerical interference in the liturgy and the new Catholic concern for a firmer social morality. They thus resemble the English upper classes in their attitude to the contemporary Church of England and they consider the assertion of orthodox (that is, novel) Catholicism to be a slur on their training at home and at school. Some are now openly secular, others still inclined to a folkish faith. On the other hand the better-off of the middling people have taken very well to the new Catholicism. They are activist and dogmatic and have cornered most offices in the Church. They, therefore, have pursued socio-religious moves analogous to the middling sort among Mayeros who gained control of the Nazarene chapel, and thereby challenged the elite *without* engaging in outright confict. They have taken advantage of the increasing differentiation of society and, in particular, the differentiation of church and social power, to take control of an ecclesiastical sector not absolutely central to the interests of the elite. There are fewer official Protestants in Flores because the 'Protestants' act under the label of reformist Catholics.

As for the Nazarene chapel in Flores, it comprises newcomers, and people in the lower middling groups of independent artisans, and small shopkeepers who could not hope to be included with those activists who have taken over the Catholic Church. The Protestants have not succeeded in converting any lowly cultivators of chicle or the milpa – or members of the elite. But they are urbanely tolerated, and more so than elsewhere, for example in San José.

What this analysis suggests is that power can be culturally circumvented in discrete sectors, and this is precisely what Protestantism does, as also does some version of reforming Catholicism. The latter is more likely overall to arouse tension among the elites because Catholicism is traditionally bound up in the system as a whole. The former is framed by historic forces which fit it for a limited and specific sector of activity, and in this case for innovative shifts shielded behind an apolitical stance. The people involved in these shifts will not be in the lowest or highest reaches of the social system, but among those of lower middling status who seek new spheres of influence and activity and have some modest independence with respect to social relationships and economic resources. Apart from that, the people involved may include the footloose migrants, those in positions of painful inconsistency, and members of ethnic minorities who are permanently denied honorific roles in the established socio-religious hierarchy.

As indicated, this kind of analysis, pursued here at the level of comparative studies of structures of community, seems to offer basic insights into the openings available for Protestantism. It shows clearly the importance of several rival Protestant organizations emerging to cater for the sheer number of rival deviant groups seeking openings and satisfying roles. It also shows clearly how close reformist Catholicism is in its appeal to Protestantism. A map of Protestant incursions needs to be placed over another map of the incursions of reformed Catholicism to see where they directly compete and where one is operative rather than the other. Nobody has done that, and to do so on a large scale is an almost impossibly difficult venture. Nevertheless, in the study of microclimates such as that in El Petén, it is quite easy to see how the Protestant and Catholic versions of reform express and propel similar social changes and perform closely analogous roles. Certain groups will turn to religious reform because they are not rendered complacent by power or deferential through a combination of social incorporation, indigence and ignorance. Short of the dangerous, doubtful and bloody alternative of armed political revolution, the religious vehicles of change which they chose will alter the landscape in such a way that one day a landslip may occur. Such after all was the relationship of the Great Awakening to the American Revolution; at least as understood by some historians.

Accounts of a Second Birth: A Puerto Rican Case Study

What has just been described is a cultural and structural paradigm of the shifts to which people resort, focused on the channels of religious innovation. One must not use mechanistic terminology about these processes, or phrases which imply that the transformation of the affections is just some means to a social end. People do have such ends but they are admixed with more comprehensive notions of 'betterment', and wider notions of 'goods' as these are conveyed by 'visions and revisions'. Nor must the paradigmatic processes so well illustrated in El Petén be blown up and subjected too mechanically to a process of generalizing abstraction. They are based in particular 'life worlds' where people negotiate for meanings and purposes, and where hopes jostle against the pricks and pains of social and physical constriction.

It is to that world of life as it is lived that we have to turn to understand conversion, and in Sidney Mintz's *Worker in the Cane* we have an older study which illuminates turning points in the life of a man and wife in Puerto Rico.[5] It is important that whereas in El Petén the missionaries mostly came from a distant North America, in Puerto Rico the local people are already poised between the Hispanic and the Anglo worlds. Indeed, there are earlier studies concerned precisely with the role of Protestantism in making easy the transition to the American way of life soon after the island was incorporated in the US sphere of influence.[6] Puerto Rico also offers ideal material for understanding this transition as worked out in the USA by Puerto Rican migrants.

Sidney Mintz sets the scene, beginning with an account of the kind of Catholicism found in Puerto Rico and for that matter over much of Latin America. In Barrio Jauca, Puerto Rico, most people are Catholics but many have little to do with the church and its rites.

> The 'average' Jauca Catholic, if a male, has not been confirmed, has never taken communion, has never gone to confession, is not married in the church, and has an attitude toward official Catholicism which is neither enthusiastic nor violently critical. . . . The walls of his shack are decorated with saints' pictures, a cross, and bit of palm from the preceding Holy Week. He has his children baptized, though the official baptism may take place years after the children are born. He has no objection if his wife goes regularly to church so long as it does not interfere with her household duties – though the likelihood of her going is slight . . . He may tell you that the Catholic Church is 'the church of the rich', but he is not likely to change his faith.[7]

Taso was just such a Catholic, baptizing his children, giving alms and colouring his speech with religious phrases. What mattered for him was baptism and the choice of godparents for his children and the maintenance of respect for these *compadres*. 'But though he had over fifty compadres – both godparents to his children and parents to whose children he was padrino – he did not concern himself about the connection between the godparental custom and Catholicism.'[8]

In 1949 Taso was 41 years old. His economic situation was better than it had been during preceding decades and his political party had been confirmed in power by a majority in the 1948 election. Nevertheless, he was becoming disillusioned with the party, and had worries about illness and guilt with which no political salve could deal. His wife's persistent and extreme jealousy also greatly troubled him. As for Protestantism he had heard preachers as a child and liked their message for its clarity and simplicity, but the sight of young girls entranced at Pentecostal services he found comical and shamefully lacking in proper control. Yet, even while he retained such attitudes, he was reorganizing his understanding of religion and preparing the way for a view of his own life which would see conversion as its natural culmination.

While he was turning these things over in his mind, his daughter, Carmen Iris, attended Pentecostal services and returned home with sensational stories of 'how the lame walk and the blind see'. Then his wife Eli did the same, and she made the events she saw directly relevant to Taso. Something motivated her to urge him to attempt to cure himself of iguinal pains by supernatural agency, and she must have supposed that he was by now disposed to listen. He went at her urging, experienced an overwhelming physical sensation, and the disabling condition disappeared for good. 'Just as Carmen Iris and Eli attend the important revival meetings in Ponce before him, so Blanca and Eli precede him in making professions of faith within the church. . . . When Eli joins she first tests Taso by saying she had joined when she really had not', so that she could withdraw her commitment had he objected.[9] He did not.

When Taso himself made a profession of faith somewhat later, he said it was a test to see whether the visitation of the Holy Ghost was genuine. Then when Eli received the blessing of the Spirit he experienced the *promesa* or promise and knew he had entered into 'everything that the prophets had foretold'. He also felt discharged from his guilt. When the pastor at a service placed his finger on acts of ill-will in the family, Taso recognized them as his own. He saw himself as 'culpable', meaning by that 'guilty as charged'. His wife, too, felt 'convicted' of her jealousy. So the Pentecostal experience became a discharge for both of them in every sense of the word.

Both Taso and Eli gave accounts of that discharge, though in what follows more use is made of Eli's narrative than of Taso's. Both should be read *in extenso* in Mintz's seventh chapter since they offer narratives of remarkable power. Indeed, the sequence in which Eli is first converted, and then Taso, reminds one of the way John and Charles Wesley, as well as their sister and mother, were converted in swift succession in the course of 1738. The accounts by Taso and Eli could well be placed alongside the account in Wesley's Journal, since almost every element is identical, including the feelings of intense warmth and the relationship felt to exist between fears for the body and spiritual disease.

Taso describes his healing by the Holy Ghost:
'Well – they tell one to close one's eyes. One is in complete communion while they pray; and the ecstasy is as if one were seasick; what I felt that night was something like that. I didn't see anything. I felt as if they had put something before my eyes, as if I had left the world. Even when he said, "Open your eyes", I still felt something big in my head – it was as if one were in a faint. But you know that when you faint you are about to fall, while I had my feet firmly planted. Elisabeth says she saw stars and things. I saw nothing like that. Rather, I felt this big thing in my head, this ecstasy. Now, when he told me to open my eyes, I opened my eyes but I still felt something like an ecstasy. Then I didn't feel anything – anything more. I only felt that thing in my body, that ecstasy in my whole body. Now, I know there was something in me. Because before I had never had that sensation, never until that moment; and then afterward the sensation went away. Something was in me at that moment.'[10]

Taso talks about his baptism in the Holy Ghost:
'It was – a short period of time passed – a matter of one week or two, something like that. The night I received it, it was in this church here. Yes. In that place here; there it was. That night they told us to pray and we were praying. And while one is praying one feels as if something comes and fills one – a thing that comes and fills one. And then I received a blessing, and I was moving myself about, and as it happened here on my knees – since it was concrete – I skinned my knees while we were praying. That was the night I received the blessing, over there.'[11]

'One feels most content, one feels full of that. Truly, when one receives the blessing that way, when a person thus receives the blessing of the Holy Ghost, it is a great joy that a Christian feels. And frequently you can arrive at a Pentecostal church and hear a brother who has just received the blessing talking in tongues from moment to moment. Now see, afterward, the brother gets to control himself better. For when one is converted, when one thus receives the blessing, one's desire is to be in communion always, and one is always seeking it.'[12]

Taso also talks about speaking in tongues:

'It can be – I have heard some brothers speak sometimes in such a way that you can understand them. Yes, at times one can understand some. We have heard some brothers in the course of the blessing order the church to pray. And some things you understand, although others you do not. As the Scriptures say, in tongues one speaks mysteries that no one will understand. But many times one understands. You feel a thing – as if you have – some say they feel something that enters through their feet and fills them; now, I felt as if a thing came through my head and filled me. There are those who feel it through – through different parts of the body. The body trembles, you see, and one always has a continuous movement while one feels this.

'One feels no pain at all. We were kneeling and praying. They ordered us to kneel, and we were praying. Then one receives the Spirit, you see; that comes and fills one, and you have that demonstration; then it is during the demonstration that one receives the blessing.

'From there on one feels nothing more. One feels this thing that filled one, one feels *full*.'[13]

Eli's narration began by her explaining that when she was little her father took her to the evangelical church and to Bible school. There her father lost his faith, began to drink and to give her mother such a bad time that they separated. As a young woman, Eli herself enjoyed 'the things of the world'. 'I only came to have more interest in the things of God since I have the capacity of a grown woman, you see – after I had had my children.'[14]

As already mentioned, Carmen Iris, her daughter, was the first to go to the meetings in Ponce and came back to tell her parents what had happened. Eli explained how that night

we have already gone to sleep when she came back and she woke us up to tell us what she had seen. She told us of a child who was deaf and had recovered his normal hearing, and of many blind men who had regained their sight. She came home very happy. At that time I was already listening to the services here. I would approach the services that were then being held in Mora's family store. I'd walk up close to the door. But I wouldn't stay long, I'd just listen a little while.[15]

Eli gave a vivid account of dancing in the Spirit, and of healings of tumours which filled her 'with even more faith'. Then she went to a service at which Brother Juan Hernandez, the pastor, said 'Come, Eli.' 'Then I felt as if I were carried from where I was sitting, carried to where the pastor was.' That moment brought about her conversion. Then for some weeks she prayed with more and more intensity, experiencing overpowering feelings of warmth and cold which the pastor assured her were intimations of something more to come. Eli then went to an all-night vigil at which she experienced light, wind and fire and a cumulative upheaval of a 'second birth' by the impregnation of the Holy Spirit.

'Well, then we went to that vigil, Taso and I. We passed the whole night in prayer and singing, and it was a lovely thing – for the vigils are beautiful, and one spends the whole night in meditation with the Saviour, and praying – praying and honoring the Saviour and singing beautiful hymns.'[16] About twelve there was a break for a little coffee, and then as the second part started,

I felt those waves of heat coming more rapidly. In the place where I was sitting, I would feel something that came over me that was not – that was something that – I don't know, I can't explain what it was like. But I know that each time this thing approached me, it filled me – from my feet to my head – some cool thing came over me and blew upon me. And I felt at times that my body [she laughs slightly] – as if it wanted to move; I felt my body tremble – quiver. I felt as if each time something surrounded me, as when one is caught in a light shower. I felt as if my heart were growing bigger, as if my heart wanted to jump out of my chest. I was receiving those things [she moves her hands in front of her face] – thus, over one, now and again. Something comes to where one is; one sees nothing but one feels it.

It was already getting light; morning was already coming. And we began to pray again, and when – I know that when I kneeled, there came this peculiar thing. It invaded my whole body [her voice becomes tense and excited] and I began to tremble, to move my body. I didn't want to move it – something was moving me. When I knelt they asked the brothers who were not baptized with the blessing to form a group. We did – men and women – to seek the blessing. In the prayer I was raising I beseeched the heavens – I asked the Lord to stamp me with the blessing that the pastor said He had for us.

By then my body was moving more, moving more, until at last something [her voice rises almost to a shriek] compelled me to dance, something carried me about, so that I was struggling this way and that – I could not control myself, I could not because this was a tremendous thing. This was something tremendous. And the joy one feels – because it is not a thing that frightens one, no. I didn't feel the slightest bit frightened; I felt instead that I wanted to hurry to receive it, to receive the blessing. I wanted to hurry, to be filled completely with it. And the more one danced, the more one felt it. And I know that this thing, this peculiar thing, was in me – you see – that it was in me. When one receives such a strong blessing, at times the other sisters rejoice in the same sanctification. They spoke in tongues alongside me, and they were telling me to glorify – to glorify more, and the pastor was saying to me, 'Glorify! Glorify the Lord still more! You are going to receive the promise now.'

And while I was glorifying, I know that at one point I wanted to say, 'Glory to God, Hallelujah,' and I could not. I swallowed my tongue; and then I spoke in other languages, like Hebrew or something like that. The pastor said I was going to say something in tongues; and then I heard Brother Juan say, 'She has received it! She has received it! She has spoken in tongues, in spiritual tongues.'[17]

The Social Consequences of Second Birthing: A Move to the United States

Such accounts give some idea how a turning point was experienced by two people in Puerto Rico. But, of course, the Puerto Rican nation is divided into two groups: those who live on the island and the two million or more who now live in the United States. For them the transition from Hispanic culture is far advanced and many have simultaneously retained their roots and made their adjustments to the USA through their participation in the Pentecostal faith. Alex Huxley Westfried's study of how Puerto Ricans cope with the problems of being an ethnic minority in New England focuses on four ethnic leaders, Octavio, Pedro, Maria and Tom. They all had a college education, and a professional career – and they all knew their way around American institutions. Westfried was concerned to show how they dealt with difficulties in education, housing and employment, and also adjusted to the US while maintaining their own traditions.[18]

The scene of his research was a small New England town in which about 5 per cent of the population was Hispanic, and in which the Puerto Ricans were much more likely to be unskilled or semi-skilled than the Dominicans or Cubans. His chosen leaders were a hospital administrator, a policeman, a community organizer and a minister. Three of these are evangelicals (two of them Pentecostal) and it is on them that I concentrate.

Westfried begins with an account of how family respectability is understood among most Hispanics, because this is highly relevant for understanding his life histories. Children must respect, and obey, their elders, or else expect to be beaten. Kin are expected to raise children of their own kin group, and children are expected to support their families and eventually to take care of aged and retired parents. Girls should remain virgins until married and boys should protect the virginity of their sisters. The roles of man and wife are separate, especially in the working class; and there is a double standard about extra-marital affairs. Men have the authority in the family, but in the domestic sphere the mother is in control, and she is the focus of intense loyalty. To this should be added that respectable families do *not* exhibit emotion in church, but aspire to decent formal behaviour and a 'good appearance'. This, then, provides something of a context for the adjustments, social and religious, made by Puerto Ricans in the United States.

Octavio's father had fought on the republican side in Spain and then escaped to settle as a mayordomo on a sugar estate in Puerto Rico. He was something of a rake, he beat his wife, he was a gambler, a drunk and a womanizer, and he expected honour and '*respeto*' from his children rather than love and esteem. Octavio's mother worked immensely hard and often intervened to save him from paternal abuse. Indeed, his mother helped him become independent and, as so often, the family became anchored around the relationship of mother to son.

In this way Octavio gained an unusual sense of what advancement might be possible for him, and through the resources of his mother's uncles and parents was able to prepare for a professional career. His early independence can also be attributed to his religious conversion at the age of seventeen, which followed on the conversion of his mother. 'When he had a crisis or a personal problem he did not normally need to consult his kin; instead he would walk in the hills,

Bible in hand, and come back to his grandfather's house, calm and contented.'[19]

With great financial difficulty Octavio trained for the ministry. Then he enlisted with the hope of further advancing his education, and at the end of a prolonged period in the army he completed a master's degree in Hospital Administration through New York University. In 1972 he took up a position as hospital administrator in New Castle, New England. This gave him a chance to serve the local Hispanic community as an associate Baptist minister. From time to time, Octavio curbed his father's excesses and also helped him, and eventually converted him, so that he gave up drinking. Earlier Octavio had observed the conversion of four of his brothers, but they relapsed back in to alcoholism and wife-beating on the model of their father.

His strict standards governed how he brought up his own family and how his own kin had to behave when they visited him. He still thought in terms of *respeto* – as well as of love. In raising his son and daughter he insisted on obedience and sexual continence. At the same time, his wife Josephine helped him in his ministry and he diverged sharply from Puerto Rican custom in revealing his weaknesses to her and in making decisions in consultation with her. He also tried to help his daughter, Juanita, to be an independent person, to have the educational means for supporting herself, and even to engage in athletics which traditional Puerto Ricans consider not ladylike. At eighteen his daughter gave up scholarship offers to study marine biology at Wheaton and Columbia, and instead studied theology at Thomas Lee University in South Carolina. In the education of his son, Francisco, Octavio encouraged seriousness, self-discipline, educational aspiration, and manual skills – and laid less emphasis on strength and sexual aggression than is usual among Puerto Rican males. After a somewhat Bohemian episode, Francisco was accepted at Cornell and Yale but found the permissiveness not to his liking. So he attended the Divinity School of the University of South Carolina, and in his turn trained for the ministry.

Here, then, we can see the pattern of discipline, independence and aspiration established on a religious basis and a mutation in family relationships away from female subordination and machismo towards sexual equality. Octavio also gave up beating his children as a means of family discipline.

As to Octavio's church, it was mainly attended by working-class Hispanics, so he had to stay close to his origins, even though his own peers were mostly middle-class. He stressed education and female equality more than is usual among his congregation, but also preferred the Protestant Ethic to middle-class permissiveness. His church was, in fact, a synthesis of the Anglo and Puerto Rican cultures. Everything about Octavio and his family offers the reader an advanced version of the values inculcated and embraced at conversion by most poor Protestants in Latin America.

Westfried's account of Maria and her son Pedro is called 'The Castros: The Search for a New Vision' and it illustrates not only the shift to Pentecostalism but also to a semi-political secularization of evangelical zeal. This emerged in a greater emphasis on nationalist and political concerns in the third generation. Maria is a character who very much resembles Eli and has something of her eloquence. One can sense in her precisely how religious faith and vision is passed down the distaff side whatever happens among the errant males.

The stories of Maria and Pedro are, of course, almost completely intertwined, but it is useful first to look at Maria primarily on her own account. Maria's father was a railroad engineer and mason who cared a great deal about the education of his daughters. He cared about strict standards and about learning, and both concerns were rooted in the Pentecostal faith to which he and his wife had been converted. Maria spent two years at Puerto Rico University, but at her father's death she moved to New York to help support the rest of the family. There she heard a young Mexican missionary and determined to become herself a minister, taking particularly to heart the advice of St Paul to the Romans (chapter 12), 'be ye *transformed* in the renewing of your mind'.

Maria's husband, Francisco, was brought up in a much less strict atmosphere and spent some time in the US navy. He became a Pentecostal through coming to watch Maria sing in the choir, and also because during his time in the navy he made a promise to give his life to God if he survived (as also, in fact, did Octavio while in the army). When he and Maria married, they dedicated themselves to religious teaching and missionary work and always moved their home under the inspiration of the Holy Spirit. Maria first did missionary work among Hispanic migrants in Florida, providing them with food and clothing, and then she and her husband were offered a two-year course at the American Bible Institute in Northport, New England. In the event, Francisco became a skilled operative; and Maria became a community worker, educator and Pentecostal missionary running a church in 'Devonshire', New England. Maria stressed cleanliness, neatness, seriousness in work, education, interaction with people, staying away from rough or violent individuals, and commitment to the Puerto Rican community. These commitments were to create some difficulty for her son Pedro, whom she saw in a vision as 'preaching the word' all over the world. The vision for Pedro she interpreted as prophecy in the sense spoken about by Paul in his first Epistle to the Corinthians (14: 2–15). In that text, Paul rates prophecy, that is vision, as more important than speaking in tongues. Pedro did not see it that way, but his mother had no doubt that the prophecy would come about. Like Monica, mother of Augustine, Maria did not believe the child of such prayers could finally be lost.

Pedro holds to a version of his mother's faith but, in part, translates it into politics, nationalism and mixing with the street-wise inhabitants of the ghetto. He is a missionary in a different mode. In Pedro we can see the kind of second transformation which often occurs when religious commitments are shaped and directed by the influences of modern liberal education, particularly as those might influence someone with dual national roots.

In grammar school Pedro was a difficult student and found some of the prohibitions of the Pentecostal faith absurd. He became involved for a while in drug culture, and when he went to Queen's College found himself passionately absorbed by the writings of Cleaver, Fanon and Campos. He became fully aware of his roots and the destiny of his people through meeting and working with Abd-l-Akimm, a director of youth services and a follower of Malcolm X. He described himself as 'black' so far as his political alignment was concerned. All his closest friends were *independentistas*. However, his work for Hispanics required expert knowledge of law and so he secured a scholarship to Bangor University. Eventually he acquired a BA in Social Welfare and went into the Youth Services Programme.

Yet Pedro remained a religious individual, even though he did not go to church. What he rejected were only those aspects of his mother's definition of respectability which might cut him off from his own people and from any attempt they might make to achieve a distinctive style of life. He did not reject the drive to obtain education and to achieve professional standards at work. One incident is highly instructive. He and his close friends encountered two *santeros* (spiritist healers) who assaulted their spirits, but it was Pedro who successfully drew on his personal faith to ward off the danger.

Pedro always remained a street-wise person who could find his way around the ghetto. He took a hard line with people who tried to 'give him a bad time' – whereas his parents would have tried to keep away from any violence. As for women, Pedro believed that they were entitled to a career; and he has had relationships with women that have ended in abortion. His moral world is more complex, uncertain and fractured than that of his parents.

Some of his experiences were so morally ambiguous that he became unhappy about the way he was living. He went to a retreat in

Pennsylvania and there received that 'discharge' in every sense which
was clearly experienced by Eli and Taso. He felt 'culpable' just as they
did. This experience in Pennsylvania offered him the transformation
with which this chapter has been primarily concerned.

> This experience was so complete my whole life turned
> around . . . I am almost completely at peace with myself
> right now. We had a very non-religious service Saturday,
> everyone sat in a cricle. The spirit . . . had been hitting me
> . . . touching me, making me aware that I was not living the
> way He wanted me to. The spirit of God was so real that in
> that building you could reach it – touch it almost. It was
> like heaven.
>
> I went to the lake, this was ten o'clock at night and I'll
> remember that for ever, for the clouds were making a
> fantastic formation with the light of the moon. I went to the
> lake and I sat down on that bench. As soon as I sat down on
> that bench, I started weeping uncontrollably. And I had not
> shed a tear for five or six years *for anything*. I started
> weeping and heaving, I could not stop. All I could do was
> praise God, Alleluja, Amen, Praise be the name of God.
> That is all I could do.[20]

Peaceable Cultural Transformation

What follows from all this is the way Protestantism emerges at a
certain point in the opening up of a society, particularly among people
above the lowest level of indigence and with some independent
resources of mind or money or skill. It enables such people to edge
sideways into religious forms of participation, expression and
reponsibility which do not have directly to threaten the central stem of
hierarchical power. Even where Catholicism adopts religious reforms
and extends those into political reform, it retains a long-term historic
identification with the socio-religious hierarchy and, indeed, the very
sophistication and organic nature of its critical approach reflects that.
Protestantism picks up sectors beginning to detach themselves
through classic processes of differentiation or marginality, and is itself
shaped by its history to fit in with a differentiated society. It is this
which restricts its political scope and provides the push and shove for
individual or group advancement rather than for political revolution.

Nevertheless, the shift to Protestantism does represent a revolution
within the self: an ecstasis, a breaking beyond the static. In many

cases it literally breaks down and breaks through the structured nature of social boundaries and the settled limits of ordinary received behaviour. It 'fills' and 'fulfils' personalities deeply infected in their physical and psychic being with dis-ease and unease. By exactly what linkages of mind and body we do not know, but there is sufficient evidence from the New Testament to the present time of a double release or discharge acting simultaneously on spirit and physical substance to restore harmonies long distorted and disturbed. When a Pentecostal speaks of life as delivered once again by a second birth in experiences of light and wind and fire, he or she dramatically symbolizes dissolutions of the past in catalytic and cataclysmic recoveries of wholeness. In Pentecostal language, that is an achievement of holiness. Such recoveries spread like forest fires along linked chains of kin and neighbours, re-forming families or creating communities which are themselves extended families-in-God. The importance of these networks for facilitating conversion can hardly be exaggerated. Rodney Stark, working in the different contexts of Mormon missions and early Christian missions among Jews of the Diaspora, has shown how faith spreads from relative to relative, neighbour to neighbour, but rarely from door to door.[21]

All the foregoing evidence illustrates another generalization proposed by Stark which is the continuity between what missionaries and carriers of the faith have to offer and what is already in the inherited background. Though Pentecostalism maintains a rigorous rejection of Catholicism, it also activates elements which are actually latent in the Catholic faith. Kin relations are forged 'in God', the *promesa* or promise is tested and realized in the gifts of healing and of the spirit, and godparenthood is extended to all the *hermanos* and the *hermanas*. Indeed, the women of Pentecostalism form something which is very close to a sisterhood. As they are brought into the circle of participation they more and more actively relate to each other and sustain each other.

At the same time, elements of the classic Protestant Ethic are realized, since discipline and sobriety are as vigorously embraced in ordinary life as ecstasy and release are achieved in the sphere of worship. Protestantism perhaps offers education, as it did in El Petén in the 1930s, or else it may motivate its followers to seek after education once there is the slightest chance such education is available. It may well be that the combination of discipline and educational aspiration is already stirring in some people and then, as they cast their eyes to new horizons, Protestantism emerges as one marker of a whole new way of life they propose to follow. The role of Protestantism is to reinforce and, indeed, sanctify their vision of comprehensive betterment. Clearly it provides them with a raft on to which people bound on the same journey may lash themselves.

That raft lies in a current which often slews in an American direction, at least for those in the immediate proximity of the United States. This is not to suggest, as many nationalist intellectuals would argue, that conversion to Pentecostalism is the straight path to Americanization. It roots often lie, after all, in the oral traditions and oratory of black cultures and to that extent it does not inculcate the American concern with the written word. But it does bring people from all kinds of background into contact with North Americans, and with their expectations, and provides channels along which American ideas and ideas of America may move. The brothers and sisters communicate and pick up influences travelling from another world, mostly the joys of heaven but also the promise and power of the United States. Pentecostalism, after all, is about spiritual power and empowerment, and it would be surprising if some believers were not impressed by the United States as a fount of power. It may even be that Protestants from Puerto Rico, and elsewhere in Latin America, like Protestants in Korea, are more likely to migrate to the United States.

Whatever may be the truth about the pull of US power, it is evident that Pentecostalism (as well as other forms of evangelicalism) enables many of its followers to achieve a power in their lives which can simultaneously infuse them with the possibility of 'betterment' and of new goods of every kind, spiritual and material, and also put them in touch with spiritual charges and discharges lodged deep in the indigenous culture, black, Indian or Hispanic. The long-term resources now drawn upon in people's lives run back both to the traditions of Protestant revival and to the ancient spirit worlds of Indian peasants and African slaves.

Chapter 11

Protestantism and Economic Culture: Evidence Reviewed

There is a general, indeed notorious, supposition in sociological and anthropological studies that Protestantism is associated with economic success. This supposition derives in a loose way from Max Weber and the endless debate about how the Protestant Ethic influenced, and was influenced by, the Spirit of Capitalism. But that debate has been mainly focused on the first wave of Calvinist Protestantism in the sixteenth, the seventeenth and (marginally) the eighteenth century. The debate has been less concerned with the second wave of Methodist Protestantism; and so far as the third and Pentecostal wave is concerned, the evidence we have is recent and rather fragmentary. When it comes to the second and third waves of Protestantism, they have been discussed more in terms of their contribution to democracy, to individualism and to the avoidance of violent revolution than in terms of their capacity to promote economic success. The *locus classicus* of debates over Methodism is not so much Weber as Halévy.[1] If Weber is invoked, it is on account of his essay on 'The Protestant Sects and the Spirit of Capitalism' rather than 'The Protestant Ethic and the Spirit of Capitalism'.[2]

That essay is a useful starting point because Weber stresses the way in which membership in a church, especially after a period of probation, provides a guarantee of moral qualification and, therefore, of credit. Doctrine he regards as comparatively unimportant so long as the moral qualifications required enshrine the Puritan virtues. Weber also notes, as did de Tocqueville earlier, the fantastic variety of associations to which Americans belong. They include, for example, masonic lodges as well as churches. These associations provide a means of contact, a source of mutual assistance and information, and a form of insurance. As a result, the USA is not a formless sandheap of individuals, but rather a buzzing complex of voluntary organizations. It is the transfer of that buzzing complex to Latin America (and South Korea) which is currently under way. Time and again in the studies here reviewed the emphasis falls on the importance of the fraternal network.

Of course, we are not, in fact, dealing just with small so-called sects, even though many of the groups concerned only have a few thousand adherents. As we have seen, the phenomenon of contemporary Pentecostalism has a wider provenance than ever Calvinism had in the past, and certainly more than Calvinism has today. The scale is 'small' only in the sense that the people who become Pentecostals are small people and their 'capitalism' is at the moment mostly 'penny capitalism'.

There have been a reasonable number of localized investigations concerned with the effect of contemporary evangelical religion, in particular Pentecostalism, on economic behaviour, or at least touching on that issue as a major concern. There are, however, some problems about obtaining really firm evidence and these need to be set out. Once this is done it will become clear that we are dealing only with cumulative indications and with more or less sensitive observations about likely outcomes. We cannot expect to find more than plausible likelihoods. But, at least, it is not necessary to rehearse that part of the classic debate concerned with whether Protestantism or capitalism came first. *What we do need to probe are the complicated feedbacks whereby people perceive the possibility of change and so grasp and are grasped by religious ideas which can accelerate that change and/or help them to cope with it.*

A question which has arisen crucially in the original debate, and now arises once more, is the contingent nature of the connection between evangelical religion and economic advance. It is clear that capitalism in the past *could* occur without Protestantism and vice versa. Scholars have asked themselves complicated questions, for example, about pious Calvinist communities in certain parts of Holland and also in Scotland which did not appear to bring forth the fruits of the capitalist spirit. Then, and again now, there is no necessary connection. The posited linkages and plausible likelihoods have to be couched in terms of frequent concurrence and mutual reinforcements. Evangelical religion and economic advancement do *often* go together, and when they do so appear mutually to support and *reinforce* one another.

Economic Advance by Non-evangelicals: 'Strangers'; Mormons

The capacity shown by people of religious persuasions other than evangelical to advance themselves needs some further discussion. To take the example of the Lebanese (or 'Syrians'), their ability to make good in the Caribbean, in Brazil, in the Ivory Coast and in North America presumably derives from a long historical experience of commerce in the Levant, and from the way many minorities – though not all – are in a position to exploit a particular corner of trade. A group of ethnic 'strangers' willing to assist one another and to act cohesively can build up economic resources rather in the manner of the sects described by Max Weber. This they are well able to do even if they arrived, as most Syrians did, with only the resources of a hawker or a pedlar. The Chinese, too, are notoriously capable of forming a cohesive community of prosperous minor entrepreneurs, without the extra assistance from evangelical religion. Examples can be multiplied, for example the achievements of Asians in Kenya and, after their expulsion from Kenya, again in Britain.

This phenomenon is, however, easily understood and familiar, and it need not erode any propositions we may tenatively put forward specifically about evangelicals and the improvement of material fortunes. Evangelicals are not usually migrant members of historic trading communities, though, of course, they *can* be. The Huguenots who went to England, Holland, South Africa and North America after 1685 were precisely such, though they can only broadly be classified as 'evangelicals'.

Less easily disposed of are instances of groups arising in a similar manner to evangelical Protestants and in similar environments whose members achieve comparable advances without being 'Protestant'. The main groups in question are the Witnesses, the Mormons and the Adventists. They need briefly to be considered.

With regard to the Witnesses there is a lack of material so far at least as concerns Latin America, though evidence gathered elsewhere suggests the same kind of capacity for economic and social improvement as found amongst evangelicals. James Beckford's fine study of Witnesses in England documents their capacity in a general and impressionistic way.[3] Norman Long has provided further supporting documentation with regard to Witnesses in Zambia.[4]

There are general grounds for supposing that Adventists also improve their positsions somewhat, though the evidence directly derived from Latin America is fragmentary. Certainly material cited later from studies by Lewellen and Birdwell-Pheasant suggests that Adventism assists social mobility.[5] In the America (North, Central and South), the Adventists build hospitals and provide schools, as well as encouraging certain practices with regard to health and diet. They constitute a kind of small-scale welfare system which can hardly fail to help forward their community.

The Mormons are an interesting case. In the first place, Rodney Stark has maintained that they are a *new* religion rather than a semi-Christian sect.[6] Therefore, he argues, they make their maximum impact where modernization has advanced sufficiently to create a religious vacuum. This means, presumably, that they are expanding on the whole in environments already prosperous, for example Uruguay.

The position with regard to the Mormons is complicated further, and in a way highly relevant to our overall problem, by certain aspects of their proselytizing style. They have emphasized their US character and origin, and this has made them attractive to persons already well-disposed to the US way of life and even, maybe, seeking connections in the USA. These persons clearly form a distinctive subgroup. As Mark Grover in his study of Mormonism in Brazil puts it, 'The number of cars that have recently become prominent at Mormon chapels provides extra visual evidence of the success of members in following the American-influenced middle class dream.'[7] Mormons are urged to follow the original US model as closely as possible. A curious outcrop from the stress that Mormons place on their US character is that blacks were not a target population for conversion up to quite recently, and this has meant that many of those who belonged to the poorest sections of society did not, and could not, become Mormons. Indeed, in the early stages of Mormon activity in Brazil, the missionaries concentrated on the German community, which was unequivocally white, and moreover already equipped with the skills necessary to become better-off.

Another aspect of Mormon missions which helps their converts to assimilate the norms of middle-class America is the teaching of English, which may in turn facilitate visits to the USA, and lead to attendance at Brigham Young University. Salt Lake City is a kind of Mecca for Mormons, even though they are no longer expected to migrate to Utah. Those who make the trip rapidly acquire new horizons as to what prosperity can offer, and ideas about how prosperity is to be achieved. To such pilgrims the USA has appeared attractive, superior, powerful and modern. The approved style among Mormons for presenting oneself in public has been based on the US businessman, and no doubt the outer style proclaimed and moulded the inner attitude. Indeed, at one time in Brazil missionaries were identified by the fact that they wore hats.

Those who became converted also had to live according to the Mormon code of health, which included abstention from coffee and tea, as well as from alcohol and tobacco. In general, the fruits of faith were seen as cleanliness, home improvements and decent diet. When women met in what was known as the Relief Society they were taught the skills of motherhood, of arts and crafts, and of social relations. The Relief Society also encouraged home industries and communal gardening. Clearly, these characteristics of Mormonism simultaneously hindered and helped the promotion of faith. It requires great fortitude and persistence to reject your background in favour of a religious group which absorbs nearly all your time and cuts you off from almost all outside connections. Again, while some people are attracted to the image of Americanism, others are repelled. But for those who *did* make the transition to the Mormon religion, the resocialization was very extensive, and it involved an orientation to the USA and to US ways and styles. This inevitably raises the question as to whether perhaps we are really talking as much about religious vehicles for making Latins into North Americans as about the effect of a specific Mormon ethos.

A study carried out by David Clawson in Mexico largely confirms on a small scale what Mark Grover suggests for Mormonism in the whole of Brazil.[8] Clawson remarks, in a preliminary way, that insofar as Catholics in the USA have been shown to be socially and educationally on a level with Protestants, this is a reflection of the way North American Catholics have become assimilated to the dominant Protestant ethos of pristine America. The study which he then presents is of a Nealtican community in central Mexico.

Clawson describes how converts to Mormonism were first made in the inter-war period. Then in 1948 a Mormon became municipal President. This led many Catholics to fear reprisals for previous persecution, but in fact it simply opened a free space for Mormon activity which non-resident Catholic priests could do little to counteract. About 8 per cent of the community became converted to Mormonism (nearly 600 people), while a few became converted to the Pentecostal Church of God.

Clawson's conclusions confirm all the conventional expectations of differences between Catholics and 'Protestants' (so-called). He took a stratified random sample of farmers from each religious group and found major differences with regard to literacy, leadership, readiness to participate in cooperative economic ventures, attitudes towards outsiders – and wealth. 'Protestants' placed great emphasis on reading, initially the Bible, but eventually magazines. Of the seventeen youths in post-elementary education thirteen were Protestant. Protestant women were trained in how to save their domestic money. So far as outside contacts went, they had strong ties with US missionaries. They became increasingly open to visits from health and development personnel, and – as mentioned above – they gained experience and acquired new aspirations by excursions to Salt Lake City. Clawson concludes that similar changes might follow the introduction of Catholic base communities, but success would depend there on the availability of priests, whereas for Protestants success was quite independent of any clerical presence.

Of course, one cannot generalize on the basis of one study, however much it reinforces prior expectations. It does suggest, nevertheless, that Mormons, soaked in the Protestant ambience of their historic and geographical origins, do act as carriers for the Protestant Ethic equally with those who are 'proper' Protestants. Witnesses and Mormons, though theologically at the margins of Christianity, carry forward the general tendencies of the Protestant sectarian backgrounds from which they emerged. These tendencies are fused more broadly with the spirit of America. As to the Adventists, it is likely that the same is true of them, but in their case one is inclined to include them within the scope of evangelical Protestant Christianity.

Clawson, in his comments, raises a question relevant to most of the studies now to be reviewed as well as to his own. It may well be that those who choose a new religion are already the more active members of a given community. Their predisposition to try something new, should it become available, makes them opt for the moulding which their new faith provides. They will not usually be knowledgeable enough to distinguish between varieties of Protestantism and movements which are only marginally Christian. Rather, they will, amongst other things, perceive the presence of a novelty which for them carries the aura of modernity including (maybe) technical opportunity and welfare provision. In short, they enter a wider world through the narrow door of sectarian membership, discipline and mobility.

The study by Clawson, even though mainly of Mormons, provides the classic outline of the effects attributed to Protestantism. The four studies now to be looked at were all made in Mexico and bring out different aspects of the varied situations in which Protestantism makes an impression. In discussing them, I omit inessential elements and concentrate on such novel features as the studies may present.

Case Studies: Mexico

A study by Mary O'Connor of Mayos compares the impact of evangelical Protestantism with the impact of a nativistic millenarian movement.[9] At the time of the study in the mid-seventies the Mayos numbered some 20,000 and were much better-off than most other Mexican Indians because they lived in an agriculturally developed area. They were also more integrated into Mexican society. Most spoke both Spanish and Mayo, and had acquired modern consumer goods and clothing. Those Mayos who became Protestant, which effectively means Pentecostal, initiated a major change of life, notably by gaining freedom from the fiesta system and from the obligation of *fiesteros* to give away huge quantities of food. To reject the obligations of the fiesta helped them get together more money for consumer goods and the education of their children. They also saved money by their rejection of all entertainment, especially drinking. Yet the rejection of waste and indulgence was not a rejection of wealth. Pastors encouraged their congregations to work hard, educate their children and improve their material conditions. It was not accounted a reproach to own a tape recorder or a car. Mary O'Connor claims: 'Rationality in general is encouraged, a beliefs in witchcraft, ghosts, buried treasure and folk curing, common among the general population, are ridiculed.'[10]

The nativistic millennarian movement among the Mayos has some points in common with Pentecostal. The participants are an elect to be saved when God destroys the world; and they refuse drink and secular entertainment. However, the nativistic movement aims to regain economic and political control for Mayos and rejects all aspects of the mestizo world as evil. O'Connor identifies those who take part as having few opportunities for economic and social progress. The Protestants, on the other hand, see a chance of advancement for themselves and their families. Indeed, they already have an adequate economic base. They can become Protestant without losing their Mayo identity, which means that they can make the best of both the mestizo and Mayo worlds. O'Connor adds that traditional folk-Catholicism will probably remain the faith of the majority, though the fiestas will become increasingly secular. She also mentions that those who cease to be Protestant often do not revert to Catholicism. (That is an important point noted in some other studies and bears on the relationship of Protestantism to secularization.)

Paul Turner's study 'Religious Conversion and Community Development' has to do with some remarkable mass conversions among Tzeltal Indians in the municipality of Oxchuc, Chiapas, in southern Mexico.[11] The study is additionally interesting because it offers a sympathetic account of the work of the Wycliffe Bible Translators which needs to be put in the balance when considering the recent criticisms of the translators by anthropologists. The missionary work here described was passive and low-key. Indeed, the initial converts responded after hearing the new religion explained on records.

Prior to these conversions the Oxchuc municipality was considered the most backward. Afterwards, however, it came to exceed all other Indian communities in education and acceptance of scientific medicine. The Tzeltals now buy washbasins and soap. Previously they resisted education. But now they read bilingual materials written in their own language and in Spanish: primers, story-books, health booklets, a dictionary – and the New Testament. Adult literacy classes are eagerly sought out.

In his analysis of these changes Turner lays stress on the tensions which had existed through high and growing population, the expropriation of land by Ladinos, and consequent pressure to borrow land. The tensions manifested themselves in excessive drinking and accusations of witchcraft, and the religion of the Tzeltals was not capable of coping with them. Rather it emphasized the maintenance of past traditions and of cosmic harmony with gods and shamans. Catholicism reinforced this with an other-worldly concern and by passively accepting the linkage between social, political and religious hierarchies. By contrast, Protestantism emphasized direct access to the God and the possibility of change.

Being freed from fears of evil spirits and from drink, the converts adopted a sober style of life which included hard work, punctuality, fulfilment of promises, honesty and thrift. 'The exercise of these minor virtues,' says Turner, 'led to wealth accumulation and a rising standard of living.'[12] The Protestant clinic even became something of a medical shrine for the Tzeltals. Not only did they seek out scientific medicine, but they looked increasingly to the future and to personal improvement. Tzeltals became more responsive to governmental development programmes and, therefore, came to receive a dispro-portionate amount of federal aid. (Turner adds that a counter-reformation which was initiated by some young Catholic priests produced similar, if not superior, fruits of the 'Protestant' ethos. In Turner's view this is because they had absorbed and incorporated the Protestant challenge.)

The next study of change was made among the 90,000 Chols of northern Chiapas and it also concerns the Wycliffe Bible translators.

The general situation is described by Henry Wilbur Aulie in a study done for Fuller Theological Seminary.[13] Initially a couple of missionaries arrived in Chol country and converted a few mestizos, who in turn influenced a few Indians. These Indians formed a group of lay evangelists who travelled from village to village. Their work was accelerated by the arrival of Wycliffe translators who provided the Bible in the local language. The overall result was an increase in ethnic self-respect, linguistic vitality and economic independence. Aulie goes on to discuss later breakaway Protestant movements, notably of Pentecostals, and to note the emergence of a local Roman Catholic counter-reformation.

As in the case of the Indians studied by Turner, the Chols have experienced rising population and hunger for land. Aulie makes several points pertinent to social and economic advancement. He stresses the beneficent effect of learning to read and preparing to preach. Both these slipways of Protestantism threaten the authority of the father and may in the long run take the son out of the ambit of his family. He also stresses the growing feeling that the communal obligation to sustain the fiestas is wasteful. Clearly, the Chol people, like many other 'Indian' groups, were in a state of partial disintegration which manifested itself in alcoholism. They were also fearful of shamans and spirits. It seems that Protestantism, when it arrived, restored a sense of power, and this might manifest itself in dispersing spirits, or in improved production and learning to keep bees and cattle, or in cleanliness and temperance. (When the conversions took place, they normally did so by segments and whole families.)

Yet the sense of power could begin to tail off with the second generation. And the local language might once again go into a decline, particularly as people took to singing hymns in Spanish and continued to pursue advancement by hankering after the culture of the mestizo. Pastors in particular may come to have a strong sense of their own personal dignity and seek a house in a mestizo town as well as mestizo schools for their children. Presbyterian forms of organization assist this separation of pastor from people. Aulie expresses the classic dilemma of success lamented by John Wesley. Those who pull themselves up by their bootstraps feel they 'are not as other men are'. 'No longer spending their money on intoxicating liquor,' says Aulie, 'the Christians now use their income to buy clothing, medicine, mules, radios, and trips to the outside world.'[14]

Two interesting and connected developments discussed by Aulie are the dramatic changes in the music used, and the arrival of the Pentecostals in what had hitherto been designated Presbyterian territory. Initially, hymns in the local language were very popular, but now there is great increase in the use of Spanish choruses. These are accompanied by the guitar and follow the rhythms of radio and mariachi groups. When the Pentecostals arrived many of those in favour of the new participatory styles left the Presbyterians to join the new denomination. Some of the divisions between Presbyterians and Pentecostals followed the fault-lines of local political rivalries, between villages and inside them.

These issues cannot be followed up here, since they lead away from the issue of economic advancement. Nevertheless, a relevant question does arise because of the relationship between social or geographical mobility and the status of being mestizo and speaking Spanish. The arrival of missionaries was initially part of the opening up of the whole area, but as the opening up accelerated, it pulled the Chols and their native culture not only upwards but also outwards, away from the little chapels and the Chol community. And although the Protestant emphasis on literacy and on the native tongue renewed the sense of Chol culture, the new faith also helped break up the community into rival groups comprising the Christo-pagans, the secularized, the Catholics – and the various evangelical rivals.

A fourth study, significantly also among Maya, throws a different sidelight on the role of Protestantism in development. In general, the number of Protestant believers has increased thirteen times in the period of Mexico's economic take-off between 1940 and 1980. Jean-Pierre Bastian describes how Protestantism bifurcates into a written urban culture and an oral rural culture.[15] At the same time, economic development in Mexico has stimulated the formation of a rural bourgeoisie whose members try to monopolize commerce and who exploit their workers. Rural Protestantism finds itself ranged against this rural bourgeoisie. Clearly, this bears more directly on the political than the economic aspect of Protestantism, but it helps underline the complexity of the economic situation and the difficulty of locating the relationship of Protestantism to economic change and advance. Patricia Fortuny, in her work on rural Protestantism in the Yucatan, shows that Protestants are concentrated in the least developed part of the countryside, while Catholicism is strongest in the area of capitalist agriculture.[16] This simply means that where the current of Protestantism seeps into the political and economic divisions of the countryside, it may become concentrated in out-groups trapped in economic backwardness and fighting for survival. That fact need not in itself alter the general tendency of Protestantism to promote some economic advance, though this is not an issue on which Fortuny comments.

Case Studies: Guatemala

The four studies just surveyed have indicated the diverse ways in which Protestantism may infiltrate different groups. All the groups discussed are Indian, mostly Maya, and that reflects the relatively greater expansion of Protestantism among the Indian peoples of Chiapas, Tabasco, and the Yucatan in southern Mexico, as well perhaps as the distribution of missionary investigators and anthropologists. The two studies which follow now offer analyses of groups in Guatemala which are almost continuous ethnically with the peoples of southern Mexico. One of them, by Schwartz and Reina, I discuss in more detail in the chapter on conversion because it is really a study of microprocesses rather than an enquiry into economic aspects of Protestantism.[17] (Indeed, I use the study there to indicate in a much more precise way the persistent relationship of new Protestant groups to struggles between local factions.)

The study by Schwartz and Reina begins by drawing on a point made over two decades ago by Emilio Willems. It is that Protestants are found not only among migrants to the new rural frontiers or among those otherwise isolated in the city, but among people who own middle-sized plots of land. These constitute a kind of frugal land-working peasantry who farm for subsistence and are fairly independent of markets. What makes the difference in such instances is relative freedom from ecclesiastical and social authority combined with adequate means for sustaining an independent existence. Schwartz and Reina approached three communities in El Petén, northern Guatemala, equipped with an interest in such semi-independent middle groups. Does their susceptibility to conversion vary in some way in relation to their independence, their tendency to migrate, and their openness to change in general?

Schwartz and Reina comment on the weakness of the Roman Catholic Church in El Petén up to 1954. People still distinguish sharply between the religion of the clergy and the social identity of being Catholic. The three communities they studied are in an isolated frontier area which was spared any traumatic conquest and was never subject to patron–client relationships or to the hacienda system. The area ought theoretically to be ripe for conversion, but in fact this is mediated and canalized by the precise nature of the different social systems. In the town of Flores, which is the main local centre, there is a system of marked social stratification which prevents some potential converts opting for innovation. Those who do become converted are middle-class, but less secure and less able to compete with the elite than are the 'new' Catholics nurtured by the priests. The main arena of conflict is between the old and the new Catholics, who respectively comprise the elite and the counter-elite. In the community of San Andrés, by contrast, the system of stratification is less marked and people are more willing to work out their frustrations. 'There is consequently more religious activity in San Andrés than in Flores and proportionately more people opt for innovation. There is, moreover, a base in the community culture for innovative agents'.[18] This brief sketch and the sentences just quoted do at least show how difficult it is to do statistical comparisons between Protestants and Catholics. Who is available for economic and/or religious innovation depends on the shape of the social structure.

Nevertheless, an empirical study has been attempted by James Sexton of two towns in Guatemala called Panajachel and San Juan.[19] Panajachel is 58 per cent Indian and San Juan 96 per cent. Protestant church membership in both towns is almost entirely Indian. Since Catholic cargos were organized by the confraternities, participation in them was utilized in the study as one measure of traditional behaviour. 'Modern' behaviour was defined as it related to changes in clothing, houses, furniture, child-spacing and migration, as well as to job aspirations and degree of fatalism.

Sexton's interests were focused on the direction of causation. He states that he does not see religious values having a major impact on socio-economic behaviour, as the starting motor. He argues rather than in Panajachel, at least, relatively well-off Indians acquire certain Ladino cultural traits such as the wearing of Western clothing and living in more modern houses. They then become more exposed to the outside world and, *at this juncture*, become converted to Protestantism. There is a feed back in changes which are linked one to another. In Panajachel, and to some extent in San Juan, the Protestants are better-off, more literate, live in more modern houses, work more often in non-agricultural occupations, are more inclined to sobriety, and are in their attitudes less fatalistic. Thus, all the main elements of 'achievement' motivation are present and Protestantism cooperates with other elements in a complicated dance of mutual reinforcement helping along modernization. He mentions in passing, as do other sources, that the highland Maya have long been noted for industriousness and self-denial. They are 'penny capitalists'. What Protestantism does is to harness these qualities and reinforce them in the context of a more forward-looking and active world-view. It is part of the process of opening out. That process makes Protestantism possible and is, in turn, helped forward by Protestantism.

This, perhaps, is the point at which to insert a small but interesting item of evidence drawn from Belize, adjacent to Guatemala. Donna Birdwell-Pheasant studied an area originally settled by refugees from the Caste Wars in the Yucatan, mostly mestizo interspersed with some Maya Indians.[20] The local religion was based on fiestas and novenas, the latter being mostly under the control of the sugar ranchers and bosses. In the 1920s the sugar ranchers collapsed; and at the same time the religious culture disintegrated under the impact of Adventism. By the late 1920s the religious scene comprised a small group of traditional Catholics concerned with syncretic practices, some lay Catholic brothers, a religiously disillusioned group, some Adventists and some newly established Pentecostals. The traditional Catholics comprise a faction opposed to the group controlling the village council, and are linked politically to a Senator in the north who has preached socialism, and who also has some commitment to a modest revival of Maya culture. The 'brothers' by contrast are linked to the Catholic Church as an institution and, therefore, to the urban centres of Belize, where the political and commercial elites are mostly Catholic. The nominal Catholics are by definition without a religious power base, but are relatively well-off and powerful within the village council. The Adventists also have links with the council and are all possessed of above average economic means. They are relatively self-sufficient and their main ties outside the village are political. The Pentecostal group is distinctive, comprising people from outside or from broken families or otherwise of low status. Pentecostalism acts as a substitute for the family rather than as a form of political alliance or even a means of upward mobility. What this example offers is, once again, a glimpse of the detailed way in which the varied religious groups are linked up to the economic and political divisions of the village.

This kind of evidence drawn from rural and largely Indian contexts can be complemented by an older study carried out by B. R. Roberts in a neighbourhood of Guatemala City.[21] Roberts lays his stress on the usefulness of belonging to a tight-knit religious network when trying to survive in the city. He argues that 'It is the social relationships and social organization made available in one of these groups that explains their effects on an individual's economic position and public behavior.'[22] These effects are both negative and positive from an economic point of view. As regards the negative effects, Protestants were too few and too poor (in the mid-sixties, that is) for their network to give them serious advantages. Their churches were so recently founded that they absorbed a great deal of the time and money of their members. Furthermore, some of the better-off among Protestants tended to become less active in their faith. Of course, this tendency has always made it difficult to measure how far 'sectarian' Protestantism provides a social escalator, since success may mean that people step off the escalator. At any rate, the evidence Roberts cites does not show Protestants at that period more advanced than their Catholic neighbours in economic or educational standing. He also points out that most low-income workers in Guatemala City are strongly motivated to improve their position. The problem is that the means to do so are pitifully lacking. (It is worth remarking that several of the studies reviewed here mention the existence of strong motivation in the general population toward improving one's economic position as well as the importance of networks for Roman Catholics).

Yet the Protestant network of mutual assistance which he describes clearly has considerable potential, and we know that these networks are today very much more extensive in Guatemala City and, for that matter, in most of the other mega-cities of Central and Southern America. It was, of course, the mutual assistance provided by reliable and credit-worthy fellow Christians which Weber stressed in his remarks about the American Baptists. Roberts describes how

> Funds attached to the central headquarters of these groups pay for funeral expenses when a family member or a believer dies. When a Protestant in one of the neighborhoods is sick, members of his congregation join together to provide money for the affected family and frequently visit the sick person. Should a Protestant in one of the neighborhoods need help to improve or repair his house, install drainage, or obtain a loan, other members of his congregation join together to give help. If a Protestant is out of a job or wants to change his work, other members of his congregation help him find work.[23]

The Protestant networks, then, provide an intensive and extensive information service and offer a kind of insurance as well as the emotional support of stable relationships. Beyond that they inculcate North American norms of behaviour and educate members in such matters as household budgeting, social comportment and table manners. To this one would add the way in which membership in Protestant groups provides a marriage and sexual discipline and along with that some break in the cycle of endemic corruption. It is also amazing that today so many Protestant churches can provide a clinic and some access to skilled medical help. As in Hong Kong the Protestant churches offer a significant part of a welfare system. What does not, however, arise from membership of the Protestant – or rather of the Pentecostal – churches is active leadership in projects for community improvement. This sphere is one where Catholics, with their more organic traditions of broad communitarian concern, are much more conspicuous.

Some more general comments on the evidence in Guatemala are found in the work of Virginia Garrard Burnett, and these are particularly useful because they touch on a much later state in the development of Protestantism than does Roberts. Virginia Burnett emphasizes, in particular, the rapid growth of Protestantism since the earthquake in 1976. Burnett uses evidence from several anthropological studies which I do not attempt to specify individually. In summarizing what she has to say I shall try to keep the focus on economic advancement, although it is significant that such a focus very easily broadens out into diffuse considerations about conversion and the wider appeal of Protestantism.[24]

Protestantism attracts converts because it combines material and spiritual improvement, as indeed it has done since Presbyterian 'ragged schools' were established in the late nineteenth century. Discussing the superior wealth and industry of Protestants compared to Catholics in San Antonio Aguascalientes, Virginia Burnett quotes the local Protestant view of the link between conversion and material improvement: 'del suelo al cielo' – from the dirt floor to the sky. The prospect of such improvements naturally appeals particularly to the marginalized and the poor.

Burnett adds that during the period of acute social distress following the earthquake of 1976, the poor saw that 'the austere moral and economic rules of the Protestant churches offered an enticing – and well-defined – route for upward mobility.'[25] This was a time of increasingly concentrated land tenure, civil violence, inflation and rising population; and the indigenous communities in particular were forced out of their isolation. The old *milpa* technologists were replaced by dispossessed peasants and petty capitalists, many of them receptive to fresh religious motivations.

From 1976 on, these frustrations were by no means confined to marginalized people. The Guatemalan middle class also found itself cut off from access to the political arena and experienced acute status inconsistency. For the first time, substantial numbers in the Guatemalan middle class became converted to Protestantism (though some also began to entertain a more intense and meditative attachment to Catholicism). A church like Verbo, for example, has a strong middle-class component in its membership. Its facilities and style are reminiscent of North America, and it offers educational facilities. In fact, the organization associated with Verbo resembles many large churches in the USA. It provides a complete protective and insulated environment: an orphanage, a school, medical and dental clinics, sports facilities, family entertainment and recreation, not to mention a women's magazine called 'Ester' designed 'to help women fulfil their God-given feminine destinies'.[26] There is considerable emphasis on restoring the integrity of the family.

The material assistance and training provided by Verbo is apparently not restricted to members, and whatever may be said about the politics of Verbo, it seems difficult to deny the extent of the social first-aid work in which its members and leaders are engaged. One does not have data on how this kind of integrated and familial environment assists personal and economic advancement, but on general grounds it seems likely to do so. And one must underline the way in which Latin American cities are beginning to abound in organizations of this kind. Many of them are independent initiatives even when they have North American connections and draw on North American support. A non-denominational (?) organization like Shekinah run by Dr Charlotte Lindgren, and known to the author, would provide another example from among many in Guatemala City. Dr Lindgren is responsible for the El Refugio home for abandoned and needy children.

Case Studies: Ecuador and Colombia

It is now useful to turn to the evidence to be found in South America, though that is perhaps even more fragmentary than the evidence found in Mexico and Guatemala. Nevertheless, it provides pointers. We begin with studies undertaken in the adjacent Andean countries of Ecuador and Colombia.

Ecuador has not provided a very fertile soil for Protestantism. In any case, Protestant missions were late arriving. Most of their converts lived on the coast, where there was a large number of small or medium-sized farms. By 1979 there were in Portillo, for example, some eighteen congregations. Kent Maynard, in his study, says that evangelicals often belong to secular organizations. 'Artisans are particularly likely to be members of their professional cooperative, while other evangelicals have been involved in savings and loan cooperatives, and housing cooperatives.'[27] This participation in wider organizations provides a channel of social and economic mobility for them, and is simultaneously an expression of their responsibility as artisans. What is worth taking from this small study is that the attitudes of evangelicals to secular memberships vary according to the country, the social context and, of course, denominational emphasis.

Whereas in Guatemala the attitude may be inturned, in Ecuador it may be more outgoing. In Ecuador the secular memberships are a means whereby some evangelicals make their way in the wider society. Of course, they observe the same rules of abstinence which define evangelicals everywhere and give them additional capacity for economic advancement.

In Colombia, as in many other Latin American countries, the initial relationship of Protestantism to economic and social advancement was mediated through prestigious schools, especially those run by Presbyterians. These, of course, belong to the early phase of missions promoted by the historic denominations. Elizabeth Brusco, in her study of El Cocuy, a town in northern Boyaca (discussed in more detail elsewhere in relation to Protestantism and the role of women) mentions that the personality promoted by Protestantism is regarded as the antithesis of the Colombian personality, which is seen as undisciplined, vicious and lacking in respect for others.[28]

In El Cocuy, Protestants were divided between the 'historic' denomination of the Lutherans – and the Pentecostals. What Elizabeth Brusco provides is an intimate picture of precisely those psychological and social changes, especially the taming of machismo, which might give Protestants some assistance in a quest for social advancement. Machismo is a major drawback because the more women a man 'conquers' the less he can provide. In her view, the effect of Protestantism is to reduce drinking and fighting and to increase concern for the home and the family. Whereas Catholics aimed to acquire a radio, the first priority of Protestants was a domestic table. Their concern, she says, was with wholesomeness, with learning, and with being productive. Evangelical households ate better and exemplified new priorities in consumption. In addition, the Lutherans provided music, pianos, and games and sport, by way of family recreation.

Dr Brusco comments: 'The early missionaries were also involved in what might be viewed as small-scale development work, and their interest in "progress" was a main selling point of the new doctrine that continues to characterize evangelical activities in Colombia.'[29] She goes on to add, which of course is more generally true: 'Modernization for its own sake, as well as class mobility and status achievement, are not the goals of these evangelical community activists.'[30] What her study shows more clearly than most is the way mutations at the level of the personality and the culture of the family are capable of altering the 'tone' of a society. The possibility of advancement follows as a byproduct, which is not to say that believers are indifferent to the material blessings associated with their new faith.

The other three studies of Protestantism in Colombia are focused respectively on Medellín, Bogota and Palmira. Thornton's study of Medellín suggests that people seek out Protestant churches because of loneliness and a desire to belong, and because many priests do not make themselves sufficiently available to help with such problems as sickness, marital breakup and difficult teenagers.[31] Catholicism seemed too vast and impersonal and tied in to the social, educational and economic system. So the individual had little opportunity to exercise his own spiritual gifts, or to read, or to help create a warm, concerned, participatory and friendly community. Thornton also comments that in Colombia prestige is the basis of association and some lower-class Protestants are glad to acquire prestige by making genuinely cross-class contacts at a Protestant church in a middle-class neighbourhood.

Clearly, these attractions of Protestantism are at least such as to assist survival in the economic conditions of the modern Colombian city. Thornton goes on to discuss economic advancement.[32] He says that no Protestant he interviewed ever mentioned economic security or material gain as a motive for conversion, and some mentioned their acceptance of economic costs or even loss of a job. At the same time, they said they could be sure of assistance in time of need or unemployment. Here we observe, once again, the help provided by a network.

Most Protestants felt assured that God provided them with 'material blessings' not experienced before their conversion. These blessings came the more easily from their commitment to a strict code and their vocational attitude to work. When a piece of repair work needs to be done Protestants recommend a member of their own fraternity. Thornton also mention the 'blessings' found among Adventists, in particular through an emphasis on diet, and through the provision of health and educational services.[33]

Karl W. Westmeier, in his study of Bogota, notes the early association of Protestantism with liberal politics in Colombia, as in so many other Latin American countries.[34] He also suggests that Pentecostal ecstasy takes over from older experiences of trance and that Pentecostal healers draw from more ancient traditions of healing. He views ecstasy as providing a form of integration for people dealing with new experiences in mega-cities like Bogota. The Protestant communities of Bogota provide solutions for those held in bondage by vices and by household squabbles. One solution, of course, is for the husband to restrict himself to one woman, which, as mentioned above, restricts his outgoings.

Frequent meetings in the church provide Protestants with an all-absorbing life-style which holds meaninglessness and anomie at bay. When Colombian *creyentes* speak about 'power' they mean the experience of moral victory. They also gain a rather different sense of power when they participate in a mass meeting. The severity of their dress and behaviour serves to mark them off and to put behind them the old style of life. *Creyentes* feel that in every respect they have become different. Their new mystical identity parallels the acquisition of a new identity for dealing with the difficulties of urban life. It seems that this new identity does not lead to the kind of withdrawal from politics found among many evangelicals in some other countries.

Westmeier's summary of evidence about economic advancement begins by suggesting that when Colombian Protestants save they do so not to 'prove their election' but in order to have time to labour for the Lord.

> Betterment of external physical conditions (their house, some additional furniture) happens incidentally. Although Protestantism has been Colombia for more than a hundred years, the truly indigenous and enthusiastic breakthrough has occurred very recently. At this developmental stage, it is not yet clear whether and/or to what extent processes of embourgeoisement can be distinguished. On the other hand, enthusiastic Protestantism is making successful evangelistic inroads into the Bogotá middle class.[35]

The incursion into the middle class bears out evidence already cited for Guatemala City.

The study carried out by Cornelia Butler Flora in Valle del Caula offers mildly negative conclusions about the economic opportunities opened up by Pentecostalism. She comments that the Pentecostals she encountered did not perceive any likely connection between conversion and improved personal circumstances.[36] Their belief in the efficacy of their personal efforts was not more marked than among Catholics, nor did they have an increased sense of the power of their own personal voice. On the other hand, they were not, as some have suggested, any *less* aware of what was going on in the world around them.

At the same time, Flora does point to certain distinctive aspects of Pentecostalism. In common with Elizabeth Brusco she stresses new consumption patterns and a sense of family solidarity. It common with Rolim (to be discussed later) and with Roberts, she finds Pentecostals strongly represented among the self-employed, or else located in small enterprises. And this finding can be regarded as showing them outside the truly modern (large-scale), sections of society. The data presented by Cornelia Butler Flora lead to the kind of conclusion found in Roberts, which emphasizes the central importance of the network. What the network offers is a safety net and – quite often – some work. In Latin American conditions the advantages of such a system of mutual support may take a generation or two to be realized.

Contrasting Case Studies: 'Indians' in Peru and Bolivia

Before considering material which has to do with the major population centres in South America, it is worth looking at a couple of contrasting studies of Andean 'Indian' communities. These run parallel to the work on the Maya discussed earlier. There are, in fact, many studies of 'Indian' communities. These range from the kind of work done by Elmer Miller on the Argentinian Toba, which focuses on the way evangelical religion reduces stress and restores harmony, to analyses which accuse missionaries of propagating 'maladaptive' responses, undermining the practices which sustain group viability and identity, encouraging social division, and acting as agents of US culture.[37] This is not the place to enter into that debate, which tips one way or the other according to varied conditions in different areas and often owes something to the predilections of the author.

Of course, the focus of analysis in these studies is on terms like 'adaptation' and 'development', and economic advancement is just one aspect of development. The work of Ted Lewellen deals with the relationship of 'deviant religion and cultural evolution', and the vocabulary he uses reminds us how saturated with theory are the concepts deployed in any study of this kind, even those expressly dedicated to the 'facts'.[38]

In his discussion of the Aymara of Peru, Lewellen refers to the one circumstance affecting the vast majority of such groups: the shift from subsistence agriculture to a money economy. Increasing population, as elsewhere, has outrun the availability of land and many of the Aymara have had to leave their ancestral locality high in the mountains by Lake Titicaca and engage in wage labour on the coast. Lewellen comments: 'Exactly coincident with this sudden and severe economic change was the emergence of a small group of Seventh Day Adventists as the power elite in the community.'[39] Though making up only 18 per cent of the population, the Adventists have come to hold most of the top political offices. They are better educated, take out more bank loans, engage in more profitable jobs during time spent on the coast and have greater possessions. These differences do not arise in any important measure because the Adventists have withdrawn from the fiesta system, which is anyway not all that expensive, but as a consequence of their more favourable evaluation of education. Adventists have always valued education (as well as health) and already by 1950 there were 166 Adventist schools in the southern Peruvian highlands. Such education was not relevant while the old social system remained intact, but once it collapsed local government was reorganized on a national model with direct links to district, department and national agencies. It was also secularized and thereby opened up to non-Catholics. Only the Adventists were educationally ready for these changes, and they soon became the elite in their community and acted as the mediators of modernity. Lewellen describes them as 'preadaptive', that is, ready and apt for change.

The other study is of 'Social Change and Pentecostalism is an Aymaran Community'. It is by Gilles Rivière and he begins by referring to the 'spectacular growth' of non-Catholic religious groups in Bolivia, and to the fact that by 1986 200 of them were registered with the Bolivian Ministry of External Relations.[40] The study offers an account of how individuals were originally guaranteed integration into the traditional community, and rights to the exploitation of the local means of production, as well as participation in arrangements for the redistribution of surplus accumulation. Festivals and rituals reinforced this egalitarian social system and celebrated the historic identity of the group. But then the old order started to disintegrate as population increased and put pressure on the available land. Part of the community started to operate in a wider commercial network, traded on the black market, migrated for work, bought trucks, and generally secured economic power at the expense of the other *communarios*. Aymara identity and language lost prestige, and the community became divided into those who had gained from the changes and those who were left behind. The urban model to which the Aymara were attracted was Chilean, since Chile was just across the nearby frontier. And so too was the new faith to which part of the community gravitated. About one in four joined the Evangelical Pentecostal Church of Chile (EPC), and were conspicuous as being the older and the poorer people, those who had no trucks and had not joined in the commercial and black-market activity. These people violently rejected older traditions and set themselves apart, recovering their personal dignity through evangelical consolation and messianic hope. They eschewed all festivities and offices, all profane activities and all contact with secular communication. They took no part in development projects, avoided political commitments, and refused to send their children to school beyond what was needed to read the Bible.

This situation both assists and retards 'development'. It is clearly at one level a protest whereby people endeavour to recover some personal dignity and to create a new social solidarity. At the same time, the Pentecostal Church provides many contacts with examples of middle-class Chilean values, and the local brothers clearly identify admiringly with their white fraternal colleagues in Chile. The 'temple' faces Chile, so breaking with the traditional orientations. Unfortunately, this identification with, and orientation to, a distant and superior culture is also a kind of alienation from whatever can be put in hand by the local Aymara community.

A study of this kind underlines the way in which evangelical religion may trickle into any line of social fault, and (as in the situation analysed by Donna Birdwell-Pheasant discussed above), this may happen to be among groups thrown off balance by socio-economic disruption as well as those exceptionally apt for it. Even so, the crucial element for present concerns may still be located in the way Aymara Pentecostals are now integrated into a wider social system in Chile, offering them urban and middle-class models for emulation.

Studies in Developed Sectors of South America

Most of the materials to be covered now refer to relatively developed sectors of Brazil, Chile and the Argentine, in particular Brazil.

One has to begin in the case of Brazil by referring back to the role of Protestantism in Brazilian society about a century ago. At that time the missions became linked to the liberal middle classes, partly because people in those classes associated Protestantism with democracy and progress, and partly because, as Ronald Frase puts it, 'The Protestant education institutions offered accessibility to the one resource that promised social mobility – education.'[41] Though these institutions primarily served the middle (and even upper) classes, they often provided aid to promising children of lower-class Protestant parents, and indeed much of the pastorate was recruited in this way. Ronald Frase has pointed out that a whole new network of relationships between patrons and clients was created around a complex organization of churches, schools, seminaries, hospitals, orphanages, publishing houses and retreat centres. At the centre of this organization the pastor performed the critical role of broker, dispensing aid and influence. Thus the open and democratic promise of Protestantism was partly diminished by the pressures and exigencies of the system in which it had to operate. It therefore offered mobility party in traditional Brazilian terms, but with a fresh injection through the style and content of Protestant schooling. Clearly, the role of networks in contemporary Protestantism duplicates what happened a century ago but on a much larger scale and on the level of migrant workers.

The question about economic advancement in Brazil has partly to be posed in terms of the effectiveness of networks, as indeed it was posed earlier in relation to Guatemala City. In making some comment about that, I draw on an unpublished paper by Cecilia Mariz comparing the relative effectiveness and varying styles of the rival networks associated with Pentecostalism and with the base communities.[42] She argues that while Pentecostals are quite distinct from the base communities with regard to their individualistic rather than socialistic approach, and also with regard to the inward rather than communal character of their concerns, nevertheless the two groups offer rather similar experiences and opportunities to their members. Both groups require a conscious choice and a conscious rationale from those who join them, which must mean some shift away from passivity and fatalism. They also depend on participation, which implies learning to speak, to organize, and maybe also to read. They assume a connection between belief and action, religion and living, and expect sobriety and discipline from their members. The skills acquired and the life-style adopted, and especially the new sense of personal worth, must confer some advantage and some cutting edge on those who belong to Pentecostal churches or to base communities. (Some commentators even suggest they draw from precisely the same social constituencies, though others, for example Rolim, consider that the base communities contain relatively greater numbers of industrial workers.)

However, Cecilia Mariz comments that self-help is actually quite common among poor Brazilians whether or not they belong to base communities or Pentecostal churches. In her view, Pentecostal churches and base communities offer *alternative networks* parallel to family and neighbourhood networks. Of course, they also reinforce the working of their particular network by adding a national scope and a sacred sanction. They provide not only psychological support 'but also material support such as a place to live, jobs, the payment of children's schooling etc.'[43]

One study relevant to the concerns of this chapter is Rolim's *Pentecostais no Brasil*.[44] Rolim's concern is with the Pentecostalism which has burgeoned since 1930 and especially so since 1960. This is a grassroots and indigenous Christianity now accounting for two-thirds of the Protestant sector, and 12 per cent or more maybe of the whole population.

Rolim has some interesting things to say. Most Pentecostals – over half – are in work and they are concentrated disproportionately in the spheres of commerce and services, rather than among direct producers. Rolim refers to porters, independent masons, watchmen, mechanics, electricians, tailors, chauffeurs, street vendors, non-commissioned officers, office boys etc. these are mostly occupations involving self-employment or some degree of autonomy or minor responsibility. Pentecostals were mostly of lowly education.

Rolim goes on to say that Pentecostals rarely wanted to gain money. They economized partly to improve their diet and their home, and partly to support the church. They worked for their churches, helped repair them, gave spare time to them, and such donations weighed on their scanty resources. One Pentecostal commented that God gave him the skills of a mason and he in turn gave back the fruits of those skills. The burden of Rolim's evidence would seem to weigh against any extensive socio-economic mobility specifically among Pentecostal Protestants. It suggests by implication that those Protestants who most advance themselves belong to the other older 'historic' denominations. Thus, Pablo Deiros in his comments on Baptists, at least in the Argentine, says that 'they generated an ethic conducive to a disciplined, hard-working life', so that second and third generations of converts were 'mostly integrated in the middle and lower middle class'.[45]

Writing of Protestantism *generally* some twenty years ago, Read (et al.) and Willems held that its followers in Latin America did achieve some economic and social advancement.[46] Willems emphasized the effects of ascetic behaviour, though he also mentioned the asceticism displayed by participants in messianic movements in Brazil prior to any serious Protestant incursions. Read laid stress on the way vigorous integration in a universe of meaning led to a desire for personal improvement. He underlined once more the way self-esteem and sense of purpose make for economic improvement. Read et al. comment that 'the sense of community, purpose, direction, hope for betterment, responsibility and authority' help to make life better for the worker.[47] Of course, as D'Epinay originally pointed out, the opportunities for advancement in Latin America have been limited and this has restricted what religious mutations at the level of personality and culture can achieve.

A rather different emphasis emerges from the works of Lalive D'Epinay, again mostly produced nearly two decades ago.[48] In these major studies of Chilean Pentecostalism, Lalive D'Epinay placed less weight on social mobility and economic advance, precisely because he was concerned with Pentecostals rather than with Protestants as a whole. In common with Willems, Lalive D'Epinay rejected any

Weberian connection of the classical type between Pentecostalism and the growth of large scale capitalist activity. That, anyway, is not the contemporary issue, since Pentecostals are not within striking distance of the social position that would make such a connection possible. In Lalive D'Epinay's view, moral regeneration takes clear precedence over material advance. The kind of moral regeneration espoused does not necessarily lead even to increased savings.

Lalive D'Epinay draws attention to what he regards as elements of closure in Pentecostalism. While it undoubtedly inculcates participation and offers equality and individual dignity through the gifts of the Spirit, it also echoes the authoritarianism and the patron–client relationships of the society in which it emerges. Lalive D'Epinay sees strong resemblances to the relationships which held on the hacienda: the importance of face to face relationships, the belief that the 'master' will solve and resolve all difficulties. The powers and authority of the master are reproduced in the powers and authority of the pastor. In such circumstances, the mobility of the Pentecostal remains largely on the spiritual plane and is mostly confined to his new spiritual home. Moreover, Pentecostalism remains a faith for the 'habitat' whereas Marxism is a faith for the work-place. The two pass by each other rather than competing. The Pentecostal is on 'social strike' *from* society and the Marxist on strike *against* society.

It is not appropriate at this point in a chapter concerned with economic advancement to pursue the analysis by Lalive D'Epinay further, since it takes us into the political stance of Pentecostalism and raises fundamental questions of meta-interpretation. But clearly the kind of understanding offered by Lalive D'Epinay, which analyses Pentecostalism as a 'haven' strongly resembling the hacienda, does not see it as offering all that much by way of material advance, even in terms of 'penny capitalism'.

A Korean Aside

In parenthesis it is worth observing that though Protestants have increased dramatically in numbers in Korea as well as in Latin America, there seems to be little evidence of economic advance specifically associated with them. The point will be reiterated in chapter 8 devoted to the phenomenon of Korean Protestantism. Certainly when Protestantism arrived in Korea it was associated with the USA, with the assertion of individuality and with modernity in general. That association remains. Protestantism also came to be associated with the early struggles of Korean nationalists against the

Japanese and with the survival of the Korean language. To that extent there are analogies with the spread of Protestantism among the Maya.

But as to the association of Protestantism in Korea with a work ethic and economic advancement, the consensus of opinion seems to be that the Confucian work ethic provides all the motivation necessary. Yet converts in the early period at the turn of the last century were conspicuously industrious. Perhaps their sense of inner purpose and meaning gave them additional confidence at a time of social dissolution. In more recent times, the rapid growth of Protestantism has run alongside the rapid economic growth of Korea, but it could easily be that Protestantism provides communitarian support and creates an enclave of meaning against the rigours and anxieties of change. Thus, Protestantism switches social roles and provides shelter and some psychic security while the whole society tries to mend its fabric and move simultaneously into an era of rapid technological change.

The preaching of a gospel of success among many conservative Protestants is not in itself evidence that they are noticeably more successful than people of other faiths or none. Commentators seem mostly agreed that a population imbued with the Confucian work ethic needs no further inducements to industry from Protestantism. They are, so to say, Protestants *naturaliter*.

Summary

If we try now to bring these disparate observations together, it seems clear that the Protestantism which first lodged in South and Central America provided a vehicle of autonomy and advancement for some sections of the middle class, conspicuously so in Brazil, and provided channels for mobility for some who would otherwise have been condemned to poverty. Mortimer Arias has aptly commented that this Protestant seed came with its flowerpot – 'the world view, the ethos and the ideology of the prospering and the expanding capitalistic countries, the image of democracy, progress, education, freedom, and material development. And it was the flowerpot, not the seed itself, that the liberal politicians, the members of the Masonic lodges, and the young Latin American elite were looking at.'[49] But this foreign packaging prevented the seed taking deep indigenous root. So, too, did the educational ethos which Protestants promoted. The whole Protestant style remained remote from the largely illiterate millions of Latin America. A pastorate imbued with this style, either from birth or inducted into it by clerical training, was incapable of establishing easy communication with the people. Even when Protestantism acquired something in the nature of its own network of patron and client, this meant only its own subversion by the 'host society' and not the conversion of the indigenous people.

Pentecostalism by contrast be came truly indigenous and independent and also lacked the alienating character of educational advance. Being truly indigenous it was also more truly embedded in the local cultures and reflected them even as it altered them. It came close enough to be moulded in the local image as well as to recreate that image.

The clearest instance of the way Pentecostalism takes on local colour is where it creates a protective network and reproduces some of the solidarities and the structures of authority found on the hacienda. Nevertheless, the network offers participation and equality in the gifts of the spirit. It also offers opportunity for developing skills of expression, organization, propagation and leadership. Such skills cannot, in the long run, be irrelevant to survival and modest advancement in the conditions of contemporary Latin America, especially for the pastorate. This is true even if much of the time, money and labour of Pentecostals is expended on sustaining the group. By moulding individuals with some sense of their own selfhood and capacity to choose, it may well be building up a constituency well-disposed to a capitalistic form of development. It is also, as we have seen, often building up a constituency open to American modes and techniques, particularly by reason of the technical means for propagating the message now available, such as television, radio, film and cassette. The speed and scope of modern communications may well be accelerating cultural mutations which previously moved much more slowly.

Of course, the impact of Pentecostal Protestantism varies according to the local channel most receptive to it, and this is true both economically and politically. In certain circumstances the impact may be translated in terms of a dispossessed group in a backward social condition seeking a measure of autonomy and, maybe, redress. At another time the translation may be made in terms of binding up distressed and/or isolated persons, restoring the family or offering new ties of religious kinship. In yet other instances, Protestantism may be aligned with an ethnic identity. It can provide a shelter from the rigours of very rapid social and economic change. According to circumstance, different aspects of the Pentecostal message will be efficacious. In one situation it may console and buttress those who lose from social change; in another situation it may select precisely those who can make the most of chances that change offers to them. The framework within which it acts will normally be a dualistic one and one derived from American models separating religious organizations from politics as well as from the state. But the personality it nourishes will be one with a new sense of individuality and individual worth and, therefore, possessed of a potential for assessing its own proper activity, in which will be included activity in the economic realm. Experience of the way social mobility has come about elsewhere, as well as common sense, suggest that the capacities built up and stored in the religious group may take two or three generations to come to fruition. Much depends on the balance which Pentecostalism maintains between its ability to expand among the masses, by remaining of the masses, and its ability to advance their condition. If the former remains powerful the latter must operate at the margin.

Chapter 12

The Body Politic and the Spirit: Evidence Reviewed

The political stances of evangelicals in Latin America have given rise to a great deal of controversy, particularly when the stances have been apolitical. Indeed, it is not too much to say that the kind of commentary evangelicals have received has been strongly coloured by the way their politics are assessed. Whatever changes in culture they may represent or accelerate, the overall estimate of their significance is often definitely reviewed from the political standpoint. They, for their part, may see themselves as offering salvation and also, perhaps, as promoting self-improvement, but the academic (and theological) debate about and around them is mostly pitched in terms of their contribution to 'liberation' understood in a comprehensive manner and their putative role as agents of alien cultural styles.

Thus the case against them is an essentially political case turning on the way evangelicals, more especially the Pentecostals and the representatives of the various faith missions, are held to be agents of cultural colonialism and barriers to liberation. They are a sector of 'the poor' who advance forward only to enter a cul de sac of other-worldly compensations and who raise their consciousness only to evade the conditions which hold them in thrall. They give tongue to hope in an alienated and quasi-universal religious speech, but do not address their real problems or help create the solidarities which may assist the solution of those problems on the political plane.

In touching on debate at this meta-level of theoretical interpretation, I anticipate a final chapter partly concerned with such interpretations. But clearly a chapter focused on the political question is already moving into the domain of large-scale meta-interpretation. After all, political debate itself is framed in terms of organizing perspectives, the aim of which is to order events and processes according to their threat or promise. Some things are 'sinister' and some exhibit rectitude. Thus the debate about the Pentecostals has some paradoxical characteristics, since the criticism of their dualistic division between a 'church' and 'world' is itself inclined to another dualism between liberation and enslavement.

Historical Retrospect

With that preliminary warning about a potential shift in the level and colour of discourse, it is worth reiterating one or two points made earlier about the origins of Pentecostalism. Pentecostalism arose as a religion mainly of the poor in the USA, and at least some of its roots lie among those who were not only poor but black. It certainly creates a 'free space' wherein new priorities and statuses are created and celebrated; and it anticipates a great reversal whereby the lowly are exalted and the rich sent empty away. At the same time, it is dualistic not only in the general sense of dealing in 'mighty opposites' but in dividing 'the church' from 'the world'. It fosters a contempt for the world and that includes the political struggle in which the world is so constantly engaged. (Of course, this indifference to 'the political' is not all that unusual. For most of humankind most of the time the primary category is not 'political' in any developed way. The Pentecostal expression of an apolitical stance is special because it is principled and based on transcendental foundations.)

Such an enclosed dualism arose in the organicist societies of the European past among, for example, the Anabaptists. At that time it encapsulated social alienation and embodied reversals of the ways of 'the world' inside a religious enclave. It therefore attracted all the available engines of repression. Where religion and society were nearly coextensive a dissident faith was inherently anti-social. But in England and Holland, and above all in the United States, the separating out of political and religious elements meant that a dualistic kind of religion eventually came to exist alongside all other denominations in the voluntary sector. It was inherently confined to the cultural, and any lack of interest in politics was not subject to much by way of animadversion. Religious enthusiasts were, in any case, not so highly prized that their political views needed to be brought peremptorily into the public forum. Much liberal opinion in the 'West' accepts the idea that you have a right to contribute and equally a right to indifference, and adds (*sotto voce*) that if you are unenlightened then your indifference is not all that lamentable.

A problem, therefore, arises when a religion, nurtured among the poor of a highly differentiated and more or less 'liberal' society, gains a large constituency in societies much less differentiated and subject to comprehensive political polarization. In the upper levels of such societies one finds all-embracing political world-views, especially so among the intelligentsia, and at the lower levels one finds a complex mixture of so-called 'pre-political' movements, the politics of patronage, intermittent and ambiguous populism (for example, Peronism), and a kind of numb sense of fatality. The intelligentsia, in particular, seeks to raise the consciousness of the masses in terms of the comprehensive political world-views they have themselves created and adopted. The existence of a growing number of people who are dualistic and whose pluralism and voluntarism is transferred from highly differentiated Protestant cultures with large apolitical margins is clearly problematic. They represents a mobilization that goes so far *precisely* in order to go no further. I suggested earlier that things are less simple than that. This kind of mobilization has historically represented a latent potential released according to social circumstance: the slave wars in Jamaica, Anabaptist and Quaker critiques of war and slavery, and Martin Luther King. But the question of latency need only be noted in the margin here. It has a piquant, even poignant, aspect in contemporary Latin America in that many of the politically radical and non-Pentecostal evangelicals represent groups that themselves went through periods of 'latency' at earlier priods, likewise protected in a dualistic capsule. They now embrace a union of 'church' with 'world' and criticize Pentecostalism for being slow to make the desired transition. They are more 'modern', more sophisticated, more aware of the social structural problem, more concerned *about* 'the poor' – but less successful *with* the poor. From their point of view, it is of the nature of poverty that the poor are too conceptually impoverished to know where their earthly treasure is located.

Contemporary Prospects and Options

What then are the political options which the spirit-filled evangelicals of today may embrace? They may, of course, stay out of 'the dirty game' believing that all political promises are deceptive will-of-the-wisps. They may make some tenatative assessment based on how they perceive the interests of their social group. The evidence shows, for example, that many supported Allende's Popular Unity Party. They may support a party which distances itself from any Catholic identification and comes out in favour of religious freedom and the social equality of all faiths. They may be pulled into the politics of anti-clericalism or, alternatively, of anti-communism: after all, they are equally opposed to the Pope and to Marx. They may engage in local politics, either by pulling out of the social hierarchy or by actual participation in movements for peasants' rights. They may stay within the old tradition of clients seeking patrons, and create their own network for the dispensing of favours. They may suppose that the national security state offers political and economic stabilities which are worth the cost in terms of liberty of expression and association. All these options have been explored by some Pentecostals. There is no route which Pentecostal doctrine absolutely precludes, except adherence to a movement which is doctrinally atheist.

However, there is enough in their indigenous local origins to make anti-Catholicism a prime political consideration, and enough in their US connections to make anti-communism also a major political consideration. Looking first at their anti-Catholicism, it stems not from the polite demurrals of liberal Protestantism but from a root and branch view of the Roman Church as the enemy of Christian truth. It involves a particular dislike for those features of Catholicism which are most distinctive, like papalism or Marian devotion, and also a contempt for the syncretic amalgam of Catholicism with indigenous faiths known as 'Christo-paganism'. This total opposition to 'Rome' was fuelled up until quite recently by persecution, by devices and laws which stated or implied that Protestants were only second-class citizens, and by an attitude which defined Protestantism as 'the problem of the sects'.

This mutual repulsion at the theological level is fed into, perhaps even maintained, by a repulsion at the social level. A Protestant (or an 'evangelical' to use the more usual term) has opted out of a social system, thereby, claiming his or her social autonomy. This really is a radical step even if mainly 'symbolic', and it must engender and/or express an acute rejection of the religion which is bound up in that system. No matter that Catholicism has in many places prised itself out of the system, or been prised out by external forces, the Protestant still reacts to an ancient image of an ecclesiastico-social hierarchy. Like the English Puritans he thinks in terms of 'no King, no Bishop'. This means that Protestants are likely to support whatever is the non-Catholic party. While the historic denominations often work in cooperation with Catholics, socially, politically and theologically, the new evangelicals do not.

So far as concerns communism, they are very wary indeed. The fate of believers in most communist states is minatory. Their US colleagues, where they have them, offer constant reminders of the menace of godless communism and its persecution of the faithful. Moreover, the only rapprochement between Marxism and Christianity of which they know is the Catholic one of 'liberation theology', and for them that combination hardly holds much attraction. Both Catholicism and Marxism look hegemonic: put together they do not look less so. (Of course, if a Marxist government were to be in power long enough to gain legitimacy, then evangelicals might assume it was in power by divine ordinance. In that case, they would fear God and honour the party as well, because 'the powers that be are ordained of God.' Only under extreme pressure would they reverse this and revert to another key text: 'It is better to obey God than man.')

Case Studies: Chile and the Argentine

In what follows I intend to proceed from south to north, starting with the southern cone. Naturally, the evidence is fragmentary and will have to be deployed to illustrate the range of political positions. I begin with the southern cone: Chile and Argentina. Both Chile and the Argentine offer some evidence about Protestantism under 'national security' regimes; Chile also offers evidence about Protestantism in the complicated period leading up to the deposition of Allende. It is, therefore, worthwhile examining the Chilean evidence in comparative detail.

Commenting two decades ago on the earlier history of Protestantism in Chile, Frederick Turner described Protestants as 'very far behind Christian Democratic activists in terms of their religious motivations for constructive political activity'. That is true 'in spite of some increased interest in voting, some concern for religious liberty and support for an occasional Protestant candidate'.[1] He emphasizes that the 'unprecedented pace' of Pentecostal growth already evident in the 1960s was definitely not related to any overt concern for social and political reform. Their stress was on personal purity as well as sometimes on the connection they thought they perceived between spiritual conversion and some modest material improvement. He quotes the results of a questionnaire administered by Lalive D'Epinay which show that Pentecostals are far more removed from political action than other Protestants. Four out of five Pentecostal pastors thought they should never discuss social problems in their sermons, whereas only one in four of other Protestant pastors agreed. Turner then makes the crucial point, which is that although Catholicism may only hold some of its middle- and upper-class members by adopting a progressive ethos, 'For the lower groups whom progressive Catholicism is designed to help . . . the psychological functionality of new religious norms may have more importance than the official Christian Democratic emphasis on politics, trade unionism, or "social reforms".'[2] (However, a minority among Pentecostals does show interest in social reform and something will be said of them below.)

Evidence about the earlier political identifications of Chilean Pentecostals is sparse, though it was suggested in the *Christian Century* (27 March 1968) that in the 1964 Presidential election some of them deserted a traditional affiliation with the anti-clerical Radical Party to vote for Eduardo Frei and the Christian Democrats. This may have been because the *freistas* stressed they were now non-sectarian and managed to dramatize the idea of a simple choice between Communists and Christian Democrats.

The only extensive evidence is that collected by Johannes Tennekes between 1971 and 1973 immediately prior to the right-wing military coup d'état.[3] Tennekes did not concern himself with the 'historic' denominations, who anyway only account for one in five of Chilean Protestants. His fundamental conclusion was that pastors held – or struck – much more right-wing attitudes after the coup than was consonant with the views of their flocks prior to the coup. He first recounts evidence of the relative concentration of Pentecostals in the south and in the two main cities as indicating their overwhelmingly 'popular' character. His specific evidence on their political views was gained by interviewing members of three communities belonging to the Methodist Pentecostal Church and comparing their responses with those of non-Pentecostals living alongside them. The area chosen for the study was on the edge of Santiago, and was occupied by a marginal population. For various reasons, the results could not be assumed to be representative of elsewhere, but they were at least suggestive, particularly in their comparison of Pentecostals with non-Pentecostals.

Tennekes reported several findings. The involvement of evangelical believers in community organizations and union meetings was slightly less than that of non-believers. The believers were also considerably more inclined (60 to 45 per cent) to suppose that political participation did not really lead anywhere. Again, interest in social and political questions was lower among the evangelicals, a finding associated with less exposure to newspapers. In other words, the

Pentecostals were somewhat more passive than others found in their particular milieu.

It is here that the argument is of particular interest. Tennekes notes that though quite a large number of Pentecostals were not all that closely involved in their church, for the faithful it was an all-absorbing activity. That left little time for other organizations. Moreover, this absorption was all the more understandable and necessary given that their neighbours regarded them as distinctly odd. To be on ordinary terms with 'the world' of their neighbours and their community would mean insensibly slipping into worldly ways. The 'dualistic' division between 'church' and 'world' is sociologically indispensable. They *had* to respond negatively to the general perception of them as somewhat bizarre and ignorant fanatics.

However, Pentecostals were also perceived with respect as well as with disdain, but it was a respect turning once again on their distinctive commitment and distance from 'the world'. Committed Pentecostals were regarded as good and honest workers. They had abandoned the normal masculine life-style with its attendant vices, had given up drink, and stayed at home with their wives and children. They were, therefore, both respected on account of difference and disdained on account of difference, and both the respect and the disdain jointly help maintain social barriers.

Leaving aside such questions as the availability of time apart from church commitments and the need to maintain strong frontiers against a threatening or seductive 'world', there is a more general suspicion of political life as corrupt, as based on hate, controversy, manipulation, self-interest and deceit. Whereas participation in community organizations might be for social benefit, the life of a politician was inevitably bound up with sordid bargains and self-interested considerations. So it is not that positions of responsibility in society are to be abjured automatically. It is rather that the conditions of contemporary politics make the participation of Christians difficult. In that connection, Tennekes notes that members of the small Wesleyan Church, though they are well-known as socialists, nevertheless avoid involvement in political life. Indeed, most Chileans hold that the church should avoid political entanglements. Perhaps one is encountering here a general scepticism about political life in Chile, and maybe in Latin America, which achieves ideological expression and some mild reinforcement in the Pentecostal faith. It is also important always to keep in mind the extent to which any member of the 'popular classes' is bound to be absorbed by the problems of daily life.

Yet Pentecostals *do* vote and are not much below non-Pentecostals in their electoral participation. As mentioned earlier, they were a generation ago inclined to support the centrist Radical Party as aligned with liberty of conscience. Leading Pentecostals had often advocated such support, though the actual response to their advice is unclear. By 1970 at any rate, the Christian Democrats had ousted the Radical Party and there was a choice between an atheistic socialist, a catholic Christian Democrat and a reactionary. At that juncture the Pentecostal leaders recognized that to state any overt preference would cause division and jeopardize their own power.

Tennekes comments that behind the overt neutrality of the Pentecostal leaders lay a discernible preference for the right. They saw Marxism as incompatible with their view of society and from their US co-religionists they derived a suspicion about the intentions of any future Marxist government towards the churches. And beyond that the absorption of the population in political conflict meant that less attention was accorded to the proclamation of the gospel.

Yet, apparently, the sympathies of the great mass of Pentecostals did not correspond to those of their leaders. The distribution of their votes accorded with their social position or, at any rate, with the distribution among comparable non-Pentecostals. More than that, 80 per cent of Pentecostals preferred Allende to Frei, compared with 60 per cent of non-Pentecostals. At the same time, the views of Pentecostals were moderate, in that they rejected violence and class warfare, and did not desire the abolition of private property. They wanted change within the limits of law and of order. Other investigations also showed that participation in the left-wing struggle for a new society was stronger among non-believers than among either Catholics or Pentecostals.

Why this disparity between the Pentecostal pastors and their flocks? Tennekes suggests that the view of the pastors is influenced by their concern for the organizational survival of the movement, a concern which also happens to coincide with their personal interests. The movement provides the outer limit of their horizon. Their flocks, by contrast, are influenced by the interests promoted in and by their social milieu. Insofar as their votes are influenced by specifically religious considerations, these appear more anti-Catholic than anti-Marxist. This is, of course, a major motivation among evangelical voters throughout Latin America: to make the anti-Catholic choice.

After the coup d'état the situation became shadowy. The only remaining means of expression were now religious. The Junta attended the dedication of a sanctuary to the Virgin at Maipu; and the immense Pentecostal cathedral at Jotabeche was solemnly inaugurated in the presence of General Pinochet. This appearance of the Head of

State was a kind of recognition of the Protestant presence and represented something of a quid pro quo with regard to declarations of support for the new regime from some prominent Pentecostal pastors. The pastors wanted some recognition, hitherto largely denied, and the regime saw that here was a social pillar they might attempt to co-opt, especially if part of the Roman Catholic Church was becoming unreliable. At the same time, the broad declarations of Pentecostal support acquired an equivocal character on such matters as political refugees and prisoners. It is difficult to judge just how far the pastors were pressed to make these broad declarations, though there is no doubt that some such pressure was exercised.

Before proceeding to look at the classic work of Christian Lalive D'Epinay on the Chilean situation, it is worth noting first of all the existence of a radical minority among Pentecostals and, second, the special religious situation found in the army. With regard to the former, they may be seen as parallel to the radical groups which grew up in the Methodist milieu during the late eighteenth century and Napoleonic period, such as the Kilhamites. Some idea of their approach may be gained from an interview with them conducted by William Cook when they attended the World Council of Churches. They belonged to the Mission Pentecostal Church and the Evangelical Pentecostal Church of Chile. Of course, their presence at the WCC and their 'open-door' attitude towards other Christian bodies marks them out as atypical. As one interviewee put it, 'We have many, many Pentecostal churches in Chile who do not have this [political and social] dimension. . . . Only our two churches belong to the WCC.'[4] The political and social dimension involves a breakdown of the barrier between 'church' and 'world', social work in the community at large, solidarity programmes, and programmes to deal with hunger and unemployment. (It is interesting that Sister Palma from the Evangelical Pentecostal Church referred to being a pastors's daughter and how this led to her taking up a profession. That transformation was, she suggested, quite a frequent one among Pentecostals.)

Among the other Protestants of Chile, perhaps comprising some 15 per cent of the Protestant minority, there was more opposition than among Pentecostals. Most notable was the opposition of Bishop Helmut Frenz, a church leader among a minority ethnic church. The Evangelical Lutheran Church was seriously split by Frenz's support for Allende and by his leadership of an ecumenical committee to assist refugees. The evangelical Confraternidad Cristiana de Iglesias has called for a return to full democracy.

A comment by Victor Alfredo Quezada in a dissertation on the Baptist Church in Chile indicates that some degree of opposition was located there. He comments, however, that evangelicals have no model to deal with human rights, with political prisoners, and with the imposition of martial law. He adds ruefully: 'After 65 years refusing to identify with the society, a good number of leaders of Protestantism have made the decision to support a government that is condemned world-wide.'[5]

Material on the position of religion in the Chilean army is extremely valuable. Clearly the disposition of faith and adherence in the armed forces is pretty crucial in current struggles, but rarely looked into. Humberto Lagos Schuffeneger and Arturo Chacón have produced almost the only available evidence in their 'Religion en las Fuerzas Armadas y de Orden'.[6] This evidence refers to the mid-eighties and pre-dates the political changes set in train by the 1988 referendum.

According to Kenneth Aman, Lagos argued that Chile 'experienced a forceful appropriation of religious symbols which seeks to bring about an internalization of the political order through the mechanism of faith'.[7] Shortly after achieving power the military government confirmed freedom of religion in Chile, provided that religious faiths were not opposed to morals and public order and did not seek to subvert Christian principles. These Christian principles are part of the inherent character of Chile. They are opposed to materialism and made incarnate in the military.

Part of the Roman Church, more especially that influenced by Vatican 2 and Medellín, broke with the regime over its denial of human rights. However, there is a Catholicism found in most of the military chaplains which is intensely patriotic and which is crystallized in the devotion to the Virgin of Carmen. In the services conducted under the auspices of this kind of Catholicism, General Pinochet himself plays a quasi-liturgical role. An enquiry initiated by the chaplaincy found the soldiers, enlisted and conscripted, 'profoundly united to God'. However, the soldiers were far from orthodox. Only 24 per cent receive Communion at all frequently and 60 per cent do not believe in life after death. Among enlisted men 15.8 per cent are not Catholic, and among conscripts 21.1 per cent; Lagos goes on to argue that there has been an even more remarkable increase of evangelicalism in the armed forces than in the population as a whole. However, the figure of 15 per cent seems not out of line with current estimates of the Evangelical population of Chile.

Evangelicals had complete freedom to evangelize in the army, and even in the Escuela Militar, and this policy may possibly have derived from a desire to punish the Roman Catholic Church for opposition. These evangelicals have links with brethren in the USA. They are happy with hierarchical organizations and stress the importance of being faithful to God and to His commanders. They make conversions from the bottom up, and have so far reached no higher than major. (Two members of the joint chiefs of staff are Lutherans, but that presumably tells us more about the status of the German ethnic minority than about Pentecostalism.) In Lagos's view, there is debate going on in the military as to whether or not the military should diversify in its use of 'spiritual shelters'.

The discussion of Chile can be concluded by reference to some general theoretical remarks by Christian Lalive D'Epinay. These remarks summarize the views of the principal student of Chilean Protestantism, working on that topic since the mid-sixties and were most recently presented in 1979 at the Venice meeting of the International Conference of the Sociology of Religion.[8]

Christian Lalive D'Epinay defines his problem as that of the functional role of a sect in a dependent capitalist society. The evolution of neo-dependency and of Pentecostalism he sees as advancing almost hand in hand. The crisis of Chilean society began in the 1930s; and since that time the number of evangelicals has about doubled every decade, though population growth in general has been only marginally less. He locates Pentecostalism among all the exploited classes found in conditions of unstable employment: the urban lower proletariat, the rural proletariat, and the lower middle-class strata.

As is well known, Christian Lalive D'Epinay sees Pentecostalism as a refuge for the masses which reproduces much of the closeness and the patronal relationships of the hacienda. Pentecostalism offers a religious image of society through the categories of spirit and matter, church and society. It cuts society into two, and while it allows a man to be alienated from society, it also offers him a free space wherein he may retain at least some dignity.

He recounts the Christian Democratic project in Chile in terms of reformism and participation, and places it parallel to that of the Roman Catholic 'base communities'. During that period (1965–70), popular political mobilization reduced the dynamic of Pentecostal expansion. Then between 1970 and 1973 Chilean society entered a period of transition under the Popular Unity government of Allende, and this opened up rival possibilities for the hitherto enclosed society of Pentecostalism. The dualities of Pentecostalism might have become complementary rather than antagonistic and mutually exclusive. He cites the instance, mentioned earlier, of the Iglesia Wesleyana Pentecostal, located in the coal-mining district of Lota-Coronel, which developed a political dimension and one which was actively socialist. Alternatively, dualism might be projected on to the global situation, and Pentecostalism enter into a war as partisan of Christ versus the Marxist anti-Christ. That alternative might be accompanied by an imitation of the old-style Catholic Church, above all the building of a vast cathedral in Santiago capable of holding 18,000 people.

The Argentine offers much less material for comment, partly because Protestantism has only experienced rapid growth since the mid-eighties.[9] The initial incursions of Protestantism came with British and American Methodist and Baptist missions, and some mild successes were achieved among the Spanish and Italian migrants arriving between 1880 and 1914. Many of the converts found their way into the lower middle or middle class and went through the universities. As in almost all other countries of Latin America, Protestantism moved in the atmosphere of modernization projected by the liberal elites. Where Protestants formed cultural and linguistic communities as, for exmple, among the Scots Presbyterians or Dutch Reformed, they kept out of politics. Where they were theologically 'conservative' they maintained a dichotomy between religion and politics. Where they were influenced by the social gospel, they gave support to the laicist parties, such as the Partido Democrata Progresista and the Partido Radical. They appreciated the politics of religious liberty found in those parties and felt broad sympathy with social democratic ideas. However, the advent of Peronism aroused an almost visceral antagonism among Protestants, partly because it was at one period in alliance with the Catholic Church and ill-disposed to religious liberty, and partly because it included some fascistic (and, therefore, anti-Anglo-Saxon) elements.

With the advent of chronic instability, radical insurgency and military governments of left and right there emerged for the first time Protestant groups in the middle class aligned with the military regimes. Probably most middle-class Protestants saw their interests in stability and liberty, and thoroughly disliked Peronism, terrorist insurgency and the more obvious forms of military brutality. In short, they were in the middle and wanted peace and quiet. With the arrival of military dictatorship in 1976, the middle class in general saw the army as messianic agents of order. Such opposition as was possible turned around the issue of human rights, and certain sectors of Protestantism (such as the Reformed Church, the Methodist Church, the Disciples of Christ) worked in tandem with Catholics in the Movimiento Ecumenico por los Derechos Humanos. With the coming of the war over the Falklands, the people in these sectors generally condemned imperialism (meaning by that British sovereignty over the islands) but also questioned the motives of the invading forces.

These activities, notably the protests against the dictatorship, came from the ecclesiastical leadership and small lay groups. Much of the Protestant middle class together with the Pentecostal leadership sided with the government, seduced by its anti-communist propaganda. Only defeat by the British forced the military dictatorship toward the restoration of due political process, and with that there emerged once again the liberal and social democratic values associated with classical Protestantism. The price of opposition had been paid in terms of people exiled, murdered, or 'lost' without trace. In both the Catholic and Protestant churches the opposition had come from a minority, while the majority of leaders and laity kept silent. And it seems that the Pentecostal leadership was almost entirely part of that silent majority. Perhaps the leadership of the Pentecostals was as much to the right of its constituency as the leadership of the older evangelicals was to the left of its constituency. That would be the case if the Chilean evidence is a secure guide.

Some further illumination of the processes involved in transposing religious styles nurtured in US culture can be gained by a brief examination of the political stance of just one of the older evangelical denominations in the Argentine. The history of the Baptists in the Argentine prefigures elements in the history of the Pentecostals who are just now emerging as a major force. The Baptist experience precisely illustrates the effect of a mind-set created by an advanced social differentiation, based on a separation of church and state, when combined with a suspicion of the political order and reinforced by strong boundaries between 'church' and 'world'. The importance of the Baptists is not entirely exemplary: they are, after all, one of the two largest 'historic' denominations.

The Baptist ideal as originally adumbrated was very advanced: a Free Church in a Free State. It was part of the 'emancipatory project' of nineteenth-century liberals, including the anti-clerical liberals of Latin America. The Baptist ideal was also rooted in the idea of local democracy. There was, however, an ambiguity in the repertoire of legitimate Baptist responses concerning politics, which has been exploited in the past to support or reject political activism and which is also available in the conservative theological tradition as a whole, including Pentecostalism.

On the one hand there is an emphasis on separation and on indifference to power. On the other hand, it is possible to view politics as an interim condition, divinely ordained within the temporal order. This 'interim condition' can include ordinary political activity to promote civic interests, and as such is based on individual competence and conscience. The individual conscience is arbiter. It is his conscience which the Christian man brings to his political vocation. The 'interim condition' may also include the idea that the powers that be are ordained of God, an idea which will become relevant later when we consider Nicaragua.

Pablo A. Deiros, in his study of 'Argentine Baptists and Politics', describes how the first Baptist pastor arrived in 1881.[10] Whereas Baptists were politically active elsewhere, in the Argentine they tended to abstain. There were several reasons for this: a certain vulnerability in a country where Catholicism and the state were closely linked, and a sensitivity about being castigated as agents of a foreign cultural style inimical to Argentinian nationalism. Moreover, they were influenced, as were Baptists elsewhere in Latin America, by the roots of the Baptist Church in the South of the USA. The 'conservatism' of the post-bellum South spilled over into the Protestantism of Latin America. In any case, the Baptists were either migrants or they were converts from rural areas, so they lacked political experience and had few political opportunities open to them.

But, of course, their North American 'conservatism', leaving aside their political withdrawal and indifference, was still South American liberalism. Baptists wanted political freedoms, and sought an education which was free and lay. They had to face some restrictions and some legal discrimination, and in that respect were inherently political in their attitude since clericalism (and the Roman Catholic monopoly) was a major focus of political contention. Baptists approved of moral values in politics and saw political action in terms of personal probity, and they were well disposed to the rising middle class. Indeed, they generated an ethic conducive to a disciplined, hard-working life, so that second and third generation Baptists were mostly integrated into the middle or lower middle class. (That last point reinforces the general contentions of the previous chapter, and is worth a further emphasis here.)

Baptists, therefore, fitted into the classic confrontation between the conservatives, who were landed, military and clerical, and the liberals. Like the liberals they were for democracy, liberty, constitutional government and laicization, especially in such sensitive areas as marriage law (which is still a matter of contention) and education. They were above all peaceable, and this trait was simply not consonant with South American traditions of political violence. Peaceability (in the limited context indicated in chapter 1) is a cultural oddity derived from Anglo-American conditions and traditions, and it cuts all Protestants off from both the Latin American right and the Latin American left.

Certainly this peaceable and constitutional liberalism did not prepare Baptists for the problems of Peronism. Syndicalism and demagoguery had burgeoned in Latin not Anglo-American soil and Baptists were in an alien cultural context. Indeed, the appearance of a rising tide of Latin American nationalism, which was particularly strong in the Argentine, made this very clear. They were urged to 'nationalize' their work; they were attacked as an extraneous cultural influence by the extreme Catholic right; and their activities were restricted by the Peronist regime.

Peronism is an ambiguous phenomenon. On one side of its face are the marks of the ancient oligarchical alliances of church and army; on the other side there is a mobilization of the less privileged classes in conjunction with a sector of the military. The ambiguity of Peronism produced a varied response among Baptists. Some thought Peron might bring back democracy. Many were sympathetic to Peronism, at least during the period (in 1962) when he clashed with the Roman Catholic Church, restricted clerical education and laicized divorce. Quite a number of Baptists simply wanted order and stability. Yet the negative associations of militarism were always very real to them and they disliked military interventions. Middle-class Baptists and the denominational leadership in particular tended to be opposed to Peronism and in 1966 the denominational newspaper *El Expositor Bautista* deplored the cessation of democratic process.

As in Chile the liberal and middle-class Radical Party appealed to many Baptists; some of the better educated were attracted by Social Democracy, though put off by the atheism of many leading Social Democrats. Inevitably, Christian Democracy and Communism were unattractive, as respectively Catholic and Marxist. Marxism was especially unattractive, being associated with the guerrillas and with Castro.

The position adopted by Baptists is not so very different from that adopted by Pentecostals, except that the Argentinian Baptists can be seen as parallel to Billy Graham, whereas perhaps there is some parallel between the Argentinian Pentecostals and Jimmy Swaggart. This is not to suggest direct political and cultural connections with the United States: it is rather to point to different stages and styles in the apolitical and 'devotional' traditional. Currently, of course, the availability of US television means that the cultural incursions are indeed direct, since programmes associated with Jimmy Swaggart and with Pat Robertson's Club 700 are shown quite widely. That these are greatly objected to by cultural nationalists can be taken for granted. (Swaggart also had free access to the media in Chile.)

Contrasting Case Studies: Nicaragua and Guatemala

The comparison between Chile and Argentine can now be extended by a comparison, not to say a contrast, between Nicaragua and Guatemala. The interest of Nicaragua lies not only in the obvious problem of evangelicals under a left-wing regime, which is itself under intense North American pressure, but also in the evidence it offers of the variability of evangelical responses, especially where the political powers 'ordained by God' turn out to be Marxist. Given that the events concerned have occurred so recently, much of the material is fragmentary and it is difficult to indicate the numbers involved holding this or that position. Things change and the Nicaraguan situation is notoriously volatile. It is also shrouded in propaganda of all kinds.

It is worth emphasizing that the Protestant presence in Nicaragua has been a substantial one, perhaps including up to 15 per cent of the population. That is slightly surprising given that the Catholic Church over recent years established a much more effective popular base than in Guatemala or pre-revolutionary Cuba. It is also a matter for some surprise that evangelical expansion has continued under the present government, at least according to some evangelical sources. Of course, the divisions within the Catholic Church between the 'People's' Church and part of the hierarchy may have some deleterious impact on Catholic effectiveness. That, like so much else, is speculation.

In my account of the earliest phase of the Nicaraguan situation, I rely for balance on an article by Tom Minnery in *Christianity Today* (8 April 1983) which has less of a propagandist ring about it than usual. Minnery begins by referring to a pastor of the Assembly of God who worked with the Sandinistas in procuring assistance for *campesinos*. This 'illustration' contradicts both what one expects of 'conservative' evangelicals and implies unexpected tolerance of such evangelicals on the part of Sandinistas. Minnery claimed that since the revolution the distribution of Bibles increased fivefold and of New Testaments ninefold. In 1987 officials of Verbo in Guatemala City assured me their own work was allowed to expand in Nicaragua, and I do not think their political colour is such as to involve undue tenderness towards the Sandinistas. (They maintained the Sandinistas put up with preaching provided there were some social benefits as well.)

The evolution of evangelical attitudes apparently leads back to the great earthquake of 1972 and to the expropriation of the relief funds by the Somoza family and their associates. Evangelical pastors in the city organized some 1,100 volunteers who cooked 30,000 hot breakfasts in the days following the calamity. This was the beginning of the Evangelical Committee for Aid and Development (CEPAD), a nation-wide alliance of Protestant churches which is now the largest non-governmental relief agency and is led by a US-trained Baptist physician, Gustavo Parajón. In 1974, some 300 Protestant pastors went into retreat to reflect on what they had learnt from their cooperation following the earthquake concerning social responsibility. The upshot was a degree of cooperation with the Sandinista movement, such as was also extended by the Catholic Church. Some time after the Sandinistas took power in 1979, the CEPAD evangelicals were at pains to explain themselves to (mostly sympathetic) visiting evangelicals from North America. Perhaps slightly less than half of the evangelicals in Nicaragua share the view of the CEPAD group concerning social responsibility, though CEPAD apparently 'represents' some 80 per cent of nearly half a million Protestants. Only a few evangelicals work within the framework of liberation theology, which is viewed as a Catholic development. (It has also been stated that a number of evangelicals were in Somoza's National Guard.)

Before continuing with an account based on Minnery, it is worth just indicating the content of the meeting between the visiting North America delegation and the indigenous evangelical pastors. I utilize an account from *Sojourners* (20 March 1983). Alvino Melendez of the Baptist Church, Rodolfo Fonseca of the Church of God, Nicanor Mairena of the Nazarenes and Antonio Videa of the Assemblies of God emphasized the extension of traditional evangelical concerns towards a 'new man' and an 'integral gospel', linking spiritual and material. Thelma Pereira, of the Waves of Light radio station, emphasized that the churches actually grew after the revolution.

The history of the Sandinistas' treatment of the Miskito Indians is variously reported, not surprisingly given that it has figured largely in the international propaganda war. The Miskitos inhabit the north-western Atlantic coastland. They live in an area remote from the rest of the country and have always been resistant towards 'Spanish' power. In the mid-nineteenth century, they became Protestant Moravians (having earlier resisted Methodism) and they have managed to maintain their ethnic and religious distinctiveness with the help of distance. But the Sandinistas tried to integrate them into their literacy and health programmes, which might well have meant final integration into Hispanic culture. Incidents on both sides set up a spiral of suspicion and violence, until the government for its part forcibly evacuated 10,000 Indians to new villages, and most of the remaining Miskitos fled, some of them to join with the contras. The

Sandinista government recognized its mistakes to some degree, but the situation was still bedevilled by the propaganda aspect of the whole issue and by CIA involvement.

Other incidents affected relationships between evangelicals and the government, notably the unauthorized (?) seizures of some churches, and these incidents followed on fears that evangelicals were being used by the USA, and one or two incidents that seemed to feed that fear, such as the pronouncements of an evangelist, Morris Cerullo, who proposed visiting Nicaragua. However, CEPAD met with President Ortega, who apologized, and saw to it that all occupied churches were returned, except those belonging to the Jehovah's Witnesses.

It seems that CEPAD has maintained good relationships with the Sandinista government from the first. On 5 October 1979, some three months after the fall of Somoza, 500 evangelical pastors associated with CEPAD endorsed a document supporting the goals of the revolution, but adding that their participation was relative to their loyalty to Christ. On the first anniversary of the revolution, representatives of the evangelical churches again affirmed their support. On 4 July 1986 the Baptist Convention of Nicaragua issued a pastoral letter which contained an appeal against US intervention in Nicaragua and the economic embargo. From outside Nicaragua, the Latin American Council of Churches (CLAI), based in Mexico City, issued similar statements in favour of the Nicaraguan government.

What such statements amount to in terms of the evangelical population in Nicaragua is difficult to say. No amount of reading clarifies the situation beyond doubt, and the author has read sources as different as Shirley Christian, *This World* and Walter LaFeber.[11] Perhaps one can only conclude with two opposed viewpoints. One is derived from the Instituto Historico Centroamericano (5 September 1982) and is entitled 'La lucha ideológica en las iglesias evangélicas nicaraguenses'. The other is derived from *Christianity Today* (13 December 1985) and is entitled 'The Government's Heavy Hand Falls on Believers'. The former suggests that religion has been utilized to destabilize radical governments in Latin America, and offers a 'space' for similar activity in Nicaragua. It goes on to say that the denominations which have come to predominate on Nicaragua's Pacific coast are mostly Pentecostal. One gathers that the Adventists have cooperated with the government and the Jehovah's Witnesses have not (as indeed is their tradition in every country). One also gathers that there have been other tensions in connection with the activities of some evangelicals ranging from advice not to participate in communal activities, or in 'revolutionary vigilance', to complaints about the use of powerful electronic instruments. Exception is also taken to over-frequent reference to the adverse judgement of God. The nub of the complaint seems to be that some evangelicals do not want to join in the 'organization of the masses' and treat their faith as a useful means to keep themselves to themselves. The blame for this is in part attached to their mother churches in the USA and to the influence of US missionaries. The strongest condemnation is reserved for those who side with the 'contras'. This seems to be mainly a reflection of the problem of the Miskitos, though mention is made of the 'abuse of religious liberty' by certain pastors and the way they link faith to anti-communism and the 'destabilization' of the 'popular process'. (Of course, there are complex elements at work here, not perhaps excluding the desire of some Catholics to blacken evangelicals by exaggerating their complicity with counter-revolution.) The article concludes, interestingly enough, with noting the difficulty of knowing how many people actually belong to the various 'temples' plainly proliferating within the country, and referring en passant to the efforts of the Panamanian government to counter the spread of sects and to control the movements of their leaders.

The opposing viewpoint in *Christianity Today* spoke of the harassment of Catholic and Protestant leaders by the Sandinista government. The article by Beth Spring refers to restrictions on evangelistic activity 'particularly among church groups that have remained politically neutral by their refusal to endorse the 1979 revolution'.[12] The kind of group whose leaders could find themselves interrogated or held temporarily or restricted in their activities is broadly sketched in the article. There has been pressure on Campus Crusade for Christ, the Evangelical Pastors' Council, the Assemblies of God and the largest Protestant church – La Primera Iglesia Centroamericano de Managua. The article mentions that 'the Sandinistas reportedly suspect some church leaders of encouraging counter-revolutionary activities.'[13] The latest turn of events (May 1989) is a Sandinista invitation to Pat Robertson to preach on Nicaraguan television.[14]

Before making a comparison between Nicaragua and Guatemala, it is worth mentioning, by way of aside, some fragments of evidence concerning Puerto Rico and El Salvador. What this evidence suggests is that the Protestantism currently spreading in those countries is either politically conservative or apolitical, and in either case linked to the United States. Anti-communism seems to be a primary motif, and social repsonsibility is defined in terms of ambulance work and individual charity. Exceptions are found in the interdenominational Seminario Biblico Latinamericano in Costa Rica, the ecumenical

centre for research and training in leadership known as DEI, a
Pentecostal church in Cartago, Costa Rica, and the influential
Emmanuel Baptist church in San Salvador. The last-named was
founded in 1964 and has about 500 members on its roll. It seeks to be
a 'people's church' acting out its faith in a social 'practice', which
includes a kindergarten, an orphanage, a food cooperative, a women's
centre, an institute for theological training, and a large ecumenical
programme to distribute medicine, food and clothing. A missionary
programme is carried out involving some fifty-four congregations
from various denominations ranging from Pentecostal to Roman
Catholic. Its pastor is, or at any rate was, in exile in Mexico City. In
his comments the pastor mentions that 'churches such as ours are in a
minority.' That conclusion can probably be applied throughout most
of Central America, with the possible exception of Nicaragua.

There is, perhaps, more material available on Guatemala than on
any other country, at least relative to size. There are good reasons for
that. It has always been a potential 'centre' of the whole region and
La Feber comments that many researchers view it as a bell-wether for
Central American developments.[15] Guatemala is also a country where
Protestantism has made the deepest inroads and where the Catholic
Church is exceptionally weak. (One places the strength of Protestantism
and the weakness of Catholicism side by side without making any
strong inference about the connection. As we saw in Nicaragua, it is
possible for the Catholic Church to be strong and for the expansion of
Protestantism to be considerable. And in Dominica it has been
possible for both Catholicism and Protestantism to be weak. The
interplay of influences and factors is very complicated.)

In this chapter the focus is on the more recent political aspects, and
so far as Guatemala is concerned, the broader picture has been
covered earlier in chapter 6. What follows offers the minimum
recapitulation and the minimum context necessary to assess the
political roles played by Protestantism in Guatemala.

Initially Protestantism was associated with the policies of liberal
and anti-clerical governments and with the deposition of the church
in 1871, but its converts after 1871 still remained confined to the
socially disfranchised. Protestantism was regarded as a faith of US
inspiration and that meant that by the end of the 1920s it was running
into a wave of nationalism. Then the promotion of the 'good
neighbour' policy on the part of the USA improved matters
somewhat, and during the presidency of Arevalo Protestants worked
with the government in literacy programmes and in attempts to
improve the plight of labour. But then with President Arbenz tension
recurred as the government proceeded against the United Fruit

Company. The US missionaries were mostly alienated by this move and, in consequence, found themselves somewhat restricted. At the same time, some missionaries, more especially the Lutherans, cooperated with the reforming initiatives, and many local Protestants rose to positions of leadership in the land reform projects and in peasant organizations. By contrast, some of their Catholic counterparts, organized in the *cofradias*, regarded their landholdings as under threat.

Then the Arbenz government was toppled with US connivance, and the Roman Catholic Church was partially reinstated as a reward for complicity. Catholic social action was viewed as a possible alternative to communism, even though the organization of the church was often sclerotic. Most Protestants were not radicals, but they were, all the same, sometimes subjected to local violence or watched as possible communists. There followed a new surge of largely fundamentalist Protestantism which removed any serious suspicion of subversive connections. The Presbyterian Church took a stance favouring democracy and opposed to communism and encouraged evangelicals to go into politics. And then in the 1960s, indigenous churches started to grow rapidly, maybe expressing explicitly a rejection of imported US religious styles. Most of these churches were Pentecostal or became Pentecostal, and many of them were tiny community sects. Such churches had lost the foreign taint and were frequently sources of medical, economic and psychological help for the newly arrived migrant in the city, especially after the great earthquake of 1976. They were less educationally demanding and also less democratic in their organization than the older Protestant churches. They presented a familiar – and appealing – patriarchal image to Guatemalans.

According to Virginia Garrard Burnett, the apolitical stance of these churches only increased their attractiveness as the country experienced massive political violence and intense guerrilla activity.[16] To many the evangelical sects were a relatively safe alternative to the radicalized sector of the Roman Catholic Church. This shift was not lost on Guatemalan army officers who saw the possibility of a new base of support in the countryside to replace that previously enjoyed with the Roman Catholic Church. They sought to capitalize on evangelical respect for the powers that be. In 1980 the Minister of Education made a widely publicized conversion to one of the large Pentecostal churches in Guatemala City.

Ordinary Protestants were deeply divided. Many were passive and some even acted as informers for the army; others were sympathetic to the guerrillas or even supporters. Dr Burnett comments that 'in every case it was individuals or factions which became involved in radical politics and not the institutional church itself.'[17] The main exception was the rural Indian Presbyterian Church, which was autonomous and open to liberal and, therefore, eventually to radical influences. The Primitive Methodist Church in the war-ravaged departments of El Quiché and Totonicapán was also Indian and likewise deeply affected by radicalism. This church was the only one actually to split over the political issue, with the result that there emerged a fiercely anti-American splinter known as the Iglesia Nacional. What happened more usually was the development of a parallel radical church. By 1981 enough evangelicals were active among the guerrillas to form an autonomous auxiliary organization called the Confraternidad Evangelica de Guatemala. However, by 1983 the army, led for part of the time by the evangelical President Rios Montt, had the situation under control. Many radical evangelicals, along with radical Catholics, left the country for Costa Rica, Mexico and Nicaragua, to form the Iglesia Guatemalteca en Exilo. However, the overall conclusion of Virginia Burnett is: 'Most Guatemalan Protestants . . . used the churches as a spiritual refuge from the turmoil of their world. Thus as the turmoil increased, the numbers of Protestants grew proportionally.'[18]

The period in which Guatemala was run by an evangelical President is worth a brief characterization for the sake of completeness, even though referred to earlier. The President vigorously attempted to restrain random murder which had defamed the previous regime, and to reduce graft and corruption. This made his popular with the urban masses. He also adopted a new policy in the campaign against the guerrillas, offering 'beans' and an amnesty to those who submitted, and death to those who did not. Though radical Catholic catechists suffered from his campaign, so equally did Protestants suspected of radicalism, for example, the thirty members of a Pentecostal Church in El Quiché killed while at worship.

The role of Protestants was located not so much in the 'beans or guns' policy as in the distribution of beans and a programme of emergency relief. At the request of two Wycliffe Bible Translators who had worked in the Ixil Triangle for many years, the government sponsored a programme of relief through a private foundation known as FUNDAPI which operated mostly on money from US fundamentalist sources. Indeed, money poured in from conservative Protestants in the USA.

It seems likely that at least part of the Protestant growth in the worst-hit areas owed something to implicit governmental support. Again Dr Burnett's comment is that the apolitical evangelical churches were a useful foil for the politicized sector of the Catholic Church, and were able to duplicate its social programmes without the inconvenient radicalization. Further than that, many evangelicals supported the concentration of the population in 'model villages' and acted as local leaders.

Yet, when right-wing political forces ousted Montt, Pentecostals were divided, as they were in all else. One group – Verbo – had been associated with the President, another group – Elim – with the President of the Council of State, and the rest felt somewhat excluded. A combination of sectarian groupings who were themselves deeply divided did not amount to a secure political base even for an evangelical President.

It seems that Montt was ousted, not so much for his religious proclivities as for his attacks on graft and corruption. Evangelicals were only briefly inconvenienced when he was removed and continued to enjoy phenomenal growth. What perhaps his presidency had shown was that Protestantism was now a sufficiently large presence in Guatemala for a Protestant to become head of state. Moreover, it may be that Protestantism was now finding an ethos within which Guatemalan nationalism might express itself safely and apolitically. That, if true, is a sure sign of a faith become fully indigenous, whatever the US connections and financial assistance.

Case Study: Brazil

When we consider Brazil we are, of course, dealing with the largest country in South America. Protestantism originally took root there as a movement associated with democracy and progress, and in some way responsible for the successful evolution of the United States. The main impact which Protestantism achieved was through schools which broke the traditional moulds of education, replacing fatalism by curiosity and by problem-solving. Protestants introduced a culture sympathetic to rational economic development and to laboratory experiment. All these elements placed Protestantism in the camp of liberal republicanism and of the incipient middle class; and when the monarchy was overthrown the Protestant community saw that this offered a chance to prove its commitment to the nation. By contrast, the Roman Catholic Church was portrayed as inherently monarchical in constitution.

One further aspect of the advent of Protestantism is worthy of political note: Brazil was a second 'frontier' for many US missionaries because some Southern colonists sought refuge in Brazil after the

Civil War. The churches which came with the migrants had a Southern flavour in some ways consonant with Brazilian culture. They were theologically conservative and often came to be even more so. They were, comments Ronald Frase, 'disenchanted with political solutions to social problems'. 'In general it can be said that [Protestantism] has assumed a posture of support for the status quo because of its unqualified acknowledgement of the principle of the separation of powers and the subsequent autonomy of the state.'[19] Frase goes on to say that this explains its uncritical acceptance of the Vargas regime in the 1930s and its silence about the military coup in 1964. Once again we see the consequence of transplanting churches nurtured in a highly differentiated society to one in which religion and society are more closely bound together. The result, as has been emphasized many times, is that any social change connected with Protestantism is restricted to the level of culture rather than structure. Apart from the educational impact just described, the cultural change has been associated with individual piety and self-discipline. To that must be added, of course, the propagation of the North American ethos.

This leads Frase to summarize the political stance of Brazilian Protestantism as follows. 'Aside from protests to the government regarding the violation of the constitutional provision for the separation of church and state, there was little evidence of a political ethic in Brazilian Protestantism.'[20] Frase quotes a view expressed by Alvaro Reis in 1915 to the effect that the political influence of Protestantism was nil and that virtue depended on its remaining so. He adds that this apolitical attitude derives not only from a separation of church and world, but from an intense anti-Catholicism which sees a high political profile as characteristically Catholic.

Frase offers as an illustration of the apolitical stance of Protestants the support provided by the military government to a literacy campaign in the late 1960s led by missionaries of the Southern Presbyterian Church. This campaign took place in the area of Recife which not only harbours intense anti-American sentiment, but is the home of the Catholic pioneer in literacy, Paulo Freire. Frase adds that Brazilian Protestantism is just not equipped to understand structural as distinct from personal violence. It was, however, equipped to understand the implications of Brazilian nationalism. The first thirty years of this century saw a struggle for Brazilian Protestant independence of outside control and a struggle to create a culture which was not just an extension of the North American model.

Another struggle is that between the youth organizations of the churches and their central bureaucracies, which does have political implications, even though the issues are largely those of church government not secular government. The underlying issue was that of centralized authority, and the issue was joined between younger pastors of the Presbyterian Church interested in reform and an older group in control of the extensive bureaucracy. Once the 1964 coup occurred, the atmosphere shifted so rapidly toward authoritarian solutions of all kinds that the proposed reforms were soon stifled. The whole incident illustrates the extent to which institutional forms with democratic implications in Anglo-Saxon cultures can be modified in an authoritarian direction once transplanted. The same modification occurs in relation to the networks of corruption and patronage. Even among the historic Protestant churches these networks continue to operate. So-called universalistic criteria of competence and authority are only applied in part in the older religious bodies. Primary loyalties are to families and friends.

The Presbyterian Church also experienced more overtly political disagreements during the period of military rule which have been described by one of the participants, Rubem Alves.[21] In July 1966, the conservative leadership of the Brazilian Presbyterian Church captured power so completely that they were able to harass liberal elements, and did so with a sense of legitimacy conferred by the style of the new military regime. Alves described the process after having previously been obliged to resign from his pastorate and the Presbyterian Church. In his view, the current condition of the Presbyterian Church represented 'a grotesque resurrection of the most repulsive aspects of medieval Catholicism'.[22] It was, he argued, a triumph of authoritarianism over the community, structures over the person, past over the future, law over love, and death over life.

This partial assimilation of historic Protestantism to the indigenous culture places in even more paradoxical light the much more extensive and successful acculturation of Pentecostalism. Pentecostalism made itself at home in Brazilian culture, and was not troubled by some of the alien constitutional paraphernalia, not to mention educational demands, which constricted the workings of the Presbyterian Church. Pentecostalism went native precisely in the way that many missiological theorists prescribe, but in doing so it reproduced some of the features of Brazilian society that one would expect Protestantism to challenge. The argument that the hacienda reappears transmogrified within Pentecostalism recognizes the extent to which an Anglo-American faith can become indigenous. The culture of patron and client and even of honour and shame, as well as the general climate of spiritism, can be all too successfully accommodated.

The serious beginnings of Pentecostalism are located in the 1930s when Brazil ceased to be dominated by the interests of agricultural exporters. In those years a programme of industrialization was undertaken which achieved its most dramatic take-off in the 1950s. In 1962 the pace slackened and inflation grew apace. The concomitants of this whole process were a southward shift of power and wealth from the north-east, in particular to the area of São Paulo, and with that very rapid urbanization or, to be more precise, a very rapid growth of urban agglomerations and disconnected neighbourhoods. This urbanization proceeded whether or not industrial production increased and is a major context for the growth of Pentecostalism. It involved not the foreign migrants of the earlier period, but the internal migration of rural Brazilians, and the *favelas* created in the cities were often rural subcultures looking out on to an alien urban world of high-rise apartments and supermarkets. These broad elements of change need, briefly, to be recapitulated here as a background to the Pentecostal phenomenon. All that needs adding is the way in which the populist politics of Vargas rested on these new urban masses, together with the removal of their role as political actors by the coup of 1964.

The very rapid growth of Pentecostalism occurs against this background. It offers participation, mutual support, emotional release, a sense of identity and dignity, and though authoritarian it does not offer authority to those who also have status in the outside world. Pentecostalism provides a substitute society, and within that society cares largely for its own, by way of schools, orphanages, homes for the elderly and informal employment exchanges. Different Pentecostal groups may vary in what they offer. Brasil para Cristo is nationalistic and holds vast rallies on national holidays. The Congregacão Crista had its original base earlier this century in a national subculture of Italian migrants.

There are similar variations in political involvement. The Congregacão Crista forbids its leaders to take up political involvements and asks its members to refrain from any political activity beyond voting. Many Pentecostal leaders warn their members against activity in unions. They see the outcasts beyond their own borders as individual failures. Though they abhor violence, they may on occasion unconsciously collaborate with violence by support for the military regime and by acting as informers against those unfriendly to the state.

Yet Brasil para Cristo, like the Evangelical Pentecostal Church of Chile, provides a massive exception, at least in the years up to 1976. Its charismatic leader, Manõel de Mello, praised the Roman Catholic bishops for their criticism of the regime and chided the Brazilian

Protestant Federation for its timidity. He believes in denouncing injustice and has co-opted a couple of pastors trained in Methodist seminaries to help him formulate a social critique and to raise the consciousness of the impoverished. The huge temple built by Brasil para Cristo includes a 'Migrant Integration Movement', as well as a hospital and an Education Centre offering courses in law and business administration.

One characteristic of Protestant (and of Pentecostal) political activity is worth reiterating, and that is the way many Protestants reproduce the pattern of relationships based on authority and patronage. Even in the historic Protestant churches members may ask pastors how to vote. Hoffnagel, in her study of the Assemblies of God in Recife, remarks: 'not only does the pastor exercise the role of the traditional 'patrão' within the church itself, but he conditions the way the church articulates with the dominant political power-structure.'[23] In order to obtain benefits from the civil authorities, like public lighting or paved streets near the church, or to secure municipal and state jobs for their members, the pastors approach politicians bargaining with their influence over votes. Souza makes similar comments about Pentecostalists in São Paulo. In spite of taking up apolitical attitudes, pastors frequently stand as candidates in elections for municipal councils.

No only are Protestants involved in municipal elections: since the partial restoration of the democratic process in Brazil, Protestants have emerged in considerable numbers in state politics. They number up to forty deputies and clearly they are beginning to constitute a distinct Protestant political presence. What that presence portends appears from new evidence assembled by Paul Freston of Campinas University, São Paulo, and given to the author in personal conversation. There are some thirty-three deputies identified in his research as constituting an evangelical group since 1986, and among these the Pentecostals have increased eightfold. The trade union organization DIAP has rated the evangelicals with respect to issues of concern to workers, and their rating is somewhat more favourable that that of the generality of deputies. Of course, evangelicals have strong views on family and moral issues such as abortion, but attitudes reminiscent of the Moral Majority are largely confined to Baptists. Pentecostals are fairly middle of the road, while 'historical' Protestants are strongly left or strongly right in their attitudes. Like all other groups, evangelicals extract their pound of flesh in return for support over such issues as the extension of the Presidential term; in other words they are clients and they have clients. Certainly, the evidence gathered by Freston corrects current stereotypes and is consonant with evidence already cited about Pentecostal attitudes in Chile during the Allende period.

Case Studies: Colombia and Mexico

In the remaining sections of this chapter the focus will be initially on Colombia and on Mexico, before we step back somewhat from the material in order to entertain wider perspectives. It should, perhaps, be emphasized that the overall aim is to indicate some kinds of evangelical action (or inaction) in selected social situations, not to provide a comprehensive summary of contemporary Protestant politics country by country or to offer any kind of historical narrative.

There is some scattered evidence on the political attitudes of evangelicals in Colombia, worth citing at least because it seems to indicate a somewhat more positive approach to the political realm in spite of the appalling nature of Colombian politics in quite recent times. Cornelia Butler Flora, in her comments on Colombian Pentecostalism, agrees with other authors that 'Pentecostals are not in the vanguard of revolutionary action' but they will not, in her view, 'oppose groups they see as acting in the instrumental interests of their class'.[24] Pentecostals are likely 'on the local level to take anti-establishment actions in such things as water strikes, protection of prisoners and other locally based protests against day-to-day living conditions'.[25]

Karl Westmeier, in his studies of Protestantism in Colombia, offers interesting background information to the effect that apathy towards voting is evident in over half the population.[26] There is widespread distrust of the electoral machinery. Colombia's two-party system has historically made the successful emergence of a third party unlikely. When, however, the former dictator, Rojas Pinilla, tried to weld together a third force, the ANAPO (Alianza Nacional Popular), many evangelicals supported it. The ANAPO embraced all kinds of elements from former supporters of the MRI (Movimiento Revolucionaria Liberal) to Neo-Peronists, but the broad image projected was populist and hostile to the traditional oligarchies. Evangelical leaders saw the popularity it attracted as a 'judgement' on the old system. When it failed some Protestants in Bogota formed their own party with a similar-sounding name – the Alianza Nacional Patriotica. This Westmeier describes as a 'characteristic expression of the genuine Colombian-Evangelical longing for a society of justice',[27] even though Protestant churches did not give it general backing and many church members continued to support the liberals. Westmeier adds that

Protestants are more active politically than Catholics of similar background. So, although there is usually a tendency to an apolitical attitude among evangelicals, nevertheless, they do participate. They keep themselves informed – and they have shown a capacity to join forces with attempts to break up the control of the old oligarchies.

The extensive studies by Jean-Pierre Bastian on Protestantism in Mexico bear directly on the issue of Protestants and politics. Bastian is at pains to bring out how Pentecostals in particular can resist the status quo, as well as submit to the divinely ordained authority of the powers that be. In an article entitled 'Dissidence religieuse dans le milieu rural méxicain', Bastian argues that Mexican anthropologists have too easily seen the rapid spread of Protestantism as the advance guard of ideological penetration by the USA.[28] They treat Pentecostalism almost exactly as they treat the Wycliffe Bible translators. Bastian cites, in particular, Erwin Rodríguez, 'Un evangelio segun la classe dominante', published in 1982.[29] In his view this is a work more of propaganda than analysis.

However, Bastian's own field-work in the south-east of Mexico where Pentecostalism is strongest suggests other possibilities. In this area the new religious groups are mostly rural, and they also offer some continuity with the old symbolic universe of healing through their practice of *Sanidad Divina*. Bastian suggests that these groups represent a political resistance to the *caciques*.

Given that in Mexico, as elsewhere in Latin America, subsistence farming is giving way to a market economy, the *caciques* have put pressure on the local peasants in order to build up their own capital. The *caciques* are part and parcel of an integrated and hierarchical politico-religious system and they effectively 'pocket' the local Catholic practices for their own advantage. Those who are at the margin of subsistence, or in the process of being made marginal, manifest their opposition by refusing any more to participate. They often adopt Protestantism, usually in one of its Pentecostal forms, but their new faith turns out to be very practical, retaining the old magic and even the rituals. Indeed, the new pastors are often the old magi writ large. Clearly, the combination of elements found here is very different from what happens when a Pentecostal group expresses its sense of displacement by a total destruction of the old symbolic order.

The withdrawal of the peasants and the breakup of the all-embracing sacred canopy brings 'class warfare' into the open and violence follows. The clash spills over into a party political difference between those who support the Catholic Party of National Action and those aligned with the Party of Institutional Revolution. It also spills over into an ecological separation between the Protestant and

Catholic sectors of villages. Sometimes a village will forcibly eject or reject the missionaries of the new faith; sometimes a village will go completely over to the new faith, including its juridical apparatus; and sometimes the members of the new faith simply have to found a new village. A little village 'Jerusalem' emerges, just as a 'Bethesda' emerged in the terrain of North Wales.

This tendency of the old system to break up in whole segments is quite normal in many parts of Latin America. Indeed, in some cases the local evangelists actually insist that conversions take place by families or by integral social sectors rather than individually. In other words, the culture is not yet fully individualized. Protestantism represents a break in social uniformity, but has not so far realized its potential for creating the autonomous free-standing individual. Nevertheless, to set these shifts in motion, or at any rate to be the medium and the means through which such shifts are manifest, is to initiate the changes which will eventually alter the bases of political action. The Welsh countryside was fragmented in a very similar manner two centuries ago by the arrival of rival evangelical groups.

Bastian adds that the leaders of the Protestant groups have recourse to their national and international organizations for aid in their local battles. He also gives an example of how an evangelical leader may be forced to assume local authority. In Tabasco, which is an area rich in oil and one where the Protestant proportion of the population is very high, the leadership of an organization to redress wrongs suffered by the country people was taken on by the Presbyterian pastor, Eulogio Mendez Perez. Of course, such leadership does not have to fall to a Protestant. Bastian mentions how in a particular part of Guatemala the same roles were taken on by Maryknoll Catholic priests. Like the pastor they could act as persons outside of the current symbolic system.

However, Bastian also indicates a different variety of Protestantism which is mainly urban and is part of a transmission belt for US culture and conservative political attitudes. It is bureaucratic and technocratic in organization, and uses the electronic media to spread its message. In his article 'Protestantismos latinamericanos entre la resistencia y la sumisión, 1961–1983',[30] Bastian contrasts it with an older and more liberal Protestantism. Since the early sixties the advocates of the new model have become more successful and aggressive, and the liberals for their part have absorbed quite a lot of liberation theology. The result is a Protestant world more and more sharply divided. The various moral and evangelical crusaders, together with articulate spokesmen like Kenneth Strachan of the Latin American Mission and Peter Wagner of the Church Growth

Movement, stand in contention with those who proclaim the importance of social concern like Emilio Castro, Mortimer Arias and Rubem Alves. For two decades or so the rival religious multinationals have confronted each other, divided over the proper articulation of social concern and over the extent of ecumenical cooperation.

Bastian sees a connection between the reformist approach and the kind of cooperation which has taken place between Protestants and the Nicaraguan government. Equally, he sees a connection between the apolitical, anti-communist approach and the cooperation between Protestants and General Efraim Montt over his 'beans or death' campaign in Guatemala.

In the course of time the use of technology by the new evangelism has moved on from radio to television and to the products of the Electronic Church, in particular Oral Roberts, Jimmy Swaggart, the PTL Club and Pat Robertson's 700 Club. The last of these has been particularly concerned to transmit political messages with regard to the Panama Canal Treaty and the sale of arms to the Guatemalan government. Alongside these politico-religious crusades, Bastian places the Cruzada Estudiantil y Profesional para Cristo (which receives economic support from the Crusade for Christ), and the Summer Institute of Linguistics. A further analysis which generally supports Bastian's view is provided by Hugo Assman's recent book *A Igreja Electronica e seu impacto na America Latina* (1986).[31] Assman discerns links between what he calls the neo-conservative offensive and such bodies as the Institute for Religion and Democracy and the American Enterprise Institute.

It is, perhaps, worth while adding here that one of the precipitating elements in the drive against communism must have been events in Cuba. The Cuban Revolution aroused US fears in general which were certainly transmitted along Protestant networks. But beyond that, in 1961 some 90 per cent of the Cuban pastorate emigrated to Florida, accompanied by two-thirds of their flocks, the fruit of sixty years' missionary work. This accentuated the anti-communist fervour both of local Latin American Protestants and the anti-communist approach of those North Americans in charge of religious television and radio.

A Critique and a Counter-instance

Clearly, all this amounts to a propaganda war of some intensity over the Protestant role in politics. It may be useful, therefore, to insert here a brief summary of the kind of political criticism advanced by those associated with the historic churches against the new wave of evangelism. For that purpose I select a piece by Jane Cary Peck based, to some extent, on research undertaken by Robert Craig in Costa Rica.[32] Jane Cary Peck is a Methodist who works at the Andover Newton Theological School. She was sometime visiting professor at the Seminario Bíblico Latinamericano at San José, Costa Rica, and has been connected with the WCC and the American National Council of Churches.

Jane Cary Peck begins by quoting Robert Craig's findings to the effect that most local Protestant groups in Costa Rica have their headquarters in the USA, and rely on the USA for literary, radio and televisual materials. They represent, in short, the religious version of a more general 'dependency' and provide slipways for Americanization and the moulding of (petit) bourgeois man. This, then, is the cultural 'project' of contemporary evangelical Protestantism, incidentally exemplified in Costa Rica, but in fact visible all over Latin America. This project is well served by a radical dualism promoted by evangelicals between body and soul, earth and heaven, world and church, structure and person, and also by an indifference to history and society. Their style is authoritarian and this makes them useful allies for the national security state and its military rulers, as well as pawns for the 'Manifest Destiny' of the United States.

Given that this critique is so all-inclusive I insert at this point a piece of concrete evidence as to how the latent symbolism of Pentecostal can be realized politically. I utilize here a paper by Bobby C. Alexander on the 'House of the Lord' led by Herbert Daughtry.[33] Alexander's research shows how a largish Pentecostal community in New York can become a political force. Under the leadership of its pastor there has grown up a union of the brotherhood expressed in participatory worship and in a unity of political purpose manifested in lobbying and demonstrating. The Pentecostals stand plainly in solidarity with other African-Americans. Alexander concludes that there is enough evidence from his own research and that of others to refute the notion that the release of tension in the worship of the congregation necessarily diverts psychic power from the pursuit of political redress.

Summary

This scattered information and comment on the political attitudes of Protestants, more particularly of Pentecostals, needs now to be reviewed at two levels. First, it is useful just to set down what kind of overall impression is conveyed. Second the information needs setting in a wider framework of interpretation.

As regards the overall impression, Protestants as a whole, and Pentecostals in particular, clearly tend to be apolitical. They suspect the machinery and the processes of politics, though in that they are at one with many not of their faith. On occasion the Pentecostal churches offer some legitimacy to the national security state in return for recognition, and the temptation to do this is specially strong in the pastorate. Indeed, Pentecostals have a strong respect for the 'powers' ordained of God, even those ordained of God in Nicargua and Cuba. In spite of these leanings towards support for the civil power, and in spite of an apolitical stance often skewed in a conservative direction, they are not necessarily committed to quietism or to conservatism. There is a minority in most places committed to political activity, and in the case of Brasil para Cristo flamboyantly so. The evidence set out by Tennekes for Chile under Allende suggests that Pentecostals sympathized with Allende's political objectives. Of course, there has always been a tendency among Protestants to invert whatever was, or is, the political position of the Roman Catholic Church, so that 'liberalism' was favoured up to the mid-century and conservatism thereafter.

It is this central orientation running diametrically counter to the positions taken up by Catholicism which provides the starting point for comment at an interpretative level. A religious minority organized against such a mammoth and overarching system is likely to be automatically opposed to Catholic policies, practices and political identifications or alliances. That, in part, is how the early Protestant schools became places for training liberal and radical leaders, and how Protestant social programes came to be seen as progressive. At the same time, Protestants rarely took their liberalism much beyond a somewhat self-concerned interest in questions of church and state. To pursue further political involvement would have been dangerous, since it might mean receiving foreign support, which would be fatal, or at least embarrassing for the foreign missionaries.

The primary opposition to Catholicism arises partly for classical theological reasons and partly because Catholicism symbolizes integration into a complete socio-religious sytem. Even if Catholicism is in fact disentangling itself from this system (or being ejected from it), for Protestants it is still part and parcel of a society they decisively reject. Whatever their political attitudes, Protestants desire (and express) a process of social differentiation in the direction of personal choice and egalitarian participation. From their standpoint, Catholicism still appears as involved in hierarchical forms, in priestly mediation through controlled channels, and in comprehensive organic integration. Even if the Roman Catholic Church emerges in friendly ecumenical guise, that is still a threat for Protestants since they cannot cooperate except as junior and local partners to a massive religious multinational.

Not only does the (very recent) alteration in Catholic attitudes towards 'the sects' cause a problem. So, too, does the Catholic readiness to entertain radical social philosophies. Those philosophies are put forward by radical middle-class Catholic intellectuals in concert with other social and political analysts in the middle class. They are *ipso facto* remote from the world of the Protestant poor up to their eyes in a day to day struggle for survival. The Catholic readiness to rework secular philosophies, including Marxism, is inimical to the Protestant reliance on a few maxims derived from the Bible. After all, this Catholic capacity to absorb and to rework secular materials derives from a very long history of organic and hegemonic relationships to the whole of society and, as suggested earlier, its contemporary manifestations retain something of that organic and hegemonic character. A political theology rooted in the idea of liberation is inherently a product of the self-conscious and sophisticated political classes, more particularly the 'knowledge class', and contemporary Pentecostals are neither 'conscious' nor sophisticated. If they were sophisticated they could hardly appeal to large numbers of the poor as self-evidently their brothers in impoverishment.

There is a further reason why Protestantism is so far 'behind' and that is because it is so far in front. Protestantism initiates the era of the individual in his (or her) specifically religious incarnation, and the obverse of that is a view of society not easily amenable to holistic and structural understandings. A primary experience of unique personhood or of personalized interactions in the small voluntary group engenders an apolitical stance because it is affronted by all the large-scale social mechanisms, and unintended consequences, which resist individual moral action. Thus, the very 'advance' associated with Protestantism leads to a truncated understanding of the social world and one which excludes structural reform. Of course, the association of Protestantism with individuality and individualism is far from absolute but it does call on and reinforce notions of personal response, experience, conscience and individual commitment.

Once we take into account the coiled up resistance of the social mechanisms in Latin American society to any moral initiatives, it is not surprising that Pentecostals erect a dualistic wall between the safe enclosure of faith and the dangerous wilderness of the world. For them that wilderness is occupied by a 'satanic' violence from all sides which will seize upon and destroy those who stray carelessly into it.

The concentration of Protestant spiritual resources on the creation of a peaceable psyche makes Protestants very inclined to seek a middle way between a violent state and violent guerrillas. What they achieve by way of peaceability at the level of personal relationships, especially in the family, makes violent antagonism between political actors deeply repugnant. When political violence occurs they are marginally inclined to prefer it to come from the powers that be, and even if it creates a desert they are still inclined to call it peace. That is an illusion, but perhaps an understandable illusion. Like the rest of humankind they retain a vested interest in survival, and that is better promoted by coming off alcohol than by hiding sub-machine guns.

It is here, of course, that the relationship of Pentecostals to the USA plays a role. In a sense the USA is the protecting power of Protestantism everywhere, and it has for several decades conceived itself as in polar opposition to 'godless communism'. Even if Pentecostals were to approve of the accidentals of communism, they are well aware that in its foundation documents atheism is defined as of its essence. The experience of believers under Castro, let alone in most of the rest of the communist world, has hardly taught otherwise. When that is combined with a certain affinity of Protestants with the US style, and a tendency to look to the USA as a political champion, even if the champion's feet are of clay, then Protestants may well feel pushed to prefer 'national security' states to guerrilla forces. No doubt much crude propaganda about communism is deployed manipulatively to scare populations away from any move whatever towards 'peace and justice', but many Protestants, rightly or wrongly, feel that they have even less to hope for where communism triumphs than where brutal generals rule the roost. The revolutionary ethos is inherently militant, military and all-inclusive in its demands, and does not allow enclaves of conscientious objection or suffer a purely personal spiritual space. Thus, Sandinistas are opposed to the way some Protestants reject any obligatory involvement in the social cells engaged in 'reconstruction' or in military service. Of course, it may be that the Sandinistas represent a new kind of gentle revolutionary, intent on a pluralistic society and happy to cooperate with whoever will help build up Nicaragua. But Protestants do not rely on that.

The fundamental points are these. There is social and political evidence to show that evangelical religion is not inherently apolitical or conservative, and also that it passes through periods of social latency before trying to generalize peace and reconciliation from the interior of the group to the wider social world. During these periods of latency, the social changes initiated by religious faith, above all universal participation, operate at the level of culture and of symbolism. Protestantism creates a 'free space', though the free space reverberates with echoes from a patriarchal past. That 'free space' is temporarily protected by an apolitical stance, setting up a boundary with a dangerous, corrupt and amoral outside world. Nevertheless, the creation of any space in the conditions obtaining in Latin America remains inherently political. Liberation theology focuses on the idea of Exodus, and in the creation of a free space there is a kind of exodus.

PART V

Conclusions

Chapter 13

The Argument Summarized
and Extended

The Latin American heirs of the Iberian empires have suffered cumulative political and economic defeat at the hands of the North American heirs of the British empire. To point this out is not in any way to detract from the greatness or richness of Hispanic civilization, nor is it to endorse yet another covert version of the 'Whig interpretation of history' tricked out with the vulgarities of Manifest Destiny. It is only to note an obvious and extremely important fact about the impact of contrasting cultural templates. There are 'crucial events' in the history of most, perhaps all, societies, which set the general tenor of their future and either circumscribe their options or open out their potentials. These are the donations of history, givens which point towards relatively persistent outcomes.[1]

The general tenor of North American political history was set by the cumulative and largely unreversed impact of the English Civil War from 1642 to 1660 and the 'Glorious Revolution' of 1688–9, which the American Revolution of 1774–83 then continued and considerably extended. In the economic field the tenor of North America also derived from Britain. The industrial revolution began in mid-eighteenth century Britain and was quickly picked up and later dramatically extended in the United States. Indeed, the United States developed a complete set of crucial processes which were initiated in the British Isles: political democracy, industrialism – and religious pluralism. To these should be added, as Claudio Veliz has argued, the special impact of the English language and the English common law.[2] The importance of English language and law lies in the way they loosely accumulate rather than respond to centralized definition and control.

By contrast the tenor and texture of Latin American societies lacked all these elements. Even where parliamentary democracy was quite early established it eventually turned out to lack stability or staying power; religion remained a Catholic monopoly, and industrialism achieved only a partial or patchy penetration.

Such dramatically different historic profiles deriving on the one hand from the south-west European seaboard, and on the other hand from the north-west European seaboard, focused initially on religious difference. Whatever the subsequent salience of that religious difference, there have been continuous eruptions of geopolitical rivalry for four centuries. The rivalry intensified as an independent United States enthusiastically shouldered the imperial burden on its own account and either annexed parts of what Latins regarded as their historic patrimony or subjected Central and South American nations to preponderant economic power.

That is the long-term historical context within which the current overflow of evangelical religion from North to South America takes place. It is, moreover, the framework within which many Latin Americans still choose to see it, whether they happen to be old-style Catholic nationalists or intellectuals of the left. Accompanying the prolonged economic and political defeats and expropriations comes a cultural invasion spearheaded by religion. It is not necessary to endorse the nationalist or Marxist (or Marxist-nationalist) case to recognize the relevance of this rivalrous *longue durée*. In any case, the prevalence of the nationalist view is one of the facts of the current situation, providing an almost obligatory definition of Protestantism as the religious version of economic dependency or the religious guise of an alien, not to say inferior, culture. Latin Americans do not respond sympathetically to the kind of sentiment enunciated by President Bush in his acceptance speech at the Republican Convention in August 1988: 'We have whipped the world with our culture.'

But where exactly in the historic incubators of north-west Europe was the evangelical religion now crossing over from North to South America first generated? Where was this rich and potent trouble hatched? The answer is that the voluntarism came about as part of the thrust of Calvinist reform in England, which also almost simultaneously crossed the Atlantic as one element in the founding culture(s) of British North America. Channels of religious independence (and sometimes also of religions 'enthusiasm') were dug on both sides of the Atlantic. These channels were to remain countercultural in England and to become the core of the future culture of America. Of course, the dissenting and fragmented mode stood a better chance of becoming central to America because it was supplemented by rival ethnic groups, especially in the middle colonies.

The establishment of voluntarism in both cultures is a familiar cliché, but however familiar it needs once again to be underlined as a world-historical event breaking up the age old unity of faith and community, church and state. Insofar as Britain and the USA have developed in somewhat different ways the difference turns to a discernible degree on the partial retention of the overarching framework in Britain and its collapse in British North America and the United States. The same goes for an associated phenomenon: the partial retention of the aristocratic ethos in England and its collapse in America.[3]

Another common element generated in the two versions of English social and religious culture was a religious election to political destiny, which offered a path through the wilderness and an entry into lands of promise. As in the matter of voluntarism so also in the matter of special political providence, the nascent culture of North America expanded and elaborated on its English original. John Milton was its most eloquent spokesman.[4] Political messianism passed from the English 'to the American strand', and entered into the founding myths and charters of 1776. Though the notion of providence still continued to help forward British expansion for three further centuries, it was never the *raison d'être* of national existence as it was in the United States. Part of the ontological security and confidence experienced by American evangelical missionaries in Latin America had its roots in this conception of special providence and in its partial mutation into the notion of progress. In this way messianic aspirations originally generated by seventeenth century England were able to pierce the ingrained superiorities of *Hispanidad*.

The final shared Anglo-American incubation came about when eighteenth century revivalism poured along the channels of voluntary and independent religion dug more than a century before by classic Calvinist dissent. The roots of this revivalism are diverse. One major source was German pietism, the small pious cells of intense and personal faith created by Spener and his successors and by the Moravian fraternity. The evangelical revival in England combined influences from Pietism and from the Moravians, with movements for the reform of manners and reminiscences of high church piety, and these mingled and contended with a modified Calvinism. In British North America the Great Awakening(s) owed a great deal to a modified Calvinism, but much of the power generated by the Awakening(s) eventually flowed in a Methodist direction. The important point is that the channels of religious deviance were dramatically widened in both societies, creating a major channel of alternative religiosity in Britain and creating the main channel of religiosity in the United States.

What flowed in those channels was a voluntary, lay, participatory and enthusiastic faith. As on the mainland of continental Europe the groups it created might be quietist or activist, for or against established power, but the cultural logic of its forms was active, participatory, fissile, egalitarian and enthusiastic. In short, it represented an autonomous mobilization of mass-consciousness, transforming and energizing individual persons, and bringing about myriads of competitive voluntary networks for sharing and for mutual support. These networks might encompass such diverse activities as choral singing or inventing volleyball and basketball in the YMCA.

To put it in a way germane to the argument of this book: the prototypes of Pentecostal and evangelical religion now went into full cultural reproduction, ready for eventual transportation across the Rio Grande. That transportation would have to wait for some while until the same breakdown of overarching monopoly which occurred in seventeenth-century English culture on either side of the Atlantic occurred also in Latin America.

Whatever debate there may be about the details and the precise influences and sequences operating, there is little doubt that the initial creation of a voluntary, participatory and enthusiastic form of faith in England, and its realization in America, was the first and enormous step in the process of differentiation of spheres, whereby religion came increasingly to exercise its influence at the level of culture – and in discrete voluntary associations. The power of religion operated above all through its assumptions concerning the potency of individual initiative and concerning the centrality of personal experience and experiment, and from the political assonances of its organizational style. It offered the active popular supports or, minimally, the passive cultural residues above which small 'enlightened' elites might erect revolutionary structures.

It also acquired a dynamic adaptability which prevented the great cities of America becoming centres of secularity as they did in Europe and Britain. Because America lacked the association of *a* major religious institution with a class culture or cultures it was able to engender religious forms which could adapt to and reverse the anomic conditions of the city.[5] *Religion did not have to cope with a combination of anomic personal chaos and class alienation. To have reversed or at least nullified a major secularizing tendency in this way suggests that tendency is contingent on certain circumstances, not a necessary aspect of universal processes. The reversal is important because the adaptations have been passed on to the varieties of Pentecostal and evangelical religion now expanding (for example) in the megacities of São Paulo and Seoul.*

An Aside on Centre and Periphery, Centralization and Federalism

What follows is a logically detachable and even speculative section of the argument which may be omitted for the sake of cleanliness of line. It comprises two thematic elements. The first element has to do with a movement of religious intensity from centre to periphery, which is in part oscillation and in part a long-term retirement from the central and metropolitan areas of a society. The theoretical point of reference is, of course, the seminal work of Edward Shils.

Sometimes 'evangelical' religion – broadly understood – occupies the core regions of a society, and sometimes it retires to a subordinate region or periphery. Thus in seventeenth-century England it occupied the most advanced areas, and reproduced those areas on the map of New England: Boston, Ipswich, Cambridge, Braintree, Bedford, Hingham, Waltham. Later it also effected an entry into the central redoubts of culture in Victorian England.[6] At other times it has retired to the peripheries, to the small towns, the highlands and the islands, and that is where according to unilinear secularization theory it must eventually expire. In Scandinavia it was central at the court of Christian VI of Denmark, but eventually retired to redoubts in northern Jutland or Iceland. In the United States it once occupied the North East, but then established its most important redoubt in the defeated South. This oscillation, or staggered retirement, can be in part be assimilated to a general trend to secularization but not entirely.

That is because it has to be related to the second thematic element, which is the *variable* relation between centralized power and cultural vitality on the periphery. On the continent of Europe, preponderant power has resided in the centre, and that preponderance is visibly illustrated in the monumental and Baroque edifices of Europe and in the geometrical control exercised over nature. In Britain, however, the centre barely held and rarely asserted itself above an urbane Palladian modesty. In America the centre did not hold at all, and the contrast between centre and periphery can only faintly be discerned. America is federal, politically and culturally, and that gives the religion on the so-called peripheries a chance of survival and revival. The point needs further elaboration to bring out the special relationship between the evangelical peripheries of Britain and the evangelical culture of the United States.

In continental Europe the central bastions of the society press against the regions and peripheries and frequently assimilate them altogether. When the peripheries put up a successful cultural defence they do so through an intensified version of the national religion: as, for example, the militant Catholicism of Slovakia, Brittany, Flanders and the Basques, or the intensified Lutheranism of Bergen and its hinterland. In Britain the existence of alternatives in the core regions of the society and associated weakness of the central religious institution allows the peripheries and regions to adopt a *different* and more evangelical vision of Protestantism. Vigorous, participatory and egalitarian faiths have established themselves in the regional cultures of Britain – Ulster, Man, Cornwall, Scotland, Wales – and are coextensive with the more egalitarian ethos of those areas. Sometimes this faith is Calvinist or Methodist or even both combined, but in any event it is broadly evangelical in style and more genuinely popular than religion in England. Included in these resistant 'peripheries' were also Catholic cultures, above all in ('southern') Ireland but also for a long while in parts of the Scottish highlands and islands. These Catholic peripheries added a non-English weight to emigration in the USA and Australia, but that weight was only exercised in the mid-nineteenth century and thereafter.

Leaving aside the very first efflux of religious dissenters from England to America, the peripheries of the British Isles contributed more persons per head of population to emigration than did the core culture of England, for reasons partly economic, partly political, and partly religious. They went all over the world in an extraordinary diaspora and their settlements are to be traced in Australia, Canada, New Zealand, Southern Chile, Patagonia, Scandinavia – and the United States. Bangor, Ballater, Calgary, Aberdeen and Dunedin tell the tale. These migrants contributed to the way the Anglican Church maintains only a shadow of its English dominance in the 'old' Commonwealth of Australia, Canada and New Zealand, and is merely an elite if influential fragment in the United States. Of course, these politico-religious and economic associations are not to be regarded as causal, but as tangled skeins of mutually reinforcing connection. They do, however, add a significant component to the continuum from hierarchy to equality that runs from England to the peripheries of Wales, Ulster and Scotland to Canada, Australia and New Zealand – and the United States. They also add, along with other influences of course, to the egalitarian tilt.

They did that quite crucially at a particular point in the history of island Britain and British North America. In the eighteenth century, large numbers emigrated to the then colonies, in particular from Protestant 'dissenting' Ulster, and overlapped strongly both with American revival and with American rebellion. In the civil war in the English-speaking world, a war which divided not only the colonies internally but Britain itself, this Scots-Irish sector placed its weight more with the patriots than with the loyalists.[7]

Thereafter, free-ranging evangelical religion undermined such rickety establishments as remained in America. Even for people of English background Methodism provided an alternative to Anglicanism which retained an English provenance. Evangelical religion moved mightily along the frontier and eventually established its principal redoubt in the South: on the vast 'periphery' of America. But in America, as already indicated, the peripheries are large enough to compete with the centre, if indeed a centre can be said to exist at all. From the great southern redoubt came many of the first Protestant missionaries and emigrants to South America, amongst them many people of Scots origin. And today many of the most powerful impulses from 'Anglo' to Latin America emanate from the South and from Texas. Thus we have a movement of faith from periphery to periphery.

On the contemporary scene too many criss-crossing influences mingle together for the postulated movement from periphery to periphery to be more than faintly discernible. Indeed, as indicated above, the whole of this part of the argument can be eliminated without the central argument sustaining any serious damage at all.

What remains central is that the kind of religion which gave initial direction, tone and colour to the USA has crossed the Rio Grande on a truly massive scale. It has established itself as an autonomous centre of cultural reproduction and expanded so as to alter the psychic and social environment of tens of millions of the Latin American poor. *It has therefore admixed the Latin pattern of an antagonism between the faithful and secular radicals, fought out in the core institutions, with a North American pattern where religion works largely within the ambit of culture alone.* The existence of this crucial admixture will be reiterated from a different perspective in the sector of the argument immediately following. I would add that by being able to describe this hybrid pattern I complete, though from another angle, an analytic development only hinted at in my *A General Theory of Secularization.*

The Americanization of Latin American Religion?

Before this question can be properly addressed it is necessary to recapitulate and to step back to survey the whole social panorama. In Latin America, religion and the social fabric have been woven together as one, at the level of the state and the level of the local community, so that for over three centuries the continent was shut off from outside religious influence. What is now occurring is the rapid acceleration of a process of break-up which began anything from seventy to one hundred and forty years ago. This same process occurred almost four centuries ago in English cultures on both sides of the Atlantic, and it proceeded by relatively easy accretions of free social space. In Latin America today it proceeds with great speed and considerable violence.

In the technical language of sociology Latin American society is undergoing the differentiation which occurred much earlier and more slowly in 'Anglo' society. This process would have occurred independently of the earlier influence of Britain or the later influence of the United States, though, of course, those countries provided models for the protagonists of change, and by reason of their power and progress brought Latin America within the scope of their cultural radiation.

However the opening up of free space through the process of differentiation is always problematic. In the Catholic (or Latin) societies of southern Europe the monopolistic nature of Catholicism has inhibited differentiation and has tended to give rise to rival secular monopolies under the aegis of the state, some of them promoted by radical liberals, some by communists. These monopolies have mirrored Catholicism in their comprehensiveness, and there has been a war between the old and new kinds of monopoly lasting from 1789 to 1960. Even in northern Europe, the comprehensive national churches have given rise to centralized secular structures and pervasive ideologies. Social Democracy in Scandinavia is (or has been) comprehensive in its scope. In Britain, of course, there was a long tradition of religious voluntarism and an accepted area of free space, but the state church did after all remain in place and subsequent structures of communication and education like the BBC, have mirrored its comprehensiveness.

Wherever religious monopolies had historically been powerful in Europe there were persistent movements of comprehensive reintegration, especially in times of strain, some of the left, some of the right, some violently opposed to religion, some combined with it.

In general the patterns most characteristic of southern Latin Europe were replicated in Latin America, in particular movements of radical secularism, of radical populism and clero-fascism. Britain and America remained relatively free of these movements, though not entirely so, especially in the 1930s.[8]

Thus the creation of free space was by no means the inevitable result of differentiation and of the break-up of age-old monopolies exercised by state religion. On the contrary, more often some form of reintegration was quite likely, under the comprehensive aegis of secular ideology, or else society would be distracted by struggles between the old religious monopoly and the hegemonic ambitions of the new. However, these reintegrations or struggles did not occur where religious voluntarism had been most firmly established and the monopoly and/or the power of the centre most extensively undermined. Indeed, the extensive propagation of *voluntaristic* evangelical Christianity and such reintegrations or struggles were mutually incompatible. Continental Europe and Latin America remained impervious to this kind of Christianity and the Anglo-cultures of the North Atlantic remained impervious to the reintegrations and the struggles. A free, voluntaristic evangelical Protestantism is creature and creator of free social space.

If this analysis holds then it is possible to re-state what is currently happening in Latin America and then to approach the vexed and vexatious problem of Americanization. In Latin America, as in Latin Europe, the spirals of repulsion between militant secularism and Catholicism are unwinding, but in Latin America this disengagement takes place after a shorter period of struggle. Only in one or two quite small countries – Uruguay for example – has militant secularism under the aegis of the state gained control. In many countries, above all perhaps Brazil, the church has been weakened by radical governments (and/or by long periods of co-option) but the culture itself has not been secularized. However much the church has been weakened, religious understandings remain pervasive. Indeed, Brazilian culture retains a complete and free-floating atmosphere of 'spiritism'.

Now, at precisely this juncture Latin American societies have been exposed to the economic power and cultural radiation of the United States at the height of its world ascendancy. This cultural radiation includes the voluntaristic evangelical religion central to the original emergence and to the continuance of the United States. *This means that two patterns of secularization once mutually exclusive have crossed to bring about a distinctive new pattern.* In Europe the north-western pattern of Britain and the south-western pattern of Spain remained distinct; in the Americas they have mixed together. The confluence is as dramatic and revolutionary as it is unexpected. In the earlier phases of North and South American contact, it looked as if evangelical religion would simply remain as a minor element alongside other militantly anti-Catholic movements, whether political or religious. It took a minor role alongside freemasonry, positivism, and the 'societies of thought', and in general it seemed that Latin America would be as impervious to evangelical penetration as continental Europe has been.[9] That turns out not to be the case. *As the sacred canopy in Latin America is rent and the all-encompassing system cracks, evangelical Christianity pours in and by its own autonomous native power creates free social space.*

Perhaps the process under examination can be rephrased in a simpler form. Suppose an 'advanced' socio-religious system to exist, as does the United States, representing a state of radical disarticulation. The adjacent civilization of Latin America is strongly articulated, and as that articulation collapses it is convulsed by violence. What then travels across from the United States as contribution to and consequence of that crisis is precisely the kind of powerful but fragmented and competitive religiosity bound up in the very emergence of 'Anglo' civilization. It will enter into the open spaces, simultaneously enlarging them and operating as a potent competitor within them. Given that it is a disarticulated form of faith, it cannot re-form the old monopoly in a new unified Protestant format, but is able to fructify solely at the cultural level.

However, so violent are the convulsions within the old monopolistic system, that it tries to recover lost unities either under the aegis of secular radicalism, as has been the case over long periods in Uruguay, or, as is more usual, under the aegis of a bureaucratic military dictatorship. Or both, including both together. The former is resistant to evangelical penetration; the latter may tolerate evangelical religion since it initiates change solely at the cultural level, and otherwise seeks to avoid being drawn into the polarities of political violence. Thus a faith originating in a radically disarticulated system can find itself located as a silent pillar of a rearticulated system, precisely because of those radical origins. Nevertheless, its contingent and temporary political role is quite contrary to its cultural logic, and it is the long-term operation of that logic which will have to be expounded as this argument develops further.

Clearly, in the *special* sense just outlined, the influence of the United States is immense. Indeed, its influence is the precondition of the local empowerment since the fragmentation and the disarticulation inherent in American religion both imply autonomy. But the religious influence is only one aspect of a broader influence, economic, political and cultural. The religious traffic moves alongside the economic traffic, sometimes with the religious slightly ahead of the economic, and sometimes vice versa; sometimes in cooperation, occasionally in antagonism. The two kinds of traffic will have a family likeness: perhaps similar economic and political assumptions, certainly similar ideas, ideals, language, techniques, know-how and forms of communication and self-presentation. Yet none of this flow from North to South in any way depends on the specifically religious bridge, even though the religious bridge provides a definite reinforcement. The sign and symbol of this reinforcement may be the US-style supermarket at one end of the boulevard and the US-style church at the other end.

It is important to realize that Americanization is by no means limited to the expansion of evangelical Christianity. After all charismatic Catholicism began in North America. Again, the ordinary priesthood of the Latin American Church is partly drawn from abroad, and many of the partisans of liberation theology are from the USA. The business-like styles of promotion and organization found among evangelicals are also being adopted by the Catholic Church. Catholicism in Latin America is developing a committed active membership and entering into the religious competition with all the means of communication available to it. These are partly processes which belong to the autonomous development of South America, but they are speeded up and reinforced by the cultural traffic entering from the United States. You can attend mass in Rio and find yourself singing an offertory hymn to the tune of the Battle Hymn of the Republic!

So the Americanization that enters Latin America as one aspect of the incoming religious traffic reflects the reality of US cultural power in general. While the organs of nationalist opinion naturally and understandably inveigh against this, millions of simple folk simply want a share in the sources of US power whatever they may be. To put it in such a way is to make the transfer of power appear too direct and unmediated, but there are without doubt images of power behind the evangelical incursion. The aspiration for a better life, broadly understood, in terms of moral standards, economic prosperity, personal dignity, and health of body and mind, has some kind of US attachment, even though people simultaneously recognize that the United States is morally chaotic. Some commentators develop the theme of Americanization much further, and see evangelicals as really in the business of making Anglos out of Latins, in outward appearance and vesture as well as in inward disposition. If that is true of any group it is true of the Mormons.

The Latin Americanization of American Religion?

There is no precise measure of the extent of North Americanization through evangelical faith, but it is important to stress the extent of the reverse process: the Latin Americanzation of Protestantism. What historic Protestantism has lacked and still lacks is precisely the capacity to 'go native'. The first important instance of 'inculturation' occurred at the beginning of the century through the revival which brought about the Methodist Pentecostal Church of Chile. This has been the elusive goal sought by enlightened missionary endeavour over centuries, from the time of the controversy over Chinese rites, but the cost may well be less enlightenment, at least as understood by Europeans and North Americans. The total autonomy of Pentecostalism is part and parcel of its immersion in Latin American culture, and of its successful propagation by persons of roughly the same educational level as the apostles. The autocratic leadership and the partial retention of patronage networks is the other side of being a 'popular' movement in the Latin American context. To say that Pentecostalism reproduces some of the characteristics of *caudillismo* (authoritarian leadership) and of 'patriarchal relations' on the hacienda is to say that it lies close to the social roots. This is not in any way peculiar to Protestantism. Indeed, it is the incapacity of Protestantism hitherto to cross cultural divides and 'go native' that has historically given the edge to Catholicism or led to separatist native churches as in Africa. In all movements of religious conversion and change there is a dialectic of external influence and local adaptation. If local adaptation is insufficiently radical then conversions will be slow, though it must be said that the small community thus created may eventually be sustained and identified precisely by its distinctiveness.

The potent combination of external influence and radical local adaptation found in Pentecostalism is related to another characteristic source of power: the union of the very old and very modern. For example, it brings together the ancient layers of spiritism, in black Africa and indeed almost everywhere, with a modern sense of the union of psyche and soma. It brings together the ancient notion of illness as located in the community with the modern concept of community medicine. It unites the ancient layers of solidarity with the kinds of expansive organizational principles recommended by specialists in church growth. And the Pentecostal preference for stories, for gesture and oratory, belongs simultaneously to pre-literate and to post-literate society. Pentecostalism retains the participation found in the fiesta and unites that to a spiritual version of the contemporary encounter group.

Critical Paths

Through what conduits, then, does evangelical religion most easily pass into the culture of Latin America? In the past, as already emphasized, it entered as a minor motif alongside other anti-catholic elements and was most influential through its welfare and educational agencies. Its path was eased wherever the Catholic Church was already weakened by state control or governmental antagonism and wherever people were mobile or had acquired a modicum of economic and social independence.

Nowadays, of course, the number of conduits has considerably increased and they carry vastly greater numbers of people. Protestantism may in one context gain attention and adherence among those who are at the margins of subsistence and are threatened by the advance of a market economy and the depredations of local caciques. In another context Protestantism may acquire a base among small independent producers who need to band together and who are determined to assert themselves, in particular by bypassing the Ladino middle-man. Everywhere it offers a network of mutual support which may include a variety of services: groups for female interaction and for training in some skill, a source of information and communication, access to helpful contacts, a brotherhood within which to initiate economic cooperation, reliable friends to help out at home while you are away, and other friends to offer you a second home. Often the converts are those who are already ill-at-ease in their customary roles and who have begun to move out into a wider world. They see in Protestantism a new milieu in which to take an active and independent part. For such people it provides an escalator for yet further movement, and a belief corresponding to their raised aspirations.

A major conduit for evangelical expansion is provided among minority ethnic groups who have either been passed over by Catholicism or suffered too much repressive attention. The smaller ethnic groups and tribes generally exist in the remoter forest and mountain regions, and evangelization is for them a dangerous introduction to the wider world, including the wider national community. Evangelization opens up these groups and quite often offers some modest protection against the more corrosive effects of modernity and internal colonialism. Depending on circumstances, missions may lead either to cultural and linguistic revitalization or to fragmentation and collapse. On occasion pastors and local visionaries become leaders in cultural defence and act as political go-betweens. Certainly these small groups are going to be brought within the scope and impact of modern communications, whether or not their initial contact takes place through missionaries rather than through traders and prospectors. They are not going to be kept in isolation just because they are needed for theses in anthropology.

So far as the larger ethnic groupings are concerned their openness to Protestantism depends on the depth of Catholic coverage currently provided, and on how far people perceive the priest as offering genuine personal concern and continuous local involvement. It also depends on how far Catholicism has been associated with distant and foreign overlordship, as in Peru, or even with massive repression. Once alienation of this kind exists whole tribes or villages may collectively decide to adopt a non-Catholic faith. Effectively they opt to reconstitute themselves as a new society, and with that total reorientation they may perhaps acquire a hospital, or a school, or other communal facilities.

By far the largest conduit for evangelical Protestantism is provided by the massive movement of people from countryside or hacienda to the mega-city. The new society now emerging in Latin America has to do with movement, and evangelicals constitute a *movement*. Evangelical Christianity is a dramatic migration of the spirit matching and accompanying a dramatic migration of bodies. In undertaking this migration, people become 'independent' not at all by building up modest securities but by the reverse: by the loss of all the ties that bind, whether these be familial, communal or ecclesial. Pentecostalism in particular renews these ties in an atmosphere of hope and anticipation rather than of despair. It provides a new cell taking over from scarred and broken tissue. Above all it renews the innermost cell of the family, and protects the woman from the ravages of male desertion and violence. A new faith is able to implant new disciplines, re-order priorities, counter corruption and destructive machismo, and reverse the indifferent and injurious hierarchies of the outside world. Within the enclosed haven of faith a fraternity can be instituted under firm leadership, which provides for release, for mutuality and warmth, and for the practice of new roles.

In this way millions of people are absorbed within a protective social capsule where they acquire new concepts of self and new models of initiative and voluntary organization. Even if they eventually leave the capsule they still carry the imprint of these possibilities, these concepts and these models with them. Thus the template of culture undergoes a process of constant revision by the passage of people through an alternative society – as well as by the emulation of that alternative which is forced upon the Catholic Church itself. *Influence consists not only in what X does but in what X forces Y to do.*

The crucial characteristic of evangelical Christianity in the vast urban agglomerations of Latin America is self-government. People are able to devise their own social world for themselves. And as these worlds expand numerically they gain a sense of latent power, which above all becomes manifest as they come together in vast public gatherings. The growing network of chapels represents a walkout from society as presently constituted. The evangelical believer is one who has symbolically repudiated what previously held him in place, vertically and horizontally. He cannot overturn the actual structures and is, in any case, committed to non-violence, but he can emigrate from the ecclesiastical symbol of its all-inclusive claims: Catholicism. This occurs even if Catholicism itself has in fact engaged in a parallel migration. He can reject the fiesta and *compadres* in favour of his own charismatic feast and the solidarity of the evangelical brotherhood. Pentecostalism is his very *own* fiesta.

Such a fundamental shift of social location generates a very hostile psychic charge. In the countryside, for example, the new convert comes to feel that the old therapeutic techniques are powerless and the traditional Christo-pagan practices dirty and contaminating. His – or her – adoption of a new life means drinking pure and 'living water'. In the city the new convert protects his new orientation by the erection of boundaries and the acceptance of visible 'markers' which set him off as someone under new and different disciplines. And he has to be seen to obey those disciplines both by the believers and by his ordinary peers if he is not to be dismissed as a hypocrite.

This negative charge associated with social departure is matched by a counter-charge designed to extrude and exact costs. With the first arrival of evangelical Christianity in a given area the response will often be violence or extrusion or dismissal from employment. The old system and the new mutually repel each other and reinforce their boundaries, even though this repulsion may tail off with time. (Indeed, a relaxation of attitudes on the Catholic side has been known to cause serious disorientation to Protestant converts).

In these circumstances, it is not surprising that the evangelical groups, more particularly the Pentecostal ones, often restrict their reforms to the interior of the group. The achievement of radical changes in behaviour and the reversal of the hierarchies and priorities obtaining in the outside world can only be achieved in a protected environment. In any case, people without any global theory of society cannot easily extrapolate from their own situation to the complexities, compromises, and contingent twists and turns of political action. This is not to say they do not recognize the corruption of the system and the unworthiness of many of their political leaders. On the contrary, they are all too deeply aware that the political realm is deeply resistant to moralization, especially under Latin American conditions. In any case, the kind of voluntary organization represented by evangelical Christianity is contrasted with the Catholic Church precisely by its incapacity to promulgate the kind of norms which are tuned to *specific* conditions of the *whole* society. Its central priority is the recovery of moral densities and solidarities, and the regeneration of hope.

This is the root difference between the evangelical churches, or at any rate most of them, and the Roman Catholic base communities. The base communities are lay and 'Protestant' in form and style, and likewise concerned with the recovery of moral solidarities, but they are linked to a hierarchically articulated church which still has the intellectual resources, and claims the social remit, to promulgate norms governing whole societies. The Catholic Church is still adjusted to the political realm, which in Latin America is both strength and weakness. The strength arises from the universal scope of Catholic moral concern; the weakness arises from remaining implicated symbolically in the *massa perditionis*, and sometimes remaining implicated in it in practice, that is contaminated.

As already argued the evangelical groups work upon society by the 'cultural logic' they imprint and exemplify. How then, does this cultural logic operate? How are new potentials in the form of models and images and concepts of the person and of organization stored in the religious capsule, and (maybe) later released into the mainstream of society?

The Peaceable Operation of Cultural Logic

Primitive Christianity itself began as a movement active solely at the level of culture, and in this aspect, as in many others, evangelical Christianity represents a return to that primitive condition. The contemporary evangelical in Latin America has walked out of the extant structures and devised an experimental capsule or cell in the interstices of culture. Here he may reinvent himself in an atmosphere of fraternal support and give 'tongue' to his frustrations and aspirations.

This new cell can only survive and maintain its pristine character by peaceability. Peaceability is of the essence, and the poor of Latin

America may well feel that up to now political zealotry has only increased their misery. In Latin America there exists a ready-made spiral of violence such that when any group engages in physical aggression it triggers opposite and equal (or more-than-equal) aggression. Apart from the straightforward danger of annihilation, this spiral of aggression and counter-aggression will distort and perhaps reverse the messages carried by the new cell. As among the early Christians, among the monasteries, and among the sects of the radical reformation, peaceability helps ensure that the radical coding inside the cell is preserved intact. The insistence on peacability, plus protective social devices, like maximum association within the group and minimum association outside it, keep the message alive. That is why monasteries conceived themselves as remote and secret 'gardens of the Lord', and why radical sects regarded themselves as a peculiar people set aside for special purposes. Without such 'peculiarity' no serious revision of consciousness is possible.

The revision of consciousness activated within the Pentecostal or evangelical cell is remarkably thoroughgoing in that it abolishes mediations. All large-scale social organization, religious or political, is based on hierarchy and mediation, and the establishment of lay and unmediated channels of communication is a revolutionary reversal of all social order. However, this reversal itself requires a strict discipline and unequivocal leadership such as is provided by the pastor. Sheep may safely graze only when there are pastors, as well as folds and safe enclosures.

Thus enclosures and pastors constitute the paradoxical precondition of any serious revision of consciousness and social practice. A very large number of the models of change which have gone to make up our modern world were set in position in precisely this way. Women gained authority in the nunnery or the right to prophesy in the sect. Peaceability was nourished in the monastic fraternity and among Quakers and Mennonites. Food reforms were initiated among Swedenborgians and Adventists. The rejection of corporal punishment and the invention of modern schemes of educational reform originated among the Bohemian Brethren. The therapies of shared experience were devised and encouraged among the early Methodists. Religious groupings construct advanced platforms in consciousness, and test their viability in enclosed protected environments. They send out signals about what may be possible, and the wider society in time picks these up. The most powerful signals ever sent out were those which established fraternity, which abolished mediation, and which indicated how social worlds could be constructed not only on ties of blood and natural contiguity but on spiritual affinities voluntarily embraced. These are precisely the signals sent out by Pentecostalism under exemplary images: the last being the first, the lame walking, the bedevilled restored to their right mind – and the dumb singing or finding their 'tongues'.

Of course, if it is argued that culture is an impotent creature of structure then all such revisions of consciousness and innovations of practice are signals which will never be picked up and translated. However, the reverse may be true. Inductions into new worlds and socialization in symbolic reversals may in time become diffused to whole populations. The latent may be made manifest and the limited free space devised by religion may be suddenly enlarged as it was in the Civil Rights Movement led by Martin Luther King. A mutation in self-consciousness in the religious sphere, or skills in public address and in organization, may be transferred to any other sphere whatsoever. They may be transferred to whole movements, or alternatively they may be carried by individuals. They are protean in their potentials.

Catholicism and Catholic Responses

What of the Catholic Church? First, something needs to be said about the Catholicism that remained in place in most Latin American countries up to the mid-century. As has been emphasized again and again, it is perfectly possible for whole cultures to remain cradled in Catholicism and for the Catholic Church itself either to be hollowed out from the inside by total government control *or* to be ruthlessly expelled from the body politic. Thus the universal Catholicism that was once so remarked upon was the observable clothing of social practices and forms. Many central bastions of Catholic faith, such as priestly celibacy, remained remote and unintelligible. In some areas even the Eucharist had fallen into disuse.

Catholicism of this kind was too ramshackle to develop coherent strategies to deal with problems above the local level. Instead, local ecclesiastical functionaries, some of them more concerned with their careers than Catholic devotion, engaged in ad hoc manoeuvrings with adjacent political and social elites. They offered certain 'services' to society as currently constituted and had to respond to its pressures. In short, Catholicism had been incorporated, it was passive and in the strict sense of the word it was 'reactionary'. It has taken something like a century for the Church to re-collect itself as the Church and to reorganize and to plan, and to bring about some more active reference either to Roman teaching or, for that matter, to the foundation documents of Christianity. Thus, seen from a certain angle, the emergence of Pentecostalism and of evangelical Christianity generally represents a first incursion of Christianity understood as a biblically-based and personally appropriated faith, propagated by a distinct body of committed believers. Catholic observers candidly admit this when they speak of the spiritual vacuum which opens up once the external forms and localized practices collapse under the intense pressure of rapid social change.

The late Ivan Vallier described what this meant at the local level very appositely. When people came to church not only was the celestial hierarchy made manifest but the social hierarchy was also on parade. 'Those who worshipped regularly in the same church building did not constitute a solidarity based congregation but a random assortment of differential social statuses juxtaposed in proximity for the duration of the mass.'[10] He goes on to point out that there was no need to create an active and enthusiastic lay body, since everyone was gently cradled in one and the same religious universe. This, of course, was precisely the situation in England up to the eighteenth century, and for Pentecostals and Catholics today one only has to substitute Methodists and the Church of England two hundred and fifty years ago. What the Pentecostalism of today offers then is a body of committed lay persons, actively brought into being rather than passively existing, and enjoying a solidarity based on social affinity.

Of course, Catholicism has responded in various ways to the challenge of social change and the centrality of the idea of movement. It has itself tried to become a movement, notably through the vast organization known as Catholic Action. To some extent the organization of Catholic Action reflected the recovery of the Church as a distinct body all too well, since it was cast in an Italian or Roman mould and represented the militancy of the Catholic ghetto and of 'fortress Catholicism' more generally. Nevertheless, certain things are interesting about Catholic Action. Since it came into being as part of the broad process of differentiation of Church from social structure it could run counter to the interests of the secular elites who saw the Church just as a creature of their own concerns and style. Catholic Action divided the self-conscious Catholic from the automatic ritual conformity of established strata.[11] So while it was hegemonic in aspiration it was sectional in organizational form. Indeed, it was proto-Protestant insofar as it was lay and depended on specific commitment. But beyond that it could develop in a radical direction and give birth to troublesome fraternities of revolutionary Catholic youth.

Liberation theology represents a continuation both of sectarian Protestant motifs and of this political and ecclesiastical radicalism. The point is that Catholicism itself was bringing into existence elements of Protestantism through Catholic Action and Liberation Theology. What was forming outside the walls of the Catholic Church was also germinating within: a parallel development. Yet what stayed within was marked by its Catholic inheritance, in particular the idea of the Church as promulgating norms for society as a whole and acting as moral mentor. It was adjusted to political reality in a characteristically Catholic manner and was, therefore, ready to provide political translations of the Bible, especially of the Old Testament, as well as to reformulate the doctrine of the just war to encompass revolutionary violence.

Liberation theology is, therefore, a major rival to Pentecostalism. In that role it probably has a modest welcome even from the more cautious members of the hierarchy, however much they are alarmed by its attitude to traditional Catholic organization and the primacy it affords to politics. Indeed, its very sectionalism is a further alarming instalment of disarticulation.

Yet Liberation Theology is not so successful a competitor as might be expected and there are even those who see its existence as indirectly helping forward the expansion of evangelicalism. The reason is that however much it represents 'an option for the poor' taken up by hundreds of thousands of the poor themselves, that option is most eloquently formulated by radical intellectuals like the Boffs and the Cardenals. However idealistic and decently concerned and shocked the leaders of 'liberationism' may be, they are not usually 'of the people'. Liberation theology has a decided middle class and radical intellectual accent alien to the localized needs of 'the poor'. It claims to be Latin America but it is, in fact, at least as 'foreign' as Pentecostalism, if not more so, with spokesmen – yes, spokes*men* – who are part of the international circuit of theological lecturers. This means that while the language of Pentecostalism is 'odd' and many of its practices initially unattractive, the language of liberationism can easily remain remote. Beyond all that, it promises to pull poor people struggling mainly for survival into much larger and bloodier struggles of which they have often had more than enough.

There is, of course, one other response within Catholicism, which has proto-Protestant elements and which also competes with Pentecostalism, and that is the charismatic movement.[12] The Catholic charismatic movement is not on anything like the same scale as evangelical Protestantism, involving up to (say) four or five million people, but it is a significant force and derives part of its thrust from the rivalry. It offers communal warmth and solidarity, it brings the family together in strong affective bonds, and it establishes a moral density. Catholic charismatics are often aligned with the renewals proposed by Vatican 2 and they reflect on the foundation documents of Christianity. They offer a focus of loyalty which can supplement or even supplant a fideistic reliance on the magisterium. Though they are, on occasion, influenced by liberation theology, and by liberal attitudes to moral issues, they also revive some aspects of traditional doctrine. They resemble Protestant Pentecostals in their avoidance of head-on political confrontations.

Of course, from one point of view the existence of Catholic charismatics can simply be regarded as another illustration of the inauguration of the Kingdom of the Spirit, *hic et ubique*. But from a narrower and less committed perspective it is a response from the Catholic side which has its own problems. Chief among these is the confusion it creates in the minds of traditional Catholics. They are bemused by a version of Catholicism that looks superficially just like Pentecostalism, and the result is that Catholics start to attend just those local churches which happen to suit their own predilections, and thereby disrupt further the tie to the locality. In two respects Catholic charismatics differ from their separated Pentecostal brethren. They are, first of all, ecumenical. This means that if you are walking out of the old world and shaking the dust of the system from your feet, then Catholic charismatics link you too closely and irenically with what was. In the second place, they are also (maybe) relatively middle class in their social provenance. At least that is true in the USA where they originated and whence much of their leadership derives. Evidence for Latin America is sparse.[13] Thomas Chordas, in his short study, concludes that it 'includes the middle class and the very poor' and suggests that the very poor come along in the wake of the middle class.

What has just been argued concerning the Roman Catholic Church has focused in part on competition between alternative channels of new religiosity: those within and those outside the Catholic Church. That competition, now endemic in Latin America, involves constant borrowing and inventiveness. In particular, kinds of participation and types of popular music are constantly being borrowed to increase the competitive edge. It is out of this competition that forms of religious associations are being devised that may well stand up to the corrosion of religious practice traditionally associated with the city.

But there is a wider competition currently in progress with regard to money, personnel and propaganda. The churches, Catholic and

Protestant, are too little studied as rival organizations putting out propaganda, manipulating resources, disposing of personnel, and generally fighting for their share of the market. The Catholic Church in particular is opaque so far as this type of enquiry is concerned, and we know too little about the cybernetic circuits of power and influence which are eventually bound together in the Vatican. Ralph della Cava is engaged in precisely such study, but it will be some while before we fully understand how the battles are fought out and how vast resources, including financial ones, are tapped.[14] It is said, for example, that the German hierarchy is deeply involved in financing the propagation of the centre-right view in the Latin American Catholic Church. But equally considerable resources are deployed by liberationists, and also by the orders, whether like the Jesuits they are to the left or like Opus Dei to the right.

So far as the focus of the present study is concerned, the various evangelical bodies dispose of considerable resources. Some of these may be used for welfare, as they were after the Guatemalan earthquake, and some for propaganda, especially through the mass media. There are many observers, especially among Catholic nationalists, who link this propaganda to the political stand of the Electronic Church in the USA and trace other links to the positions propagated by conservative think-tanks in Washington, like the American Heritage Foundation.[15] Indeed, the whole field is fraught with propaganda, and the investigator is bound to be caught in a cross-fire whatever position he takes up. Perhaps that in itself is another indication of the social earthquake which follows as the tectonic plates of two world civilizations pass one under the other.

The main resource of contemporary evangelicalism in Latin America is people. Enquiries conducted in Great Britain show that even quite small evangelical bodies contribute surprising numbers of committed workers to the missionary task.[16] The overwelming source of missionaries is, of course, the United States. However, the really crucial factor is the ability of local churches in Latin America itself to inculcate commitment so that every lay person is propagating the message, in particular by intimate personal contact with friends and relatives. The competitive edge of evangelical Protestantism in Latin America comes from the creation of an active laity, proselytizing along chains of personal and familial contact, and working alongside a huge pastorate recruited on the basis of ability to communicate and not prolonged theological training. This is how evangelical and Pentecostal Christianity remains in contact with ordinary people.

Among the more organized sectors of evangelical Christianity this competition with Catholicism and secularism is pursued with organizational and statistical sophistication. On the Catholic side are the ecclesiastical bureaucrats and priest-sociologists but on the Protestant side are ecclesiastical business executives, church-growth experts, media tycoons and statisticians. While reliance may ultimately be placed on the Holy Spirit, during the interim there is emphasis on short and long-term planning and correct information. How wide ranging such planning may be can be gathered from the highly ambitious writings of people like Peter Wagner and David Barrett.[17] The data-banks built up in this process provide the raw materials of evangelization and a kind of practical proto-sociology dedicated to the conversion of humankind. As in earlier periods of history, major branches of evangelicalism are linked to a use of modern technology and expertise. All of that, however, is of no effect without the process of indigenization earlier described.

Secularization and the Global Perspective

Clearly this startling and unanticipated development in Latin America, now spreading to the Eastern Pacific rim and Africa, is part of much wider global changes. The first of these is a world-wide growth of religious conservatism in Judaism, and in Islam, as well as in Christianity. A balance once supposed to be tipping automatically towards liberalism is now tipping the other way.

Quite what the parallel developments in Islam and Judaism portend is much disputed. Some see it as a reaction to external pressure and a reflex of fear leading to an attempt to recover 'mechanical solidarity'. Others see it, at least in the Islamic version, as a modernization and a radical mobilization carried out inside a conservative frame. It is significant that Catholicism also tried to create a militant fortress mentality in the mid-nineteenth century, and that it came nearest to success where it was implicated in the struggles of repressed nations. It may be that Islam stands a better chance of strengthening its 'fortress', given that it has received warnings earlier in the process of disintegration and is implicated in nationalistic struggles in many societies from Algeria to Malaya.

Whatever may be the case with multiple religious monopolies like Catholicism and Islam, or even a single and weak 'monopoly' such as orthodox Judaism in Israel, the success of evangelicalism depends rather on the *reverse* process, that is on the break-up of monopolies and the restriction of religious influence to the realm of culture. This is absolutely crucial: whatever the surface similarities of conservative versions of all three monotheistic faiths, developments in Latin

America run quite counter to those in the Middle East. Evangelical religion represents an advanced form of social differentiation and can operate best where hitherto monopolistic systems are disintegrating. Once the monopolies begin to crack and to lose contact with the core structures of society, evangelical Christianity can emerge to compete within the sphere of culture. There it can stand in for what were once the local territorial units of solidarity, re-forming them in an active, mobile and voluntary format. In this way it counters chaos and restores moral densities. There is no chance it will become a substitute established church, though it may create a widely shared ethos for some oppressed ethnic group. This dramatic restriction to the cultural sphere is, of course, one aspect of secularization, but whether this means that religion has finally ceased to be socially significant depends, as suggested above, on whether culture is regarded as impotent and dependent. If culture is regarded as without serious influence then religion is indeed marginalized beyond recovery and can be dismissed as just one leisure-time activity among others.

Theories of secularization indicate how religion, and specifically Christianity, relinquishes (and/or is deprived of) its hold on the central structures of power. It ceases to be the symbolic keystone in mechanical solidarity and is released from the centripetal pull which aligns it with elite interests and explicit party attachments. Theories of secularization also specify a complementary process whereby the state takes over and develops all kinds of organizations and functions, especially in education and social welfare, which were previously under religious aegis. This advance of the omnicompetent state is associated with the growth of professions whose interests come to lie in the extension of state action, and with the propagation of ideologies which define the religious contribution as irrelevant to the efficient running of society. As Bryan Wilson has argued, a net of rational bureaucratic regulation can supplant the moral densities, the conscientious sensitivities and the commitments once generated by communities of faith.[18]

The question then becomes whether this process is contingent, i.e. dependent on specific circumstances, notably those which have obtained in Europe, or is a necessary and inevitable part of social development.[19] Clearly if the latter is the case then a certain estimate of the significance and future of the phenomena discussed in this book follows. It is simply that temporary efflorescence of voluntary religiosity which accompanies a stage in industrialization and/or urbanization. As Methodism flourished during just such a period in Britain so Pentecostalism flourishes today in Latin America. The problematic stemming from Halévy applies to them both as parallel moments in a story which will end as they shrivel at the cold touch of rationalization and the omnicompetent state.

This may, of course, be the case. But there is the alternative view based on the notion that the European experience is contingent and fails to provide the universal pardigm to which all other societies must in time approximate. According to that alternative view the effect of establishment and religious monopoly such as existed in Europe has been to inhibit the adaptability of religion to social change, above all to the industrial city. However, the North American paradigm seems to show that once religion is no longer a matter of a relation of a particular body to the elite and to the state, religion adapts quite successfully to a changing world. In all the *proper* senses of the word it becomes popular.[20] Indeed, it shows itself endlessly inventive and actually succeeds in assuaging the anomie and combatting the chaos of the megacity.

It may well be that the inventiveness displayed in North America has now been transferred to Latin America and the cycle of spirals derived from Europe thereby slowed or halted, even maybe reversed. If that is so, then secularization as understood in the European context is a particular kind of episode. If there is a universal element to it, that is restricted to the shift from structural location to cultural influence discussed earlier. Should that restricted and episodic view of secularization turn out to be correct then the crossing of the 'Anglo' and Hispanic patterns currently observed in Latin America is not a repeat performance of a sequence already played through and played out in Britain, but a new moment with new possibilities.

The matter can be put another way. The Protestant experience in Britain exhibited a religious efflorescence at the time of industrialization and urbanization that tailed away into ineffectiveness. The Latin experience in Southern Europe exhibited spirals of repulsion between the Catholic ghetto and the forces of militant secularism. In both, religion eventually receded as the state advanced. But in North America the factors which eventually curtailed the religious efflorescence in Britain did not obtain, and a new pattern emerged of immense expansive power. It is that North American pattern which has now become admixed with the Latin cultures of South America. In those cultures it so happens that certain characteristic spirals of antagonism over religion are now rapidly weakening. The long shadow of 1789 disappears and a new moment arrives in which a sizeable sector of mainstream religion rejects its old alliances on the right. It follows that as the spirals of antagonism weaken and as there is a strong admixture of the kind of religion originally generated in North America, the old tendencies may well be nullified. Should that be so then the 'tongues of fire' may not so easily sputter out.

Notes

Introduction

1 Cf. David Martin, *A General Theory of Secularization* (Oxford: Blackwell, 1978). The present book picks up the Latin American variant of the Catholic pattern of secularization indicated but not developed in the earlier book. For a treatment of the current condition of Catholicism cf. my introductory essay to Thomas Gannon (ed.), *Catholicism in Transition* (London and New York: Macmillan, 1988). For an extended treatment of the issues raised by the sociological analysis of religion cf. my 'Theology in a Social Scientific Culture', to be published in a collection of my essays on sociology and theology.
2 Claudio Veliz, 'A world made in England', *Quadrant*, March 1983, No. 187, Volume XXVII, No. 3, pp. 8–19 (8).
3 Ibid., pp. 8–9.

Chapter 1

1 James Anthony Froude, *English Seamen in the Sixteenth Century* (London: Longmans Green, 1928) p. 12.
2 Thomas Hardy, *The Dynasts* (Edinburgh: R. & R. Clark, 1931), p. 7.
3 Fernand Braudel, *The Wheels of Commerce*, vol. 2 (London: Collins, 1982), pp. 569–70.
4 Walter LaFeber, *Inevitable Revolutions* (New York and London: Norton, 1983).
5 David Martin, *Pacifism* (London: Routledge, 1965).
6 David Martin, *A General Theory of Secularization* (Oxford: Blackwell, 1978), chs 1 and 2.
7 Hugh MacLeod, *Religion and the People of Western Europe 1789–1970* (London: Oxford University Press, 1981).
8 Mary Fulbrook, *Piety and Politics: Religion and the Rise of Absolutism in England, Württemberg and Prussia* (New York: Cambridge University Press, 1983). On Pietism in America cf. F. Ernest Stoeffler, *Continental*

Pietism and Early American Christianity (Grand Rapids, Mich.: Eerdmans), 1976.

9 Stein Rokkan, 'Nation-building, cleavage formation and the structuring of mass politics' in Stein Rokkan (ed.), *Citizens, Election, Parties* (Oslo: Oslo University Press, 1970).

10 Marilyn J. Westerkamp, *Triumph of the Laity: Scots-Irish Piety and the Great Awakening, 1625–1760* (New York, Oxford: Oxford University Press, 1988).

11 Patrick Collinson, *The Elizabethan Puritan Movement* (London: Cape, 1967).

12 David S. Lovejoy, *Religious Enthusiasm in the New World: Heresy to Revolution* (London and Cambridge, Mass.: Harvard University Press, 1985), pp. 111–14.

13 Rodney Stark and Roger Finke, 'Religious economies and sacred canopies: religious mobilization in American cities, 1906', *American Sociological Review*, 53, Feb. 1988, pp. 41–9.

14 James Davison Hunter, *American Evangelicalism* (New Brunswick, NJ: Rutgers University Press, 1983), and George Marsden, *Fundamentalism and American Culture* (New York: Oxford University Press, 1980).

15 Steve Bruce, *Firm in the Faith* (Aldershot, England: Gower, 1984); Steve Bruce, *The Rise and Fall of the New Christian Right* (Oxford: Oxford University Press, 1988), ch. 2.

16 John Walsh, 'John Wesley and the community of goods', unpublished paper delivered at Southern Methodist University, Autumn 1987.

17 Casimiro Marti et al., *Iglesia y sociedad en España 1939–1975* (Madrid: Editorial Popular, 1977).

18 Kenneth Medhurst, *The Church and Labour in Colombia* (Manchester: Manchester University Press, 1984).

19 Cf. Otto Maduro, *Religión y conflicto social* (Mexico City: Crie, 1980). For a short statement by Maduro cf. 'Catholic Church, national security states and popular movements in Latin America', in *Actes* of the 17th Conference of the CISR (Paris: CISR, 1983), pp. 8–19. For further background consult Daniel H. Levine, *Religion and Politics in Latin America: the Catholic Church in Venezuela and Colombia* (Princeton: Princeton University Press, 1981).

20 Brian Smith, *The Church and Politics in Chile* (Princeton: Princeton University Press, 1982).

Chapter 2

1 Peter Berger, *The Sacred Canopy* (Garden City, NY: Doubleday, 1967). As will be evident, substantial parts of the theoretical structure underpinning this book are derived from Peter Berger.

2 Elie Halévy, *A History of the English People in 1815* (London: T. Fisher Unwin, 1924), and *A History of the English People 1830–1841* (London: T. Fisher Unwin, 1927). For a recent treatment of parallel themes cf.

Bernard Semmel, *The Methodist Revolution* (New York: Basic Books, 1973) and for further discussion cf. Theodore Runyon, (ed.), *Sanctification and Liberation*. Nashville, Tenn.: Abingdon Press, 1981, and David Hempton, *Methodism and Politics in British Society 1750–1850* (Stanford, Calif.: Stanford University Press, 1984). There is a lot of scattered material in Terence Thomas, *The British: Their Religious Beliefs and Practices, 1800–1986* (London and New York: Routledge, 1988).

3 David M. Thompson, (ed.) *Noncomformity in the Nineteenth Century* (London and Boston: Routledge, 1972), pp. 96–8).

4 Vincent Synan, *The Holiness Pentecostal Movement in the United States* (Grand Rapids Mich.: Eerdmans, 1971), p. 8; Donald W. Dayton, *Theological Roots of Pentecostalism* (Metuchen, NJ: The Scarecrow Press, 1987), ch. 2.

5 Ibid., p. 21.

6 Charles Edwin Jones, *A Guide to the Study of the Holiness Movement* (Metuchen, NJ: The Scarecrow Press and The American Theological Library Association, 1974), p. 134.

7 Ibid.

8 Walter Hollenweger, 'Methodism's past in Pentecostalism's present: a case study of a cultural clash in Chile', *Methodist History*, 20 (July 1982), pp. 169–82 (169).

9 Jean Baptiste August Kessler, *A Study of the Older Protestant Missions and Churches in Peru and Chile* (Goes, Netherlands: Oosterbaan and le Cointre, 1964).

10 Walter Hollenweger, 'Methodism's past', p. 169.

11 Cf. Ian Sellers, *Nineteenth Century Nonconformity* (London: Edward Arnold, 1977).

12 Cf. Forrest McDonald, *Novus Ordo Seclorum: The Intellectual Origins of the Constitution* (Kansas City: University of Kansas Press, 1987).

13 John Walsh of Jesus College, Oxford, in an unpublished paper 'John Wesley and the community of goods', delivered at Southern Methodist University, Autumn, 1987.

14 On the Sunday Schools cf. Thomas Walter Laqueur, *Religion and Respectability: Sunday Schools and Working Class Culture 1780–1850* (New Haven and London: Yale University Press, 1976). On the Sacred Harmonic Society cf. William Weber, *Music and the Middle Class* (London: Croom Helm, 1975).

15 Keith Wald, *Crosses on the Ballot* (Princeton: Princeton University Press, 1985), pp. 102–5.

16 Clive D. Field, 'The Social Structure of English Methodism', *British Journal of Sociology*. 28: 2 (June 1977), pp. 199–225. For the kind of materials relevant to this cf. James Obelkevich, *Religion and Rural Society: South Lindsey 1825–1875* (Oxford: Clarendon Press, 1976); Robert Moore *Pitmen, Preachers, and Politics: The Effects of Methodism in a Durham Mining Community* (Cambridge: Cambridge University Press, 1974); David Clark, *Between Pulpit and Pew: Folk Religion in a North Yorkshire Fishing Village* (New York: Cambridge University Press, 1982).

17 A discussion of the rhythm of 'work discipline' is in Edward P. Thompson, *The Making of the English Working Class* (Harmondsworth: Penguin, 1968). Discussion of the poetic and musical rhythms are to be found in Frank Baker, *Charles Wesley's Verse*, 2nd edn (London: Epworth, 1988); Bernard Manning, *The Hymns of Wesley and Watts* (London: Epworth Press, 1942); Donald Davie and Robert Stevenson, *English Hymnology in the Eighteenth Century*, William Andrews Clark Memorial Library: Los Angeles, University of California, 1980. The musical activities of local Methodists are well brought out in Roger Elbourne, *Music and Tradition in Early Industrial Lancashire 1780–1840* (with Foreword by David A. Martin) (Woodbridge, Suffolk: D. S. Brewer, 1980). The musical version of the Halévy thesis can be derived fom Henry Raynor, *Music and Society since 1815* (London: Barrie and Jenkins, 1976). Basically this variant on Halévy suggests that 'universal harmony' helps bring about social peace, especially when sung by enthusiastic Protestants. The relevance of this for Pentecostalism is brought out in ch. 6.

18 For an account of Methodist penetration in Wales cf. Griffith T. Roberts, 'Methodism in Wales', in Rupert Davies, A. Raymond George, and Gordon Rupp (eds), A History of the Methodist Church in Great Britain (London: Epworth, 1983), pp. 253–64.

19 For the relation of nonconformity to Wales and Welsh politics cf. David Martin, *A Sociology of English Religion* (London: SCM Press, 1967) and Tom Brennan, E. W. Cooney and M. Pollins, *Social Change in South-West Wales* (London: Watt, 1954).

20 For an account which stresses the lack of radicalism in Welsh nonconformist Liberalism, cf. E. T. Davis, *Religion in the Industrial Revolution in South Wales* (Cardiff: University of Wales Press, 1965).

21 Neil C. Sandberg, *Identity and Assimilation* (Washington, DC: University Press of America, 1981), p. 67.

22 Cf. Gwen Kennedy Neville, *Kinship and Pilgrimage: Rituals of Reunion in American Protestant Culture* (Oxford: Oxford University Press, 1977).

23 David S. Lovejoy, *Religious Enthusiasm in the New World: Heresy to Revolution* (London and Cambridge, Mass.: Harvard University Press, 1985); Richard W. Pointer, *Protestant Pluralism and the New York Experience* (Bloomington and Indianapolis: Indiana University Press, 1988). Cf. also William Lee Miller, *The First Liberty: Religion and the American Republic* (New York: Paragon House, 1985).

24 Lipset, Seymour Martin, 'Religion in American politics', in Michael Novak (ed.), *Capitalism and Socialism: A Theological Inquiry* (Washington, DC: American Enterprise Institute, 1979), pp. 61–80; and *Revolution and Counterrevolution* (New York: Basic Books, 1968); William Williams, 'The attraction of Methodism: the Delmarva Peninsula 1769–1820', in Richey Russel and Kenneth Rowe (eds), *Rethinking Methodist History* (Nashville, Tenn.: Kingswood Books, 1985), pp. 100–10; Rodney Stark and Roger Finke, 'How the upstart sects won America: 1776–1850', *Journal for the Scientific Study of Religion*, Oct. 1989.

25 Lipset, 'Religion in American Politics'.

26 Novak, *Capitalism and Socialism*, p. 62.
27 Williams, 'Attraction of Methodism', p. 101.
28 Ibid.
29 Ibid., p. 103.
30 Ibid., p. 104.
31 Max Weber, 'The Protestant sects and the spirit of capitalism', in Hans Gerth and C. Wright Mills, *From Max Weber* (London: Routledge, 1984).
32 Williams, 'Attraction of Methodism', p. 106.
33 Elizabeth Brusco 'The household basis of evangelical religion and the reformation of machismo in Colombia', Ph.D. diss., City University of New York, 1986.
34 Will B. Graveley, 'African Methodisms and the rise of black denominationalism', in Richey and Rowe *Rethinking Methodist History*, pp. 111–24.
35 Ibid., p. 111.
36 Stark and Finke, 'Upstart sects'.
37 Ibid., p. 37.
38 Ibid., p. 17.
39 On Canada cf. Reginald W. Bibby, 'Why conservative churches really are growing', *Journal for the Scientific Study of Religion*, 2 (1978), pp. 129–37; On New Zealand cf. Michael Hill and R. Bowman 'Religious practice and religious adherence in contemporary New Zealand', *Archive des Sciences sociales des religions*, 59: 1 (1985), pp. 91–115; on Australia see various works by Gary Bouma, Peter Glasner, Alan Black and Hans Mol, and in particular David Parker, 'Fundamentalism and conservative Protestantism in Australia 1920–1980', Ph.D. diss. University of Queensland, 1982. There is an account of Pentecostals/Charismatics in Australia in Barry Chant, *Heart of Fire* (Sydney: House of Tabor, 1984).
40 Wade Clark Roof and William McKinney, *American Mainline Religion* (New Brunswick, NJ: Rutgers University Press, 1987).
41 Kenneth Thompson and Robert Bocock (eds), *Religion and Ideology* (Manchester: Manchester University Press and the Open University, 1985), pp. 126–204; Michael Hill, *A Sociology of Religion* (London: Heinemann Educational, 1973), pp. 183–204.
42 John H. Whyte, *Catholics in Western Democracies* (Dublin: Gill and Macmillan, 1981).
43 Roger Elbourne, *Music and Tradition*.
44 Theo Witvliet, *The Way of the Black Messiah* (London: SCM Press, 1987).
45 Cf. David Edwin Harrell, Jr, *Oral Roberts: An American Life* (Bloomington: Indiana University Press, 1985).
46 Weber, 'The Protestant sects'.
47 E. P. Thompson, *English Working Class*.
48 Merle E. Curti, *Peace or War: The American Struggle, 1636–1939* (New York: W. W. Norton, 1936); Charles Chatfield, *For Peace and Justice: Pacifism in America 1914–1941* (Knoxville: University of Tennessee Press, 1971).

Chapter 3

1 Matthews Ojo, 'Charismatic cults in Nigeria', *Africa* 58: 2 (1988), pp. 175–92.

2 Wade Clark Roof and William McKinney, *American Mainline Religion* (New Brunswick, NJ: Rutgers University Press, 1987).

3 Richard Millett, 'The perils of success: post-world War II Latin American Protestantism', in Lyle C. Brown and William F. Cooper (eds) *Religion in Latin American Life and Literature* (Waco, Tex.: Baylor University Press, 1980), p. 52.

4 Ibid., p. 53.

5 Bastian, Jean-Pierre. *Protestantismo y sociedad en México* (Mexico City: CUPSA, 1983), p. 200, and 'Protestantismo y política en México', *Revista Mexicana de Sociología*, 43: Special Issue (1981), pp. 1947–66.

6 Orlando E. Costas, 'Church growth as a multidimensional phenomenon: some lessons from Chile', *International Bulletin of Missionary Research*, 5 (Jan. 1981), pp. 2–8 (5).

7 *Directorio de Iglesias, Organizaciones y Ministerios del Movimiento Protestante*, San José Costa Rica: Procades/Imdela, 1987); Jean Pierre Bastian, 'Protestantismos latinamericanos entre la resistencia y la sumisión 1961–1983', *Christianismo y Sociedad*, 82 (1984), p. 65.

8 Official Statistics for 1986, Assemblies of God, Division of Foreign Missions, 1446 Booneville, Springfield, Missouri, 65802, published 1987.

9 Kurt Bowen, Acadia University, Wolfville, Nova Scotia: Canada BOP 1X0, personal communciation.

10 Elizabeth E. Brusco, 'The household basis of evangelical religion and the reformation of machismo in Colombia', Ph.D. diss., City University of New York, 1986, ch. 1.

11 Marvin Alisky, *Uruguay* (New York, London, Washington, DC: Praeger, 1969) and Otto Maduro, 'Le Catholicisme au Venezuela', *Amérique Latine*, 11 (July–Sept. 1982). Cf. also Juan Carlos Navarro, Too weak for change: past and present in the Venezuelan Church', in Thomas Gannon (ed.), *Catholicism in Transition* (London and New York: Macmillan, 1988).

12 Wilton M. Nelson, *Protestantism in Central America* (Grand Rapids, Mich.: Eerdmans, 1984), ch. 6.

13 Pablo A. Deiros, 'Argentine Baptists and politics: an analysis of relations' Ph.D. diss. Southwestern Baptist Theological Seminary, 1985, p. 190.

14 John N. Vaughan, *The World's Twenty Largest Churches* (Grand Rapids, Mich.: Baker Book House, 1984), ch. 20. For an account of a large independent church, the Christian Crusade Church of Santa Isabel, Bogotá cf. *Latin American Evangelist*, Oct.–Dec, 1986.

15 Hugo Assman, *A igreja electronico e seu impacto na América Latina* (Petropolis: Vozes, 1986). Cf. an account of Trans World Radio on a Dutch island off Venezuela, *New York Times*, 20 Sept. 1988, p. 15.

16 José Valderrey, 'La cuestión de las sectas religiosas en la prensa

mexicana', paper presented to the Conference on Religious Sect Activities in Mexico, Oaxaca, 1986.

17 For an example cf. Jane C. Peck, 'Reflections from Costa Rica on Protestantism's dependence and non-liberative social function', *Journal of Ecumenical Studies* 21, (Spring 1984), pp. 181–98.

18 Christian Lalive D'Epinay, *Religion, dynamique sociale et dépendance: les mouvements Protestants en Argentine et au Chile* (Paris, The Hague: Mouton, 1975), ch. 11.

19 Pablo A. Deiros, (ed.), *Los evangelicos y el poder politico en América Latina* Grand Rapids, Mich.: Eerdmans, 1986.

20 Cf. Nicos P. Mouzelis, *Politics in the Semi-Periphery* (London: Macmillan, 1986).

21 Calvin Redekop, *Strangers Become Neighbours: Mennonite and Indigenous Relations in the Paraguayan Chaco*, Studies in Anabaptist and Mennonite History, 22 (Scottsdale, Ariz.: Herald Press, 1980).

22 David Barrett, (ed.), *The World Christian Encyclopedia* (Oxford: Oxford University Press, 1982), p. 188.

23 Karl Franklin, *Current Concerns of Anthropologists and Missionaries* (Dallas, Tex.: International Museum of Cultures, 1987).

24 Bruce Johnson Calder, *Crecimiento y cambio de la Iglesia Católica en Guatemalteca 1944–1966* (Guatemala City: Editorial José de Pineda Ibarra, 1970), p. 17.

25 Roger Bastide, *The African Religions of Brazil* (Baltimore: Johns Hopkins University Press, 1978); Ralph Della Cava, *Miracle at Joaseiro* (New York: Columbia University Press, 1970).

Chapter 4

1 David Gueiros Vieira, 'Liberalismo, masonería y protestancismo en Brasil en el siglo XIX', *Christianismo y Sociedad*, (1987), pp. 9–32.

2 Rubem C. Fernandes, 'Aparacida, our Queen Lady and Mother, Sarava!', *Social Science Information*, 24: 4 (1985) pp. 799–819

3 Marli Geralda Teixeira, 'A familia protestante na sociedad baiana', *Christianismo y Sociedad*, 85 (1985), pp. 91–6; Ronald Frase, 'The subversion of missionary intentions by cultural values: the Brazilian case', *Review of Religious Research*, 23: 2 (Dec. 1981), pp. 180–94.

4 Ronald Frase, 'A sociological analysis of the development of Brazilian Protestantism', Ph.D. diss., Princeton University, 1975. For a complementary account of the Roman Church in Brazil cf. P. Ribero de Oliviera, *Religão e dominacão de classe: genese, estructura e funcão do catolicisimo romanizado na Brasil* (Petropolis: Vozes, 1985).

5 Emilio Willems, *Followers of the New Faith* (Nashville Tenn.: Vanderbilt University Press, 1967), pp. 93–8.

6 Frase, 'Brazilian Protestantism', p. 504.

7 Francisco Cartaxo Rolim, *Pentecostais no Brasil* (Petropolis: Vozes, 1985), pp. 52–4.

8 Ibid., p. 250.
9 Madeleine Villeroy, 'Enquête sur les églises protestantes, dans le Brésil en crise des années 1963–73 *Cahiers de Sociologie Economique*, 12 (May 1975), pp. 18–80.
10 Bastide, *African Religions of Brazil*, p. 372.
11 Ibid.
12 Gary Nigel Howe, 'Capitalism and religion at the periphery: Pentecostalism and Umbanda in Brazil', in Stephen Glazier, *Perspectives on Pentecostalism: Case Studies from the Caribbean and Latin America*. Washington, DC: University Press of America, 1980, pp. 125–41 (135).
13 Peter Fry and Gary N. Howe, 'Duas respostas a aflicão: Umbanda e Pentecostalismo', *Debate e Critica* 6 (1975), pp. 75–94; and Diana de G. Brown, with Mario Bick, 'Religion, class, and context: continuities and discontinuities in Brazilian Umbanda', *American Ethnologist*, 14: 1 (1987), pp. 73–90.
14 Ibid., p. 87.
15 Howe, 'Capitalism and religion'.
16 Rolim, *Pentecostais no Brasil*, pp. 177–9. The suggestion that their social constituencies were similar was made to me by Dr Pedro de Oliveira at the Institute ISER in Rio.
17 Sandra J. Stoll 'Pulpito e palanque: religião e política nas eleições da Grande São Paulo', Master's diss., Unicamp, Campinas, São Paulo, 1986.
18 W. E. Hewitt, 'Basic Christian communities of the middle classes in the Archdiocese of São Paulo', *Sociological Analysis*, 48: 2 (1987), pp. 158–66 (165).
19 Scott William Hoefle, 'Continuity and change in the northeastern Sertão of Brazil', D. Phil. diss., University of Oxford, 1983. Most of the material used here on religion in the Sertão derives from Hoefle.
20 Ibid. and Regina R. Novaes, *Os escolhidos de Deus*, Cadernos do ISER, 19 (Rio de Janeiro: (booklet) ISER, 1985).
21 Carlos Rodrigues Brandão, 'Creencia y identidad: campo religioso y cambio cultural', *Christianismo y Sociedad*, 93 (1987), pp. 65–106 (78).

Chapter 5

1 Lalive D'Epinay, *Religion, dynamique*.
2 Arno, W. Enns, *Man, Milieu and Mission in Argentina* (Grand Rapids, Mich.: Eerdmans, 1971), p. 129.
3 Ibid. p. 76ff.
4 Ibid. p. 143.
5 Lalive D'Epinay, *Religion, dynamique*, p. 60.
6 Ibid. p. 86.
7 Ibid. p. 81.
8 Ibid. pp. 81–9. The paragraphs immediately following depend on Lalive D'Epinay

9 The characterizations of Colombian Catholicism here are mostly derived from Daniel Levine, *Religion and Politics in Latin America* (Princeton, NJ: Princeton University Press, 1981).

10 José Sánchez, *Anticlericalism. A Brief History* (Notre Dame, London: University of Notre Dame Press, 1972), p. 182.

11 Levine, *Religion and Politics*, p. 87.

12 Cornelia Butler Flora, *Pentecostalism in Colombia: Baptism by Fire and Spirit* (Cranbury NJ: Fairleigh Dickinson University Press, 1976).

13 Karl Wilhelm Westmeier, *Reconciling Heaven and Earth*, (New York: Peter Lang, 1986). I draw this account from various materials in Westmeier.

14 Donald Palmer, *Explosion of People Evangelism* (Chicago: Moody Press, 1974), ch. 5.

15 Cornelia Butler Flora, 'Pentecostalism and Development: the Colombian Case', in Glazier, *Perspectives*, p. 85.

16 Levine, *Religion and Politics*, pp. 75–82.

17 Barrett, *World Christian Encyclopedia*, section on Venezuela.

18 Rosa del Carmen Bruno-Jofre, 'La misión metodista y la educación en Perú: 1889–1930', *América Indígena*, 41: 3 (July–Sept. 1981), pp. 501–55; and *Methodist Education in Peru: Social Gospel, Politics and American Ideological and Economic Penetration 1888–1930* (Waterloo, Ont. Wilfrid Laurier University Press, 1988).

19 Manuel Marzal, *La Transformatión religiosa peruana* (Lima: Pontifical University, 1983); and 'Iglesia Cultural y nuevas iglesias' *América Indígena*, 48: 1 (Jan.–Mar. 1988), pp. 139–64; Directorio Evangelico 1986 Lima: Concilio Nacional Evangélico del Perú, 1986.

20 Jean Baptiste August Kessler, *A Study of the Older Protestant Missions and Churches in Peru and Chile* [plus 1987 update in Spanish], Goes, Netherlands: Oesterbaan and le Cointre, 1964 and William Read et al *Latin American Church Growth* Grand Rapids, Mich. Eerdmans, 1969, pp. 109–17 and 218–20.

Chapter 6

1 Kent Maynard, 'Christianity and religion: evangelical identity and sociocultural organization in urban Ecuador', Ph.D. diss. Indiana University 1977 (Ann Arbor microfilms, 1981), p. 77.

2 An account of Protestant incursions among the Chimborazo Indians since the middle fifties is to be found in David Preston 'Pressure on Chimborazo Indians' *Geogrpahical Magazine*, 50 (July 1978), pp. 613–18 (616).

3 Maynard, 'Christianity and religion', p. 91. Most of the information in this section is drawn from Maynard, though I have also consulted Wayne Weld, *An Ecuadorian Impasse* (Chicago: Evangelical Covenant Church of America, 1968); Originally a dissertation of the School of World Missions at Fuller Theological Seminary.

4 Everett A. Wilson, 'Sanguine saints: Pentecostalism in El Salvador', *Church History*, 52 (Jan. 1983), pp. 186–98 (189). Wilson's article is partly based on his 'Crisis of national integration in El Salvador', Ph.D. diss., Stanford University, 1970. I have relied on Wilson for this whole section, together with some useful comments in Walter LaFeber, *Inevitable Revolutions* (New York and London: Norton, 1983).

5 Wilson, 'Sanguine saints', p. 192.

6 Ibid., p. 198.

7 I draw in this section on Virginia Garrard Burnett, 'A history of Protestantism in Guatemala', Ph.D. diss., Tulane University, 1986; and Calder, *Crecimiento y cambio*.

8 I take the material in this historical section almost entirely from Jean-Pierre Bastian, in particular the following: 'Las sociedades Protestantes en México 1872–1911: un liberalismo radicál de oposición al Porfirismo y de participación en la revolución maderista', Hist. Doct. diss., Colegio de México, 1987 and *Los dissidentes, sociedades protestantes y revolución en México 1872–1911* (Mexico: Fonda de Cultura Económica and Colegio de México, 1988). Also relevant are Mariane E. McKechnie, 'The Mexican Revolution and the National Presbyterian Church of Mexico, 1910–1940', Ph.D. diss., The American University, Washington, DC.: 1970 and Deborah Baldwin, 'Broken Traditions: Mexican revolutionaries and Protestant allegiances', *The Americas*, 40: 2 (Oct. 1981), pp. 229–58 and 'Variation within the vanguard: Protestants and the Mexican Revolution', Ph.D. diss., University of Chicago, 1979.

9 Jean-Pierre Bastian, *Protestantismo y sociedad en México* (Mexico City: CUPSA, 1983).

10 This research on an urban area is currently in progress and was described in a personal communication. The research on a rural area is described in Carlos Garma Navarro, *Protestantismo en una communidad totonaca de Puebla* (Mexico: INI, 1987); 'Liderazgo protestante en una lucha campesino en México,' *América Indígena*, 44: 1 (1984), pp. 127–42.

11 Gabriela Patricia Robledo Hernandez, 'Disidencia y religión: los expulsados de San Juan Chamula', licentiate diss., ENAH, 1987 quoted in Carlos Garma Navarro, 'Los estudios antropologicos sobre el protestantismo en México', *Revista Iztapalapa*, 15 (1988), pp. 53–66 p. 63. This article provides a comprehensive survey of the controversy in Mexico over Protestantism.

12 Bastian, *Protestantismo y sociedád*, p. 152.

13 Barrett, *World Christian Encyclopedia*, section on Mexico, p. 492.

14 David Stoll, *Fishers of Men or Builders of Empire? The Wycliffe Bible Translators in Latin America* Cambridge, Mass.: Cultural Survival, 1982; *América Indígena*, 44: 1 (Jan.–Mar. 1984).

15 James Hefley and Marti Hefley, *Uncle Cam* (Waco, Tex.: World Books, 1974); Lawrence Dame, *Maya Mission* (Garden City, NY: Doubleday, 1968); *The Other Side*, Feb. 1983, pp. 25–7; Franklin, *Current Concerns*.

16 Elmer Miller, *Harmony and Dissonance in Argentine Toba Society* (New Haven, Conn.: Human Relations Area Files, 1980).

17 Ted Lewellen, 'Deviant religion and cultural evolution', *Journal for the Scientific Study of Religion*, 18: 3 (Sept. 1979), pp. 243–51 (245).
18 Bryan R. Wilson *Magic and the Millennium* (London: Heinemann, 1973).
19 Stoll, *Fishers of Men*.
20 Ibid., p. 99.
21 Joanne Rappaport, 'Las misiones Protestantes y la resistencia indígena en el sur de Colombia', *América Indígena*, 44: 1, (Jan.–Mar. 1984, pp. 111–26).
22 Jean Pierre Bastian, 'Protestantismes minoritaires et protestataire au Méxique', *Itineris*, Apr 1982, pp. 45–52. Cf. Garma Navarro, 'Liderazgo protestante'.
23 Blanca Muratorio, 'Protestantism and capitalism, revisited in the rural highlands of Ecuador', *Journal of Peasant Studies*, 8: 1 (Oct. 1980), pp. 37–60.
24 Read et al., *Latin American Church Growth*, p. 84.
25 Cf. Bryan R. Wilson, *Magic and the Millennium*; and *Contemporary Transformations of Religion* (New York: Oxford University Press, 1976). It is interesting to note the consonance between the account given here and the standard analysis provided by Bryan Wilson.

Chapter 7

1 For useful accounts of Rastafarianism cf. E. Ellis Cashmore, *Rastaman* (London: Vision Paperbacks, 1983); Barry Chevannes, 'The Rastafari and the urban youth', in Carol Stone, and Aggrey Brown, *Perspectives on Jamaica in the Seventies* (Kingston, Jamaica: 1981), pp. 392–422, and Stuart Hall, 'Religious ideologies and Social Movements in Jamaica', in Robert Bocock, and Kenneth Thompson (eds), *Religion and Ideology* (Manchester: Manchester University Press and the Open University, 1985), pp. 269–96.
2 Cf. Ivor Morrish, *Obeah, Christ and Rastaman: Jamaica and its Religion* (Cambridge: James Clarke, 1982).
3 In this section I lean on Mervyn Alleyne, 'The history of African religion in Jamaica', unpublished paper presented at the 15th Conference of Caribbean Historians, University of the West Indies, Mona, Jamaica, April 1983.
4 The action of missionaries and of the local Baptists was not approved of by the Baptist Church in Britain. There are, therefore, partial parallels here with the apolitical attitudes of American missionary organizations as these are contrasted with local resistance on the part of Indian evangelical Christians in Latin America
5 Alleyne, 'African religion in Jamaica', p. 17.
6 Barry Chevannes, 'Revival and black struggle', *Savacou*, 5 (June 1971), pp. 27–37. In these sections I have also woven in material from diverse sources which I here list: Diane J. Austin, 'Born again . . . and again and again: communitas and social change among Jamaican Pentecostalists',

Journal of Anthropological Research, 37: 3 (Fall 1981), pp. 226–46; Noel Leo Erskine, 'Black religion and identity: a Jamaican perspective', Ph.D. diss., Union Theological Seminary, New York, 1978; Anita Waters, *Race, Class and Political symbols: Rastafari and Reggae in Jamaican Politics* (New Brunswick, NJ: Transaction Books, 1985); Clive Stilson Cato, 'Pentecostalism: its social and religious implications for Jamaican society', BA diss., University of West Indies, Mona, Jamaica, 1984; Brian Gates, (ed.), *Afro-Caribbean Religions* (London: Ward Lock, 1980); Vittorio Lanternari, 'Religious movements in Jamaica', in Richard Frucht (ed.), *Black Society in the New World* (New York: Random House, 1971); George Eaton Simpson, *Black Religions in the New World* (New York: Columbia University Press, 1978); Rex Nettleford, *Caribbean Cultural Identity: The Case of Jamaica* (Kingston: ACIJ 1978); Horace Russell, 'The emergence of the Christian black: the making of a stereotype', *Jamaican Journal*, 16: 1 (Feb. 1983).

7 Chevannes, 'Revival', p. 37.
8 Wedenoja, William, 'Religion and adaptation in rural Jamaica', Ph.D. diss., University of California at San Diego, 1978. I have leaned extensively on Wedenoja.
9 Ibid., p. 73.
10 Ibid., p. 70.
11 Ashley Smith, *Real Roots and Potted Plants: Reflections on the Caribbean Church* (Williamsfield, Jamaica: Mandeville Publishers, 1984); and *Pentecostalism in Jamaica*, the William Hamnett Lecture, 1975 (Kingston, Jamaica: Mark Lane, Methodist Book Centre, n.d.).
12 Francisco C. Rolim, *Pentecostais no Brasil* (Petropolis: Vozes, 1985).
13 Cato, 'Pentecostalism'.
14 Wedenoja, 'Religion and adaptation'.
15 Ashley Smith, *Real Roots*.
16 In personal conversation.
17 Wedenoja, 'Religion and adaptation' and Ashley Smith, *Real Roots*.
18 Stephen Glazier (ed.), *Perspectives on Pentecostalism: Case Studies from the Caribbean and Latin America* (Washington DC: University Press of America, 1980).
19 Stephen Glazier, 'Pentecostal exorcism and modernization in Trinidad, West Indies', in Glazier, *Perspectives*, pp. 67–80.
20 Eila Helander, *To Change and to Preserve* (Helsinki: The Finnish Society for Missiology and Ecumenics, 1986).
21 Anthony L. LaRuffa, 'Pentecostalism in Puerto Rican society', in Glazier, *Perspectives*, pp. 49–66.
22 Ibid.
23 David Nicholls, *Haiti in Caribbean Context* London: Macmillan, 1985.
24 Gordon K. Lewis, *Main Currents in Caribbean Thought* (Baltimore: Johns Hopkins University Press, 1985).
25 Nicholls, Haiti, p. 113.
26 Edward P. Thompson, *The Making of the English Working Class* (Harmondsworth: Penguin, 1968).

27 Frederick Conway, 'Pentecostalism in Haiti: healing and hierarchy', in Glazier, *Perspectives*, pp. 7–26.
28 William L. Wipfler, *The Churches of the Dominican Republic in the Light of History* Sondeos, 11 (Cuernavaca: CIDOC, 1967).
29 George M. Mulrain, *Theology in Folk Culture: The Theological Significance of Haitian Folk Religion* (New York: Peter Lang, 1984).
30 For comments on West Indians in Britain and for bibliography on that topic see David G. Pearson, 'Race, religiosity and political activism', *British Journal of Sociology*, 29: 3 (Sept. 1978), pp. 340–57.

Chapter 8

1 John Sydenham Furnivall, *Netherlands India: A Study of a Plural Economy* (New York: Macmillan, 1944).
2 Joseph B. Tamney and Riaz Hassan, *Religious Switching in Singapore: A Study of Religious Mobility* (Adelaide: Select Books [Flinders University], 1987).
3 Everett E. Hagen, *On the Theory of Social Change* (Homewood, Ill.: Dorsey Press, 1962).
4 Kim Illsoo, 'Organizational patterns of Korean–American Methodist Churches: denominationalism and personal community', in Russell Richey and Kenneth Rowe (eds), *Rethinking Methodist History* (Nashville: Kingswood Books, 1985), pp. 228–37 (229).
5 Song Kon-Ho, 'A history of the Christian movement in Korea', *International Review of Mission*, 74 (Jan. 1985), pp. 19–36 (20).
6 I have made considerable use in this section of Suh David Kwang-Sun, 'American missionaries' and 'Hundred years of Korean Protestantism', *International Review of Mission*, 74 (Jan. 1985), pp. 5–18.
7 Irving Hexham, 'Modernity or reaction in South Africa', in William Nicholls (ed.), *Sciences Religieuses*, Suppl. vol. 19 (Waterloo, Ont.: Wilfrid Laurier Press, 1987).
8 Kim Illsoo, 'Organizational patterns', p. 229.
9 Ibid.
10 John N. Vaughan, *The World's Twenty Largest Churches* (Grand Rapids, Mich.: Baker Book House, 1984).
11 there is a great deal of material available on Minjung but a short background is provided in Chi Myong-Kwan, 'Theological development in Korea', *International Review of Mission*, 74 (Jan. 1985), pp. 73–79.
12 Kim Illsoo, 'Organizational patterns', p. 229.
13 Ibid., p. 230.
14 Cf Kim Byong-Suh, 'The explosive growth of the Korean Church today: a sociological analysis', *International Review of Mission*, 74 (Jan. 1985), pp. 59–72.
15 Cf. Kim Illsoo, 'Organizational patterns'.
16 Yoo Boo Woong, 'Response to Korean shamanism by the Pentecostal Church, *International Review of Mission*, 74 (Jan. 1985), p. 73.

17 Lee Jae Bum, 'Pentecostal type distinctives and Korean Protestant Church growth', Ph.D. diss, Fuller Theological Seminary, Pasadena, Calif. 1986, p. 1. This dissertation included an extensive bibliography.

18 Ibid. p. 251.

19 Ibid. p. 252.

20 Yi Hyo-Jae, 'Christian mission and the liberation of Korean women', *International Review of Mission*, 74 (Jan. 1985), pp. 93–102. I am grateful for the background on this (and other matters) supplied by Chun Chin-Hong in his, 'A bibliographical essay on the growth of Korean Protestantism', unpublished paper, 1987, for ISEC, Boston, pp. 36–7.

21 Yi Hyo-Jae, 'Christian mission', p. 100.

22 Parig Digan, 'South Korea: cry of the people', ch. 8 in his *Churches in Contestation: Asian Christian Social Protest* (Maryknoll, NY: Orbis Books, 1984).

23 Shim Il-Sup, 'The new religious movements in the Korean Church', *International Review of Mission*, 74 (Jan. 1985), pp. 103–8.

24 Kim Kyong-Dong, 'The distinctive features of South Korea's development', in Peter Berger and Hsiao Hsin-Huang Michael (eds), *In Search of an East Asian Development Model* (New Brunswick, NJ and Oxford: Transaction Books, 1988), pp. 197–219.

25 Gill Hyun Mo, in an interview (1987) with Kim Hwan. I am grateful to Kim Hwan for obtaining this material.

26 Kim Kyong-Dong 'Explosive growth', p. 216.

27 Peter Berger, 'An East Asian development model?' in Berger and Hsiao *East Asian Development Model*, p. 9.

28 Kim Kyong-Dong, 'Distinctive features', p. 216.

29 Jan Swyngedouw, 'The role of Christianity', in Berger and Hsiao, East Asian Development Model, pp. 115–33.

30 Ronald Dore, Information provided in personal conversation.

31 Swyngedouw, 'Role of Christianity', Cf. David Reid, 'Secularization theory and Japanese Christianity', *Japanese Journal of Religious Studies*, 6: 1–2 (Mar.–June 1979), pp. 347–78.

32 Steve Bruce and Roy Wallis, 'Sketch for a theory of conservative Protestant politics', *Social Compass* 2/3 (1985), pp. 145–61.

33 Karla Poewe, 'In the eye of the storm: charismatics and independent churches in South Africa', University of Calgary: Unpublished paper, 1987, p. 3. Cf. Karla Poewe, 'Links and parallels between Black and White charismatic churches in South Africa and the States', unpublished paper, 1988.

34 Karla Poewe and Irving Hexham, 'The new charismatic churches in Durban, Johannesburg and Pretoria', *Navors Bulletin*, 17: 9 (1987), pp. 32–6.

35 Elda Susan Morran and Lawrence Schlemmer, *Faith for the Fearful?* (Durban: Centre for Applied Social Sciences, University of Natal, 1984).

36 Ibid., p. 175.

37 Ibid., p. 177.

Chapter 9

1 Walter Hollenweger, 'After twenty years' research on Pentecostalism', *International Review of Mission*, 75 (1986), pp. 1–12.
2 Friedrich Heer, *The Medieval World* (London: Weidenfeld and Nicolson, 1961), ch. 3.
3 Ioan Lewis, *Ecstatic Religion* (Harmondsworth: Penguin, 1971); Keith Thomas, *Religion and the Decline of Magic* (Harmondsworth: Penguin, 1973; James Obelkevich, *Religion and Rural Society: South Lindsey 1825–1875* (Oxford: Clarendon Press, 1976).
4 Murl O. Dirksen, 'Pentecostal healing: a facet of the personalistic health system of Pakal-Na, a village in southern Mexico', Ph.D. diss., Knoxville: University of Tennessee, 1984.
5 Hollenweger, 'Research on Pentecostalism', p. 6.
6 Ibid., p. 10.
7 Dirksen, 'Pentecostal healing', p. iv.
8 Ibid., p. 30.
9 Ibid., pp. 20–1.
10 Ibid., p. 46.
11 Ibid., p. 43.
12 Ibid., p. 80.
13 Ibid., pp. 33–4.
14 William Thornton, 'Protestantism: profile and process. A case study in religious change from Colombia, South America', Ph.D. Diss., Southern Methodist University, Dallas, Tex. 1981.
15 Kaja Finkler, 'Dissident sectarian movements, the Catholic Church and social class in Mexico', *Comparative Studies in Society and History*, 25: 2 (1983), pp. 277–305 (277).
16 Ibid., p. 278.
17 Ibid., p. 285.
18 Ibid., p. 301.
19 Felicitas D. Goodman, 'A trance-based upheaval in Yucatan', in Goodman, Felicitas, Henney, Jeannett, and Pressel, Esther (eds.) *Trance, Healing and Hallucination, Three Field Studies in Religious Experience* (New York and London: Wiley, 1974).
20 Ibid., p. 250, Cf. also Felicitas Goodman, 'Apostolics of Yucatan', in Erika Bourguignon, (ed.), *Religion, Altered States of Consciousness and Social Change* (Columbus: Ohio State University Press, 1973), pp. 198–218.
21 Jean-Pierre Bastian, *Protestantismo y sociedad en México* (Mexico City: CUPSA, 1983), ch. 6.
22 Karl Wilhelm Westmeier, 'The enthusiastic Protestants of Bogotá, Colombia: reflections on the growth of a movement', *International Review of Mission*, 75 (Jan. 1986), pp. 13–24.
23 Henry Raynor, *The Social History of Music* (New York: Schocken Books, 1972).

24 Henry W. Aulie, 'The Christian movement among the Chols of Mexico with special reference to problems of second generation Christianity', Ph.D. Diss., Fuller Theological Seminary. 1979.

25 Elmer Miller, *Harmony and Dissonance in Argentine Toba Society* (New Haven, Conn.: Human Relations Area Files, 1980), pp. 105–9.

26 P. Solomon Raj, 'The influence of Pentecostal teaching on some folk Christian religion in India', *International Review of Mission*, 75 1986 pp. 39–46.

27 George MacDonald Mulrain, *Theology in a Folk Culture: the Theological Significance of Haitian Folk Religion* (New York: Peter Lang, 1984).

28 Karla Poewe, 'Links and parallels between black and white charismatic churches in South Africa', unpublished paper, 1988, p. 4.

29 Lamin Sanneh, 'Christian missions and the Western guilt complex', *Christian Century*, 8 April 1987, pp. 330–4.

30 Ibid., p. 331.

31 Ibid., p. 332.

32 James Hefley and Marti Hefley, *Uncle Cam* (Milford, Mich.: Mott Media, 1981), p. 74.

33 Olive Banks, *Faces of Feminism: Feminism as a Social Movement* (Oxford: Martin Robertson, 1981).

34 Elizabeth Brusco, 'The household basis of evangelical religion and the reformation of machismo in Colombia', Ph.D. diss., City University of New York, 1986.

35 Dirksen, 'Pentecostal healing', p. 28.

36 For parallel developments in the role of women in a Nigerian context cf Rosalind I. J. Hackett, 'Women as leaders and participants in the Spiritual Churches' in Rosalind I. J. Hackett (ed.), *New Religious Movements in Nigeria* (New York: Edison Mellen Press), 1987, pp. 191–208.

Chapter 10

1 Sidney Mintz, *Worker in the Cane* (New York: Norton, 1974); Alex Huxley Westfried, *Ethnic Leadership in a New England Community: Three Puerto Rican Families* Salem, Wis: Sheffield Publishing, 1981).

2 Ruben E. Reina, and Norman B. Schwartz, 'The structural context of religious conversion in El Petén, Guatemala: status, community and multicommunity', *American Ethnologist*, 9: 1 (1974), pp. 157–91.

3 Ibid., p. 182.

4 James Sexton, 'Protestantism and modernization in two Guatemalan towns', *American Ethnologist*, 5: 2 (1978) pp. 280–302.

5 Mintz, *Worker in the Cane*.

6 Emilio Pantojas García, *La iglesia protestante y la americanización de Puerto Rico 1898–1917* Bayamón, PR: Prisa, 1976); Daniel R. Rodríguez Diaz, *Ideologías protestantes y misiones: El caso de Puerto Rico 1898–1930* (Mexico: UNAM, 1979).

7 Mintz, *Worker in the Cane*, p. 247.
8 Ibid., p. 242.
9 Ibid., p. 249.
10 Ibid., p. 218.
11 Ibid., p. 220
12 Ibid., p. 221.
13 Ibid., pp. 222–3.
14 Ibid., p. 229.
15 Ibid., p. 231.
16 Ibid., p. 240.
17 Ibid., pp. 240–2.
18 Westfried, *Ethnic Leadership*.
19 Ibid., pp. 89–90.
20 Ibid., p. 75.
21 Rodney Stark, 'Jewish conversion and the rise of Christianity: rethinking received wisdom', in Kent Harold Richards (ed.), *Society of Biblical Literature Seminar Papers* (Atlanta: Scholars Press, 1986), pp. 314–29.

Chapter 11

1 Elie Halévy, *A History of the English People in 1815* (London: T. Fisher Unwin, 1924) and *A History of the English People 1830–1841* (London: T. Fisher Unwin, 1927).
2 Max Weber, 'The Protestant sects and the spirit of capitalism', in Hans Gerth and C. Wright Mills, *From Max Weber* (London: Routledge, 1948).
3 James Beckford, *The Trumpet of Prophecy* (New York: Wiley, 1975).
4 Norman Long, *Social Change and the Individual* Manchester: Manchester University Press, 1968.
5 Ted Lewellen, 'Deviant religion and cultural evolution', *Journal for the Scientific Study of Religion*, 18: 3 (Sept. 1979), pp. 243–51.
6 Rodney Stark, 'Modernization and Mormon success', in Thomas Robbins, and Dick Anthony (eds), *In Gods We Trust*. New Brunswick, NJ: Transaction Books, 1989.
7 Mark Grover, 'Mormonism in Brazil: religion and dependency in Latin America', Ph.D. diss., Indiana State University, 1985, p. 10.
8 David L. Clawson, 'Religious allegiance and development in rural Latin America', *Journal of Interamerican Studies and World Affairs*, 26 (1984), pp. 499–524.
9 Mary O'Connor, 'Two kinds of religious movement among the Mayo Indians of Sonora, Mexico', *Journal for the Scientific Study of Religion*, 18: 3 (1979), pp. 260–5.
10 Ibid., p. 262.
11 Paul Turner, 'Religious conversion and community development', *Journal for the Scientific Study of Religion*, 18: 3 (1979), pp. 252–60.

12 Ibid., p. 258.
13 Henry Wilbur Aulie, 'The Christian movement among the Chols of Mexico with special reference to problems of second generation Christianity', Ph.D. diss., Fuller Theological Seminary, 1979.
14 Ibid., p. 159.
15 Jean-Pierre Bastian, 'Protestantismo y sociedad en México' Mexico City: CUPSA, 1983.
16 Patricia Fortuny, 'Movimientos religiosos minoritarios en el Yucatán rural de hoy', in *Capitalismo y vida rural en Yucatán* (Merida, Yucatán: Department of Economic and Social Studies, 1984), pp. 357–67.
17 Ruben E. Reina and Norman Schwartz, 'The structural context of religious conversion in El Petén, Guatemala: status, community and multicommunity', *American Ethnologist*, 9: 1 (1974), pp. 157–91.
18 Ibid., p. 188.
19 James Sexton, 'Protestantism and modernization in two Guatemalan towns', *American Ethnologist*, 5: 2 (1978), pp. 280–302.
20 Donna Birdwell-Pheasant, 'The power of Pentecostalism in a Belizean village', in Stephen D. Glazier (ed.), *Perspectives on Pentecostalism: Case Studies from the Caribbean and Latin America*, Washington, DC: University Press of America, 1980, pp. 95–110.
21 Bryan R. Roberts, 'Protestant groups and coping with urban life in Guatemala', *American Journal of Sociology*, 6 (May 1968), pp. 753–67.
22 Ibid., p. 765.
23 Ibid., p. 766.
24 Virginia Garrard Burnett, 'A history of Protestantism in Guatemala', Ph.D. diss., Tulane University, New Orleans, 1986.
25 Ibid., p. 193.
26 'Front Line Report', International Love Lift, 10: 6 (1986), p. 4.
27 Kent Maynard, 'Christianity and religion: evangelical identity and sociocultural organization in urban Ecuador', Ph.D. diss., Indiana University, 1977 (Ann Arbor microfilms, 1981) p. 122.
28 Elizabeth Brusco, 'The household basis of evangelical religion and the reformation of machismo in Colombia', Ph.D. diss., City University of New York, 1986.
29 Ibid., p. 115.
30 Ibid., p. 117.
31 William Thornton, 'Protestantism: profile and process. A case study in religious change from Colombia, South America', Ph.D. diss., Southern Methodist University, Dallas, Tex., 1981.
32 Ibid., pp. 71–3.
33 Ibid., p. 152.
34 Karl Wilhem Westmeier, *Reconciling Heaven and Earth: The Transcendental Enthusiasm and Growth of an Urban Protestant Community, Bogotá, Colombia* (New York: Peter Lang, 1986).
35 Ibid., pp. 231–2.
36 Cornelia Butler Flora, *Pentecostalism in Colombia: Baptism by Fire and Spirit* (Cranbury, NJ: Fairleigh Dickinson University Press, 1976).

37 Elmer Miller, *Harmony and Dissonance in Argentine Toba Society* (New Haven, Conn.: Human Relations Area Files, 1980).
38 Lewellen, 'Deviant religion'.
39 Ibid., p. 245.
40 Gilles Rivière, 'Social change and Pentecostalism in an Aymaran community', *Fe y Pueblo*, 3: 14 (Nov. 1986), pp. 24–30.
41 Ronald Frase, 'A sociological analysis of the development of Brazilian Protestantism: a study in social change, Ph.D. diss., Princeton Theological Seminary 1975, p. 185.
42 Cecilia Mariz, 'Religion and coping with poverty in Brazil: a comparison of the base communities and Pentecostal Churches', Institute of Economic Culture, Boston University, 1987.
43 Ibid., p. 10.
44 Francisco Cartaxo Rolim, *Pentecostais no Brasil* (Petropolis: Vozes, 1985).
45 Pablo A. Deiros, 'Argentine Baptists and politics: an analysis of relations', Southwestern Baptist Theological Seminary: Ph.D. diss., 1985.
46 William Read et al., *Latin American Church Growth* Grand Rapids, Mich.: Eerdmans, 1969; Emilio Willems, *Followers of the New Faith: Culture, Change and the Rise of Protestantism in Brazil and Chile* (Nashville: Vanderbilt University Press, 1967).
47 Read et al., *Latin American Church Growth*, p. 246.
48 Christian, Lalive D'Epinay, *Haven to the Masses: A Study of the Pentecostal Movement in Chile* (London: Lutterworth Press, 1969).
49 Mortimer Arias, 'Contextual evangelism in Latin America: between accommodation and confrontation', *Occasional Bulletin of Missionary Research Library*, 2 (Jan. 1978), pp. 19–28 (22).

Chapter 12

1 Frederick Turner, 'Protestantism and politics in Chile and Brazil', *Comparative Studies in Society and History*, 12: 2 (1970), pp. 213–29 (216).
2 Ibid., p. 225.
3 Juan Tennekes, 'El movimiento Pentecostal en la sociedad Chilena' (mimeo) (Santiago: La Vida Nueva, 1973); Johannes Tennekes, 'Le mouvement pentecôtiste chilien et la politique', *Social Compass*, 25: 1 (1978), pp. 55–79.
4 William Cook, 'Interview with Chilean Pentecostals' (WCC, Vancouver, 1983), *International review of Mission*, 72 (Oct. 1983), pp. 591–5.
5 Victor Alfredo Quezada, 'The challenge of growth for the Baptist Church in Chile', Th.M. diss. Fuller Theological Seminary, Pasadena, Calif., 1985.
6 Humberto Lagos Schuffeneger and Arturo Chacón, 'La religión en fuerzas armadas y de orden', Santiago, Chile, 1986.

7 Kenneth Aman, 'Fighting for God: the military and religion in Chile', *Cross Currents*, 36 (Nov. 1987), pp. 459–66 (460).

8 Christian Lalive D'Epinay, 'Régimes politiques et millénarisme dans une société dépendante', *Actes* of the 15th Conference of the CISR, Venice, 179 (Paris: CISR, 1979).

9 José Miguez Bonino, 'Presencia y ausencia protestante en la Argentina del proceso militar 1976–1983', *Christianismo y Sociedad*, 83 (1985), pp. 81–5.

10 Pablo A. Deiros, 'Argentine Baptists and politics: an analysis of relations', Ph.D. diss., Southwestern Baptist Theological Seminary, Fort Worth, Texas, 1985.

11 Walter LaFeber, *Inevitable Revolutions* (New York and London: Norton, 1983); Shirley Christian, 'Nicaragua. Revolution in the Family' (New York: Random House, 1986), ch. 12; Issue on Nicaragua, *This World*, 6 (Fall 1983).

12 Beth Spring, 'Nicaragua: the Government's heavy hand falls on believers', *Christianity Today*, 29: 18 (Dec. 1985), p. 51.

13 Ibid.

14 I have recently come upon some comments on Nicaragua by Margaret Poloma, in an article 'Pentecostals and politics in North and Central America', in Jeffrey K. Hadden and Anson Shupe, *Prophetic Religions and Politics*, vol. 1 (New York: Paragon House, 1986), pp. 319–52. Margaret Poloma comments that the situation in Nicaragua appears unclear (p. 343), but she confirms statements about rapid Protestant growth.

15 LaFeber, *Inevitable Revolutions*, p. 257.

16 Virginia Garrard Burnett, 'A history of Protestantism in Guatemala', Ph.D. diss., Tulane University, New Orleans: 1986.

17 Ibid., p. 209.

18 Ibid., p. 217.

19 Ronald Frase, 'A sociological analysis of the development of Brazilian Protestantism: a study in social change', Ph.D. diss., Princeton Theological Seminary, 1975, p. 347.

20 Ibid., p. 376.

21 Ruben A. Alves, *Protestantism and Repression: A Brazilian Case Study* (New York: Orbis Books, 1979).

22 Quoted in Frase, 'Brazilian Protestantism', p. 463.

23 Judith Chambliss Hoffnagel, 'Pentecostalism: a revolutionary or conservative movement?', in Stephen D. Glazier *Perspectives on Pentecostalism* (Washington, DC: University Press of America, 1980), 111–24 (116–17).

24 Cornelia Butler Flora, *Pentecostalism in Colombia: Baptism by Fire and Spirit* (Cranbury NJ: Fairleigh Dickinson University Press, 1976), p. 227.

25 Ibid., p. 87.

26 Karl Wilhelm Westmeier, *Reconciling Heaven and Earth, the transcendental enthusiasm and growth of an urban Protestant community, Bogotá, Colombia* (New York: Peter Lang, 1986).

27 Ibid., p. 260.
28 Jean-Pierre Bastian, 'Dissidence religieuse dans le milieu rural méxicain', *Social Compass*, 32: 2/3 (1985), pp. 245–60.
29 Erwin Rodríguez, *Un evangelio según la classe dominante* (Mexico City: UNAM, 1982).
30 Jean-Pierre Bastian, 'Protestantismos Latinamericanos entre la resistencia y la sumisión, 1961–1983', *Christianismo y Sociedad*, 82 (1984), pp. 49–68.
31 Hugo Assman, *A Igreja Electronica e seu impacto na América Latina* (Petropolis: Vozes, 1986).
32 Jane Cary Peck, 'Reflections from Costa Rica on Protestantism's dependence and nonliberative social function', *Journal of Ecumenical Studies*, 21 (Spring 1984), pp. 181–98.
33 Bobby C. Alexander, 'Pentecostal ritual reconsidered: 'anti-structural' dimensions of possession', *Journal of Ritual Studies*, 3: 1 (Winter 1989).

Chapter 13

1 Seymour Martin Lipset, *Revolution and Counterrevolution* (London: Heinemann, 1969), ch. 1.
2 Claudio Veliz, Personal Communication. Cf Claudio Veliz, 'A world made in England' *Quadrant* 187, Vol. XXVII, No. 3, March 1983, pp. 8–19.
3 Martin J. Wiener, *English Culture and the Decline of the Industrial Spirit, 1850–1980* (Cambridge: Cambridge University Press, 1981).
4 Richard W. Pointer, 'Freedom, truth and American thought 1760–1810', in Ronald A. Wells, and Thomas A. Askew, *Liberty and Law* Grand Rapids, Mich.: Eerdmans, 1987), pp. 25–42.
5 Rodney Stark and Roger Finke, 'Religious economies and sacred canopies: religious mobilization in American cities, 1906', *American Sociological Review*, 53 (March 1988), pp. 41–9.
6 Mark Girouard, *The Victorian Country House* (London and New Haven: Yale University Press, 1979).
7 Marilyn J. Westerkamp, *Triumph of the Laity, Scots-Irish Piety and the Great Awakening 1625–1760* (New York, Oxford: Oxford University Press, 1988).
8 Cf. Michael Billig, *Fascists* (London and New York: Harcourt Brace Jovanovich, 1978); David J. O'Brien *American Catholics and Social Reform* [chapter 7 on Father Coughlin] (New York: Oxford University Press, 1968).
9 Rosa del Carmen Bruno-Jofre, *Methodist Education in Peru: Social Gospel, Politics and American Ideological and Economic Penetration 1888–1930*, (Waterloo, Ont.: Wilfred Laurier University Press, 1988).
10 Ivan Vallier, 'Religious elites' in Seymour Martin Lipset and Aldo Solari (eds), *Elites in Latin America* (Londin, Oxford, New York: Oxford University Press, 1967), pp. 196–7.
11 Everett C. Hughes, 'Action catholique and nationalism' in Stewart

Crysdale and Les Wheatcroft (eds), *Religion in Canadian Society* (Toronto, Canada: Macmillan, 1976).

12 Richard J. Bord and Joseph E. Faulkner, *The Catholic Charismatic* (London: Pennsylvania State University Press, 1983).

13 Thomas Chordas, 'Catholic Pentecostals' in Stephen D. Glazier (ed.), *Perspectives on Pentecostalism* (Washington D.C.: University Press of America, 1980), pp. 143–175.

14 Ralph Della Cava, personal communication.

15 Cf. Ana Maria Ezcurra, 'Neo-Conservatism in the US and Ideological Struggle towards Central America', *Social Compass*, Vol. XXX, 1983, 2–3, pp. 349–62. Cf. Graham Howes, 'God damn Yanquis', unpublished paper given at a Conference on World Order and American Religion, University of Massachusetts, Amherst, Jan. 1989.

16 Carried out under the supervision of Dr. Andrew Walker: unpublished research for the Institute for the Study of Economic Culture, Boston University, Mass.

17 David Barrett, 'The Twentieth-Century Pentecostal/Charismatic Renewal in the Holy Spirit, with its Goal of World Evangelization', *AD2000* II, No. 5, Fall 1988, pp. 1–10; C. Peter Wagner, 'Church Growth' in Stanley M. Burgess and Gary B. McGee, (eds), *Dictionary of Pentecostal and Charismatic Movements* (Grand Rapids: Zondervan 1988). An instance of the type of detailed study undertaken would be provided by David Royal Brougham, *The Work of the Holy Spirit in Church Growth as seen in selected Indonesian Case Studies* (Pasadena, California: D. Miss. Fuller Theological Seminary, 1987).

18 Bryan R. Wilson, 'Secularization: the inherited model' in Phillip E. Hammond (ed.), *The Sacred in a Secular Age* (Berkeley and Los Angeles: University of California Press, 1985), pp. 9–20, and 'The Functions of Religion: a Reappraisal', *Religion* 18, June 1988, pp. 199–216.

19 Cf. David Alfred Martin, *A General Theory of Secularization* (Oxford: Blackwell, 1978). The present book and in particular this last chapter fill in a gap in my previous work relating to the modification in Latin America of the 'Latin' pattern of secularization. For a treatment of the general situation of Roman Catholicism cf. David Alfred Martin, 'Introductory essay' in Thomas Gannon (ed.), *Catholicism in Transition* (London: Macmillan, 1988), pp. 3–35.

20 There is also useful material in Reginald Bibby and Merlin Brinkerhoff, 'Circulation of the Saints in South America', *Journal for the Scientific Study of Religion*, 24 (1985), pp. 39–55.

Glossary

abertura	political opening
bhakti	fervent devotion
caciques	local potentates
campesinos	agricultural workers
cancionistas	singers
caudillismo	authoritarian leadership
cofradias	confraternities
compadres	godfathers
creyentes	believers
criollo	[here] of mixed blood
dirigentes	leaders
favela	impoverished, ramshackle suburb
fiesteros	revellers
hermanos, hermanas	brothers, sisters
Hispanidad	the realm of Hispanic culture
indigenista	pro-native
integrista	organicist
irmandades	brotherhoods
Nova Vida	'New Life'
peninsulares	people with Spanish roots
porfiriato	intermittently repressive regime of Porfirio Diaz lasting from 1876 to 1910
promesa	promise (of spiritual gifts)
Reglamento	Rule or Discipline
resguardos	reserves
Sanidad Divina	divine healing
La Violencia	Colombian Civil War
wa	system of harmonization (Japan)

A note on statistics for the
Assemblies of God

	1973	1982	1989
Argentine	5,034/5,000	15,000/30,000	329,100
Bolivia	6,400/4,000	12,387/10,007	42,000
Brazil	2,057,000/726,000	3,350,000/2,750,000	8,649,000
Chile	2,961/1,240	6,600/4,000	33,310
Colombia	2,895/5,861	6,636/9,282	35,727
Dominican Republic	6,665/12,359	13,276/10,213	77,290
Ecuador	780/1,489	1,559/2,704	21,550
El Salvador	12,100/69,500	43,000/95,000	210,000
Guatemala	13,431/19,300	35,909/78,015	148,514
Haiti	2,747/5,966	6,315/30,527	41,828
Honduras	1,762/3,238	8,311/18,495	45,313
Mexico	12,500/32,677	45,000/50,000	570,334
Nicaragua	2,897/7,583	10,200/6,450	64,000
Paraguay	295/250	540/860	13,250
Peru	35,500/15,250	72,000/30,000	204,750
Uruguay	2,179/3,034	5,756/8,300	23,000
Venezuela	4,386/8,113	10,000/13,000	62,965
Total: Latin America			10,705,486

Note: Although the Assemblies of God are the largest single evangelical denomination overall in Latin America, they are not always even the largest Pentecostal denomination in particular countries e.g. Chile. In the 1989 figures, the figures previously divided into Active and Other are given as a single total. I am grateful to Rosalee McMain of the Division of Foreign Missions, Springfield, Missouri, for supplying these figures.

Bibliography

Books

Alcantara Matos, Domingo. *Cien años de prescencia en Centroamerica*. Iglesia y Sociedad, Santiago, Chile. (Presbyterian Church), 1973.

Alves, Rubem. *Protestantism and Repression: A Brazilian Case Study*. New York: Orbis Books, 1979.

Aman, Kenneth. *Border Regions of Faith*. New York: Orbis Books, 1986.

Anderson, Robert Mapes. *Vision of the Disinherited: The Making of Modern Pentecostalism*. New York: Oxford University Press, 1979.

Anfuso, Joseph and Sczepanski David. *Efrain Rios Montt: siervo o dictador: la verdadero historia del controversial President de Guatemala*. Guatemala: Gospel Outreach, 1984.

Annis, Sheldon. *God and Production in a Guatemalan Town*. Austin: University of Texas, 1988.

Arias, Mortimer (ed.). *Evangelización y revolución en América Latina*. Montevideo: 1969.

Assemblies of God, General Council. *Growth Analysis of Assemblies of God Foreign Mission Fields, 1965–1975*. Springfield, Mo: Assembly of God Publishing House, 1976.

Assman, Hugo. *A igreja electronico e seu impacto na América Latina*. Petropolis: Vozes, 1986.

Barrett, Leonard. *The Rastafarians: Sounds of Cultural Dissonance*. Boston Beacon Press, 1977.

Bastian, Jean-Pierre. *Breve historia del Protestantismo en América Latina*. Mexico City: CUPSA, 1986.

——*Los dissidentes, sociedades protestantes y revolución en México 1872–1911*. Mexico City: Fondo de Cultura Económica and El Colegio de México, 1988.

——*Protestantismo y sociedad en México*. Mexico City: CUPSA, 1983.

Bastide, Roger. *The African Religions of Brazil*. Baltimore: Johns Hopkins University Press, 1978.

Beckford, James. *The Trumpet of Prophecy*. New York: Wiley, 1975.

Belli, Umberto. *Breaking Faith: The Sandinista Revolution and Its Impact on Freedom and Christian Faith in Nicaragua*. Westchester, Ill.: Crossway

Books, 1985, (Reviewed by Peter Calvert, *Journal of Latin American Studies*, Nov. 1986, p. 465.)

Berberian, Martha. *La communicación masiva y el evangelico*. Guatemala City: Ediciones Sa-Ber, 1983.

Berger, Peter. *The Sacred Canopy*. Garden City, NY: Doubleday, 1967.

—— 'An East Asian development model?' in Berger, Peter and Hsiao Hsin-Huang Michael (eds). *In Search of an East Asian Development Model*. New Brunswick, NJ and Oxford: Transaction Books, 1988, pp. 197–219.

Bermudez, Fernando. *Death and Resurrection in Guatemala*. (trans. Robert Barr) Maryknoll, NY: Orbis Books, 1986.

Berryman, Philip. *The Religious Roots of Rebellion: Christianity in Central American Revolution*. New York: Orbis Books, 1984.

Birdwell-Pheasant, Donna. 'The power of Pentecostalism in a Belizean village' in Glazier, Stephen D. (ed.). *Perspectives on Pentecostalism: Case Studies from the Caribbean and Latin America*. Washington, DC: University Press of America, 1980, pp. 95–110.

Boehm, Richard G. and Visser, Sent (eds). *Latin American Case Studies*. Dubuque, Iowa: Kendall/Hunt, 1984.

Brintnall, Douglas E. *Revolt Against the Dead: The Modernization of a Mayan Community in the Highlands of Guatemala*. New York: Gordon and Breach, 1979.

Bruce, Steve. *Firm in the Faith*. Aldershot, England: Gower, 1984.

Bruno-Jofre, Rosa del Carmen. *Methodist Education in Peru: Social Gospel, Politics and American Ideological and Economic Penetration: 1888–1930*. Waterloo, Ont.: Wilfrid Laurier University Press, 1988.

Calder, Bruce Johnson. *Crecimiento y cambio de la Iglesia Católica en Guatemalteca 1944–1966*. Guatemala City: Editorial José de Pineda Ibarra, 1970.

Cava, Ralph Della. *Miracle at Joaseiro*. New York: Columbia University Press, 1970.

Cesar, Waldo A. *Para uma sociologia do Protestantismo Brasileiro*. Petropolis: Vozes, 1973.

——*Protestantismo o imperialismo na América Latina*. Petropolis, Brazil: Vozes, 1968.

Chant, Barry. *Heart of Fire*. Sydney: House of Tabor, 1984.

Christian, Shirley. *Nicaragua. Revolution in the Family*. New York: Random House, 1986.

Clark, David. *Between Pulpit and Pew: Folk Religion in a North Yorkshire Fishing Village*. New York: Cambridge University Press, 1982.

Collinson, Patrick. *The Elizabethan Puritan Movement*. London: Cape, 1967.

Cook, Guillermo. *The Expectation of the Poor. Latin American Basic Ecclesial Communities in Protestant Perspective*. Maryknoll, NY: Orbis Books, 1985.

Costas, Orlando E. *Christ Outside the Gate*. Maryknoll, NY: Orbis Books, 1982.

——*El protestantismo en América Latina hoy: ensayos del camino*. San José, Costa Rica: Indef, 1975.

—— *Theology of the Crossroads in Contemporary Latin America: Missiology in Mainline Protestantism 1969–1974*. Amsterdam: Rodopi, 1976.

Costello, Gerald M. *Mission to Latin America: The Successes and Failures of a Twentieth Century Crusade*. Maryknoll, NY: Orbis Books, 1979.

Damboriena, Prodencio. *El Protestantismo en América Latina*. (2 vols.) Friburgo: FERES, 1962.

Dame, Lawrence. *Maya Mission*. Garden City, NY: Doubleday, 1968.

Dayton, Donald W. *Theological Roots of Pentecostalism*. Metuchen, NJ: The Scarecrow Press, 1987.

Deiros, Pablo A. (ed.). *Los evangelicos y el poder politico en América Latina*. Grand Rapids, Mich.: Eerdmans, 1986.

De Kadt, Emmanuel. Religion, the Church and social change in Brazil', in Veliz Claudio (ed.), *The Politics of Conformity in Latin America*. New York: Oxford University Press, 1965, pp. 192–220.

de la Rosa, Martin and Reilly, Charles A. *Religión y política en México*. Mexico City: Siglo Veintiuno, 1985.

Denton, Charles F. 'La mentalidad protestante: un enfoque sociologico' in Padilla, C. René (ed.). *Fe cristiana y Latinoamérica hoy*. Buenos Aires: Ediciones Certeza, 1974.

Directorio Evangelico 1986. Lima: Concilio Nacional Evangélico del Perú, 1986.

Dirksen, Carolyn. 'Let your women keep silence' in Bowdle, Donald (ed.). *The Promise and the Power*. Cleveland: Pathway Press, 1980, pp. 165–96.

Dussel, Enrique. *Hipotesis para una historia de la teologia en America Latina*. Bogotá, Colombia: Indo-American Press Service, 1986.

Emery, Gennet M. *Protestantism in Guatemala: Its Influence on the Bicultural Situation with Reference to the Roman Catholic Background*. Sondeos, 65. Cuernavaca, Mexico: CIDOC, 1970.

Enns, Arno W. *Man, Milieu and Mission in Argentina*. Grand Rapids, Mich.: Eerdmans, 1971.

Erskine, Noel Leo. *Decolonizing Theology: A Caribbean Perspective*. Maryknoll, NY: Orbis Books, 1981.

Ezcurra, Ana Maria. *La Ofensiva neoconservadora: la iglesia de USA y la lucha ideologica bacia America Latina*. Madrid: IEPALA, 1982.

Finkler, Kaja. *Spiritualist Healers in Mexico: Successes and Failures of Alternative Therapeutics*. New York: Berger and Garvey, 1985.

Flora, Cornelia B. *Pentecostalism in Colombia: Baptism by Fire and Spirit*. Cranbury, NJ: Fairleigh Dickinson University Press, 1976.

—— in Glazier, Stephen D. (ed.). *Perspectives on Pentecostalism: Case Studies from the Caribbean and Latin America*. Washington, DC: University Press of America, 1980.

Fortuny, Patricia. 'Movimientos religiosos minoritarios en el Yucatán rural de hoy' in *Capitalismo y vida rural en Yucatán*. Merida, Yucatán: Department of Economic and Social Studies, 1984, pp. 357–67.

Franklin, Karl. *Current Concerns of Anthropologists and Missionaries*. Dallas, Tex.: International Museum of Cultures, 1987.

Fulbrook, Mary. *Piety and Politics: Religion and the Rise of Absolutism in England, Württemberg and Prussia*. New York: Cambridge University Press, 1983.

Garma Navarro, Carlos. *Protestantismo en una communidad totonaca de Puebla*. Mexico City: INI, 1987.

Garrison Vivian. 'Sectarianism and psychosocial adjustment: a controlled comparison of Puerto Rican Pentecostals and Catholics' in Zaretsky, Irving I. and Leone, Mark P. (eds.). *Movements in Contemporary America*. Princeton, NJ: Princeton University Press, 1974.

Gates, Brian (ed.). *Afro-Caribbean Religions*. London: Ward Lock, 1980.

Gaxiola, Manuel J. *La serpiente y la paloma: analisis del crecimiento de la Iglesia Apostólica de la fe en Cristo Jesús en México*. South Pasadena, Calif.: William Carey Library, 1970.

Glazier, Stephen D. *Marching the Pilgrims Home: Leadership and Decision Making in an Afro-Caribbean Faith*. Westport, Conn. and London: Greenwood Press, 1983.

——*Perspectives on Pentecostalism: Case Studies from the Caribbean and Latin America*. Washington, DC: University Press of America, 1980.

Goff, James. *Protestant Persecution in Colombia 1948–1958*. Cuernavaca, Mexico: CIDOC, 1965.

——'Apostolics of Yucatan' in Erika Bourguignon, (ed.). *Religion, Altered States of Consciousness and Social Change*. Columbus: Ohio State University Press, 1973, pp. 198–218.

Goodman, Felicitas D. 'A trance-based upheaval in Yucatan' in Felicitas Goodman, Jeannett Henney and Esther Pressel (eds), *Trance, Healing and Hallucination: Three Field Studies in Religious Experience* (New York and London: Wiley, 1974.

Graveley, Will B. 'African Methodisms and the rise of black denominationalism' in Richey, Russell and Rowe, Kenneth (eds.). *Rethinking Methodist History*. Nashville: Kingswood Books, 1985, pp. 111–24.

Halévy, Elie. *A History of the English People in 1815*. London: T. Fisher Unwin, 1924.

——*A History of the English People 1830–1841*. London: T. Fisher Unwin, 1927.

Hamid, Idris. *A History of the Presbyterian Church in Trinidad 1868–1968*. Trinidad: St Andrews Theological College, 1980.

Hamid, Idris. *Out of the Depths*. Trinidad: St Andrews Theological College, 1977.

Harrell, David Edwin, Jr. *Oral Roberts: An American Life*. Bloomington: Indiana University Press, 1985.

Haselden, Kyle. *Death of a Myth: New Locus for Spanish American Faith*. New York: Friendship Press, 1964.

Haslam, David. *Faith in Struggle: The Protestant Churches in Nicaragua and their Response to the Revolution*. London: Epworth Press, 1987.

Hefley, James and Hefley, Marti. *Uncle Cam*. Waco, Tex.: Word Books, 1974.

Hempton, David. *Methodism and Politics in British Society 1750–1850*. Stanford, Calif.: Stanford University Press, 1984.

Hill, Michael. *A Sociology of Religion.* London: Heinemann Educational, 1973.

Hinshaw, R. E. *Panajachel: A Guatemalan Town in 'Thirty-Year Perspective.* Pittsburgh: University of Pittsburgh Press, 1975.

Hoffnagel, Judith Chambliss. 'Pentecostalism: a revolutionary or a conservative movement?' in Glazier, Stephen D. (ed.). *Perspectives on Pentecostalism: Case Studies from the Caribbean and Latin America.* Washington, DC: University Press of America, 1980, pp. 111–24.

Hollenweger, Walter James. *The Pentecostals: The Charismatic Movement in the Churches.* Minneapolis: Augsburg Publishing House, 1972.

——*Pentecost between Black and White: Five Case Studies on Pentecost and Politics.* Belfast: Christian Journals, 1974.

Howe, Gary Nigel. 'Capitalism and religion at the periphery: Pentecostalism and Umbanda in Brazil' in Glazier, Stephen D. (ed.). *Perspectives on Pentecostalism: Case Studies from the Caribbean and Latin America.* Washington, DC: University Press of America, 1980.

Huck, Eugene and Mosely, Edward. *Militants, Merchants and Missionaries: US Expansion in Middle America.* University of Alabama Press, 1970.

Hunka, Jack W. *The History/Philosophy of Assemblies of God in Latin America.* Western Evangelical Seminary, 1967.

Hunter, James Davison. *American Evangelicalism.* New Brunswick, NJ: Rutgers University Press, 1983.

Hvalkof, Soren and Aaby, Peter (eds). *Is God an American? An Anthropological Perspective on the Missionary Work of the Summer Institute of Linguistics.* Copenhagen: International Work Group for Indigenous Affairs and London: Survival International, 1981.

Johnson, Norbert E. *The History, Dynamic, and Problems of the Pentecostal Movement in Chile.* Richmond, Va.: Union Theological Seminary, 1970.

Jones, Charles Edwin. *A Guide to the Study of the Holiness Movement.* Metuchen, NJ: The Scarecrow Press and The American Theological Library Association, 1974.

——*A Guide to the Study of the Pentecostal Movement* (2 vols.). Metuchen, NJ: The Scarecrow Press, 1983.

Jurgen-Prien, Hans. *La Historica del Christianismo en America Latina.* Salamanca: Ediciones Sigueme, 1985.

Kessler, Jean Baptiste August. *A Study of the Older Protestant Missions and Churches in Peru and Chile.* Goes, Netherlands: Oesterbaan and le Cointre, 1964.

Kilson, Martin and Rotberg, Robert I. *The African Diaspora: Interpretive Essays.* Cambridge, Mass.: Harvard University Press, 1976.

Kim, Illsoo. 'Organizational patterns of Korean–American Methodist Churches: denominationalism and personal community' in Richey, Russell and Rowe, Kenneth (eds). *Rethinking Methodist History.* Nashville: Kingswood Books, 1985, pp. 228–37.

Kim Kyong-Dong. 'The distinctive features of South Korea's development' in Berger, Peter and Hsiao, Hsin-Huang, Michael (eds). *In Search of an*

East Asian Development Model. New Brunswick, NJ and Oxford: Transaction Books, 1987, pp. 197–219.

Kliewer, Gerd Uwe. *Das neue volk der pfingstler: religion, unterentwicklung und sozialer wandel in Lateinamerika.* Bern: Peter Lang, 1975.

LaFeber, Walter. *Inevitable Revolutions.* New York and London: Norton, 1983.

Lalive, Gerhard. *The Religious Factor.* Garden City, NY: Doubleday, 1961.

Lalive D'Epinay, Christian. *Haven to the Masses: A Study of the Pentecostal Movement in Chile.* London: Lutterworth Press, 1969

——*Pénétration culturelle et presse religieuse: le cas d'une revue protestante argentine.* Sondeos, 80. Cuernavaca, Mexico: Centro Intercultural de Documentación, 1971.

——*Religion, dynamique sociale et dépendance: les mouvements protestants en Argentine et au Chile.* Paris, The Hague: Mouton, 1975.

Lanternari, Vittorio. 'Religious Movements in Jamaica' in Frucht, Richard (ed.). *Black Society in the New World.* New York: Random House, 1971.

Laqueur, Thomas Walter. *Religion and Respectability: Sunday Schools and Working Class Culture 1780–1850.* New Haven and London: Yale University Press, 1976.

Lara-Brand, Jorge. 'Protestants and the process of integration' in Shapiro, Samuel (ed.). *Integration of Man and Society in Latin America.* Notre Dame and London: University of Notre Dame Press, 1967.

LaRuffa, Anthony L. 'Pentecostalism in Puerto Rican society' in Glazier, Stephen D. (ed.), *Perspectives on Pentecostalism: Cae Studies from the Caribbean and Latin America.* Washington, DC: University Press of America, 1980.

Leonard, Emile. *O Protestantismo Brasileiro: estudo de eclesiologia e historia social.* Sao Paulo: Aste, 1963.

Lernoux, Penny. *Cry of the People.* Harmondsworth: Penguin, 1980.

Levine, Daniel H. (ed.). *Religion and Political Conflict in Latin America.* Chapel Hill and London: University of North Carolina Press, 1986.

——*Religion and Politics in Latin America: The Catholic Church in Venezuela and Colombia.* Princeton, NJ: Princeton University Press, 1981.

Lewis, Gordon K. *Main Currents in Caribbean Thought.* Baltimore: Johns Hopkins University Press, 1985.

Lewis, Ioan. *Ecstatic Religion.* Harmondsworth: Penguin, 1971.

Lipset, Seymour Martin. *Revolution and Counterrevolution.* New York: Basic Books, 1968; London: Heinemann, 1969.

——Religion in American politics in Novak, Michael (ed.), *Capitalism and Socialism: A Theological Inquiry.* Washington, DC: American Enteprise Institute, 1979.

Long, Norman. *Social Change and the Individual.* Manchester: Manchester University Press, 1968.

Lovejoy, David S. *Religious Enthusiasm in the New World: Heresy to Revolution.* London and Cambridge, Mass.: Harvard University Press, 1985.

McDonald, Forrest. *Novus Ordo Seclorum: The Intellectual Origins of the Constitution*. Kansas City: University of Kansas Press, 1987.

McGavran, Donald. *Church Growth in Mexico*. Grand Rapids, Mich. Eerdmans, 1963.

MacLeod, Hugh. *Religion and the People of Western Europe 1789–1970*. London: Oxford University Press, 1981.

Madsen, William. *Christo-Paganism: A Study of Mexican Religious Syncretism*. New Orleans: Middle American Research University (Tulane) 1957.

Maduro, Otto. *Religión y conflicto social*. Mexico City: Crie, 1980.

Maestre, Julio R. *Las buenas obras: un imperativo de Jesús*. Buenos Aires: Certeza, 1981.

Marti, Casimiro et al. *Iglesia y sociedad en España 1939–1975*. Madrid: Editorial Popular, 1977.

Martin, David. *A General Theory of Secularization*. Oxford: Blackwell, 1978.

Marsden, George. *Fundamentalism and American Culture*. New York: Oxford University Press, 1980.

Marzal, Manuel. *La transformatión religiosa peruana*. Lima: Pontifical University, 1983.

Medhurst, Kenneth. *The Church and Labour in Colombia*. Manchester: Manchester University Pres, 1984.

Miller, Elmer. *Harmony and Dissonance in Argentine Toba Society*. New Haven, Conn.: Human Relations Area Files, 1980.

Miller, William Lee. *The First Liberty: Religion and the American Republic*. New York: Paragon House, 1985.

Millett, Richard. 'The perils of success: post-World War II Latin American Protestantism' in Brown, Lyle C. and Cooper, William F. (eds). *Religion in Latin American Life and Literature*. Waco, Tex.: Baylor University Press, 1980.

Mintz, Sidney. *Worker in the Cane*. New York: Norton, 1974.

Moore, Robert. *Pitmen, Preachers, and Politics: The Effects of Methodism in a Durham Mining Community*. Cambridge: Cambridge University Press, 1974.

Morran, Elda Susan and Schlemmer, Lawrence. *Faith for the Fearful?* Durban: Centre for Applied Social Sciences, University of Natal, 1984.

Morrish, Ivor. *Obeah, Christ and Rastaman: Jamaica and its Religion*. Cambridge: James Clarke, 1982.

Mouzelis, Nicos P. *Politics in the Semi-Periphery*. London: Macmillan, 1986.

Mulrain, George MacDonald. *Theology in Folk Culture: The Theological Significance of Haitian Folk Religion*. New York: Peter Lang, 1984.

Muratorio, Blanca. 'Protestantism, ethnicity and class in Chimborazo' in Whitten, Norman E. Jr. (ed.). *Cultural Transformations and Ethnicity in Modern Ecuador*. Urbana: University of Illinois press, 1981, pp. 506–34.

Nelson, Wilton M. *Protestantism in Central America*. Grand Rapids Mich.: Eerdmans, 1984.

——*El Protestantismo en Centroamérica*. San José: Editorial Caribe, 1982.

Nettleford, Rex. *Caribbean Cultural Identity: The Case of Jamaica*. Kingston, Jamaica: ACIJ, 1978.

Nicholls, David. *Haiti in Caribbean Context*. London: Macmillan, 1985.

Nida, Eugene A. *Understanding Latin Americans: With Special Reference to Religious Values*. South Pasadena, Calif.: William Carey Library, 1974.

Norman, Edward. *Christianity in the Southern Hemisphere*. Oxford: Clarendon Press, 1981.

Novaes, Regina R. *Os escolhidos de Deus* (booklet), Cadernos do ISER, 19. Rio de Janeiro: ISER, 1985.

Obelkevich, James. *Religion and Rural Society: South Lindsey 1825–1875*. Oxford: Clarendon Press, 1976.

Oliviera, P. Ribero de. *Religão e dominacão de classe: genese, estructura e funcão do catolicisimo romanizado na Brasil*. Petropolis: Vozes, 1985.

Orr, J. E. *Evangelical Awakenings in Latin America*. Medellin: Tipografia Union, 1978.

Ospina, A. *The Protestant Denomination in Colombia*. Bogota: National Press, 1954.

Owens, Joseph. *Dread: The Rastafarians of Jamaica*. Kingston, Jamaica: Sangster, 1976.

Palmer, Donald. *Explosion of People Evangelism*. Chicago: Moody Press, 1974.

Pantojas García, Emilio. *La iglesia protestante y la americanización de Puerto Rico 1898–1917*. Bayamón, PR: Prisa, 1976.

Pointer, Richard W. *Protestant Pluralism and the New York Experience*. Bloomington and Indianapolis: Indiana University Press, 1988.

Poloma, Margaret. *The Charismatic Movement: Is There a New Pentecost?* Boston: Twayne, 1982.

——'Pentecostals and politics in North and Central America' in Hadden, Jeffrey and Shupe Anson (eds), *Prophetic Religion and Politics*. New York: Paragon House, 1986.

Prieto, Luis C. *Las Iglesias Evangélicas da Guatemala*. Universidade Francisco Marroquim, Depto de Teologia, 1980.

Prien, Hans-Jurgen. *La historia de la Iglesia en Latin America*. Salamanca, Spain: Ediciones Sigueme, 1985. (Originally published in German, 1978 Göttingen: Vandenwoek and Ruprecht.) Extensive bibliography.

PROCADES. *Directorio de Iglesias, Organizaciones y Ministerios del Movimiento Protestante: Guatemala*. UINDEF and SEPAL, Guatemala City, 1981.

Read, William. *Brazil 1980: The Protestant Handbook*. 1973.

——*New Patterns of Church Growth in Brazil*. Grand Rapids, Mich.: Eerdmans, 1965.

——Monterroso, Victor M. and Johnson, Harmon A. *Latin American Church Growth*. Grand Rapids, Mich.: Eerdmans, 1969.

Redekop, Calvin. *Strangers Become Neighbours: Mennonite and Indigenous Relations in the Paraguayan Chaco*. Studies in Anabaptist and Mennonite History, 22. Scottsdale, Ariz.: Herald Press, 1980.

Ringenberg, Roger. *Rastafarianism: An Expanding Jamaican Cult*. Kingston: Jamaica Theological Seminary, 1978.

Roberts, Griffith T. 'Methodism in Wales' in Davies, Rupert, George,

A. Raymond and Rupp, Gordon (eds). *A History of the Methodist Church in Great Britain*. London: Epworth, 1983.

Rodrigues Brandão, Carlos. *Os Deuses do Povo: um estudo sobre religão popular*. Sao Paulo: Brasiliense, 1980.

Rodríguez Diaz, Daniel R. *Ideologías protestantes y misiones: el caso de Puerto Rico 1898–1930*. Mexico City: UNAM, 1979.

Rolim, Francisco Cartaxo. *Pentecostais no Brasil: uma interpretacão socioreligiosa*. Petropolis: Vozes, 1985.

——*Religião e classes populares*. Petropolis: Vozes, 1980.

Roof, Wade Clark and McKinney, William. *American Mainline Religion*. New Brunswick, NJ: Rutgers University Press, 1987.

Runyon, Theodore (ed.). *Sanctification and Liberation*. Nashville, Tenn.: Abingdon Press, 1981.

Russell, Horace Orlando. *The Baptist Witness* [West Indies and Latin America]. El Paso: Baptist Spanish Publishing, 1983.

Salesman, P. Eliecer. *Ciudado: Llegaron los Protestantes*. Bogota: Libreria Salesiana, 1982.

Sánchez, José. *Anticlericalism: A Brief History*. Notre Dame, London: University of Notre Dame Press, 1972.

Sandberg, Neil C. *Identity and Assimilation*. Washington DC: University Press of America, 1981.

Savage, Peter et al. *Protestant Belief Systems in Three Latin American Countries: A Preliminary Report of an Empirical Analysis*. Cochabamba, Bolivia: Board of Communication Rex Mundi', 1973/74.

Sawatsky, H. L. *They Sought a Country: Mennonite Colonization in Mexico* Berkeley: University of California Press, 1971.

Segundo, Juan L. *The Hidden Motives of Pastoral Action: Latin American Reflections*. Maryknoll, NY, Orbis, 1978.

Sellers, Ian. *Nineteenth Century Nonconformity*. London: Edward Arnold, 1977,

Semmel, Bernard. *The Methodist Revolution*. New York: Basic Books, 1973.

Siepierski, Paulo. *Evangelizacao no Brasil: Un perfil do protestantisamo brasileiro; o caso Pernambuco*. Sao Paulo SP: Ed Sepal, 1987.

Simpson, George Eaton. *Black Religions in the New World*. New York: Columbia University Press, 1978.

——*Religious Cults in the Caribbean*. Rio Piedras, PR: Institute for Caribbean Studies, 1970.

Sinclair, J. *Protestantism in Latin America: A Bibliographical Guide*. Austin, Tex.: Hispanic American Institute, 1967.

Smith, Ashley. *Pentecostalism in Jamaica*. The William Hammett Lecture 1975. Methodist Book Centre. Kingston, Jamaica: Mark Lane, (n.d.).

——*Real Roots and Potted Plants: Reflections on the Caribbean Church*. Kingston, Jamaica: Mandeville Publishers, 1984.

Smith, Brian. *The Church and Politics in Chile*. Princeton, NJ: Princeton University Press, 1982.

Smith, Michael G., Angier, Roy and Nettleford, Rex. *The Rastafarian*

Movement in Jamaica. West Indies Institute of Social and Economic Research. University of the West Indies, 1960.

Souza, Beatriz M. *A experiência da salvação: Pentecostais em São Paulo*. São Paulo: Duas Cidades, 1969.

Stark, Rodney. 'Jewish conversion and the rise of Christianity: rethinking received wisdom' in Richards, Kent Harold (ed.). *Society of Biblical Literature Seminar Papers*. Atlanta: Scholars Press, 1986, pp. 314–29.

—— 'Modernization and Mormon success' in Robbins, Thomas and Anthony, Dick (eds). *In Gods We Trust*. New Brunswick, NJ: Transaction Books, 1989.

Stoeffler, F. Ernest. *Continental Pietism and Early American Christianity*. Grand Rapids, Mich.: Eerdmans, 1976.

Stoll, David. *Fishers of Men or Builders of Empire? The Wycliffe Bible Translators in Latin America*. Cambridge, Mass.: Cultural Survival, 1982.

Sweeney, Ernest S. *Foreign Missionaries in Argentina, 1938–1962: A Study of Dependence*. Sondeos, 68. Cuernavaca, Mexico: Centro Intercultural de Documentación, 1970.

Synan, Vincent. *The Holiness Pentecostal Movement in the United States*. Grand Rapids, Mich.: Eerdmans, 1971.

Tamney, Joseph B. and Hassan, Riaz. *Religious Switching in Singapore: A Study of Religious Mobility*. Adelaide: Select Books [Flinders University], 1987.

Tax, Sol and Hinshaw, Robert. 'Panajachel a generation later'. in Goldschmidt, W. and Hoijer, H. (eds). *The Social Anthropology of Latin America*. Los Angeles: Latin American Studies Series, 1970. pp. 175–95.

Thomas, Keith. *Religion and the Decline of Magic*. Harmondsworth: Penguin, 1973.

Thompson, David M. (ed.). *Noncomformity in the Nineteenth Century*. London and Boston: Routledge, 1972.

Thompson, Edward P. *The Making of the English Working Class*. Harmondsworth: Penguin 1968.

Thompson, Kenneth and Bocock, Robert (eds.) *Religion and Ideology*. Manchester: Manchester University Press and the Open University, 1985, pp. 126–204.

Valderrey, José. *La cuestión de las sectas religiosas en la prensa mexicana*. Ponencia apresentada en el 'Encuentro sobre las sectas religiosas en el campo Mexicano'. Oaxaca, 1986.

Vallier, Ivan. *Catholicism, Social Control and Modernization in Latin America*. Englewood, NJ: Prentice-Hall, 1970.

El Vaticano y la Administracion Reagan: convergencias en Centroamerica. Mexico City: Ediciones Nuevomar y Claves Latinoamericanas, 1984.

Vaughan, John N. *The World's Twenty Largest Churches*. Grand Rapids, Mich.: Baker Book House, 1984, ch. 20.

Velasco Perez, Carlos. *La conquesta armada y espiritual de la nueva anteguerra*. Oaxaca, Mexico: Progreo Bellini, 1982.

Vergara, Ignacio. *El Protestantismo en Chile*. Santiago: Ed. de Pacifico, 1962.

Wagner, C. Peter. *Latin American Theology: Radical or Evangelical?* Grand Rapids,Mich.: Eerdmans, 1970.
——*Look out! The Pentecostals are Coming.* Carol Stream, Ill.: Creation House, 1973.
—— *The Protestant Movement in Bolivia.* South Pasadena, Calif.: William Carey Library, 1970.
Wald, Keith. *Crosses on the Ballot.* Princeton, NJ: Princeton: University Press, 1985.
Warren, Kay. *The Symbolism of Subordination: Indian Identity in a Guatemalan Town.* Austin: University of Texas Press, 1978.
Waters, Anita. *Race, Class and Political Symbols: Rastafari and Reggae in Jamaican Politics.* New Brunswick, NJ: Transaction Books, 1985.
Weber, William. *Music and the Middle Class.* London: Croom Helm, 1975.
Weld, Wayne C. *An Ecuadorian Impasse.* [Originally a dissertation at Fuller Theological Seminary.] Chicago: Evangelial Covenant Church of America, 1968.
Westfried, Alex Huxley. *Ethnic Leadership in a New England Community: Three Puerto Rican Families.* Salem, Wis.: Sheffield Publishing, 1981.
Westmeier, Karl Wilhelm. *Reconciling Heaven and Earth: The Transcendental Enthusiasm and Growth of an Urban Protestant Community, Bogotá, Colombia.* New York: Peter Lang, 1986.
Whitten, Jr., Norman E. *Cultural Transformations and Ethnicity in Modern Ecuador.* Urbana: University of Illinois Press, 1981.
Wilkie, James and Perkal, Adam (eds.) *Statistical Abstract of Latin America* vol. 3, 1984.
Williams, William. The attraction of Methodism: the Delmarva Peninsula 1769–
1820' in Russell, Richey and Rowe, Kenneth (eds). *Rethinking Methodist History.* Nashville, Tenn.: Kingswood Books, 1985.
Willems, Emilio. *Followers of the New Faith: Culture, Change and the Rise of Protestantism in Brazil and Chile.* Nashville, Tenn.: Vanderbilt University Press, 1967.
Wilson, Bryan R. *Magic and the Millennium.* London: Heinemann, 1973.
Winter, Ralph D. *The 25 Unbelievable Years, 1945–1969.* South Pasadena, Calif: William Carey Library, 1970.
Wipfler, William Louis. *The Churches of the Dominican Republic in the Light of History.* Sondeos, 11. Cuernavaca: Centre for Intercultural Documentation, 1967.
Wong, James (ed.). *Missions from the Third World.* Singapore: Church Growth Study Center, 1973.
Zapata Arceyuz, Virgilio. *Historia de la Iglesia Evangelica en Guatemala.* Guatemala City: Genesis Publicidad, 1982.

Journal Articles

Alexander, Bobby C. 'Pentecostal ritual reconsidered: 'anti-structural' dimensions of possession'. *Journal of Ritual Studies*, 3: 1 (Winter 1989).

—— 'Functión ideológica y posibilidades utópicas del protestantismo latinamericano'. *De la Iglesia y la Sociedad*, (1971), pp. 1–22.

Alves, Rubem. 'Protestantism in Latin America: its ideological function and utopian possibilities'. *Ecumenical Review*, 23: 1 (1970), pp. 1–15.

—— 'Protestantismo e repressão'. *Encontros Civilização Brasileira*, 3 (1978), pp. 199–204.

Aman, Kenneth. 'Fighting for God: the military and religion in Chile', *Cross Currents*, 36 (Nov. 1987), pp. 459–66.

América Indígena, 44: 3 (Jan.–Mar. 1984). (Complete issue on Protestantism.)

Araujo, Joao Dias de. 'Igrejas Protestantes e estado no Brasil'. *Cadernos do ISER*, 7 (Nov. 1977), pp. 23–32.

Arias, Mortimer. 'Contextual evangelism in Latin America: between accommodation and confrontation'. *Occasional Bulletin of Missionary Research Library*, 2 (Jan. 1978), pp. 19–28.

Austin, Diane J. 'Born again . . . and again and again: communitas and social change among Jamaican Pentecostalists'. *Journal of Anthropological Research*, 37: 3 (Fall 1981), pp. 226–46.

Baldwin, Deborah. 'Broken traditions: Mexican revolutionaries and Protestant allegiances'. *The Americas*, 40: 2 (Oct. 1981), pp. 229–58.

Barbieri, Sante. 'Methodism in Latin America'. Trans. B. F. Stockwell; ed. P. S. Watson. *London Quarterly and Holborn Review*, 176 (Apr. 1951), pp. 149–55.

Bastian, Jean-Pierre. 'Guerra Fría, crisis del projecto liberal y atomización de los Protestantismos Latino-Americanos 1949–1959.' *Christianismo y Sociedad*, 68: 2 (1981), pp. 7–12.

—— 'Itinerario de un intelectual popular protestante, liberal y francmasón en México: José Rumbia Guzmán 1865–1913'. *Christianismo y Sociedad*, 92: 2 (1987), pp. 91–108.

—— 'Para una aproximación teórica del fenómeno religioso protestante en América Central'. *Christianismo y Sociedad*, 85 (1985), pp. 61–8.

—— 'Protestantismo y política en México'. *Revista Mexicana de Sociologia*, 431 Special Issue, (1981), pp. 1947–66.

—— 'Protestantismos latinoamericanos entre la resistencia y la sumisión 1961–1983'. *Christianismo y Sociedad*, 82 (1984), pp. 49–68.

—— 'Protestantismo popular y política en Guatemala y Nicaragua'. Revista Mexicana de Sociología, 48: 3 (1986), pp. 181–200.

Beaver, R. Pierce. 'History of mission strategy'. *Southwestern Journal of Theology*, 12 (Spring 1970), pp. 7–28.

Belli, Humberto. 'The Church in Nicaragua: under attack from within and without'. *Religion in Communist Lands*, 12: 1 (1984), pp. 42–54.

Bertozzi, Yolanda. 'The Church's mission in countries under foreign domination: a Central American perspective'. *International Review of Missions*, 73 (1984), pp. 491–501.

'Behind the headlines, Colombia is witnessing a major religious revival' (News). *Christianity Today*, 29: 13 (1985), p. 40.

Bibby, Reginald W. 'Why conservative churches really are growing'. *Journal for the Scientific Study of Religion*, 2 (1978), pp. 129–37.

Bombart, Jean-Pierre. 'Les cultes protestantes dans une favela de Rio de Janeiro'. *América Latina*, 12: 3 (1969), pp. 137–59.

Brown, Diana de G. with Bick, Mario. 'Religion, class, and context: continuities and discontinuities in Brazilian Umbanda'. *American Ethnologist*, 14: 1 (1987), pp. 73–90.

Bruce, Steve. 'The persistence of religion: conservative Protestantism in the United Kingdom'. *Sociological Review*, 31: 3 (August 1983), pp. 453–70.

——with Wallis, Roy. 'Sketch for a theory of conservative Protestant politics', *Social Compass*, 2/3 (1985), pp. 145–61.

Bruno-Jofre, Rosa del Carmen. 'La introdución del sistema Lancasteriano en Perú: liberalismo, masonería y libertad religiosa'. *Christianismo y Sociedad*, 92: 2 (1987), pp. 49–59.

——'La misión metodista y la educación en Peru: 1889–1930'. *América Indígena*, 41: 3 (July–Sept. 1981), pp. 501–15.

Callan, Neville G. 'Invitation to docility: defusing the Rastafarian challenge'. *Caribbean Journal of Religious Studies*, 3: 2 (Sept. 1980), pp. 28–48.

Campiche, Roland J. 'Sectas y nuevos movimientos religiosos: divergencias y convergencias'. *Christianismo y Sociedad*, 93: 3 (1987), pp. 9–20.

Carrasco, Pedro E. '¿Convertir para no transformar?', *Christianismo y Sociedad*, 95: 1 (1988), pp. 7–50.

Casanova, José. 'The politics of the religious revival'. *Telos* (Spring 1984), pp. 3–33.

Castro, Emilio. 'Pentecostalism and Ecumenism in Latin America'. *Christian Century* (Sept. 1972), pp. 955–7.

CELEP, 'El Evangelio y La Religion Electronica'. *Pastorialia* San José, Costa Rica, 9, 10, July 1987.

CERI-GUA. 'Las sectas fundamentalistas y la contrainsurgencia en Guatemala'. *Servicio Especial*, Mar. 1987.

Cesar, Waldo. 'Urbanizacão e religiosidade popular: um estudo da função da doutrina pentecostal na sociedade urbana'. *Revista de Cultura Vozes*, 8: 7 (1974), pp. 523–32.

Chaunu, Pierre. 'Pour une sociologie du protestantisme latine-américain: problèmes de méthode'. *Cahiers de sociologie Economique*, 12 (May 1969), pp. 5–18.

Chevannes, Barry. 'Revival and black struggle'. *Savacou*, 5 (June 1971), pp. 27–37.

Clawson, David L. 'Religious allegiance and development in rural Latin America'. *Journal of Interamerican Studies and World Affairs*, 26 (1984), pp. 499–524.

Cook, William. 'Interview with Chilean Pentecostals' (WCC, Vancouver, 1983). *International Review of Mission* , 72 (Oct. 1983), pp. 591–5.

—— 'The Protestant predicament: from base ecclesial community to established Church: a Brazilian case study'. *International Bulletin Missionary Research Library*, 8 (July 1984), pp. 98–102.

Costas, Esdras. 'Missiology in contemporary Latin America: a survey'. *Missiology*, 5: 2 (1973), p. 89.

—— 'Protestantisme et dévelopement au nordest du Brésil'. *Social Compass*, 16 (1969), pp. 51–61.

Costas, Orlando. 'Church growth as a multidimensional phenomenon: some lessons from Chile'. *International Bulletin of Missionary Research Library*, 5 (Jan. 1981), pp. 2–8.

Curry, D. E. 'Messianism and Protestantism in Brazil's Sertão'. *Journal of Interamerican Studies and World Affairs*, 12 (July 1980), pp. 416–38.

Dann, Graham M. S. 'Religion and cultural identity: the case of Umbanda'. *Sociological Analysis*, 40: 3 (1979), pp. 208–25.

Dekker, James. 'North American Protestant theology: impact on Central America'. *Mennonite Quarterly Review*, 58: Supp. (August 1984), pp. 378–93.

Denton, Charles. 'Protestantism and Latin American middle class'. *Practical Anthropology*, 18 (Jan–Feb. 1971), pp. 24–8.

Dias, Zwinglio. 'Resistance and submission: the kingdom of the powerless (Latin America)'. *International Review of Mission*, 73 (Oct. 1984), pp. 408–16.

Dodson, Michael. 'The politics of religion in revolutionary Nicaragua'. *Annals of the American Society of Political and Social Scientists*, 483 (Jan. 1986), pp. 36–49.

Dominguez, Enrique and Huntington, Deborah. 'The salvation brokers: conservative Evangelicals in Central America'. *NACLA Report on the Americas* 1 8: 1 (Jan.–Feb. 1984), pp. 2–36.

Escobar, Samuel. 'Los evangélicos y la política'. *Certeza*, 8 (Oct.–Dec. 1967), pp. 230–2.

'Evangelicos de Nicaragua reaffirman su apoyo a la revolución Sandinista en ocasión de su primer aniversario'. *Christianismo y Sociedad*, 18: 3–4 (1980), pp. 95–6.

Falla, Ricardo. 'Evolucíon político-religiosa del indígena rural en Guatemala 1945–65'. *Estudios Sociales Centroamericanos* (San José), 1: 1 (Jan.–Apr.), pp. 27–41.

Fernandes, Rubem C. 'Aparacida, our Queen Lady and Mother, Sarava!'. *Social Science Information*, 24: 4 (1985), pp. 799–819.

—— 'Fundamentalismo a la derecha y a la izquierda: misiones evangélicas y tensiones ideológicas'. *Christianismo y Sociedad*, 69, 70: 3, 4 (1980, pp. 21–50.

—— 'O debate entre os sociologos a proposito dos Pentecostais'. *Cadernos do ISER*, 6 (1977), pp. 49–60.

—— 'Os Deuses do Povo'. *Religião e Sociedade*, 6 (1980), pp. 226–31.

Field, Clive D. 'The social structure of English Methodism'. *British Journal of Sociology*, 28 2 (June 1977), pp. 199–225.

Finkler, Kaja. 'Dissident religious movements in the service of women's power'. *Sex Roles*, 7: 5 (May 1981), pp. 481–95.

—— 'Dissident sectarian movements: the Catholic Church and social class in Mexico'. *Comparative Studies in Society and History*, 25: 2 (1983), pp. 277–305.

Floriano, Maria das Gracas and Novaes, Regina. 'O negro evangelico'. *Comuniçacões do ISER*, 4 (1985).

Fortuny, Patricia. 'Insercion y diffusion del sectarismo en el campo Yucateca'. *Yucatan: Historia y Economica*, 60: 33 (1982).

Frase, Ronald. 'The subversion of missionary intentions by cultural values: the Brazilian case'. *Review of Religious Research*, 23: 2 (Dec. 1981), pp. 180–94.

Fry, Peter and Howe, Gary Nigel. 'Duas respostas a aflição: Umbanda e Pentecostalismo'. *Debate e Critica*, 6 (1975), pp. 75–94.

Garma Navarro, Carlos. 'Liderazgo, mensaje religioso y contexto social'. *Christianiso y Sociedad*, 95: 1 (1988), pp. 89–99.

—— 'Liderazgo protestante en una lucha campesina en Mexico'. *América Indígena*, 44: 1 (1984), pp. 127–42.

—— 'Los estudios antropologicos sobre el protestantismo en México'. *Revista Iztapalapa*, 15 (1988), pp. 53–66.

—— 'Protestantismo en una comunidad Totonaca, un estudio político'. *Religión popular, hegemonia y resistencia* (1982), pp. 113–29.

Glazier, Stephen. 'African cults and Christian Churches in Trinidad: the spiritual Baptist case'. *Journal of Religious Thought*, 39 (Fall–Winter 1982–3), pp. 17–25.

—— 'Caribbean pilgrimages: a typology'. *Journal for the Scientific Study of Religion*, 22 (Dec. 1983), pp. 316–25.

—— 'Religion and contemporary religious movements in the Caribbean: a report'. *Sociological Analysis*, 41: 2 (1980), pp. 181–3.

Gonzalez, Nancie L. 'Una mayor recompenso en el cielo: actividades de misioneros metodistas entre los amerindios de Belice'. *América Indígena*, 47: 1 (1987), pp. 139–68.

Greenway, Roger S. 'The Luz del Mundo movement in Mexico'. *Missiology*, 1: 2 (1973), p. 113.

'Guatemalan pastors: between a rock and a hard place'. *Christianity Today*, 8 (May 1981), p. 43.

Gueiros Vieira, David. 'Liberalismo, masonería y protestantismo en Brasil en el siglo XIX'. *Christianismo y Sociedad*, 92: 2 (1987), pp. 9–31.

Handy, Jim. 'Resurgent democracy and the Guatemalan military'. *Journal of Latin American Studies*, 18: 2 (1986), n.p.

Hill, Michael and Bowman, R. 'Religious practice and religious adherence in contemporary New Zealand'. *Archive des Sciences Sociales des Religions*, 59: 1 (1985), pp. 91–115.

Hollenweger, Walter. 'After twenty years' research on Pentecostalism', *International Review of Mission*, 75 (1986), pp. 1–12.

Hollenweger, Walter. 'Methodism's past in Pentecostalism's present: a case study of a cultural clash in Chile'. *Methodist History*, 20 (July 1982), pp. 169–82.

Hopkin, John Barton. 'Music in Jamaican Pentecostal churches'. *Jamaica Journal* (Kingston: The Institute of Jamaica), 1984.

Howe, Gary Nigel. 'Representacoes religiosas e capitalismo: uma "leitura" estructuralista'. *Cadernos do ISER*, 6 (1977): 39–48.

Hurbon, Laënnec. 'Los nuevos movimientos religiosos en el Caribe'. *Christianismo y Sociedad*, 93: 3 (1987), pp. 37–64.

Kemper, Vicki. 'In the name of relief: a look at private US aid in Contra territory'. *Sojourners*, 14: 9 (Oct. 1985), pp. 12–20.

Kim Byong-Suh. 'The explosive growth of the Korean Church today: a sociological analysis'. *International Review of Mission*, 74 (Jan. 1988), pp. 59–72.

Kliewer, G. U. 'Assembléia de Deus e Eleicões num Município do Interior de Mato Grosso'. *Communicações do ISER*, 3 (Dec. 1982), pp. 21–7.

Lalive D'Epinay, Christian. 'Régimes politiques et millénarisme dans une société dépendante'. *Actes* of the 15th Conferenceof the CISR, Venice, 1979. Paris: CISR, 1979.

Lawrence, Robert. 'Evangelicals support Guatemalan dictator'. *Covert Action Information Bulletin*, 18 (1983), pp. 34–40.

Lee, Elizabeth M. 'School evangelism grows in Latin America'. *International Review of Mission*, 41 (1952), pp. 185–92.

Lewellen, Ted. 'Deviant religion and cultural evolution'. *Journal for the Scientific Study of Religion*, 18: 3 (Sept. 1979), pp. 243–51.

Lewis, Kingsley. 'United in service'. *Caribbean Journal of Religious Studies*, 7: 1 (Apr. 1986), pp. 6–17.

McDonnell, Kilian. 'The ideology of Pentecostal conversion'. *Journal of Ecumenical Studies*, 5 (1968), pp. 108–26.

Maciel, Elter D. 'Conversão ao Protestantismo'. *Cadernos do ISER*, 1 (1974), pp. 21–7.

Maduro, Otto. 'Catholic Church, national security states and popular movements in Latin America', in *Actes* of the 17th Conference of the CISR. Paris: CISR, 1983, pp. 8–19.

Marzal, Manuel. 'Iglesia Cultural y nuevas iglesias'. *América Indígena*, 48: 1 (Jan.–Mar. 1988), pp. 139–64.

Mayer, Jean-François. 'El mundo de los nuevos movimientos religiosos'. *Christianismo y Sociedad*, 93: 3 (1987), pp. 37–64.

Mendonça, Antonio Gouvêa. 'Incorporación de protestantismo y la "cuestión religiosa" en Brasil en el siglo XIX, reflexiones e hipotesis'. *Christianismo y Sociedad*, 92: 2 (1987), pp. 33–48.

Menezes, Eduardo D. 'A igreja Catolica e a proliferaçaõ das "Seitas"'. *Comunicações do ISER*, 5: 20 (July 1986), pp. 30–5.

Míguez Bonino, José. 'La actitud política de los protestantes en América Latina'. *Noticiero de la Fe*, 37 (July 1972), pp. 4–9.

—— 'Presencia y ausencia protestante en la Argentina del processo militar 1976–1983'. *Christianismo y Sociedad*, 83 (1985), pp. 81–5.

Millett, Richard L. 'Protestant–Catholic relations in Costa Rica'. *Journal of Church and State*, 12 (Winter 1970).

Minnery, Tom. 'Why the Gospel grows in socialist Nicaragua: the revolution turned against capitalism but not Christianity'. *Christianity Today*, 27 (Apr. 1983), pp. 34–42.

Moura, Abdalaziz de. 'Pentecostalism and Brazilian religion'. *Theology Digest* (Spring 1972), pp. 44–9.

Mulholland, Kenneth. 'A Guatemalan experiment becomes a model for change' (Evangelical Presbyterian Seminary). *International Review of Mission*, 71 (Apr. 1982), pp. 153–60.

Muratorio, Blanca. 'Protestantism and capitalism revisited in the rural highlands of Ecuador'. *Journal of Peasant Studies*, 8: 1 (Oct. 1980), pp. 37–60.

Nash, June. 'Protestantism in an Indian village in the western highlands of Guatemala'. *Alpha Kappa Delta* (Winter 1960), pp. 49–53.

Nelson, Reed. 'Funções organizacionais do culto numa igreja anarquista'. *Religião e Sociedade*, 12: 1 (Aug. 1985), pp. 112–25.

'Nicaragua – hearts and bellies: a discussion of Salvation' (Dialogue in Managua between North Americans and Evangelical Pastors). *Sojourners*, 12: 3 (Mar. 1983), pp. 20–1.

Niklaus, Robert. 'Latin America: counter-evangelism'. *Evangelical Mission Quarterly*, 19: 3 (July 1983), pp. 259–60.

Novaes, Regina R. 'Os Pentecostais e a organização dos trabalhadores'. *Religião e Sociedade*, 5 (June 1980), pp. 65–98.

O'Connor, Mary. 'Two kinds of religious movements among the Mayo Indians of Sonora, Mexico'. *Journal for the Scientific Study of Religion*, 18: 3 (1979), pp. 260–5.

Ojo, Matthews, 'Charismatic cults in Nigeria'. *Africa*, 58: 2 (1988), pp. 175–92.

Padilla, C. René. 'A new ecclesiology in Latin America'. *International Bulletin of Missionary Research*, 11: 4 (Oct. 1987), pp. 156–64.

Padilla J., Washington. 'La actividad de las sociedades bíblicas en el Ecuador durante el primer liberalismo'. *Christianismo y Sociedad*, 92: 2 (1987), pp. 61–89.

Parajon, Gustavo. 'Nicaragua: Evangelicals, Sandinistas and the Elections' (an interview). *Transformation*, 2: 1(Jan.–Mar. 1985), pp. 2–4.

'Parcial, El'. 'La santa contrainsurgencia: sectas protestantes en Centroamerica'. *Dialogo Social*, 17: 169 (July 1984) pp. 47–9.

Pearson, David G. 'Race, religiosity and political activism'. *British Journal of sociology*, 29: 3 (Sept. 1978), pp. 340–57.

Peck, Gary R. 'Black radical consciousness and the black Christian experience'. *Sociological Analysis*, 43: 2 (1982), pp. 155–69.

Peck, Jane C. 'Reflections from Costa Rica on Protestantism's dependence and nonliberative social function'. *Journal of Ecumenical Studies*, 21 (Spring 1984), pp. 181–98.

Petrella, Vaccaro de and Susana, Lidia. 'The tension between evangelism and social action in the Pentecostal movement (Argentina)'. *International Review of Mission*, 75 (Jan. 1986), pp. 34–8.

Poewe, Karla and Hexham, Irving. 'The new charismatic churches in Durban, Johannesburg and Pretoria'. *Navors Bulletin*, 17: 9 (1987), pp. 32–6.

Preston, David. 'Pressures on Chimborazo Indians'. *Geographical Magazine*, 50 (July 1978), pp. 613–18.

Raj, P. Solomon. 'The influence of Pentecostal teaching on some folk Christian religion in India'. *International Review of Mission*, 75 (1986) pp. 39–46.

Rappaport, Joanne. 'Las misiones Protestantes y la resistencia indígena en el sur de Colombia'. Trans P. Bonfil. *América Indígena*, 44: 1 (Jan.–Mar. 1984), pp. 111–26.

Reina, Ruben E. and Norman B. Schwartz. 'The structural context of religious conversion in El Petén, Guatemala: status, community and multicommunity'. *American Ethnologist*, 9: 1 (1974), pp. 157–91.

Rivière, Gilles. 'Social change and Pentecostalism in an Aymaran community'. *Fe y Pueblo*, 3: 14 (Nov. 1986), pp. 24–30.

Roberts, Bryan R. 'Protestant groups and coping with urban life in Guatemala'. *American Journal of Sociology*, 6 (May 1968), pp. 753–67.

Rodrigues Brandão, Carlos. 'Creencia e identidad: campo religioso y cambio cultural'. *Christianismo y Sociedad*, 93: 3 (1987), pp. 65–106.

Rodriguez Borges, Armando. 'Structural implications of the missionary heritage'. (Cuba) *International Review of Mission*, 74 (July 1985), pp. 350–4.

Rolim, Francisco Cartaxo. 'El pentecostalismo a partir del pobre'. *Christianismo y Sociedad* 95: 1 (1988), pp. 51–69. 51–69.

—— 'Pentecôtisme et société au Brésil'. *Social Compass*, 26: 2–3 (1979), pp. 345–72.

Rubenstein, Richard L. 'The political significance of Central American liberation theology'. *International Journal on World Peace*, Jan.–Mar. 1986.

Russell, Horace. 'The Emergence of the Christian Black: the making of a stereotype'. *Jamaican Journal*, 16: 1 (Feb. 1983).

Saler, Benson. 'Religious conversion and self-aggrandizement: a Guatemalan case study'. *Practical Anthropology*, 13 (1965), pp. 107–14.

Sanneh, Lamin. 'Christian missions and the Western guilt complex', *Christian Century*, 8 April, 1987, pp. 330–4.

Schuffeneger, Humberto Lagos. 'La función de la religión en el gobierno militar, en el modelo político autoritario y en las fuerzas armadas y de orden de Chile'. *Revista Andes* (1985), 34–42.

—— and Chacón, Arturo. 'La religion en fuerzas armadas y de orden', Santiago, Chile, 1986.

Seaga, Edward. 'Revival Cults in Jamaica'. *Jamaica Journal*, 3: 2 (June 1969), pp. 16–21.

Sexton, James. 'Protestantism and modernization in two Guatemalan towns'. *American Ethnologist*, 5: 2 (1978), pp. 280–302.

Shim Il-Supp. 'The new religious movements in the Korean Church'. *International Review of Mission*, 74 (Jan. 1985), pp. 103–8.

Sider, Ronald. 'Who is my neighbor: Nicaraguan Evangelicals host US Evangelicals (Dec. 12–19 1982)'. *TSF Bulletin*, 6: 4 (Mar.–Apr. 1983), pp. 11–13.

Song Kon-Ho. 'A history of the Christian movement in Korea'. *International Review of Mission*, 74 (Jan. 1985), pp. 19–36.

Spittler, Russell. 'World's largest congregation: a cathedral in Chile'. *Christianity Today* (Jan. 17 1975), pp. 33–39.

Spring, Beth. 'Nicaragua – the Government's heavy hand falls on believers: Sandinistas crack down on Protestant activity (Photo; News)'. *Christianity Today*, 29: 18 (Dec. 1985), pp. 51–2.

Stam, John. 'Christian witness in Central America: a radical Evangelical perspective'. *Transformation*, 2: 1 (Jan–Mar. 1985), pp. 14–17.

Stark, Rodney and Finke, Roger. 'American religion in 1776: a statistical portrait'. *Sociological Analysis*, 49: 1 (1988), pp. 39–51.

—— —— 'How the upstart sects won America 1776–1850'. *Journal for the Scientific Study of Religion*, Mar. 1989.

—— —— 'Religious economies and sacred canopies: religious mobilization in American cities, 1906'. *American Sociological Review*, 53 Feb. 1988), pp. 41–9.

Stoll, David. 'La iglesia del verbo en el triángulo Ixil de Guatemala, 1982'. *Civilización*, 3 (1985), pp. 83–109.

Swanson, Daniel. 'The challenge of Mexico City'. *Latin American Evangelist* (Oct.–Dec. 1987), pp. 12–13.

Tennekes, Johannes. 'Le mouvement pentecôtiste chilien et la politique'. *Social Compass*, 25: 1 (1978), pp. 55–84.

Teixeira, Marli Geralda. 'A familia protestante na sociedad baiana'. *Christianismo y Sociedad*, 25: 2 (1987), pp. 9–32.

Thornton, W. Philip. 'Resocialization: Roman Catholics becoming Protestant in Colombia'. *Anthropology Quarterly*, 57: 1 (Jan. 1984), pp. 28–37.

Tinney, James S. 'Black origins of the Pentecostal movement'. *Christianity Today*, 8 Oct. 1971, pp. 4–9.

Troutman, Charles H. 'Evangelicals and the middle classes in Latin America' (parts I and II). *Evangelical Missions Quarterly*, 7: 2, pp. 31–79; 7. 3, pp. 154–63.

Turner, Frederick. 'Protestantism and politics in Chile and Brazil'. *Comparative Studies in Society and History*, 12: 2 (1970), pp. 213–29.

Turner, Paul R. 'Religious conversion and community development'. *Journal for the Scientific Study of Religion*, 18: 3 (1979), pp. 252–60.

Urban, Greg. 'Development in the situation of Brazilian tribal population from 1976 to 1982'. *Latin American Research Review*, 20: 1 (1985), pp. 7–25.

Valderrey, José. 'Sects in Central America: a pastoral problem'. *Pro Mundi Vita*, 100 (1985), pp. 1–39.

Villeroy, Madeleine. 'Enquête sur les églises protestantes dans le Brésil en crise des années 1963–73'. *Cahiers de Sociologie Economique*, 12 (May 1975), pp. 18–80.

Wagner, C. Peter. 'The greatest church growth is beyond our shores'. *Christianity Today*, 28: 8 (May 1984), pp. 25–9.

Wallis, Jim and Hollyday, Joyce. 'A plea from the heart'. *Sojourners*, 12: 3 (Mar. 1983), pp. 3–5.

Warner, R. Stephen. 'Theoretical barriers to the understanding of Evangelical Christianity'. *Sociological Analysis*, 40: 1 (Spring 1979), pp. 1–9.

Westmeier, Karl W. 'The enthusiastic Protestants of Bogotá, Colombia: reflections on the growth of a movement'. *International Review of Mission*, 75 (Jan. 1986), pp. 13–24.

Willems, Emilio. 'Validation of authority in Pentecostal sects of Chile and Brazil'. *Journal for the Scienetific Study of Religion*, 6 (Fall 1967), pp. 253–58.

Wilson, Everett A. 'Sanguine saints: Pentecostalism in El Salvador'. *Church History*, 52 (Jan. 1983), pp. 186–98.

Yi Hyo-Jae. 'Christian mission and the liberation of Korean women'. *International Review of Mission*, 74 (Jan. 1985), pp. 93–102.

Yoo Boo Woong. 'Response to Korean shamanism by the Pentecostal Church', *International Review of Mission*, 74 (Jan. 1985), pp. 000.

Unpublished Materials

Albuquerque, Klause de. 'Millenarian movements and the politics of liberation: the Rastafarians of Jamaica'. Ph.D. diss., Virginia Polytechnic Institute and State University, Microfilm, 1978.

Amorim, N. F. M. 'Os mormons em Alagoas; religião e relacoes raciais'. Master's diss, São Paulo, USP, (n.d.).

Annis, Sheldon. 'God and production in a Guatemalan town'. Draft for Ph.D. diss., University of Chicago, 1984.

Aulie, Henry W. 'The Christian movement among the Chols of Mexico with special reference to problems of second generation Christianity'. Ph.D. diss., Fuller Theological Seminary, 1979.

Baldwin, Deborah. 'Variation within the vanguard: Protestants and the Mexican Revolution'. Ph.D. diss., University of Chicago, 1979.

Balouarte, Carlos H. 'De viciado a convertido: a experiência da salvação evangélica no "desafio Jovem do Brasil" '. Master's diss., University de Brasília, 1979.

Bastian, Jean-Pierre. 'Las sociedades protestantes en México 1872–1911: un liberalismo radical de oposición a Porfirismo y de participación en la revolución maderista'. Hist. Doct. diss., Colegio de México, 1987.

Bechtel, Alpha Gillet. 'The Mexican Episcopal Church: a century of reform and revolution'. MA thesis in Hist., San Diego State College, 1961.

Berberian, Samuel. 'Movimiento carismático en Latinoamérica 1960–1980'. Licenciate diss., Mariano Gálvez University, 1980.

Black, Alan W. 'Pentecostalism in Australia: some preliminary findings'. Paper prepared for the Australian Association for the Study of Religion, Brisbane, 1988; available from the University of New England, Armidale, NSW, Australia.

Bobsin, Oneide. 'Producão religiosa e significação social do Pentecostalismo a partir de sua prática e representão'. Master's diss., Pontificia Universidade Católica de São Paulo, 1984.

Brusco, Elizabeth. 'The household basis of evangelical religion and the reformation of machismo in Colombia'. Ph.D. diss., City University of New York, 1986.

Burnett, Virginia G. 'A history of Protestantism in Guatemala'. Ph.D. diss., Tulane University, 1986.

Carrasco Mulhue. 'Protestantismo y campo religioso en un pueblo del estado de Oaxaca'. Licenciate diss, in Sociology of Religion, Instituto Internacional de Estudios Superiores, 1983.

Cato, Clive Stilson. 'Pentecostalism: its social and religious implications for Jamaican society'. BA diss., University of West Indies, Mona, Jamaica, 1984.

Coke, Hugh M. 'An ethnohistory of Bible translation among the Maya'. Ph.D. diss., Fuller Theological Seminary, 1978.

Cook, Athyl W., Jr. 'The expectation of the poor: a Protestant missiological study of the Catholic Comunidades de Base' in Brazil'. Ph.D. diss., Fuller Theological Seminary, 1982.

Corral Prieto, Luis. 'Las iglesias evangélicas de Guatemala'. Licenciate Diss., Francisco Marroquín University, 1984.

Curry, Donald E. 'Lusiada: an anthropological study of the growth of Protestantism in Brazil'. Ph.D. diss., Columbia University, 1968

Deiros, Pablo A. 'Argentine Baptists and politics: an analysis of relations'. Ph.D. diss., Southwestern Baptist Theological Seminary, 1985.

Diaz, Jorge Enrique. 'Los Bautistas de ayer: un estudio sencillo sobre la historia de los Bautistas'. Licenciate diss., Instituto Superior Teológico Bautista de Guatemala, 1975.

Dirksen, Murl O. 'Pentecostal healing: a facet of the personalistic health system in Pakal-Na, a village in southern Mexico'. Ph.D. diss., University of Tennessee, Knoxville, 1984.

Elliott, William W. 'Sociocultural change in a Pentecostal group: a case study in education and culture of the Church in Sonora, Mexico'. Ed.D. diss., University of Tennessee, Knoxville, n.d.

Endruveit, Wilsom H. 'Pentecostalism in Brazil: a historical and theological study of its characteristics'. Ph.D. diss., North Western University, 1975.

Erskine, Noel Leo. 'Black religion and identity: a Jamaican perspective'. Ph.D. diss., Union Theological Seminary, New York, 1978.

Ferris, George, Jr. 'Protestantism in Nicaragua: its historical roots and influences affecting its growth'. Ph.D. diss., Temple University, 1981.

Frase, Ronald. 'A sociological analysis of the development of Brazilian Protestantism: a study in social change'. Ph.D. diss., Princeton Theological Seminary, 1975.

Garma Navarro, Carlos. 'Poder, conflicto y reelaboración simbólica: protestantismo en una comunidad Totonaca'. Diss., Escuela Nacional de Antropología e Historia, 1983.

Gibson, Delbert. 'Protestantism in Latin American Acculturation'. Ph.D. diss., University of Texas at Austin, 1959.

Gomes, Eliab B. 'Igreja, sociedade e política – os Batistas em Pernambuco (1955–1964)'. Master's diss., Federal University of Pernambuco, 1984.

Gomes, José Francisco. 'Religião e política: os Pentecostais no Recife'. Master's diss., Sociology, Federal University of Pernambuco, 1985.

Gouveia, Eliane H. 'O selencio que deve ser ouvido: mulheres Pentecostais em São Paulo'. Master's diss., Pontificia Universidade Católica, 1987.

Grover, Mark. 'Mormonism in Brazil: religion and dependency in Latin America'. Ph.D. diss. Indiana State University, 1985.

Hamid, Idris. 'The social witness of the Presbyterian Church in Trinidad, 1868–1968'. Ph.D. diss, Union Theological Seminary, New York, 1976.

Hoefle, Scott William. 'Continuity and change in the northeastern Sertão of Brazil'. D.Phil. diss., University of Oxford, 1983.

Hoffnagel, Judith. 'The believers: Pentecostalism in a Brazilian city'. Ph.D. diss., Indiana University, 1978.

Hogg, Donald W. 'Jamaican religions'. Ph.D. diss., Yale University, 1964.

Hurd, James. 'The socio-structural implications of Protestantism in northwestern Colombia'. Ph.D. diss., Pennsylvania State University, 1974.

Ibarra Bellon, Araceli y Lanczyner Reisel, Alisa. 'La hermosa provincia, Nacimiento y vida de una secta Cristiana en Guadalajara'. M.Phil. diss., University of Guadalajara, mimeo, 1972.

Kahn, Carl. 'Evangelical worship in Brazil: its origin and development'. Ph.D. diss., University of Edinburgh, 1970.

Keyes, Lawrence. 'The new age of missions: a study of Third World missionary societies'. Ph.D. diss., Fuller Theological Seminary, 1981.

Kuhl, Paul. 'Protestant missionary activity and freedom of religion in Ecuador, Peru, and Bolivia'. Ph.D. diss., Southern Illinois University at Carbondale, 1982.

Lloret, Albert. 'The Maya Evangelical Church in Guatemala'. D.Theol. diss., Dallas Theological Seminary, 1976.

Lockwood, George. 'Recent developments in US Hispanic and Latin American Protestant church music'. D.Min. diss., Claremont School of Theology, 1981.

McKechnie, Mariane E. 'The Mexican Revolution and the National Presbyterian Church of Mexico, 1910–1940', Ph.D. diss., American University, Washington, DC, 1970.

Malhue, Pedro Carrasco. 'Protestantismo y campo religioso en un pueblo del estado de Oaxaca, México'. Licenciate diss. in Sociolgy of Religion, Instituto Internacional de Estudios Superiores, 1983.

Maynard, Kent. 'Christianity and religion: evangelical identity and sociocultural organization in urban Ecuador'. Ph.D. diss., Indiana University, 1977 (Ann Arbor microfilms, 1981).

Melvin, Harold Jr. 'Religion in Brazil: a sociological approach to religion and its integrative function in rural urban migrant adjustment'. Ph.D. diss., 1970.

Mendonça, Antonio G. 'O Celeste Porvir. Um estudo da inserção de

Protestantismo na sociedade Brasileira'. Doctoral diss., University of São Paulo, 1982.

Miller, Elmer. 'Pentecostalism among the Argentine Toba'. Ph.D. diss., University of Pittsburg, 1967.

Mizuke, John. 'The growth of the Japanese Churches in Brazil'. Ph.D. diss., Fuller Theological Seminary, 1976.

Page, John. 'Brasil para Cristo: the cultural construction of Pentecostal networks in Brazil'. Ph.D. diss., New York University, 1984.

Perez Torres, Ruben. 'The pastor's role in educational ministry in the Pentecostal Church of God in Puerto Rico'. Ph.D. diss., Claremont School of Theology, 1979.

Poewe, Karla. 'In the eye of the storm: charismatics and independent churches in South Africa'. Unpublished paper, University of Calgary, 1987, p. 3.

Pottinger, George Fitz-Albert. 'The contribution of the Methodist Missionary Society to Jamaica 1938–1967'. Ph.D. diss., Boston University, 1977.

Quezada, Victor. 'The challenge of growth for the Baptist Church in Chile'. Th.M. diss., Fuller Theological Seminary, Pasadena, Calif., 1985.

Randall, Donna M. 'The beliefs and practices of the Pentecostal (Oneness) Apostolic People of Jamaica'. BA diss., University of the West Indies, 1983.

Robledo Hernandez, Gabriela Patricia. 'Disidencia y religión: los expulsados de San Juan Chamula'. Licentiate diss., ENAH, 1987.

Rodriguez-Bravo, E. 'Origen y desarollo del movimiento Protestante en Puerto Rico'. Ph.D. diss., 1972.

Santiago, Ricardo L. 'Religiao, classes sociais e familia: o caso do Pentecostalismo'. Relatorio preliminar de pesquisa de Iniciacao Cientifica apresentado no Seminario sobre Familia do Depto de Sociologia UF PE Recife, 1986.

Santos, Almir A. 'Os testemunhas de Jeovah'. Master's diss., Museu Nacional do Rio de Janeiro, n.d.

Stoll, Sandra J. 'Pulpito e palanque: religião et política nas eleições da Grande São Paulo'. Master's diss, Unicamp, Campinas, São Paulo, 1986.

Teague, Dennis. 'A history of the Church of God in Guatemala'. Master's thesis, Trinity Evangelical Divinity School, 1975.

Thornton, William. 'Protestantism: profile and process. A case study in religious change from Colombia, South America'. Ph.D. diss., Southern Methodist University, Dallas, Tex. 1981.

Valderrey, José. (s/d). 'El Protestantismo Fundamentalista y sectario en Centro América – un reto a las iglesias y al movimiento popular', Mexico (mimeo).

Wedenoja, William A. 'Religion and adaptation in rural Jamaica'. Ph.D. diss., University of California at San Diego, 1978.

Weerstra, Hans. 'Maya peasant evangelization'. Ph.D. diss., Fuller Theological Seminary, 1972.

Williams, Phillip J. 'The Catholic Church and politics in Nicaragua and Costa Rica'. D.Phil. diss. in Latin American Studies, University of Oxford, 1986.

Miscellaneous Papers

Alleyne, Mervyn. 'The history of African religion in Jamaica'. Paper presented at the 15th Conference of Caribbean historians, University of the West Indies, Mona, Jamaica, April 1983.

Cajas, Marco Tuli. '¿Habra guerra religiosa en Guatemala?' Rio Amazonas, 82–1, Colonia Cuacthemoc, 06500, Mexico, DF, Mar. 1987.

Chung, Chin-Hong. 'A bibliographical essay on the growth of Korean Protestantism'. Unpublished paper for Institute for the Study of Economic Culture, Boston, pp. 36–7.

Coleman, Simon. 'A study of the dynamics of the 'New Life' Pentecostal group in Uppsala, Sweden'. D.Phil. in progress at St John's College, Cambridge.

Lagos, Schuffeneger Humberto. 'Los Evangelicos en Chile'. Unpublished paper, Vicaria Solidaridad, Santiago, Chile, 1984.

Mariz, Cecilia. 'Religion and coping with poverty in Brazil: a comparison of the base communities and Pentecostal Churches'. Unpublished paper, 1987, privately available from the Institute for the Study of Economic Culture, Boston University, 118 Bay State Rd., Boston, Mass.

Orellana, Oscar. 'Evangelización-colonización'. Folleto de Confederación, Sacerdotes, Diosesanos de Guatemala.

Poewe, Karla. 'In the eye of the storm: charismatics and independent churches in South Africa'. Unpublished paper, University of Calgary, 1989, p. 3

—— 'Links and parallels between Black and White charismatic churches in South Africa and the States'. Unpublished paper, 1988.

Richardson, James E. 'A study of the leadership training programs of the Assemblies of God in South America'. 1974. (Typewritten – Springfield, Missouri.)

Smith, Dennis. 'For Evangelicals in Central America, religion is as polarized as politics'. Religious News Service Special Report, 16 Jan. 1985.

Tennekes, Juan. 'El movimiento pentecostal en la sociedad Chilena' (mimeo). Santiago: La Vida Nueva, 1973.

Name Index

Subject Index